NAOKI URASAWA'S

20th CENTURY BOYS

Naoki Urasawa's
20th Century Boys
Volume 08

VIZ Signature Edition

STORY AND ART BY NAOKI URASAWA

20 SEIKI SHONEN 8 by Naoki URASAWA/Studio Nuts
© 2002 Naoki URASAWA/Studio Nuts
With the cooperation of Takashi NAGASAKI
All rights reserved. Original Japanese
edition published in 2002 by Shogakukan Inc., Tokyo.

"Astro Boy Atom"
Lyricist: Shuntaro Tanigawa
Composer: Tatsuo Takai
©1963 by NIPPON TELEVISION MUSIC CORPORATION

English Adaptation/Akemi Wegmüller
Touch-up Art & Lettering/Freeman Wong
Cover & Interior Design/Sam Elzway
Editor/Kit Fox

VP, Production/Alvin Lu
VP, Sales & Product Marketing/Gonzalo Ferreyra
VP, Creative/Linda Espinosa
Publisher/Hyoe Narita

Printed in the U.S.A.

Published by VIZ Media, LLC
P.O. Box 77010
San Francisco, CA 94107

10 9 8 7 6 5 4 3 2 1
First printing, April 2010

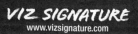

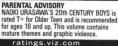

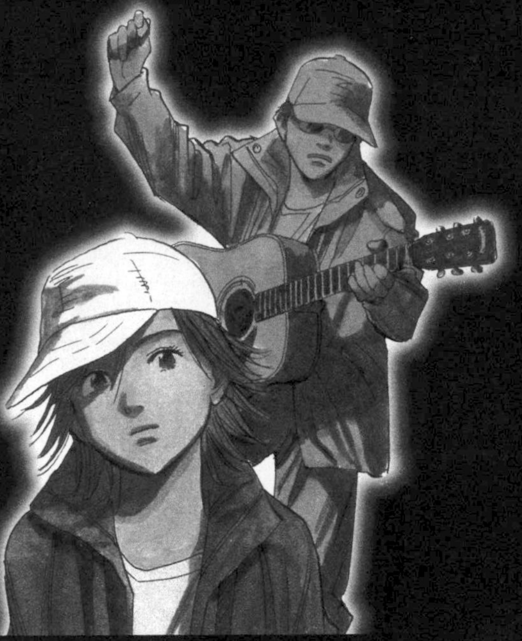

NAOKI URASAWA'S

20th CENTURY BOYS

VOL 08

KENJI'S SONG

Story & Art by
NAOKI URASAWA
With the cooperation of
Takashi NAGASAKI

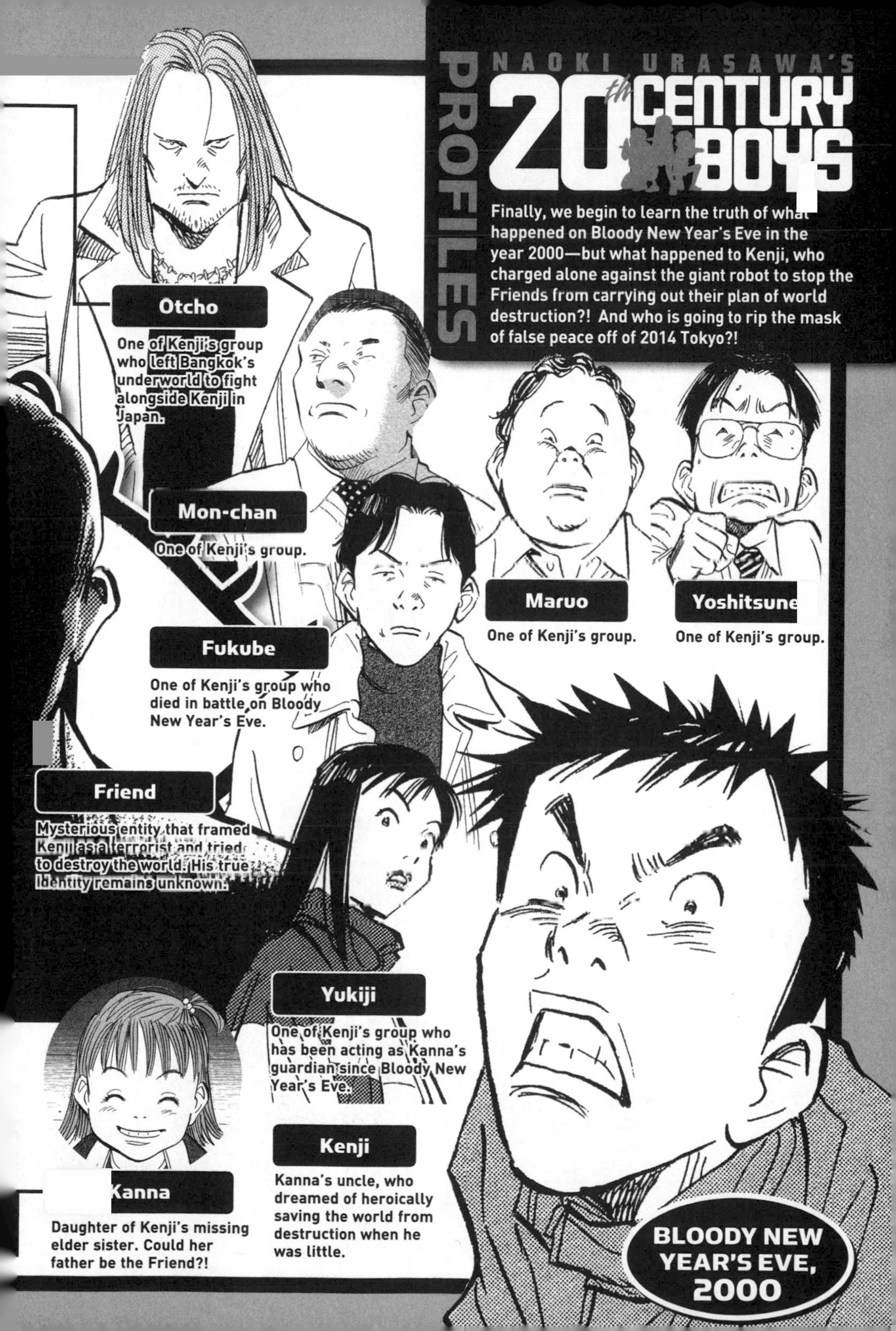

PROFILES

NAOKI URASAWA'S 20th CENTURY BOYS

Finally, we begin to learn the truth of what happened on Bloody New Year's Eve in the year 2000—but what happened to Kenji, who charged alone against the giant robot to stop the Friends from carrying out their plan of world destruction?! And who is going to rip the mask of false peace off of 2014 Tokyo?!

Otcho

One of Kenji's group who left Bangkok's underworld to fight alongside Kenji in Japan.

Mon-chan

One of Kenji's group.

Maruo

One of Kenji's group.

Yoshitsune

One of Kenji's group.

Fukube

One of Kenji's group who died in battle on Bloody New Year's Eve.

Friend

Mysterious entity that framed Kenji as a terrorist and tried to destroy the world. His true identity remains unknown.

Yukiji

One of Kenji's group who has been acting as Kanna's guardian since Bloody New Year's Eve.

Kenji

Kanna's uncle, who dreamed of heroically saving the world from destruction when he was little.

Kanna

Daughter of Kenji's missing elder sister. Could her father be the Friend?!

BLOODY NEW YEAR'S EVE, 2000

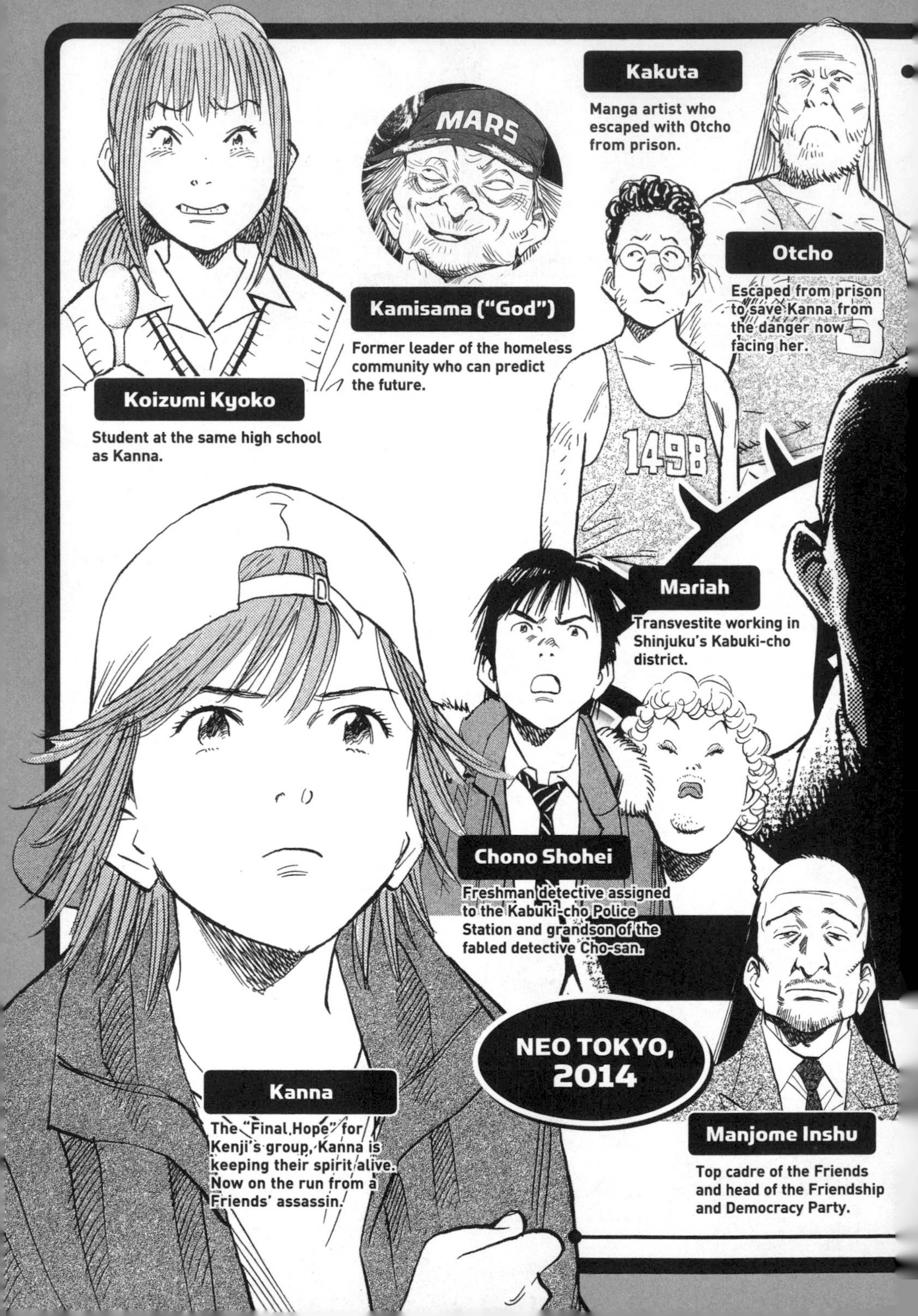
Kakuta
Manga artist who escaped with Otcho from prison.
Otcho
Escaped from prison to save Kanna from the danger now facing her.
MARS
Kamisama ("God")
Former leader of the homeless community who can predict the future.
Koizumi Kyoko
Student at the same high school as Kanna.
1498
Mariah
Transvestite working in Shinjuku's Kabuki-cho district.
Chono Shohei
Freshman detective assigned to the Kabuki-cho Police Station and grandson of the fabled detective Cho-san.
Manjome Inshu
Top cadre of the Friends and head of the Friendship and Democracy Party.
NEO TOKYO, 2014
Kanna
The "Final Hope" for Kenji's group, Kanna is keeping their spirit alive. Now on the run from a Friends' assassin.

CONTENTS
VOL 08
KENJI'S SONG

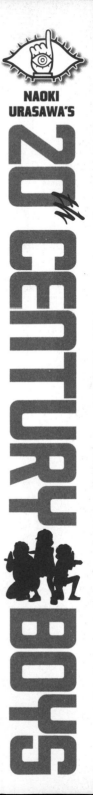

NAOKI
URASAWA'S

20ᵗʰ CENTURY BOYS

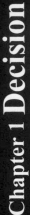

Chapter 1 Decision

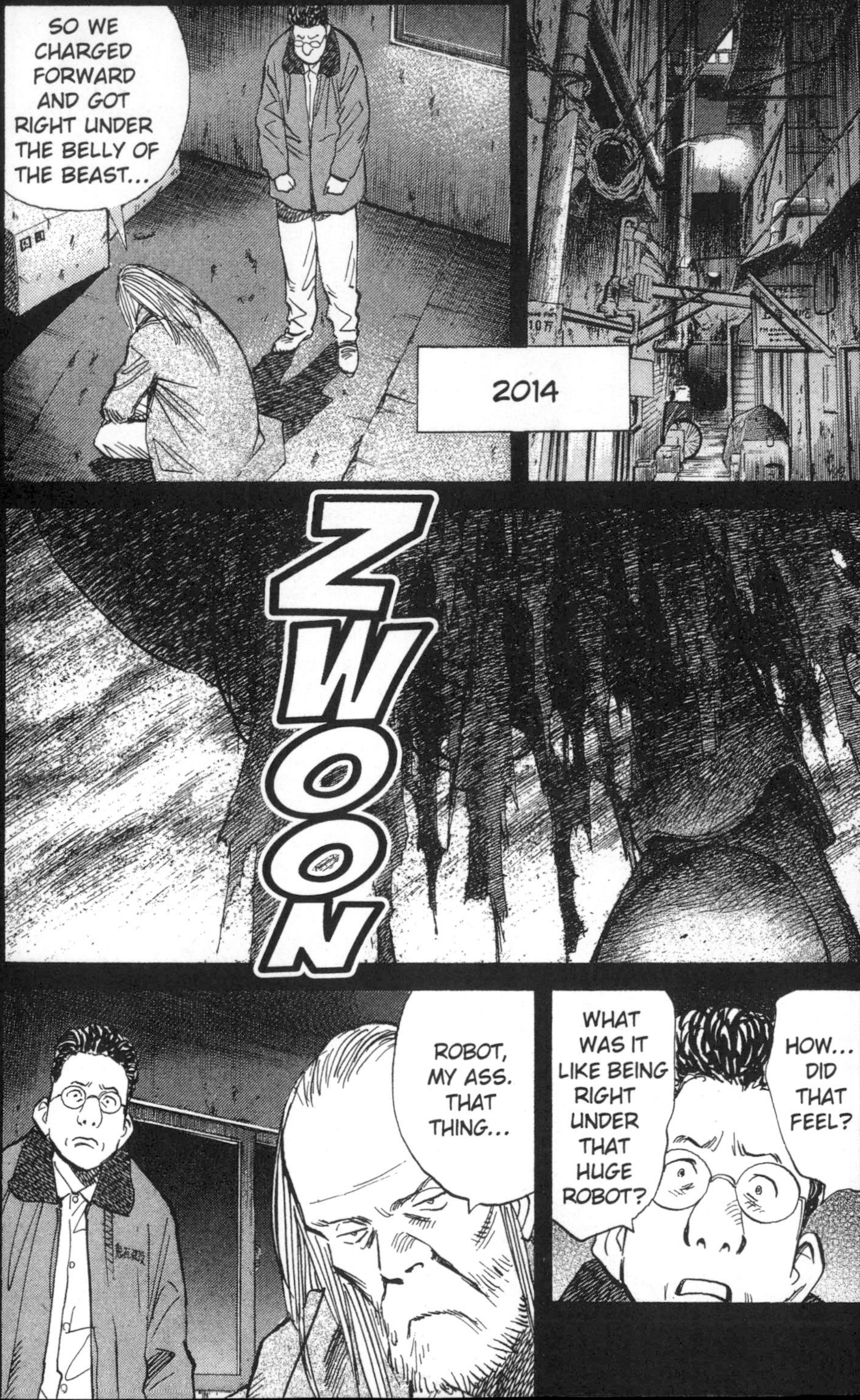
2014
SO WE CHARGED FORWARD AND GOT RIGHT UNDER THE BELLY OF THE BEAST...
ZWOON
HOW... DID THAT FEEL?
WHAT WAS IT LIKE BEING RIGHT UNDER THAT HUGE ROBOT?
ROBOT, MY ASS. THAT THING...

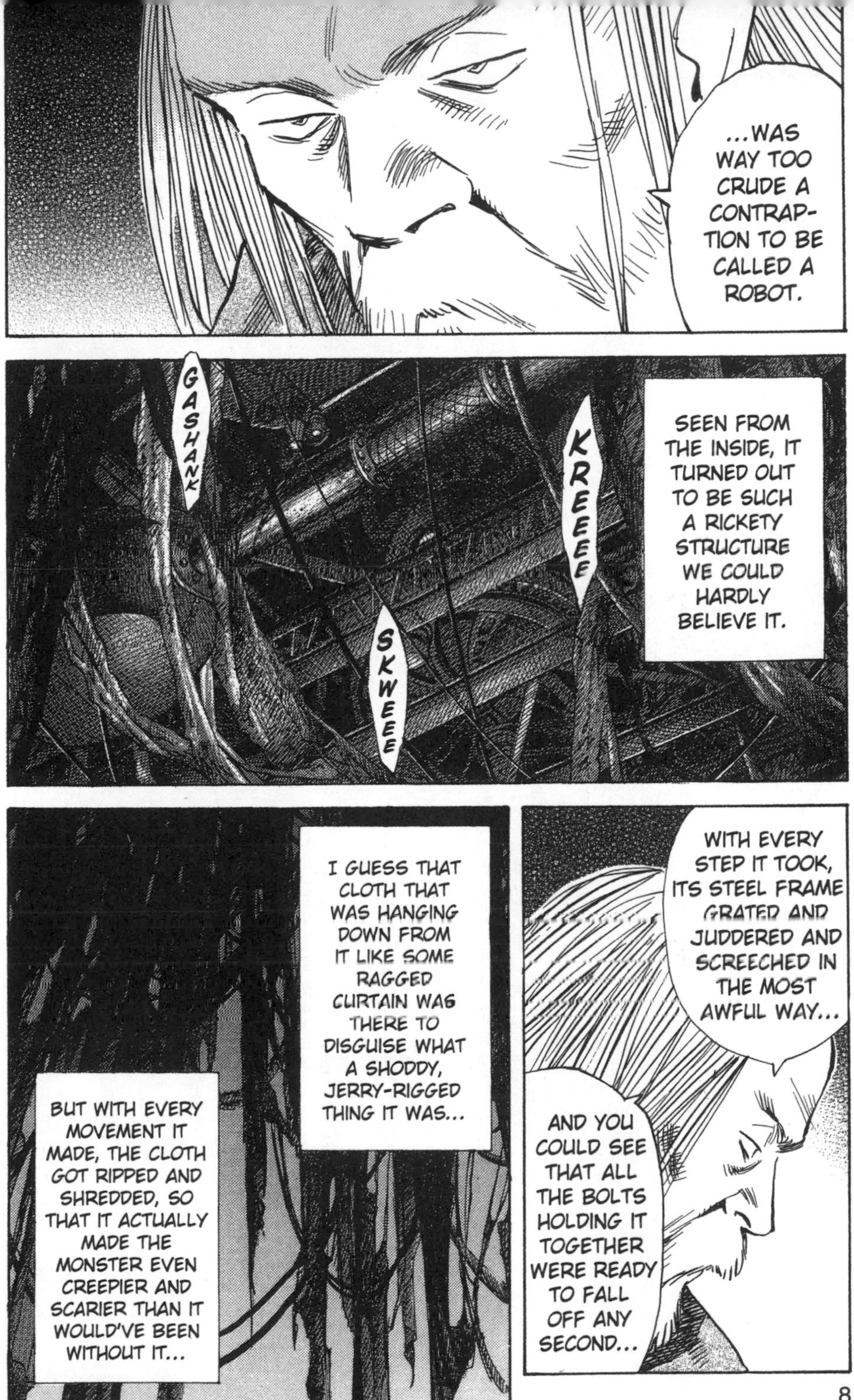
...WAS WAY TOO CRUDE A CONTRAP- TION TO BE CALLED A ROBOT.
SEEN FROM THE INSIDE, IT TURNED OUT TO BE SUCH A RICKETY STRUCTURE WE COULD HARDLY BELIEVE IT.
KREEEE
SKWEEE
GASHANK
WITH EVERY STEP IT TOOK, ITS STEEL FRAME GRATED AND JUDDERED AND SCREECHED IN THE MOST AWFUL WAY...
AND YOU COULD SEE THAT ALL THE BOLTS HOLDING IT TOGETHER WERE READY TO FALL OFF ANY SECOND...
I GUESS THAT CLOTH THAT WAS HANGING DOWN FROM IT LIKE SOME RAGGED CURTAIN WAS THERE TO DISGUISE WHAT A SHODDY, JERRY-RIGGED THING IT WAS...
BUT WITH EVERY MOVEMENT IT MADE, THE CLOTH GOT RIPPED AND SHREDDED, SO THAT IT ACTUALLY MADE THE MONSTER EVEN CREEPIER AND SCARIER THAN IT WOULD'VE BEEN WITHOUT IT...

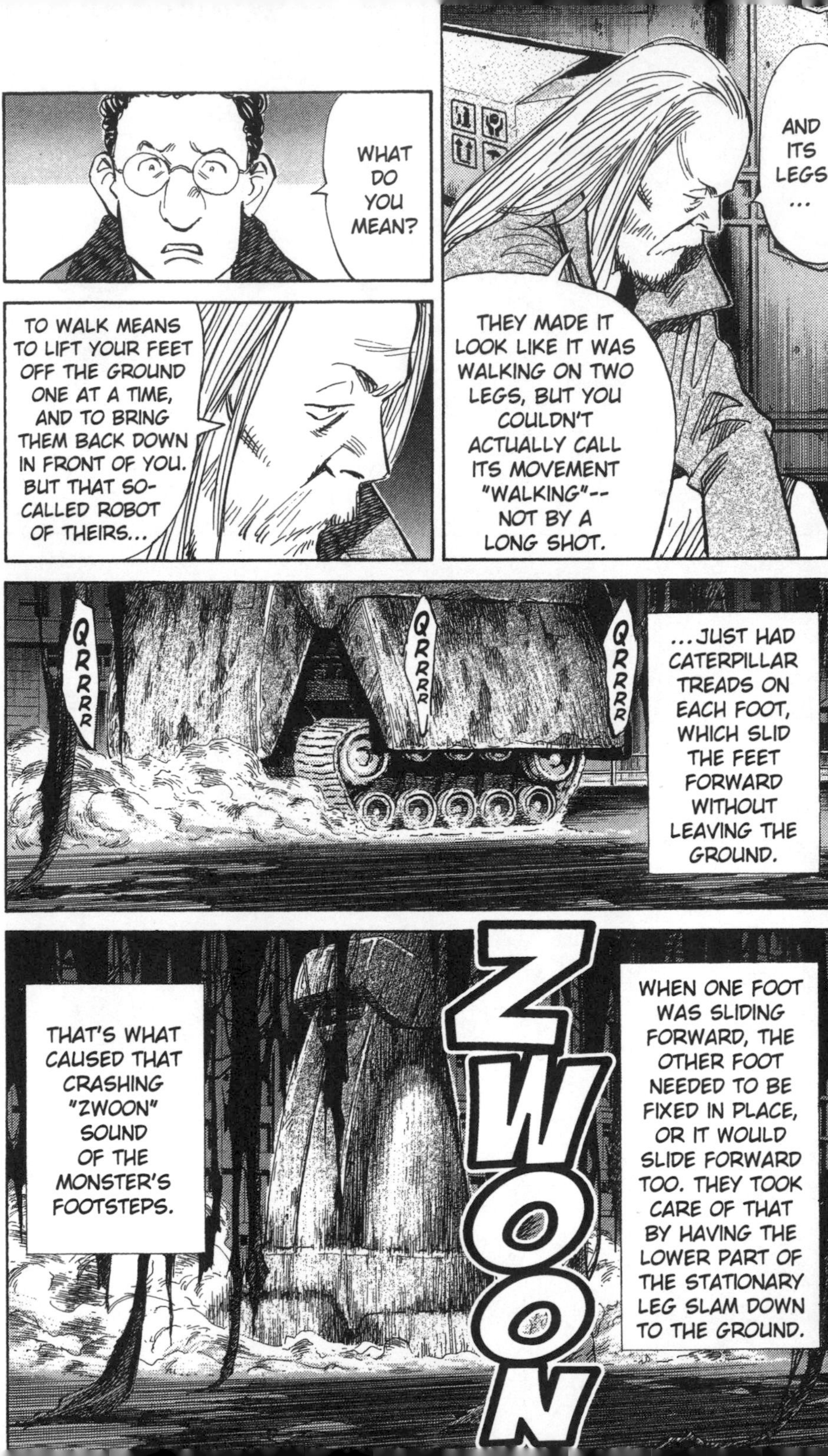
AND ITS LEGS ...
THEY MADE IT LOOK LIKE IT WAS WALKING ON TWO LEGS, BUT YOU COULDN'T ACTUALLY CALL ITS MOVEMENT "WALKING"-- NOT BY A LONG SHOT.
WHAT DO YOU MEAN?
TO WALK MEANS TO LIFT YOUR FEET OFF THE GROUND ONE AT A TIME, AND TO BRING THEM BACK DOWN IN FRONT OF YOU. BUT THAT SO-CALLED ROBOT OF THEIRS...
QRRRR
QRRRR
QRRRR
...JUST HAD CATERPILLAR TREADS ON EACH FOOT, WHICH SLID THE FEET FORWARD WITHOUT LEAVING THE GROUND.
WHEN ONE FOOT WAS SLIDING FORWARD, THE OTHER FOOT NEEDED TO BE FIXED IN PLACE, OR IT WOULD SLIDE FORWARD TOO. THEY TOOK CARE OF THAT BY HAVING THE LOWER PART OF THE STATIONARY LEG SLAM DOWN TO THE GROUND.
ZWOON
THAT'S WHAT CAUSED THAT CRASHING "ZWOON" SOUND OF THE MONSTER'S FOOTSTEPS.

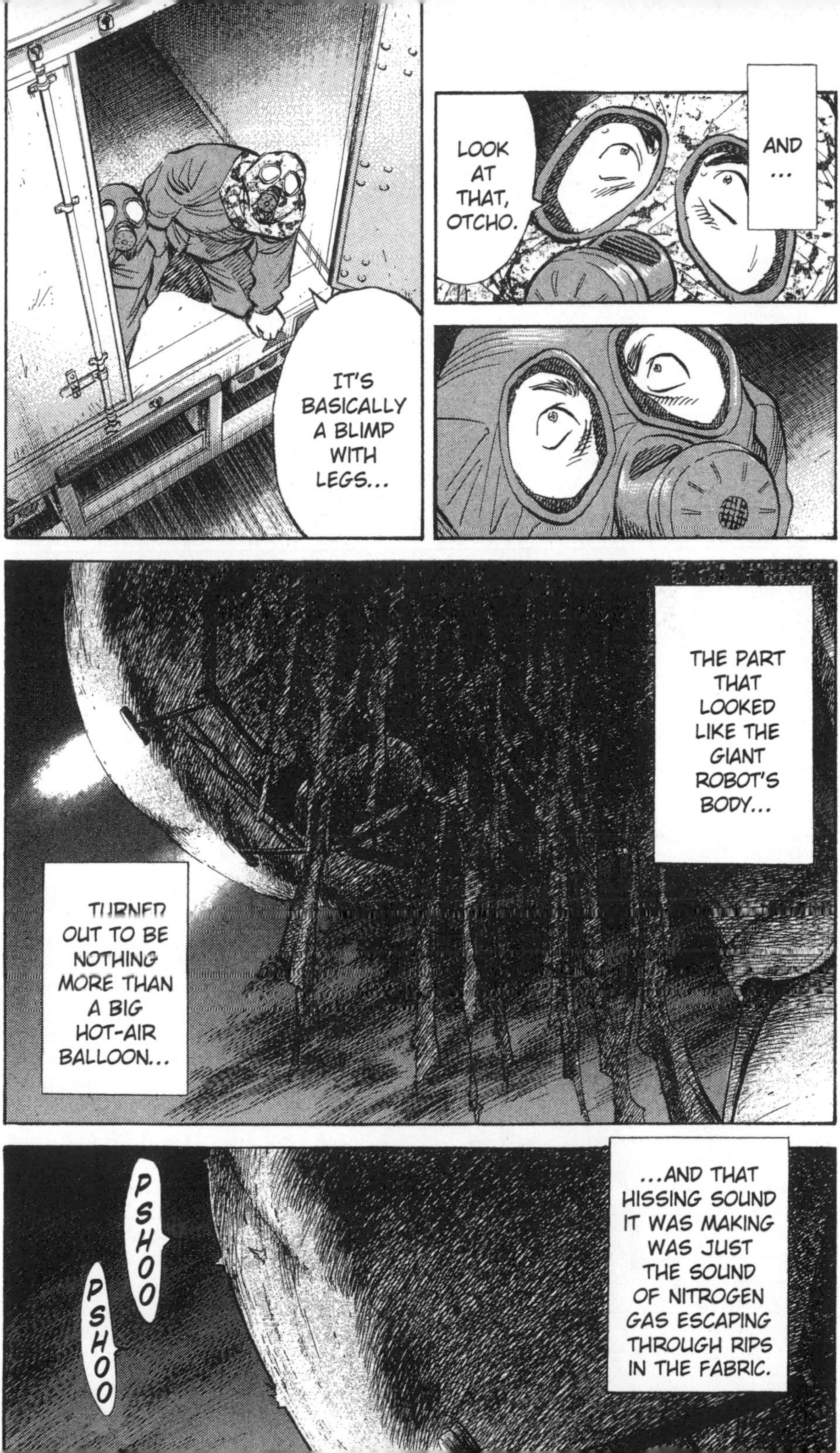
AND ...
LOOK AT THAT, OTCHO.
IT'S BASICALLY A BLIMP WITH LEGS...
THE PART THAT LOOKED LIKE THE GIANT ROBOT'S BODY...
TURNED OUT TO BE NOTHING MORE THAN A BIG HOT-AIR BALLOON...
...AND THAT HISSING SOUND IT WAS MAKING WAS JUST THE SOUND OF NITROGEN GAS ESCAPING THROUGH RIPS IN THE FABRIC.
PSHOO
PSHOO

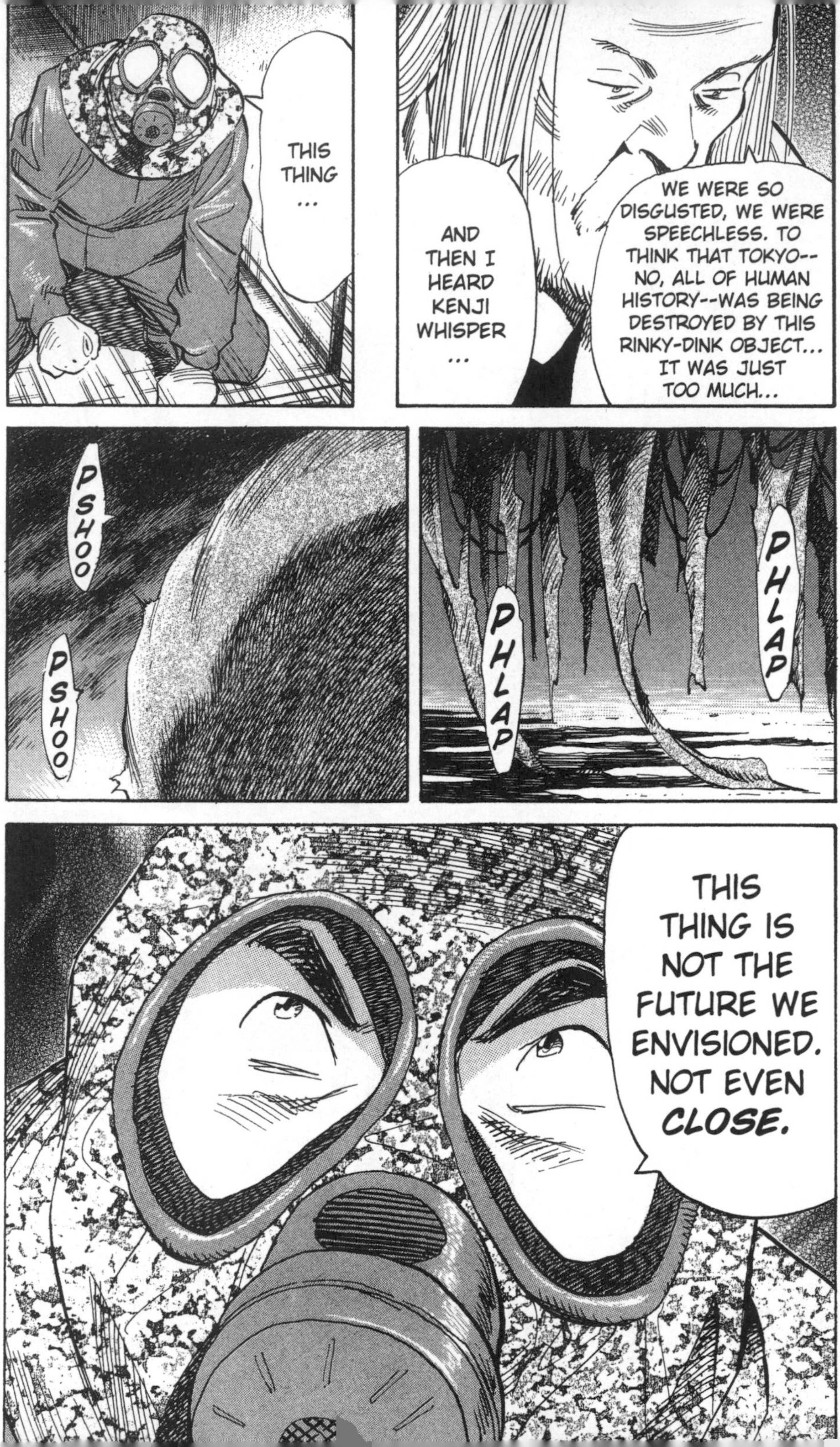
WE WERE SO DISGUSTED, WE WERE SPEECHLESS. TO THINK THAT TOKYO-- NO, ALL OF HUMAN HISTORY--WAS BEING DESTROYED BY THIS RINKY-DINK OBJECT... IT WAS JUST TOO MUCH...
AND THEN I HEARD KENJI WHISPER ...
THIS THING ...
PHLAP
PHLAP
PSHOO
PSHOO
THIS THING IS NOT THE FUTURE WE ENVISIONED. NOT EVEN CLOSE.

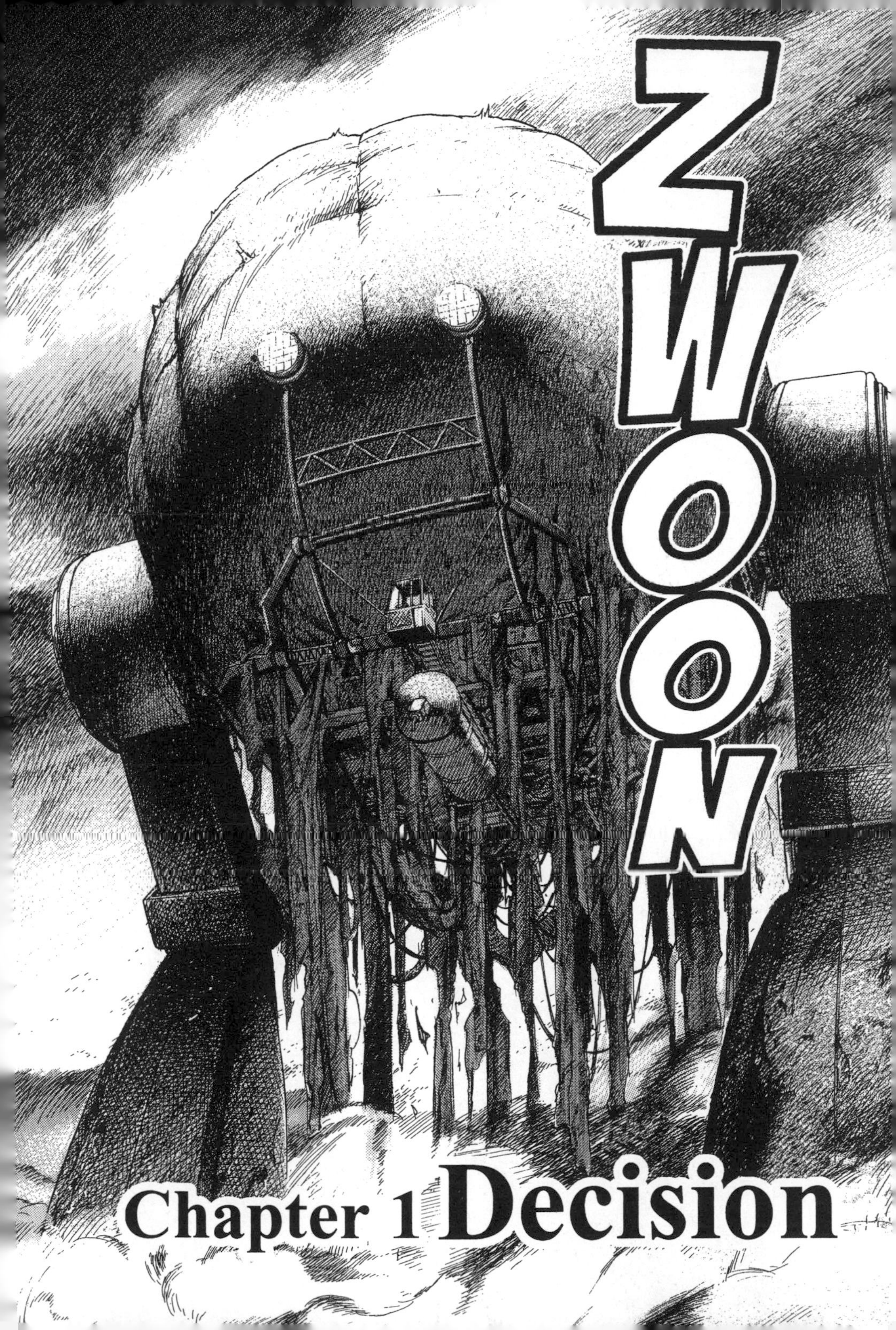
ZWOON

Chapter 1 Decision

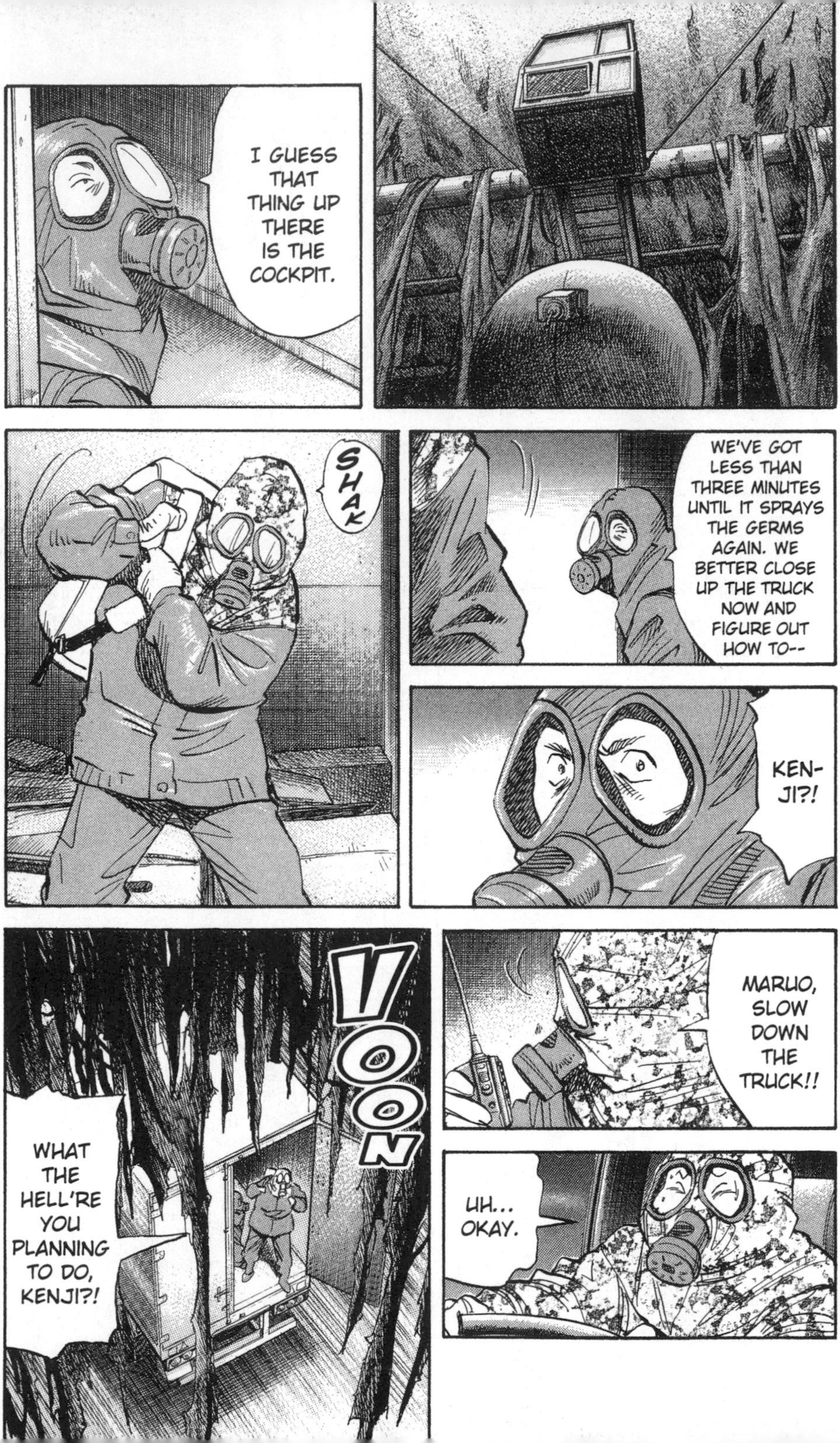
I GUESS THAT THING UP THERE IS THE COCKPIT.
WE'VE GOT LESS THAN THREE MINUTES UNTIL IT SPRAYS THE GERMS AGAIN. WE BETTER CLOSE UP THE TRUCK NOW AND FIGURE OUT HOW TO--
KEN-JI?!
SHAK
MARUO, SLOW DOWN THE TRUCK!!
UH... OKAY.
VOOON
WHAT THE HELL'RE YOU PLANNING TO DO, KENJI?!

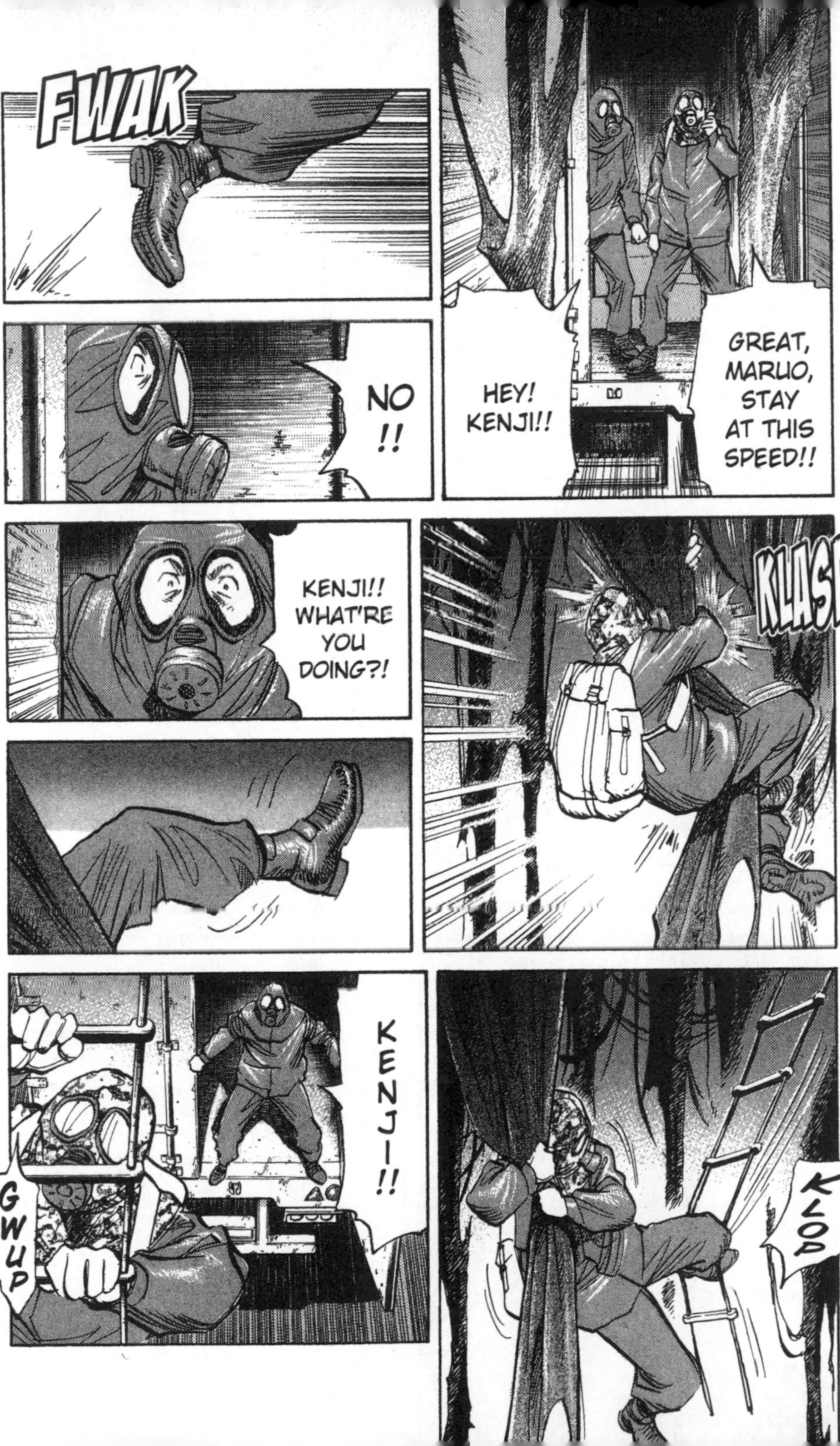
GREAT, MARUO, STAY AT THIS SPEED!!
HEY! KENJI!!
FWAK
NO!!
KLASP
KENJI!! WHAT'RE YOU DOING?!
KLOP
KENJI!!
GWUP

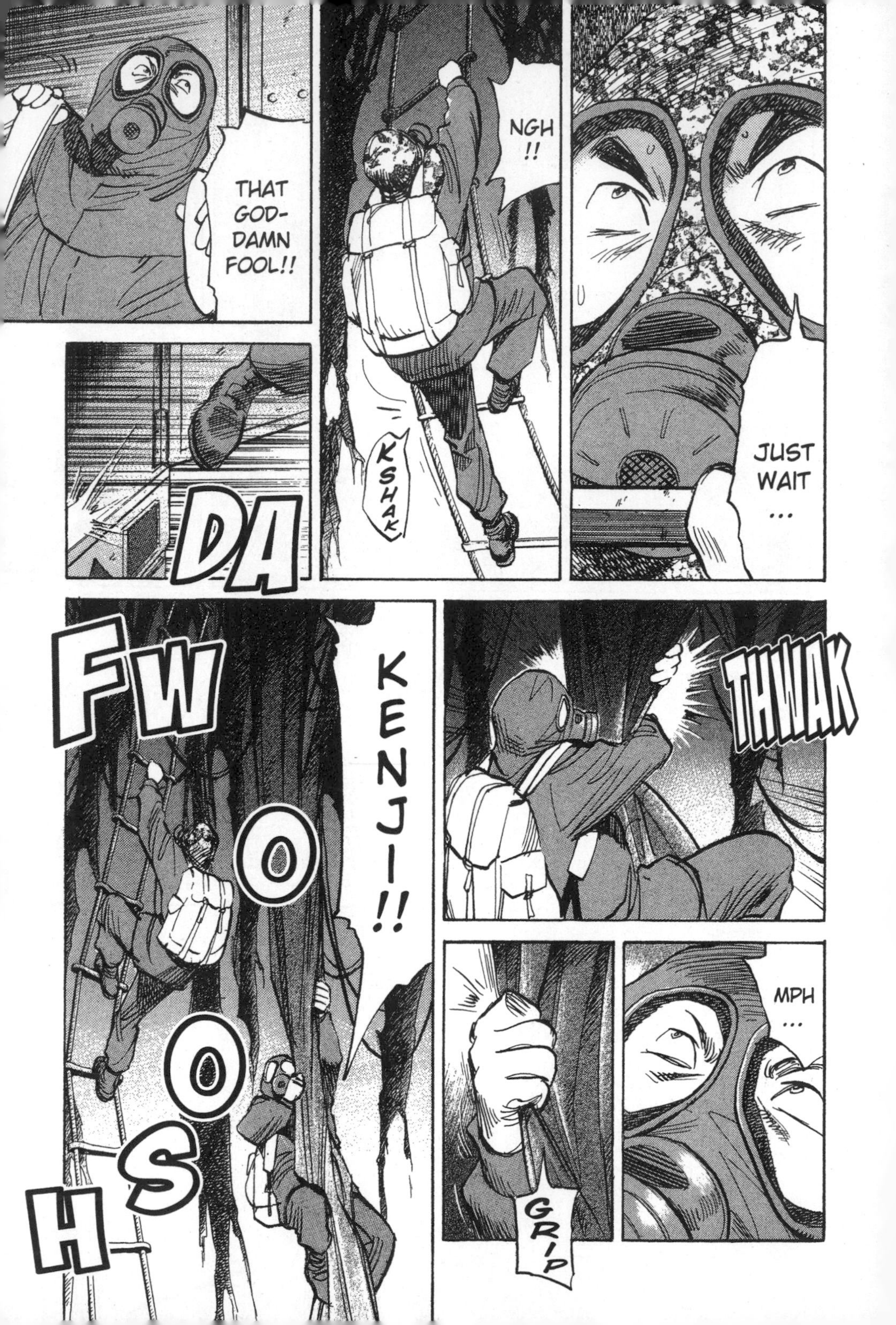
JUST WAIT ...
NGH !!
KSHAK
THAT GOD-DAMN FOOL!!
DA
THWAK
MPH ...
GRIP
KENJI!!
FWOOSH

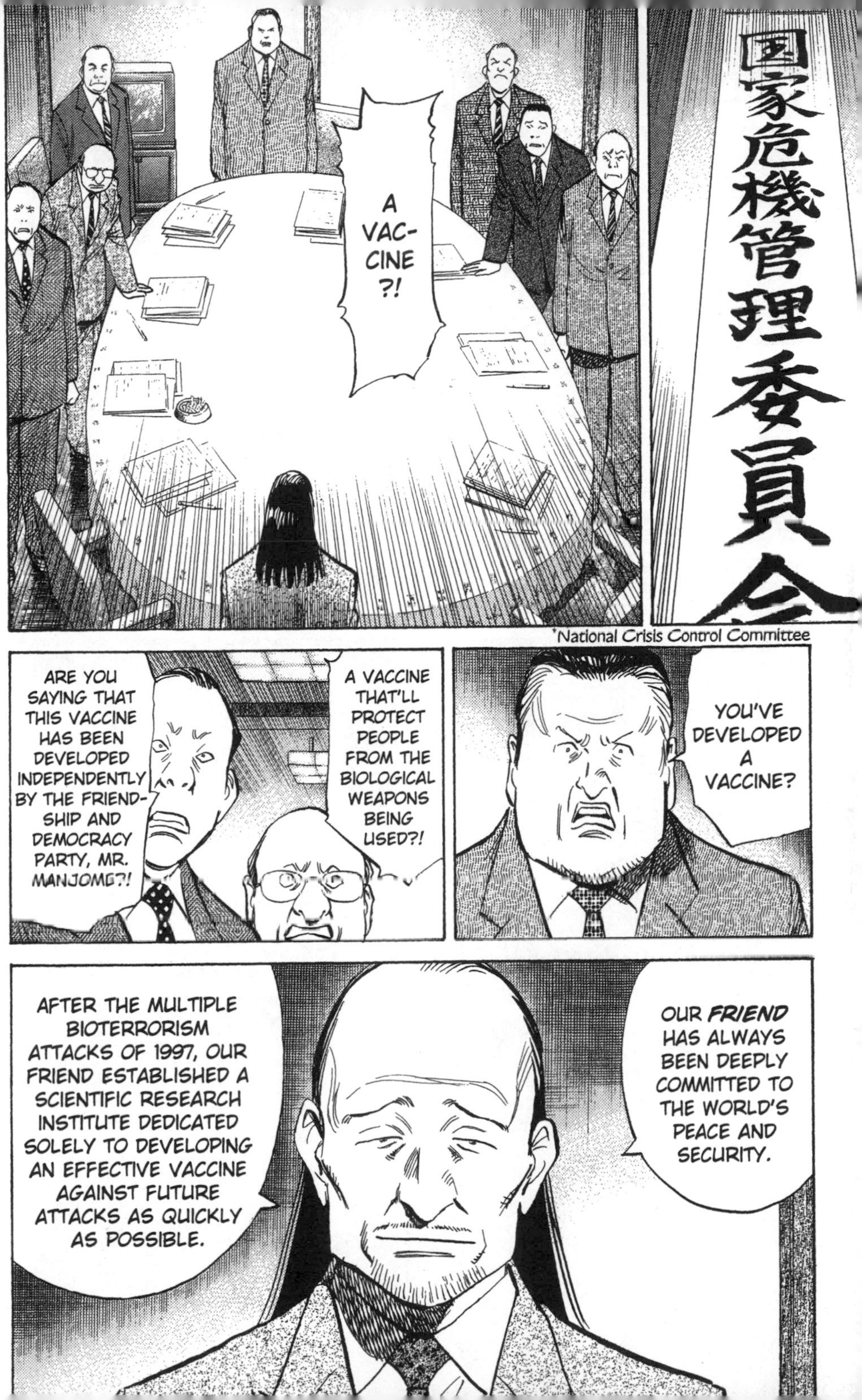
国家危機管理委員会
A VACCINE?!
YOU'VE DEVELOPED A VACCINE?
A VACCINE THAT'LL PROTECT PEOPLE FROM THE BIOLOGICAL WEAPONS BEING USED?!
ARE YOU SAYING THAT THIS VACCINE HAS BEEN DEVELOPED INDEPENDENTLY BY THE FRIENDSHIP AND DEMOCRACY PARTY, MR. MANJOME?!
OUR *FRIEND* HAS ALWAYS BEEN DEEPLY COMMITTED TO THE WORLD'S PEACE AND SECURITY.
AFTER THE MULTIPLE BIOTERRORISM ATTACKS OF 1997, OUR FRIEND ESTABLISHED A SCIENTIFIC RESEARCH INSTITUTE DEDICATED SOLELY TO DEVELOPING AN EFFECTIVE VACCINE AGAINST FUTURE ATTACKS AS QUICKLY AS POSSIBLE.
*National Crisis Control Committee

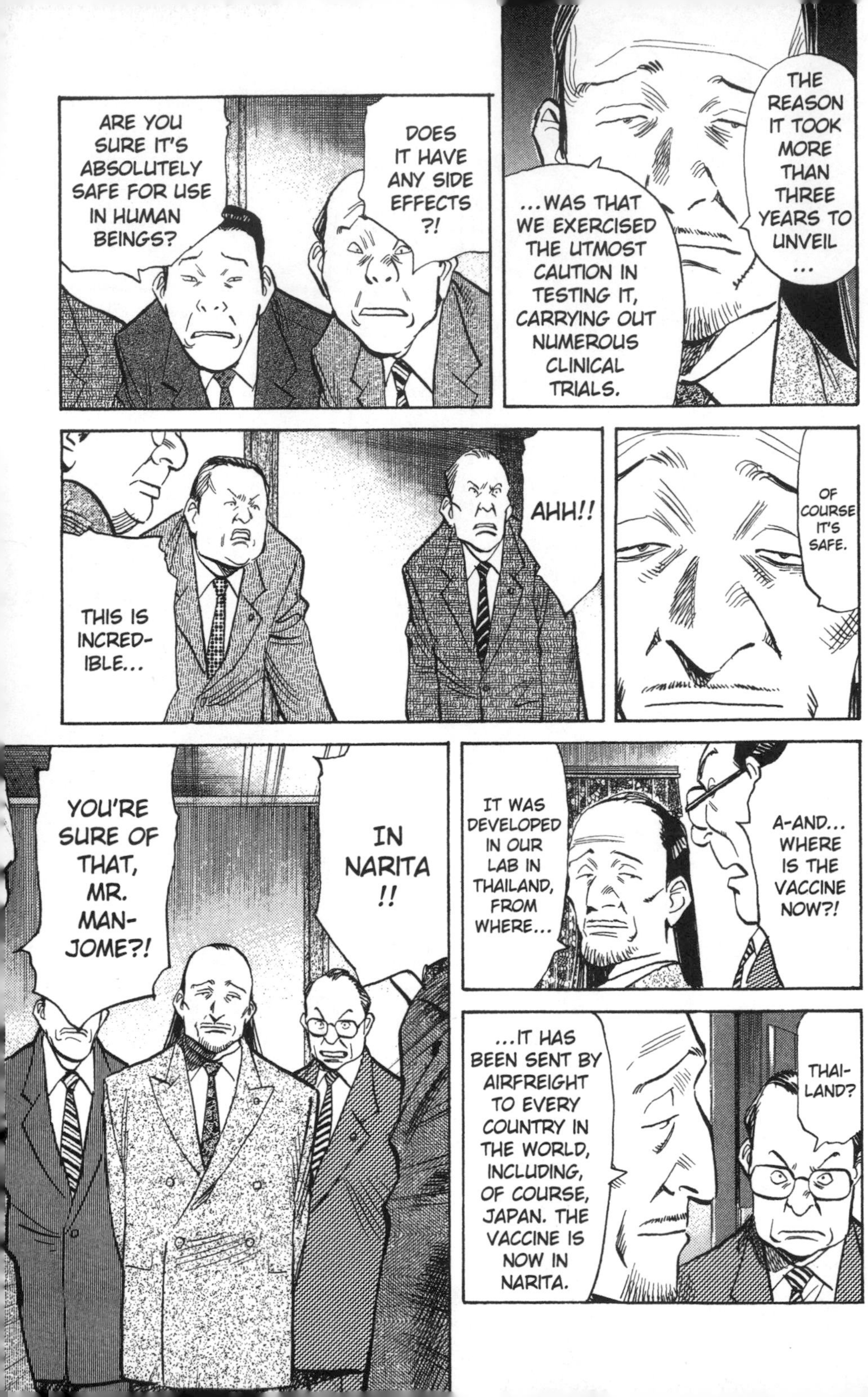
THE REASON IT TOOK MORE THAN THREE YEARS TO UNVEIL ...
...WAS THAT WE EXERCISED THE UTMOST CAUTION IN TESTING IT, CARRYING OUT NUMEROUS CLINICAL TRIALS.
DOES IT HAVE ANY SIDE EFFECTS ?!
ARE YOU SURE IT'S ABSOLUTELY SAFE FOR USE IN HUMAN BEINGS?
OF COURSE IT'S SAFE.
AHH!!
THIS IS INCRED-IBLE...
A-AND... WHERE IS THE VACCINE NOW?!
IT WAS DEVELOPED IN OUR LAB IN THAILAND, FROM WHERE...
THAI-LAND?
...IT HAS BEEN SENT BY AIRFREIGHT TO EVERY COUNTRY IN THE WORLD, INCLUDING, OF COURSE, JAPAN. THE VACCINE IS NOW IN NARITA.
IN NARITA !!
YOU'RE SURE OF THAT, MR. MAN-JOME?!

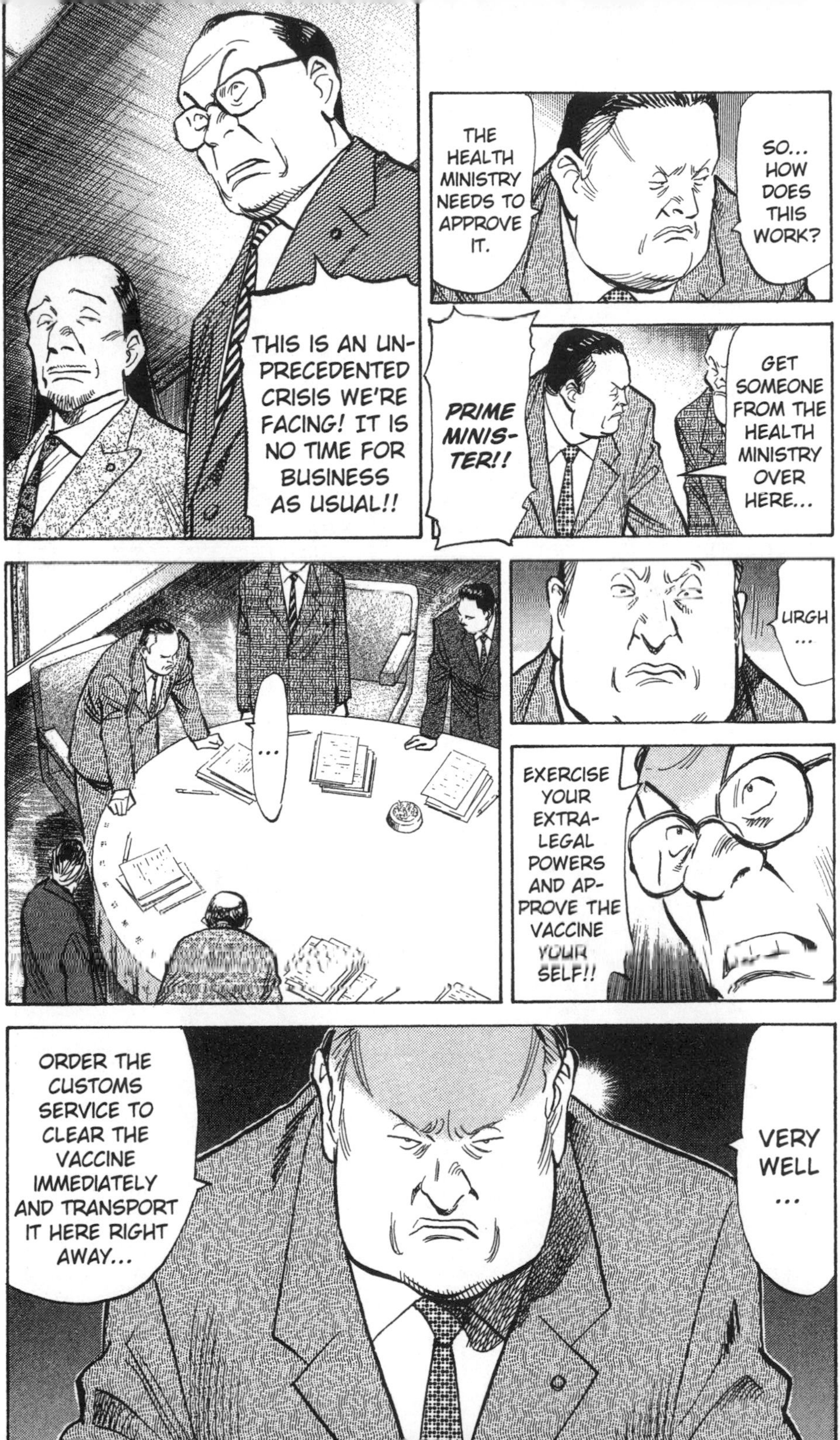
SO... HOW DOES THIS WORK?
THE HEALTH MINISTRY NEEDS TO APPROVE IT.
GET SOMEONE FROM THE HEALTH MINISTRY OVER HERE...
PRIME MINIS-TER!!
THIS IS AN UN-PRECEDENTED CRISIS WE'RE FACING! IT IS NO TIME FOR BUSINESS AS USUAL!!
URGH ...
EXERCISE YOUR EXTRA-LEGAL POWERS AND AP-PROVE THE VACCINE YOUR SELF!!
...
VERY WELL ...
ORDER THE CUSTOMS SERVICE TO CLEAR THE VACCINE IMMEDIATELY AND TRANSPORT IT HERE RIGHT AWAY...

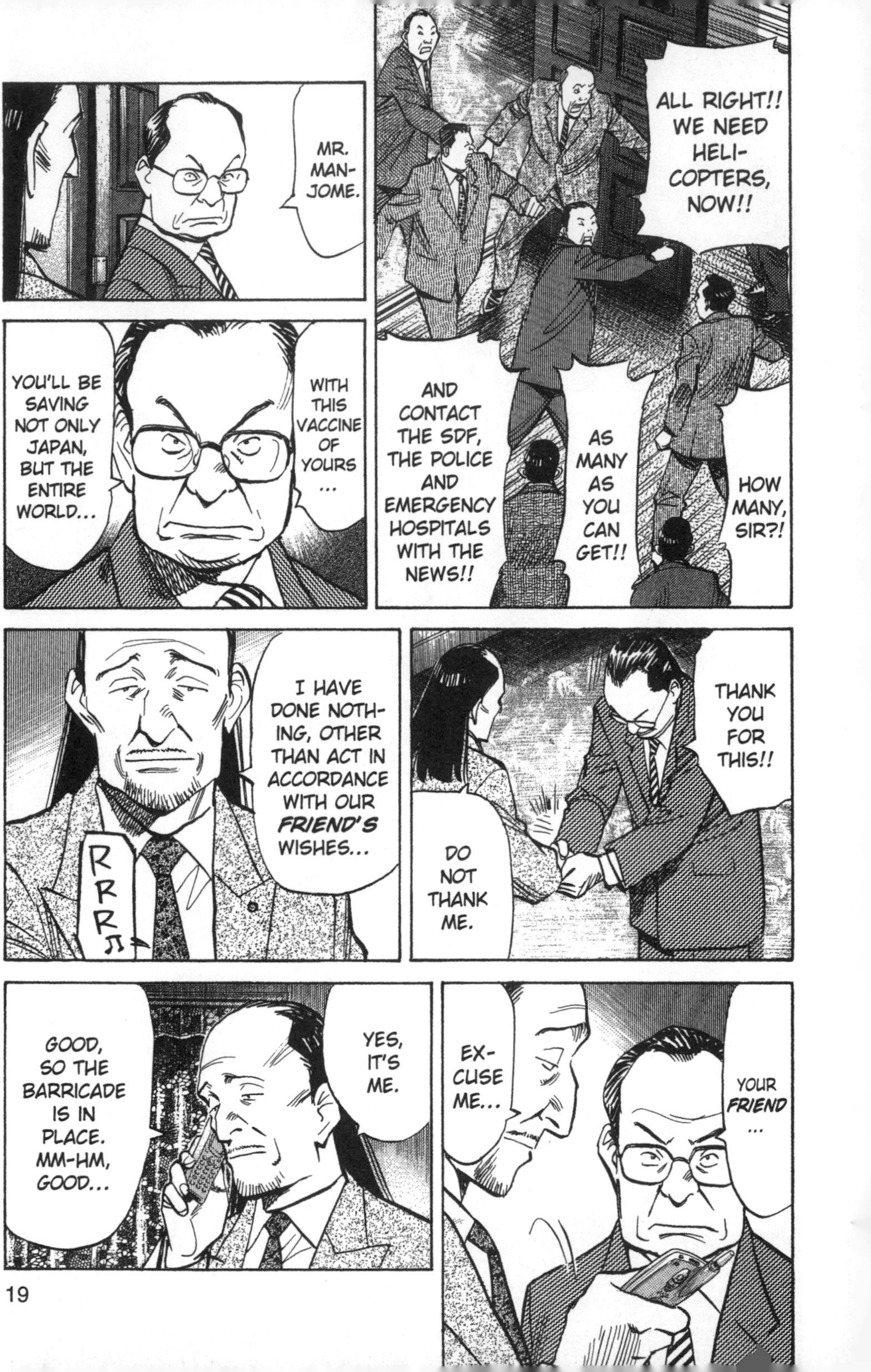
ALL RIGHT!! WE NEED HELI-COPTERS, NOW!!
HOW MANY, SIR?!
AS MANY AS YOU CAN GET!!
AND CONTACT THE SDF, THE POLICE AND EMERGENCY HOSPITALS WITH THE NEWS!!
MR. MAN-JOME.
WITH THIS VACCINE OF YOURS ...
YOU'LL BE SAVING NOT ONLY JAPAN, BUT THE ENTIRE WORLD...
THANK YOU FOR THIS!!
DO NOT THANK ME.
I HAVE DONE NOTH-ING, OTHER THAN ACT IN ACCORDANCE WITH OUR *FRIEND'S* WISHES...
RRR♪
YOUR *FRIEND* ...
EX-CUSE ME...
YES, IT'S ME.
GOOD, SO THE BARRICADE IS IN PLACE. MM-HM, GOOD...

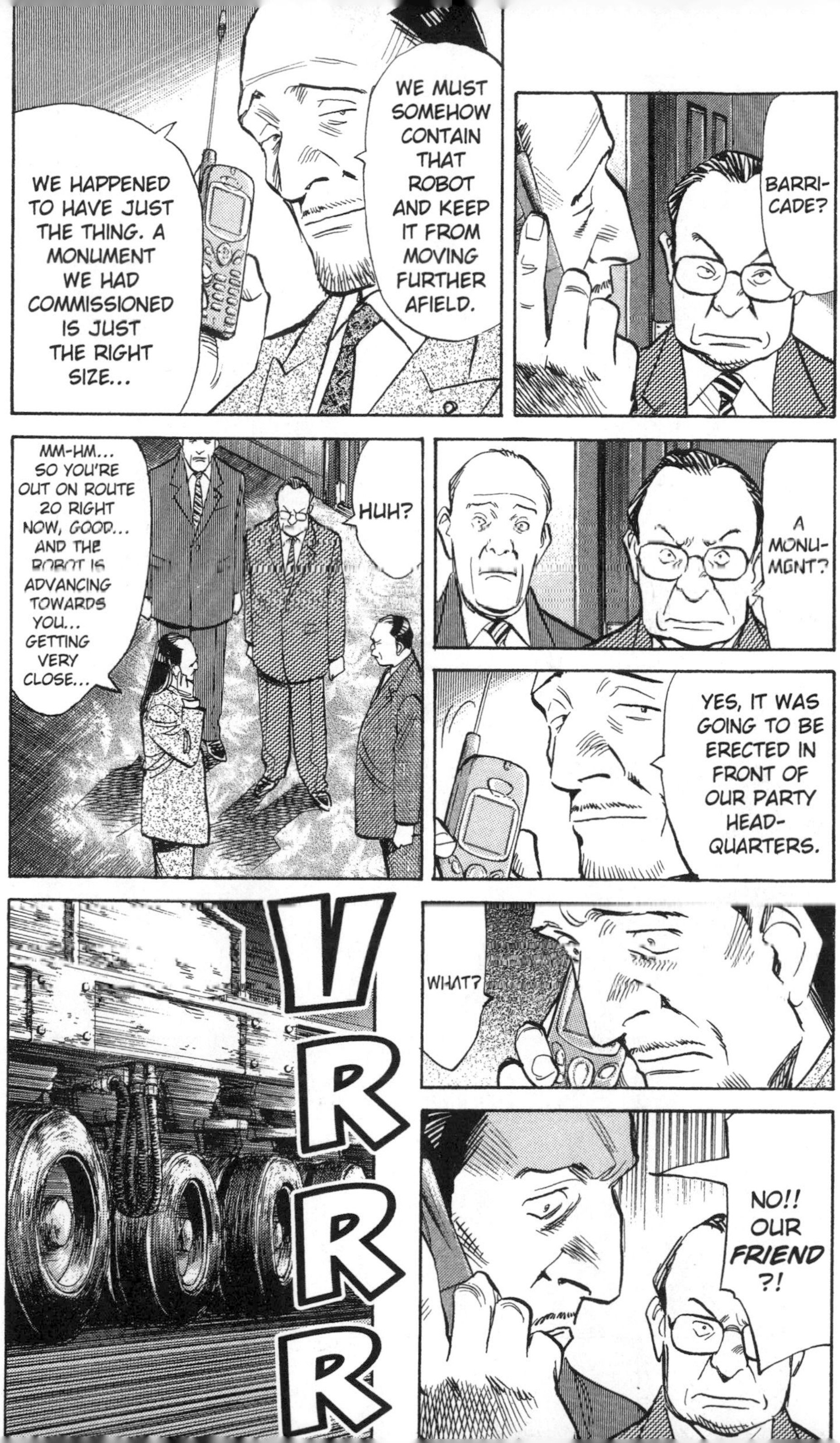
BARRI-CADE?
WE MUST SOMEHOW CONTAIN THAT ROBOT AND KEEP IT FROM MOVING FURTHER AFIELD.
WE HAPPENED TO HAVE JUST THE THING. A MONUMENT WE HAD COMMISSIONED IS JUST THE RIGHT SIZE...
A MONU-MENT?
YES, IT WAS GOING TO BE ERECTED IN FRONT OF OUR PARTY HEAD-QUARTERS.
HUH?
MM-HM... SO YOU'RE OUT ON ROUTE 20 RIGHT NOW, GOOD... AND THE ROBOT IS ADVANCING TOWARDS YOU... GETTING VERY CLOSE...
WHAT?
NO!! OUR FRIEND?!
VRRR

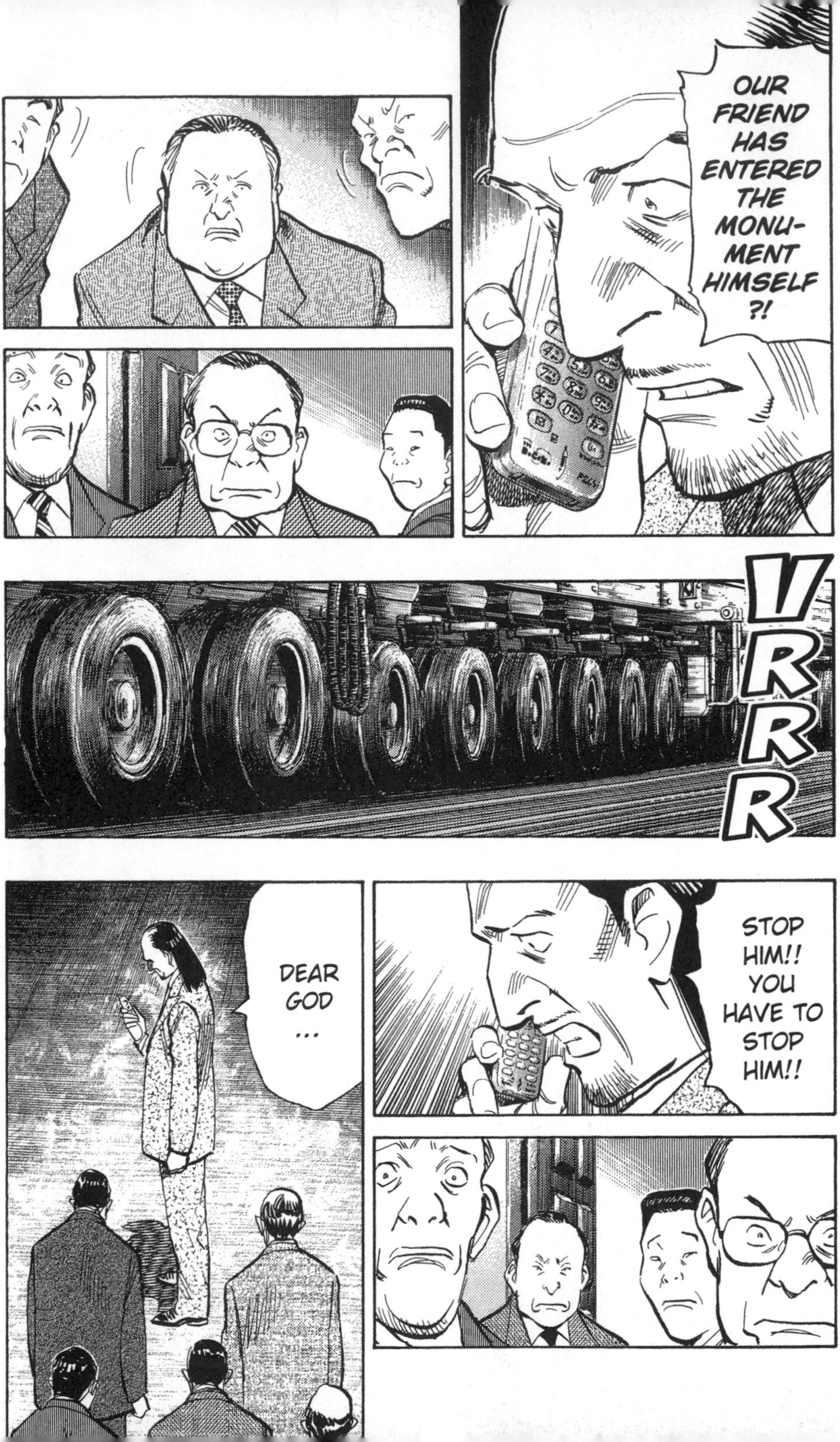
OUR FRIEND HAS ENTERED THE MONUMENT HIMSELF?!
VRRR
STOP HIM!! YOU HAVE TO STOP HIM!!
DEAR GOD ...

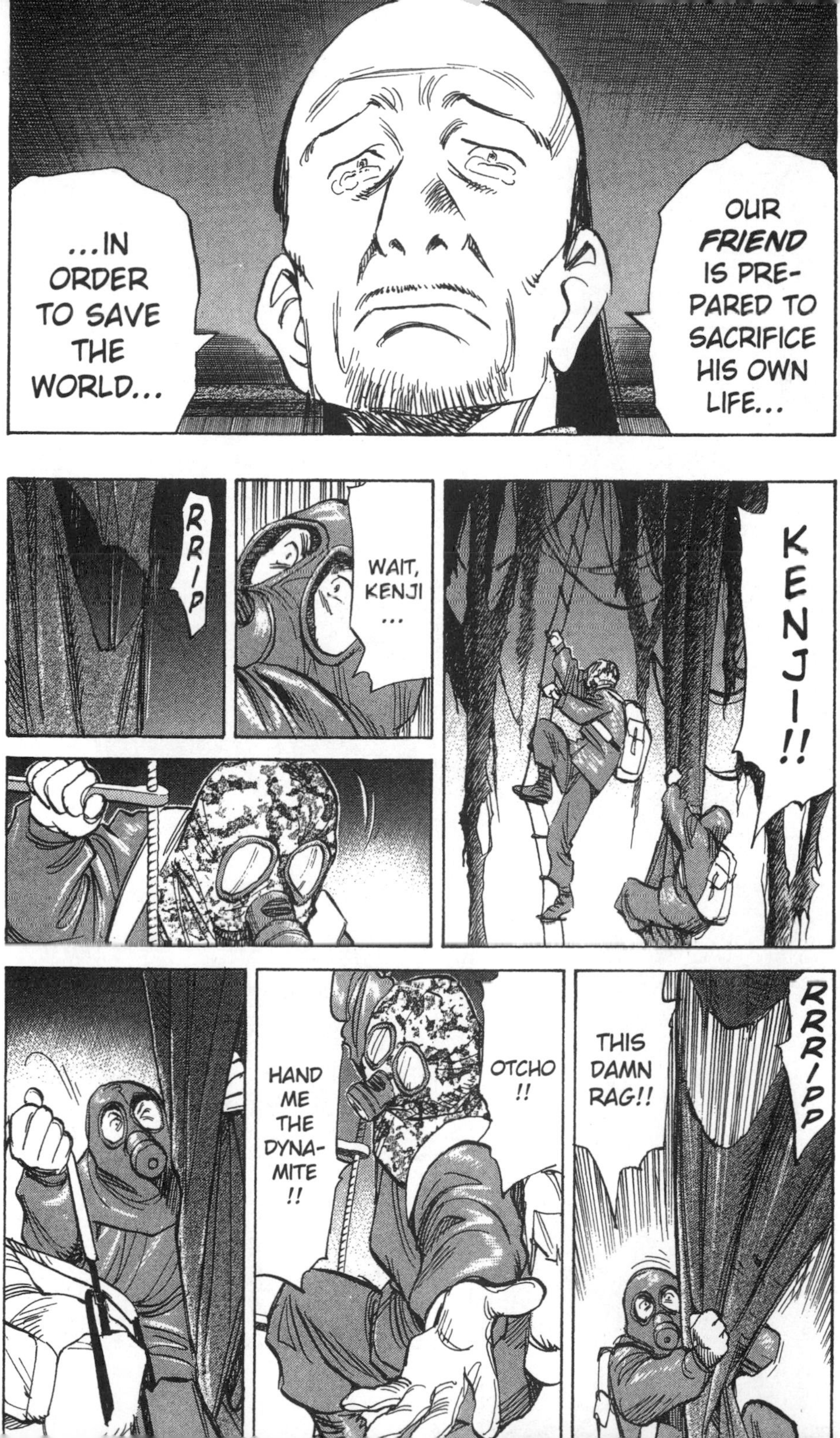
OUR FRIEND IS PREPARED TO SACRIFICE HIS OWN LIFE...
...IN ORDER TO SAVE THE WORLD...
KENJI!!
WAIT, KENJI ...
RRRIP
RRRIPP
THIS DAMN RAG!!
OTCHO!!
HAND ME THE DYNAMITE!!

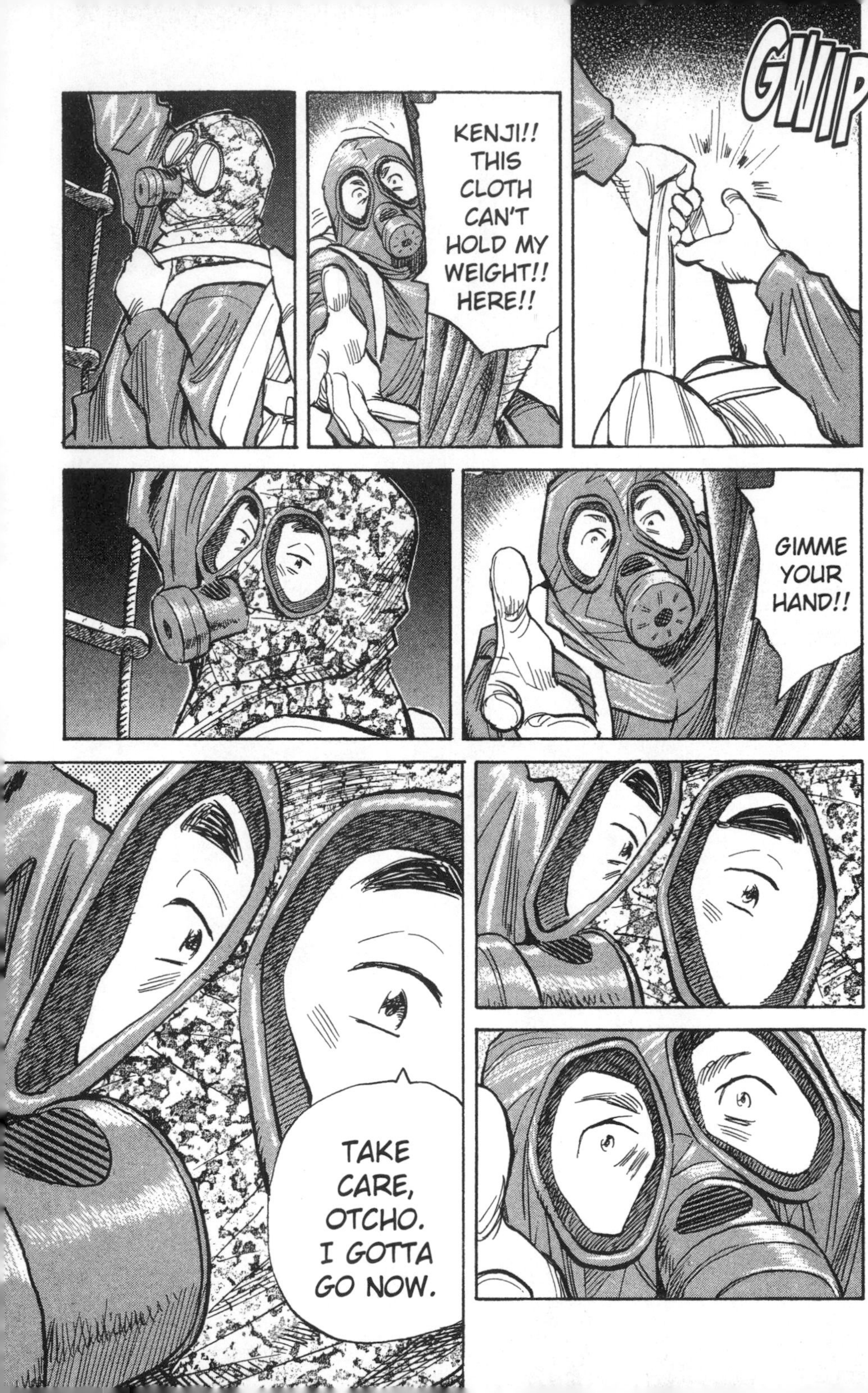
GWIP
KENJI!! THIS CLOTH CAN'T HOLD MY WEIGHT!! HERE!!
GIMME YOUR HAND!!
TAKE CARE, OTCHO. I GOTTA GO NOW.

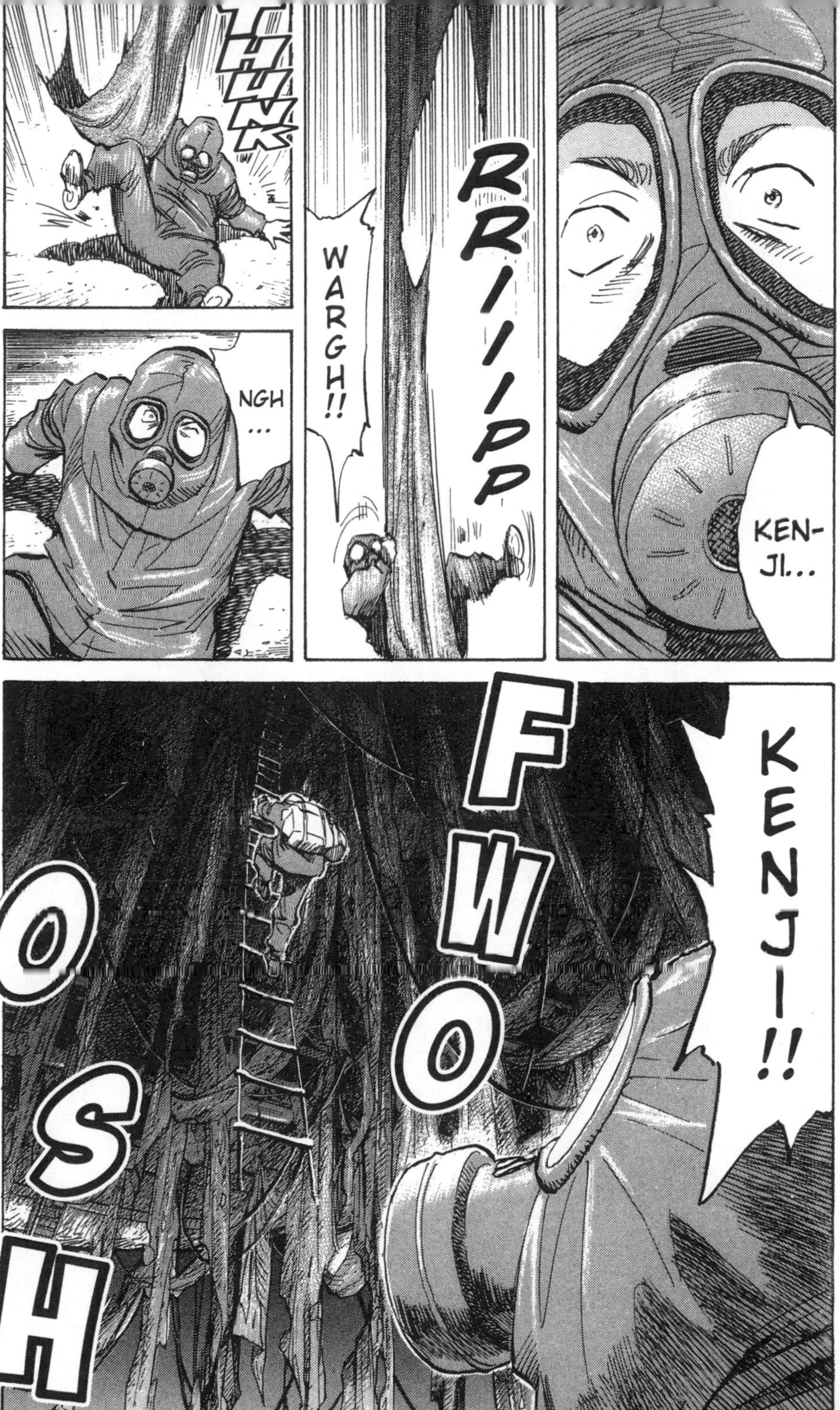
KEN-
JI...
RRIIIPP
WARGH!!
THUNK
NGH
...
KENJI!!
FWOOSH

Chapter 2 Robot

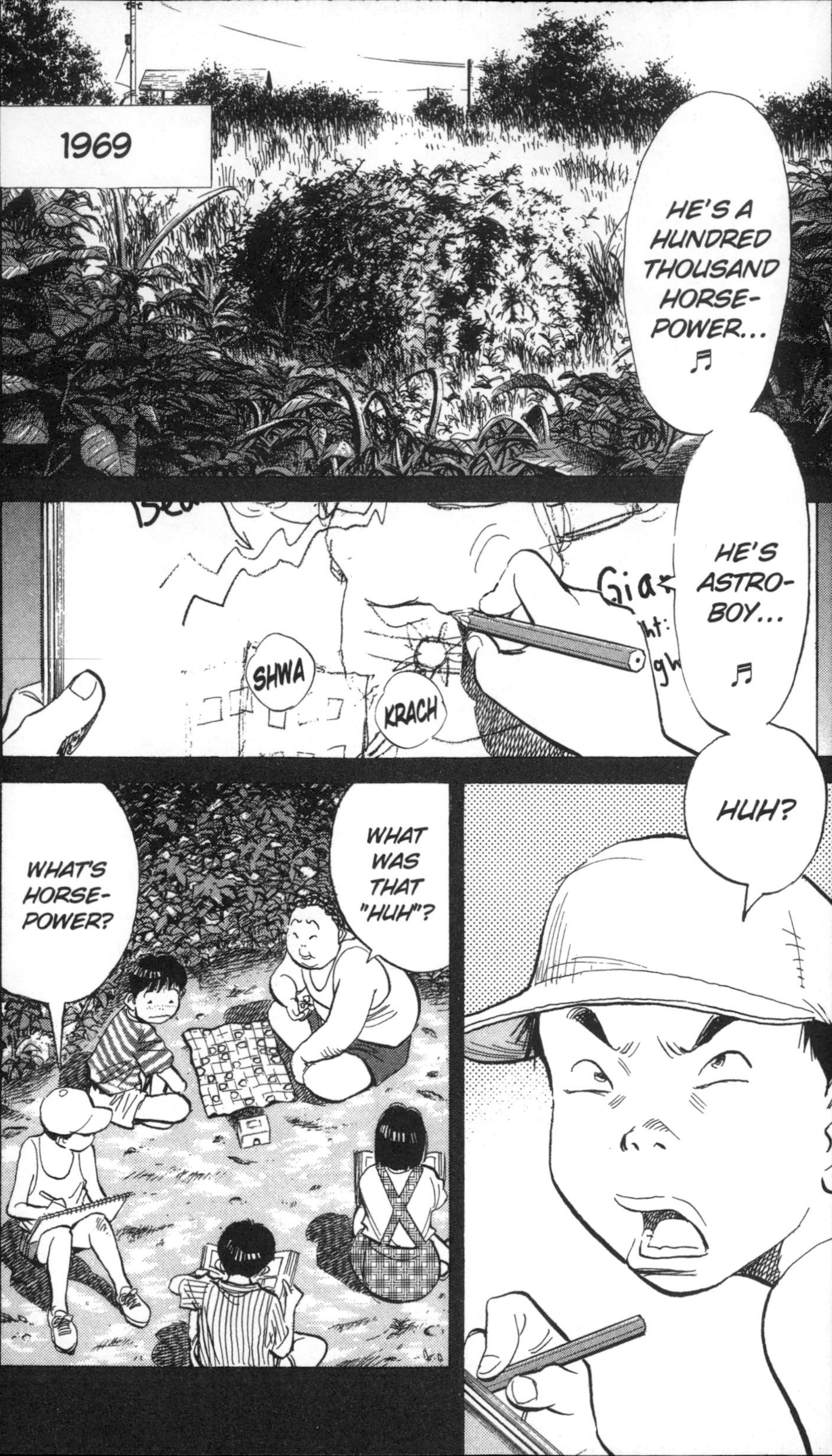
1969
HE'S A HUNDRED THOUSAND HORSE-POWER... ♬
HE'S ASTRO-BOY... ♬
SHWA
KRACH
HUH?
WHAT WAS THAT "HUH"?
WHAT'S HORSE-POWER?

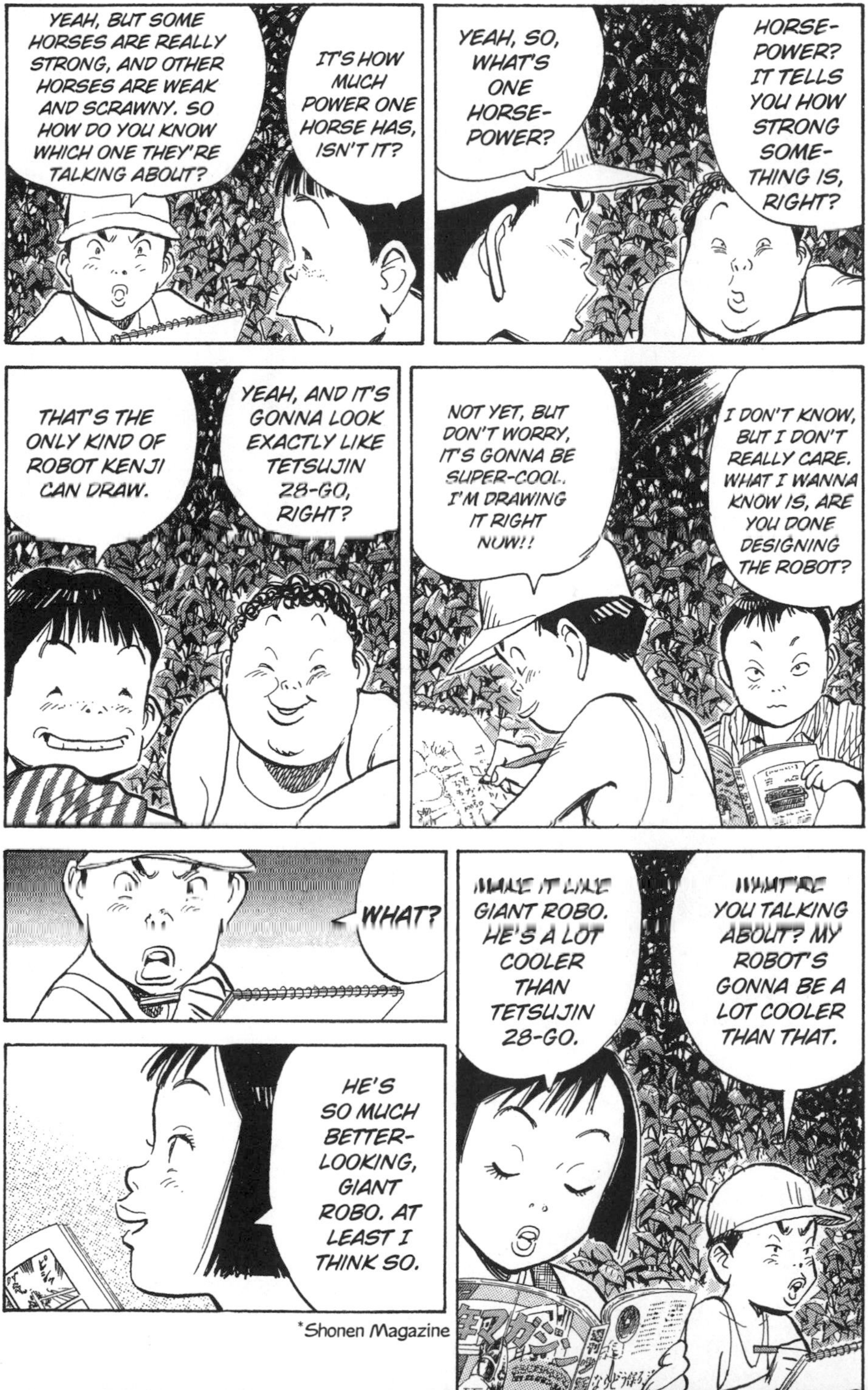
HORSE-POWER? IT TELLS YOU HOW STRONG SOME-THING IS, RIGHT?
YEAH, SO, WHAT'S ONE HORSE-POWER?
IT'S HOW MUCH POWER ONE HORSE HAS, ISN'T IT?
YEAH, BUT SOME HORSES ARE REALLY STRONG, AND OTHER HORSES ARE WEAK AND SCRAWNY. SO HOW DO YOU KNOW WHICH ONE THEY'RE TALKING ABOUT?
I DON'T KNOW, BUT I DON'T REALLY CARE. WHAT I WANNA KNOW IS, ARE YOU DONE DESIGNING THE ROBOT?
NOT YET, BUT DON'T WORRY, IT'S GONNA BE SUPER-COOL. I'M DRAWING IT RIGHT NOW!!
YEAH, AND IT'S GONNA LOOK EXACTLY LIKE TETSUJIN 28-GO, RIGHT?
THAT'S THE ONLY KIND OF ROBOT KENJI CAN DRAW.
WHAT'RE YOU TALKING ABOUT? MY ROBOT'S GONNA BE A LOT COOLER THAN THAT.
MAKE IT LIKE GIANT ROBO. HE'S A LOT COOLER THAN TETSUJIN 28-GO.
WHAT?
HE'S SO MUCH BETTER-LOOKING, GIANT ROBO. AT LEAST I THINK SO.

*Shonen Magazine

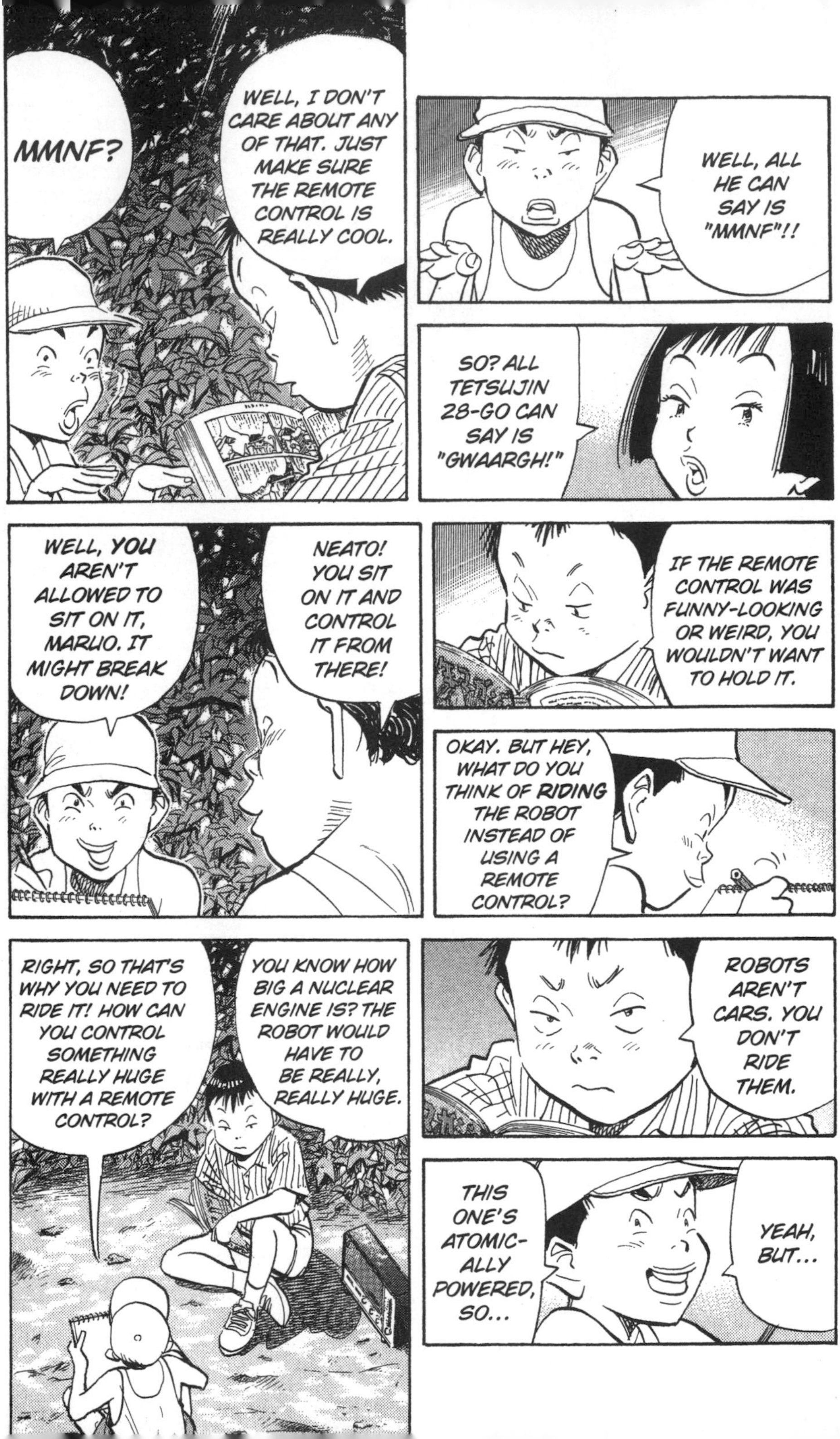
WELL, ALL HE CAN SAY IS "MMNF"!!
SO? ALL TETSUJIN 28-GO CAN SAY IS "GWAARGH!"
WELL, I DON'T CARE ABOUT ANY OF THAT. JUST MAKE SURE THE REMOTE CONTROL IS REALLY COOL.
MMNF?
IF THE REMOTE CONTROL WAS FUNNY-LOOKING OR WEIRD, YOU WOULDN'T WANT TO HOLD IT.
OKAY. BUT HEY, WHAT DO YOU THINK OF RIDING THE ROBOT INSTEAD OF USING A REMOTE CONTROL?
NEATO! YOU SIT ON IT AND CONTROL IT FROM THERE!
WELL, YOU AREN'T ALLOWED TO SIT ON IT, MARUO. IT MIGHT BREAK DOWN!
ROBOTS AREN'T CARS. YOU DON'T RIDE THEM.
YEAH, BUT...
THIS ONE'S ATOMIC-ALLY POWERED, SO...
YOU KNOW HOW BIG A NUCLEAR ENGINE IS? THE ROBOT WOULD HAVE TO BE REALLY, REALLY HUGE.
RIGHT, SO THAT'S WHY YOU NEED TO RIDE IT! HOW CAN YOU CONTROL SOMETHING REALLY HUGE WITH A REMOTE CONTROL?

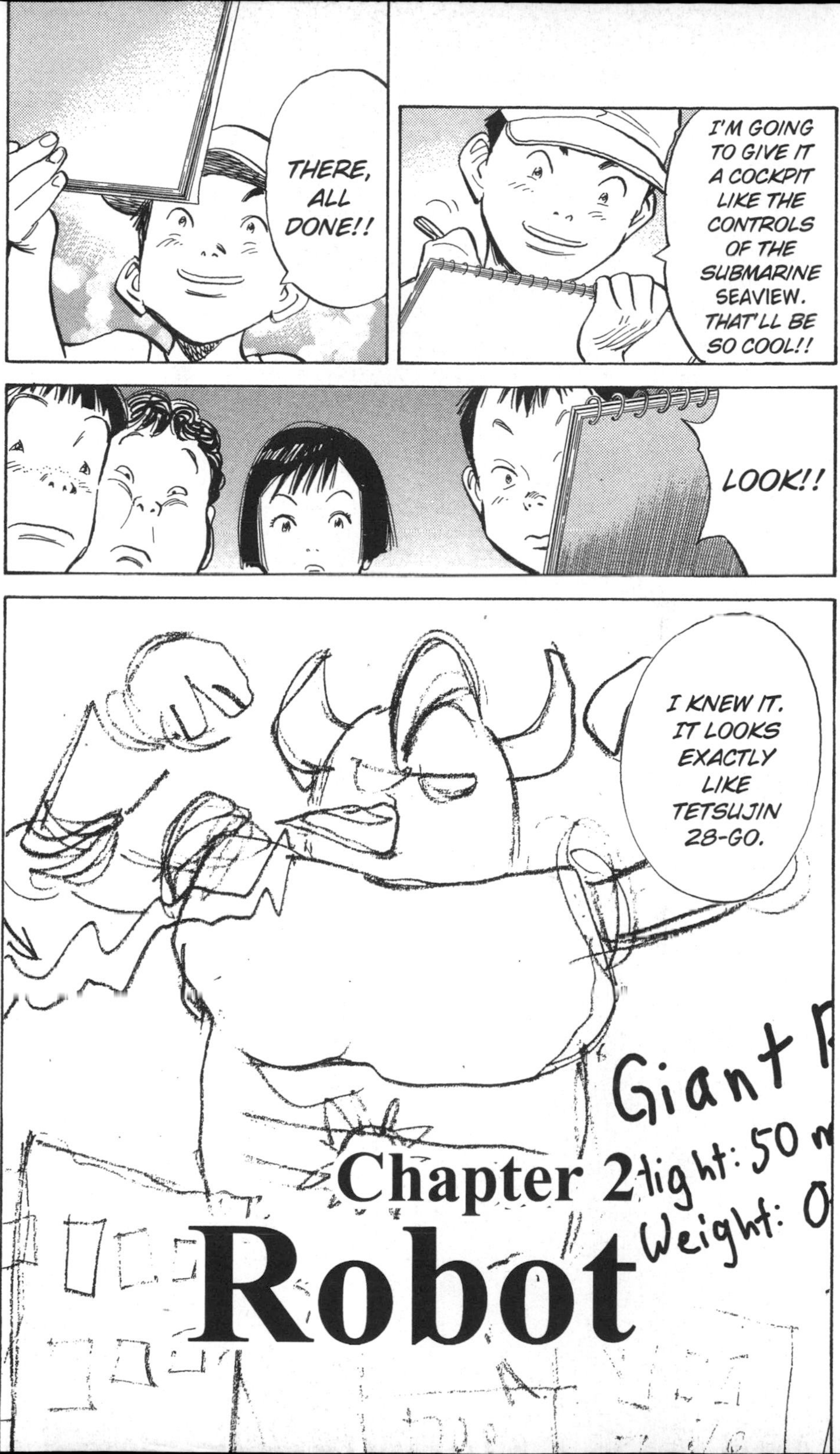
I'M GOING TO GIVE IT A COCKPIT LIKE THE CONTROLS OF THE SUBMARINE SEAVIEW. THAT'LL BE SO COOL!!
THERE, ALL DONE!!
LOOK!!
I KNEW IT. IT LOOKS EXACTLY LIKE TETSUJIN 28-GO.

Chapter 2
Robot

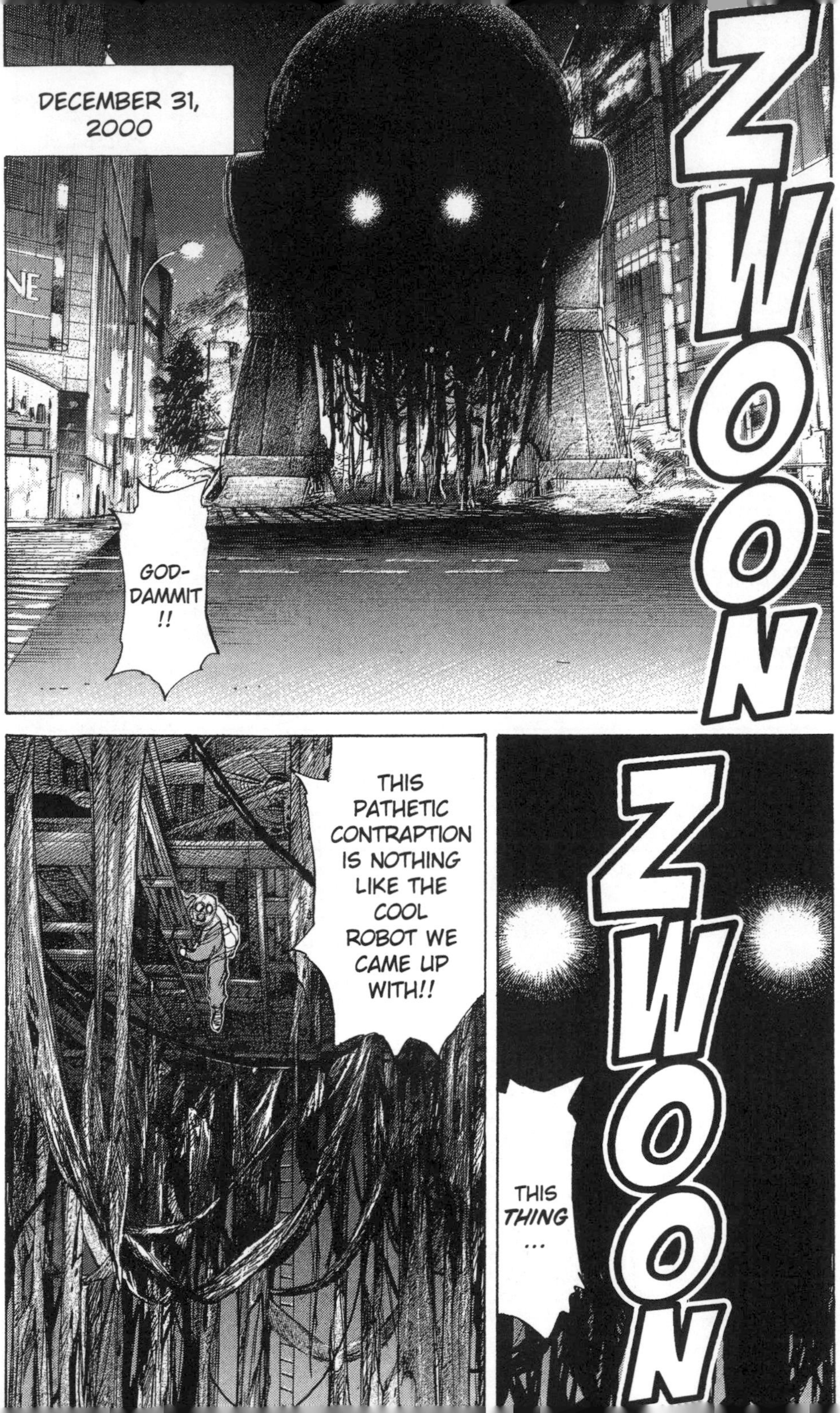
ZWOOON
DECEMBER 31, 2000
GOD-DAMMIT!!
ZWOOON
THIS *THING*...
THIS PATHETIC CONTRAPTION IS NOTHING LIKE THE COOL ROBOT WE CAME UP WITH!!

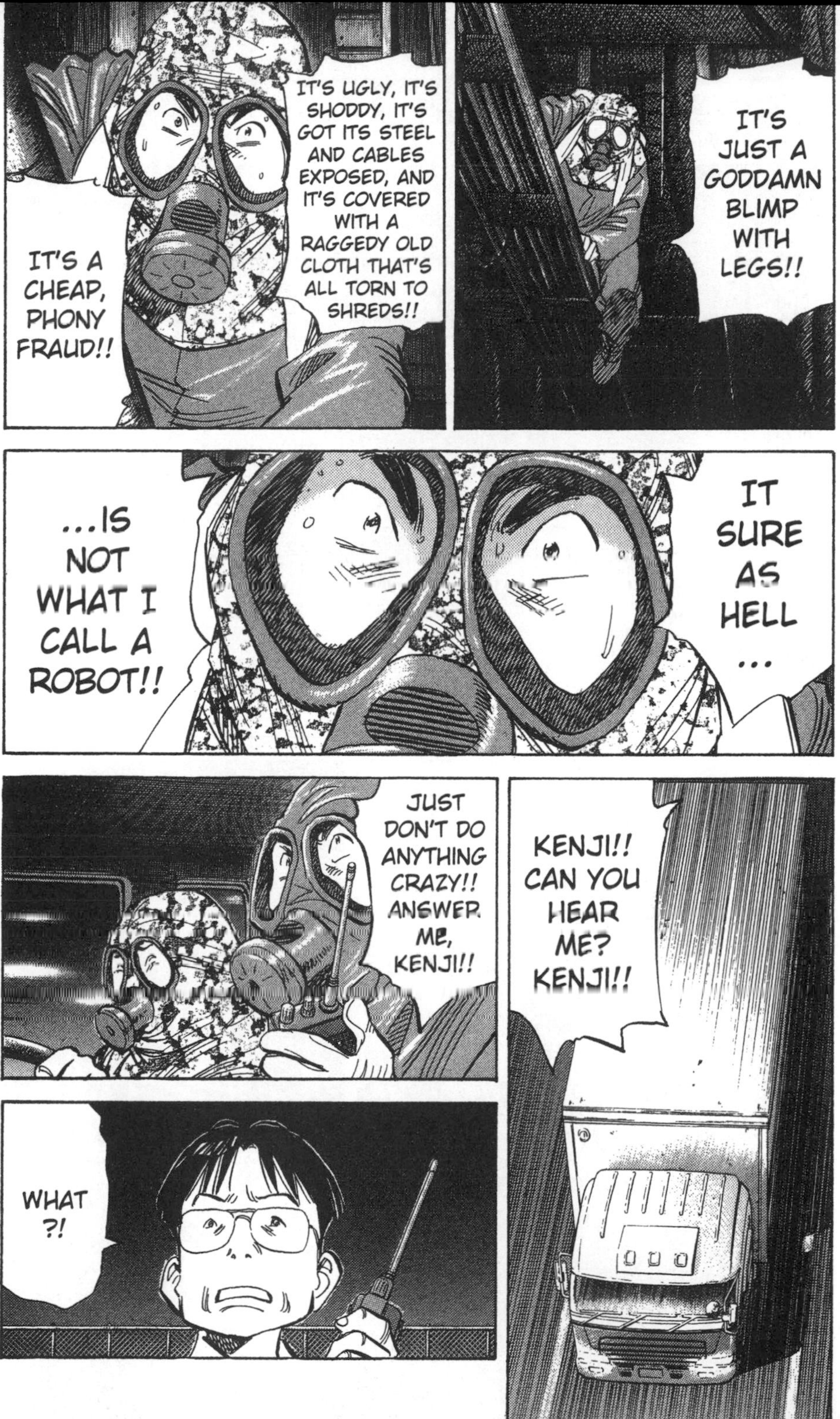
IT'S JUST A GODDAMN BLIMP WITH LEGS!!
IT'S UGLY, IT'S SHODDY, IT'S GOT ITS STEEL AND CABLES EXPOSED, AND IT'S COVERED WITH A RAGGEDY OLD CLOTH THAT'S ALL TORN TO SHREDS!!
IT'S A CHEAP, PHONY FRAUD!!
IT SURE AS HELL ...
...IS NOT WHAT I CALL A ROBOT!!
KENJI!! CAN YOU HEAR ME? KENJI!!
JUST DON'T DO ANYTHING CRAZY!! ANSWER ME, KENJI!!
WHAT ?!

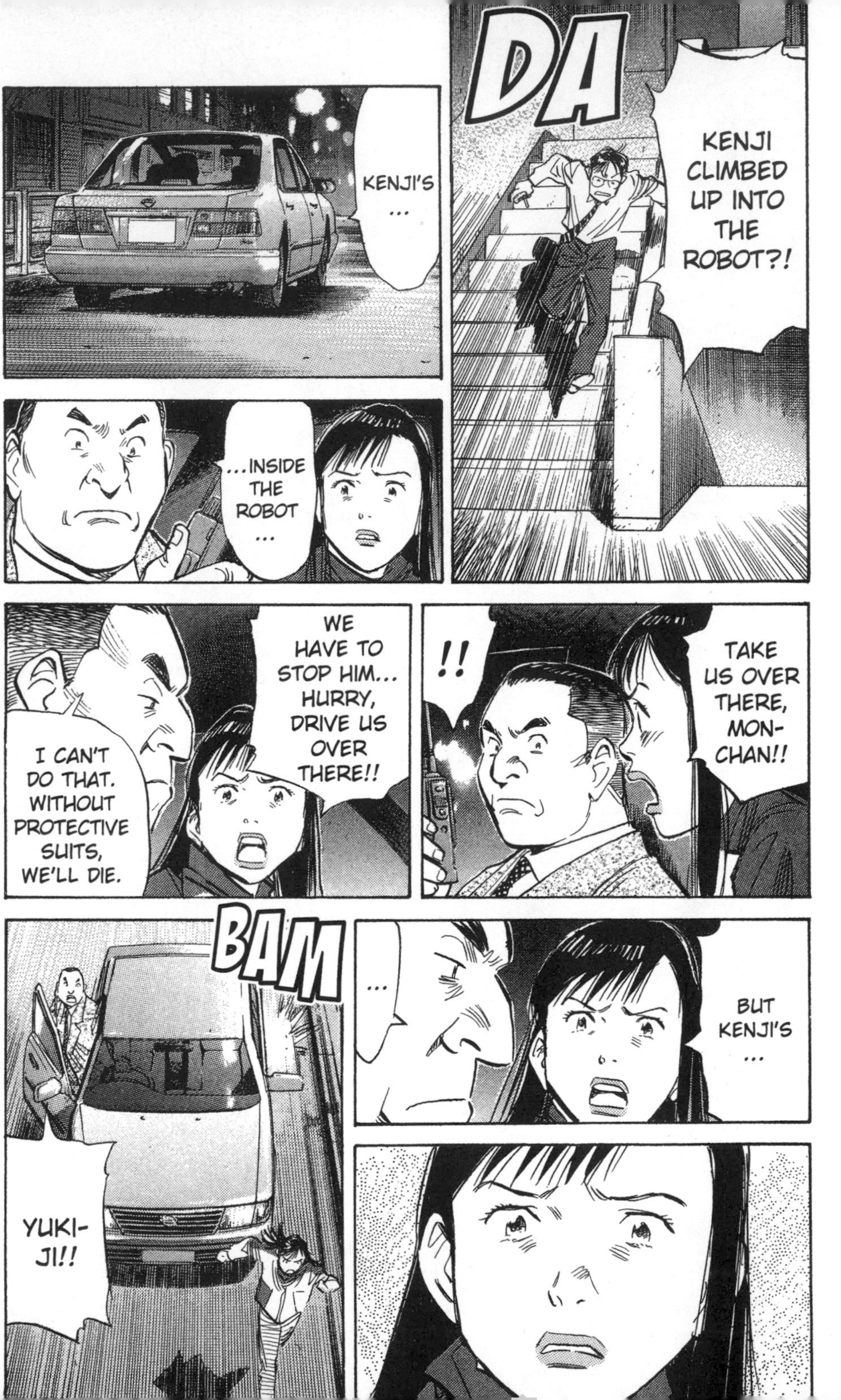
DA
KENJI CLIMBED UP INTO THE ROBOT?!
KENJI'S ...
...INSIDE THE ROBOT ...
!!
TAKE US OVER THERE, MON-CHAN!!
WE HAVE TO STOP HIM... HURRY, DRIVE US OVER THERE!!
I CAN'T DO THAT. WITHOUT PROTECTIVE SUITS, WE'LL DIE.
...
BUT KENJI'S ...
BAM
YUKI-JI!!

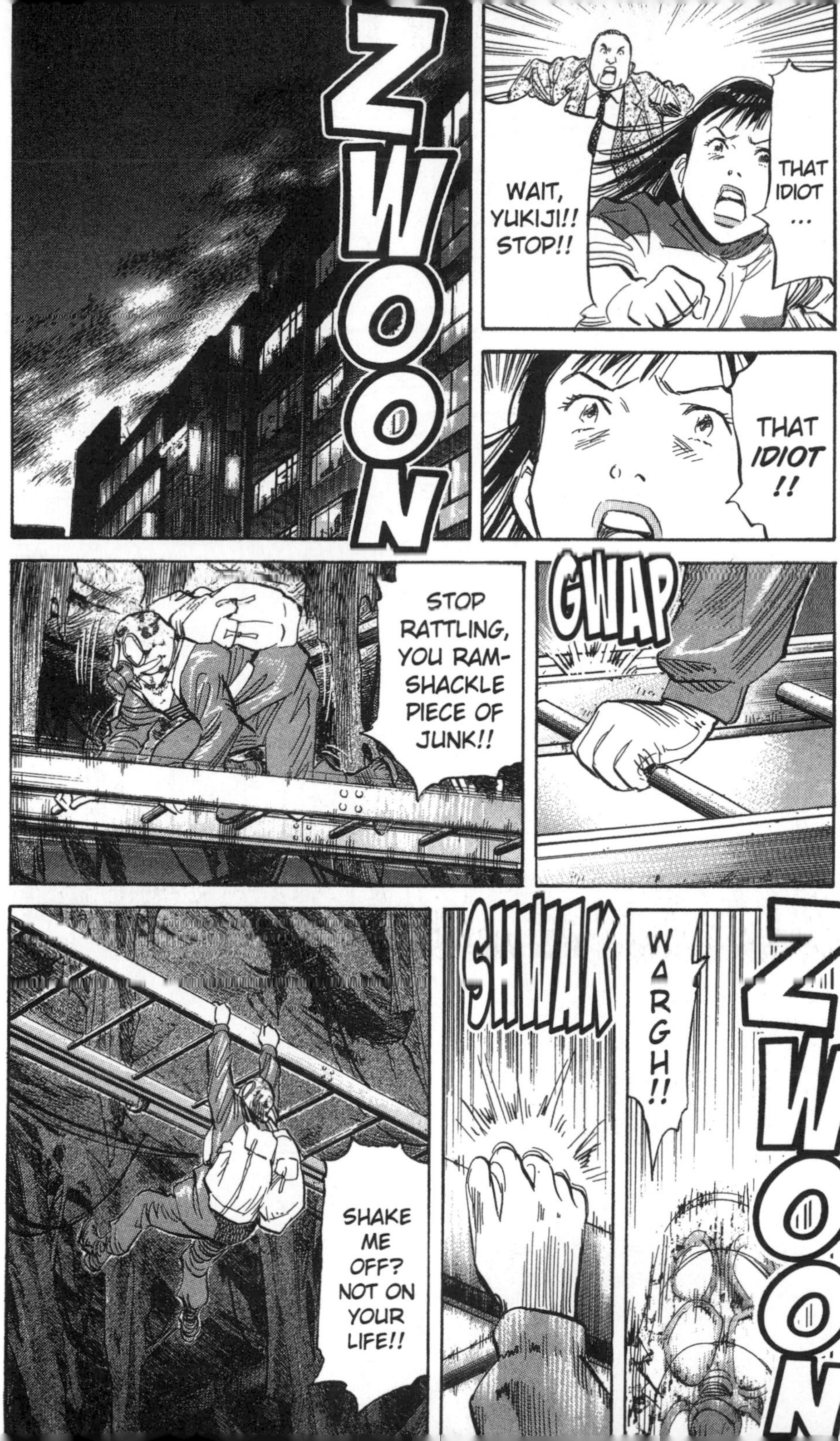
THAT IDIOT ...
WAIT, YUKIJI!! STOP!!
THAT IDIOT !!
ZWOON
GWAP
STOP RATTLING, YOU RAM-SHACKLE PIECE OF JUNK!!
ZWOON
WARGH!!
SHWAK
SHAKE ME OFF? NOT ON YOUR LIFE!!

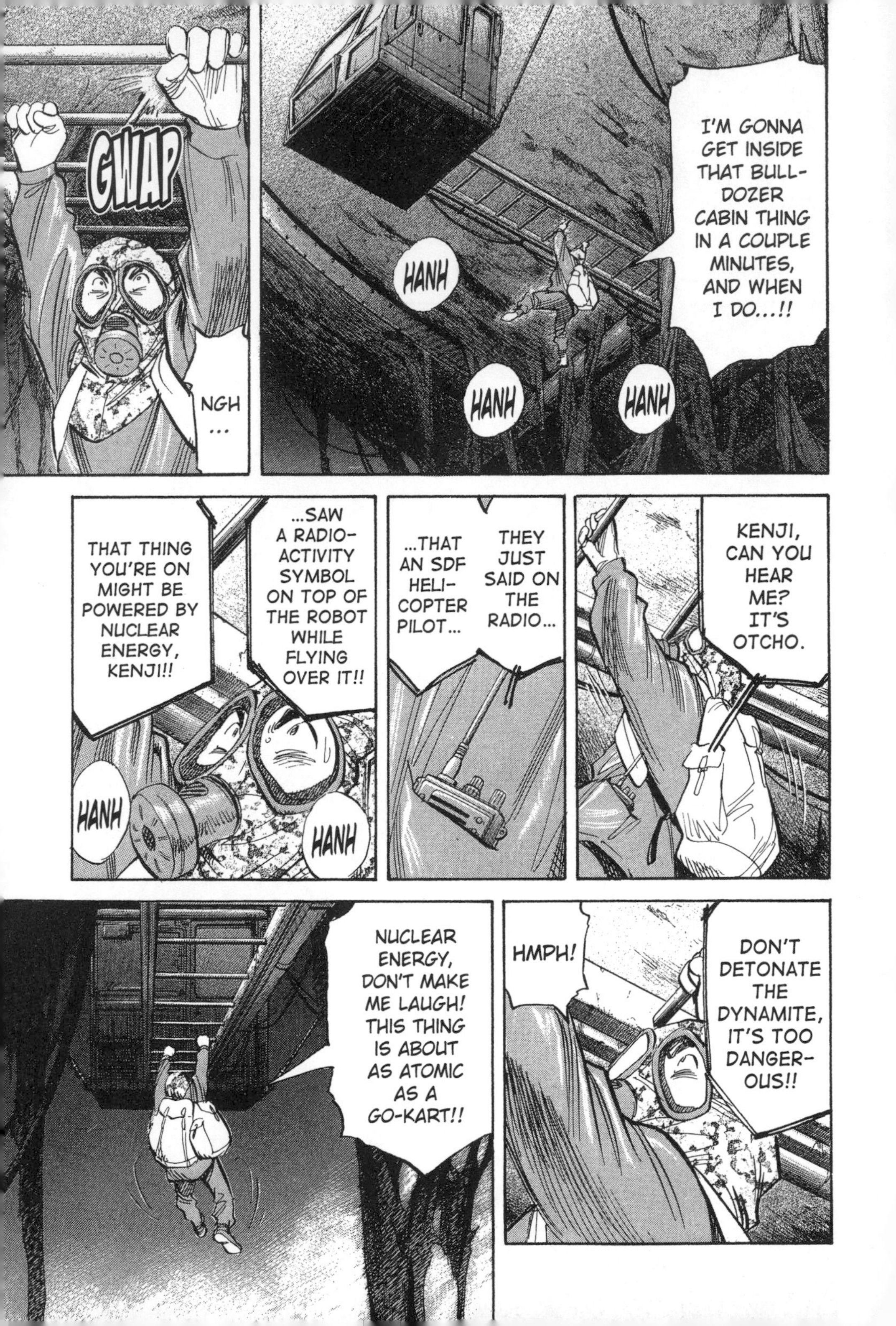
I'M GONNA GET INSIDE THAT BULL-DOZER CABIN THING IN A COUPLE MINUTES, AND WHEN I DO...!!
HANH
HANH
HANH
GWAP
NGH...
KENJI, CAN YOU HEAR ME? IT'S OTCHO.
THEY JUST SAID ON THE RADIO...
...THAT AN SDF HELI-COPTER PILOT...
...SAW A RADIO-ACTIVITY SYMBOL ON TOP OF THE ROBOT WHILE FLYING OVER IT!!
THAT THING YOU'RE ON MIGHT BE POWERED BY NUCLEAR ENERGY, KENJI!!
HANH
HANH
DON'T DETONATE THE DYNAMITE, IT'S TOO DANGER-OUS!!
HMPH!
NUCLEAR ENERGY, DON'T MAKE ME LAUGH! THIS THING IS ABOUT AS ATOMIC AS A GO-KART!!

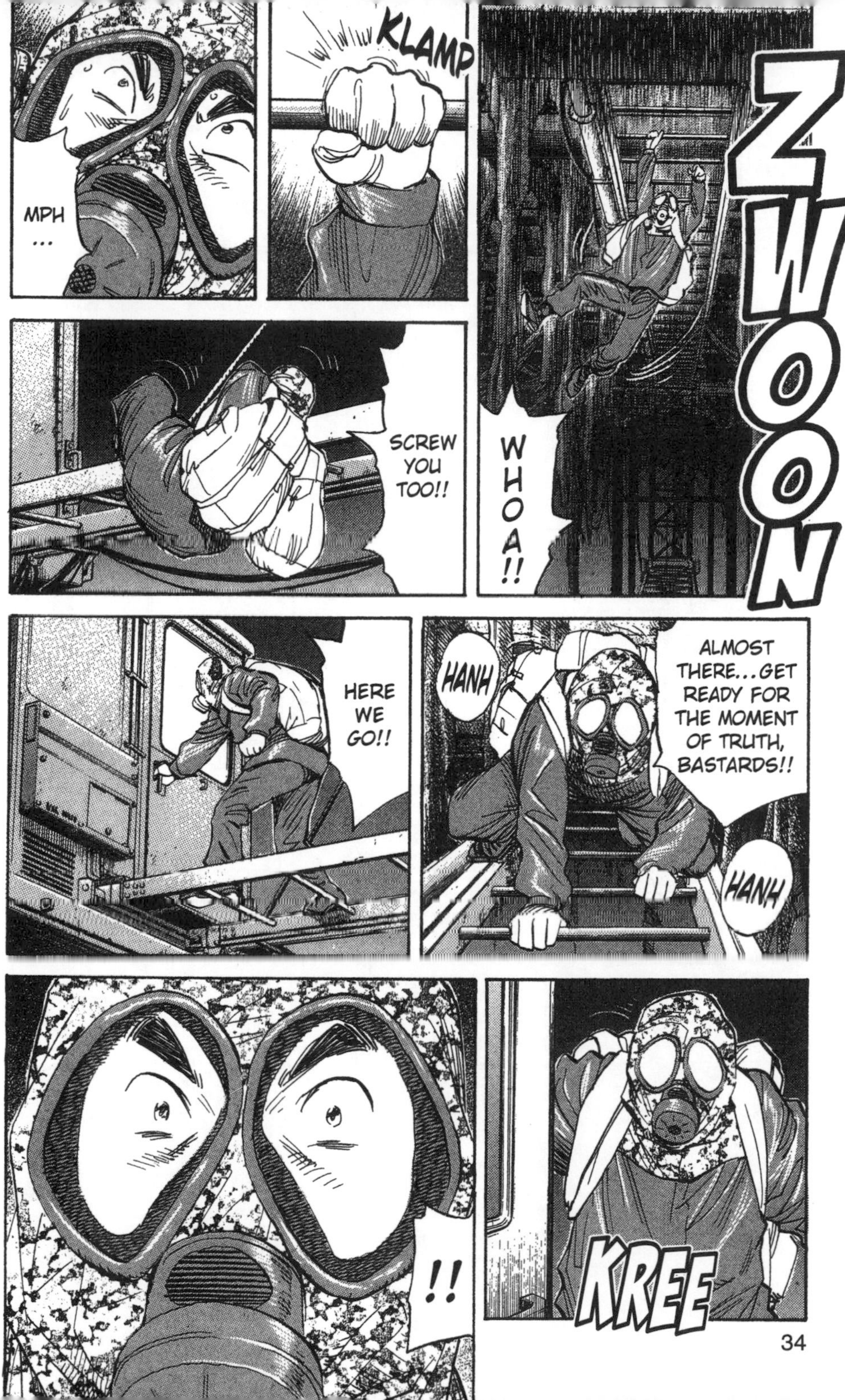
ZWOON
WHOA!!
KLAMP
MPH ...
SCREW YOU TOO!!
HANH
ALMOST THERE...GET READY FOR THE MOMENT OF TRUTH, BASTARDS!!
HANH
HERE WE GO!!
KREE
!!

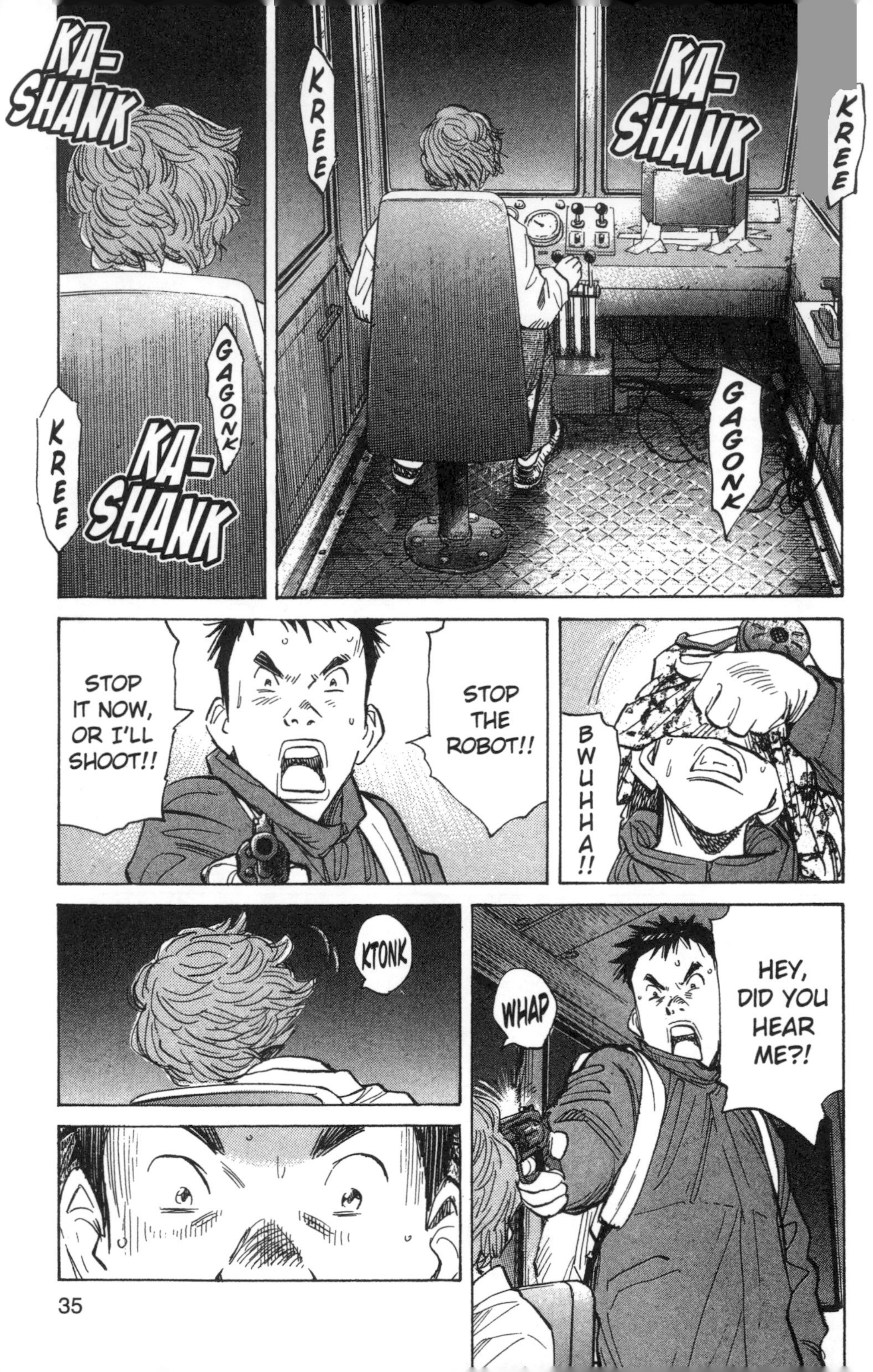
KREE
KA-SHANK
KREE
GAGONK
KA-SHANK
GAGONK
KREE
KA-SHANK
BWUHHA!!
STOP THE ROBOT!!
STOP IT NOW, OR I'LL SHOOT!!
HEY, DID YOU HEAR ME?!
WHAP
KTONK

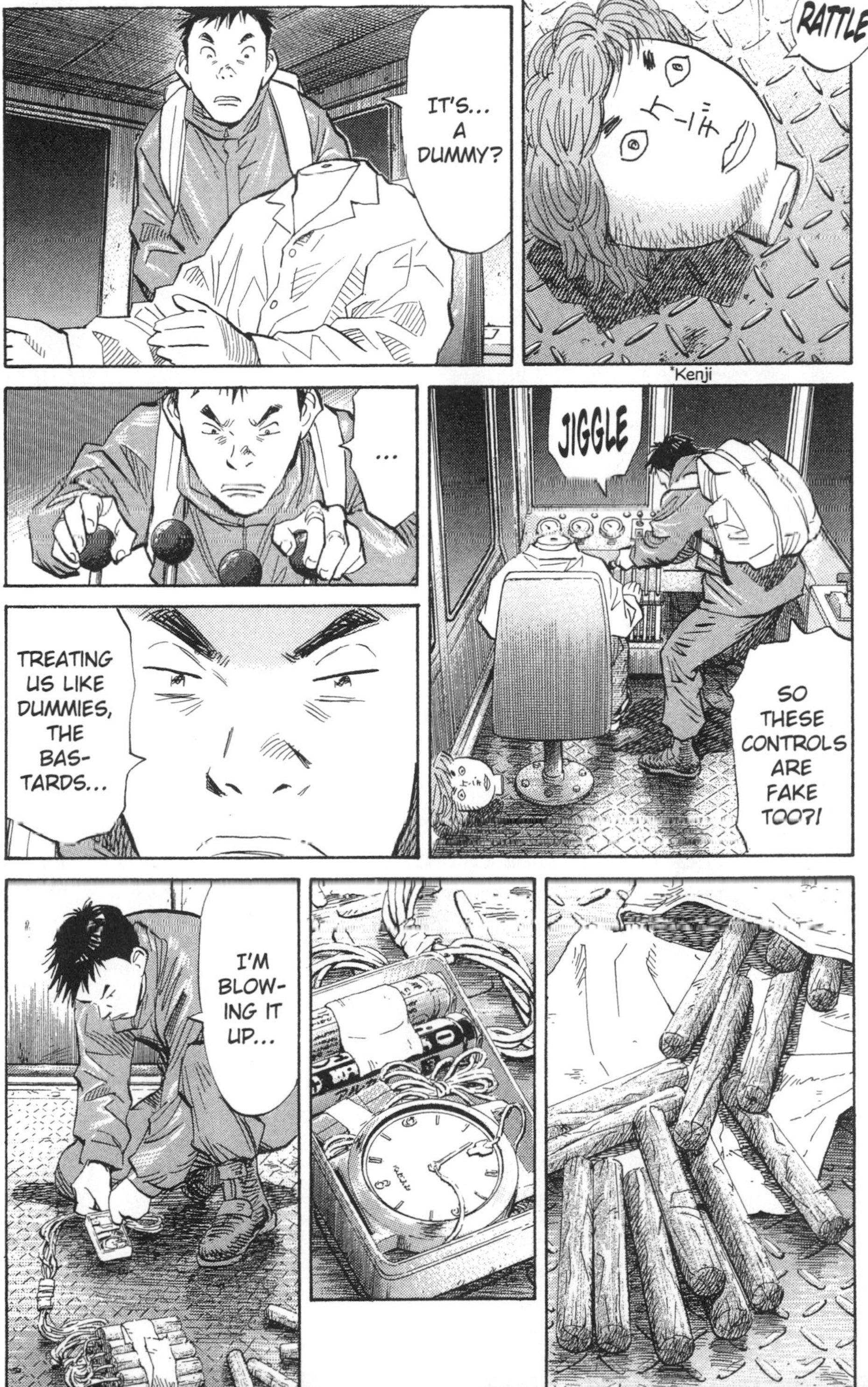
RATTLE
*Kenji
IT'S... A DUMMY?
JIGGLE
SO THESE CONTROLS ARE FAKE TOO?!
...
TREATING US LIKE DUMMIES, THE BAS-TARDS...
I'M BLOW-ING IT UP...

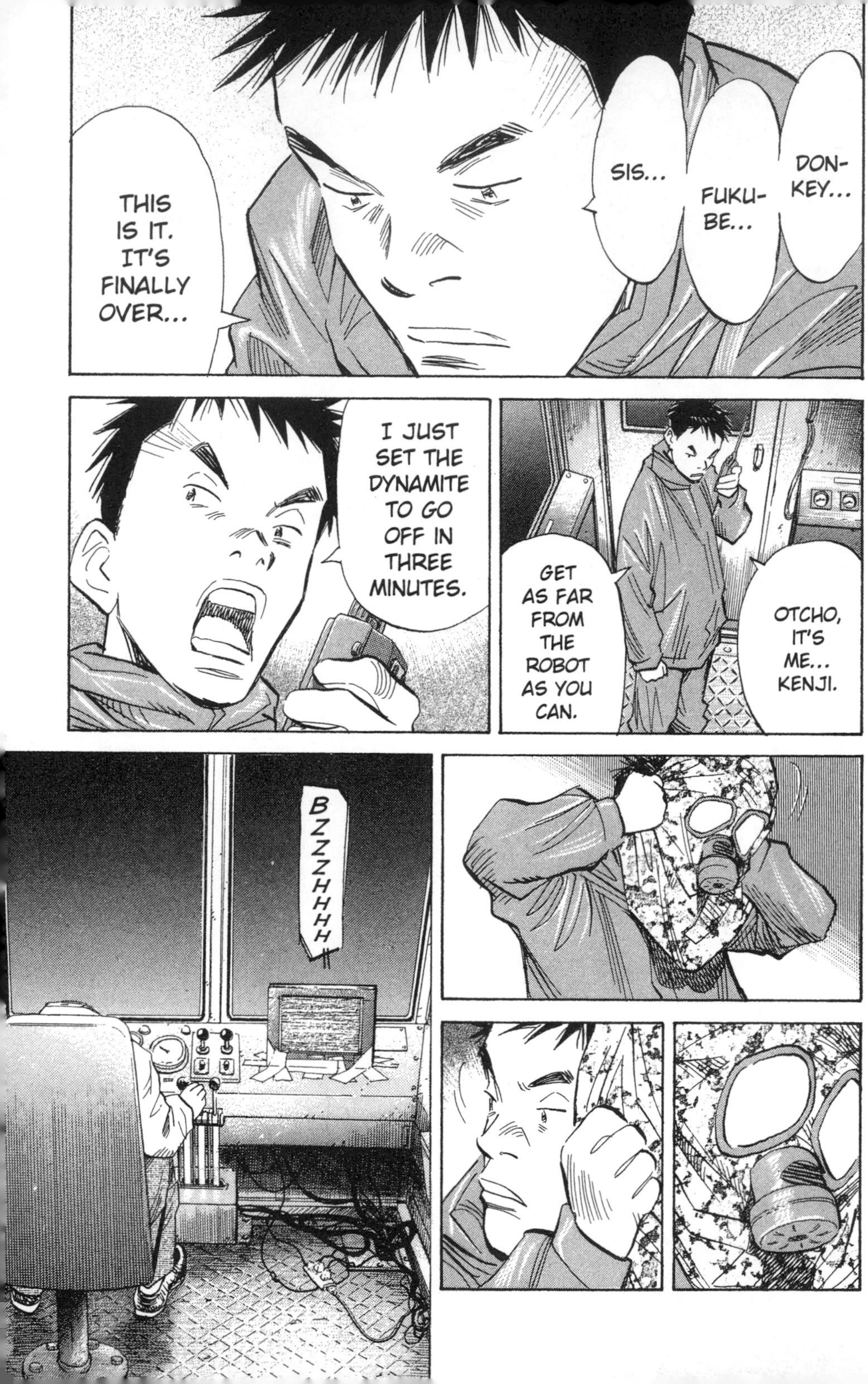
DON-KEY...
FUKU-BE...
SIS...
THIS IS IT. IT'S FINALLY OVER...
OTCHO, IT'S ME... KENJI.
GET AS FAR FROM THE ROBOT AS YOU CAN.
I JUST SET THE DYNAMITE TO GO OFF IN THREE MINUTES.
BZZZHHHH

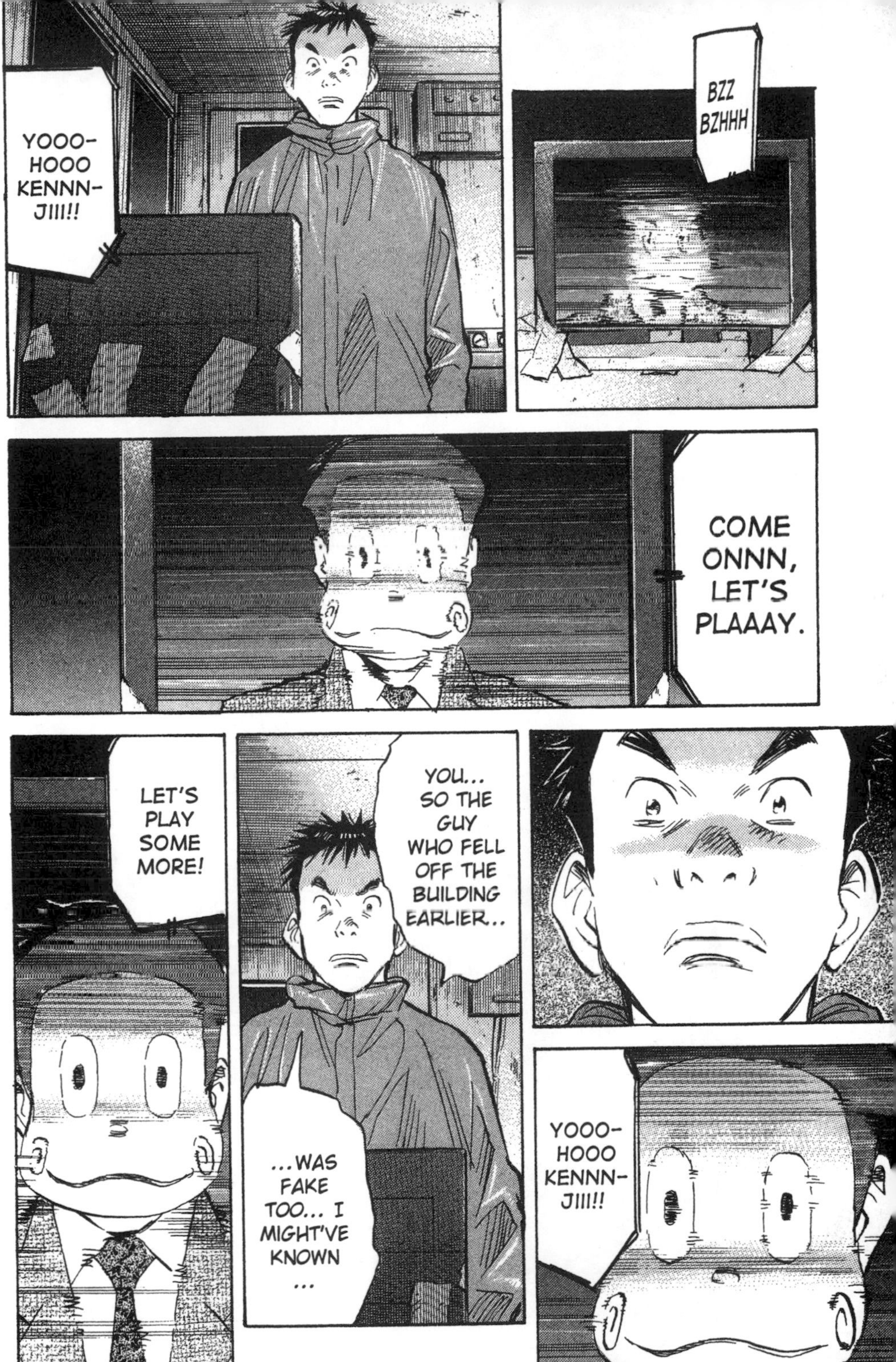
BZZ BZHHH
YOOO-HOOO KENNN-JIII!!
COME ONNN, LET'S PLAAAY.
YOOO-HOOO KENNN-JIII!!
YOU... SO THE GUY WHO FELL OFF THE BUILDING EARLIER...
...WAS FAKE TOO... I MIGHT'VE KNOWN ...
LET'S PLAY SOME MORE!

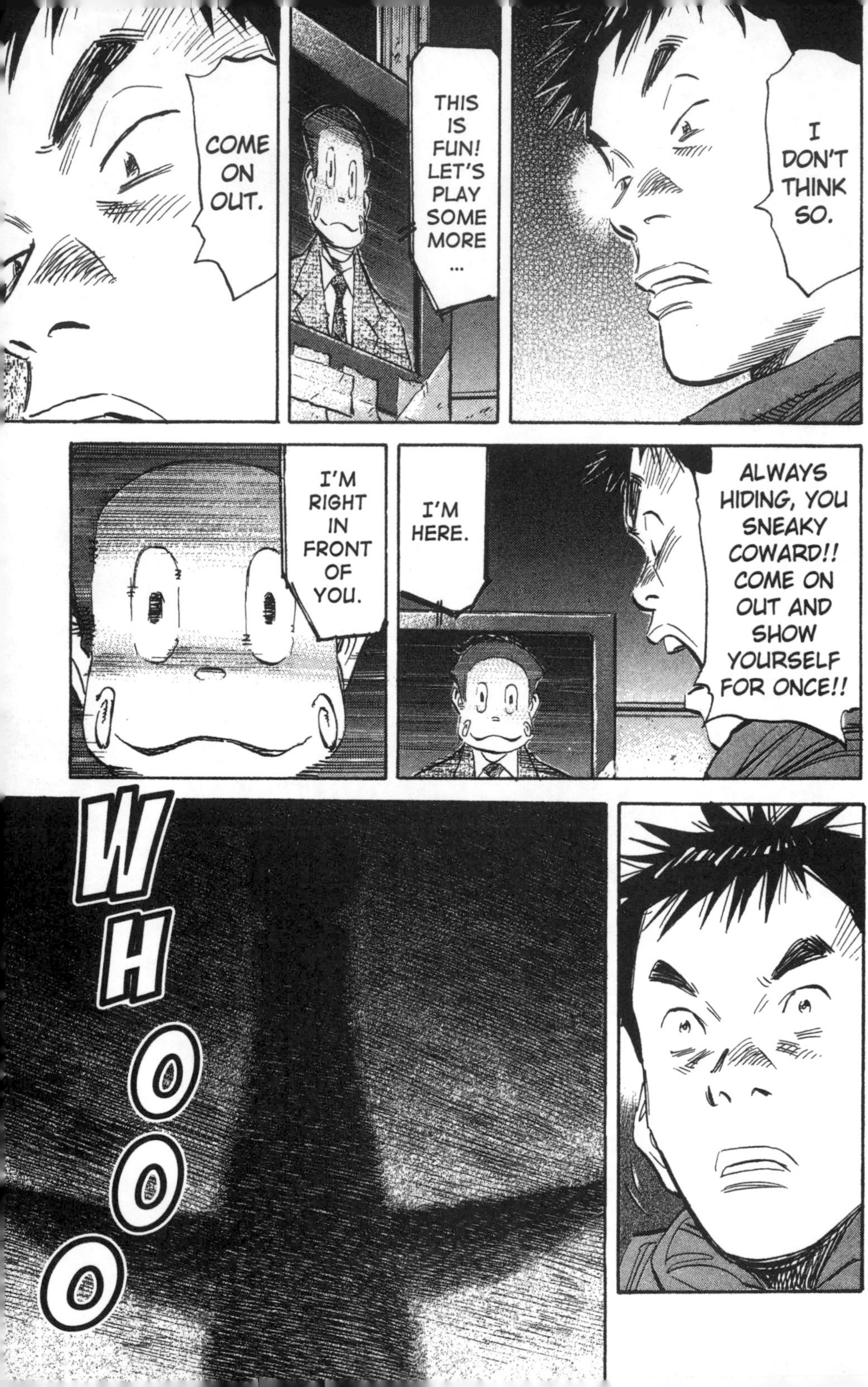
I DON'T THINK SO.
THIS IS FUN! LET'S PLAY SOME MORE ...
COME ON OUT.
ALWAYS HIDING, YOU SNEAKY COWARD!! COME ON OUT AND SHOW YOURSELF FOR ONCE!!
I'M HERE.
I'M RIGHT IN FRONT OF YOU.
WHOOOO

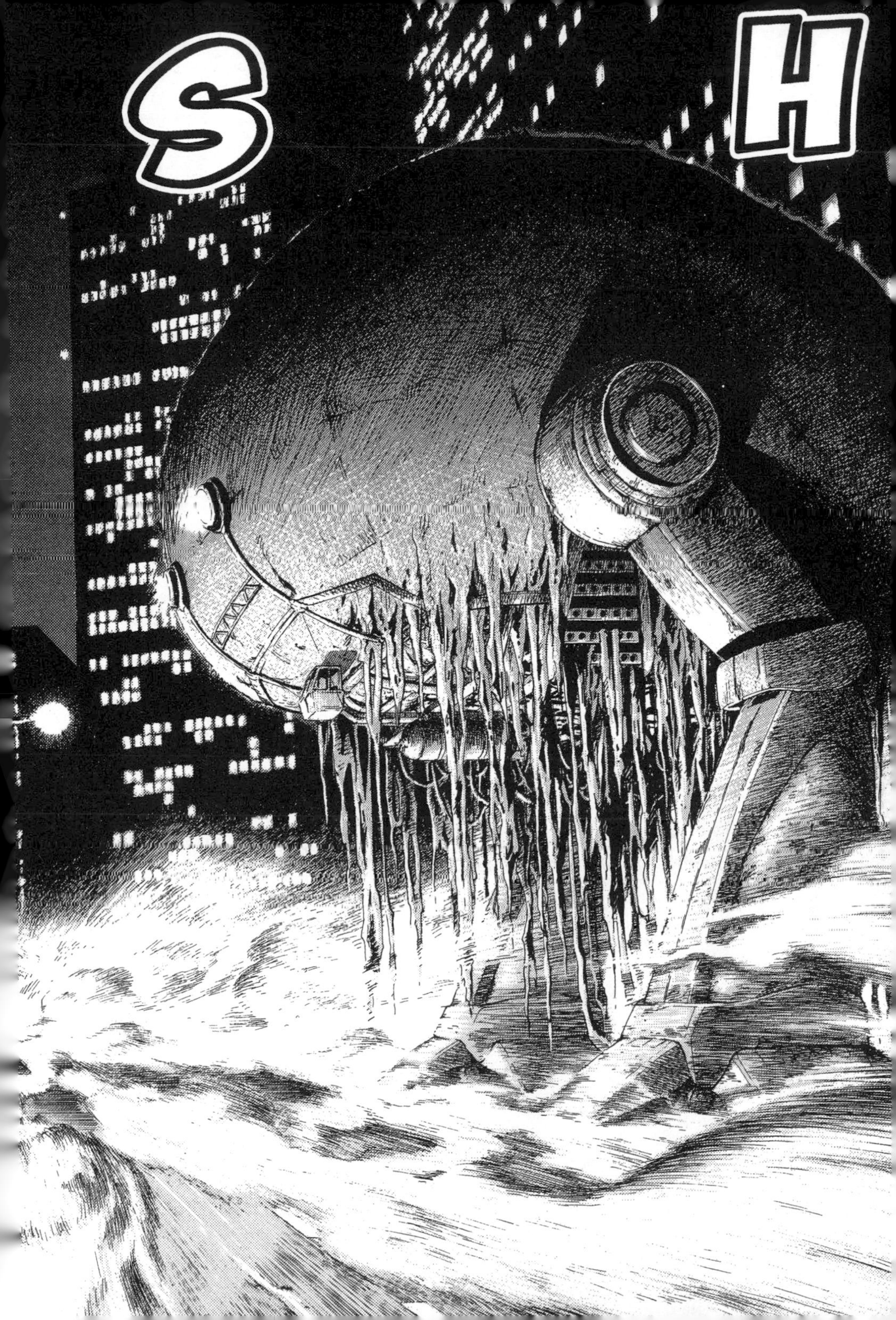
H
S

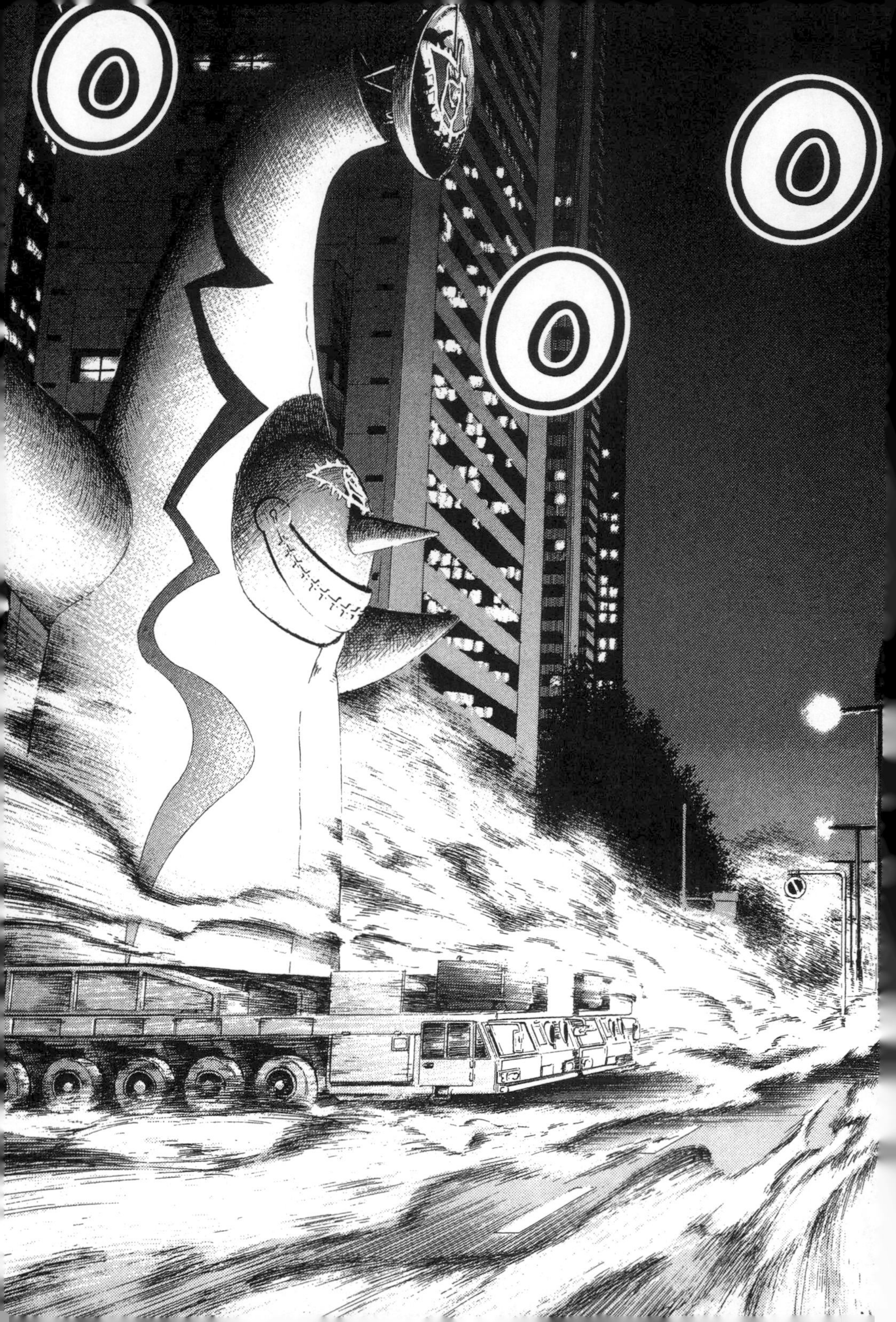

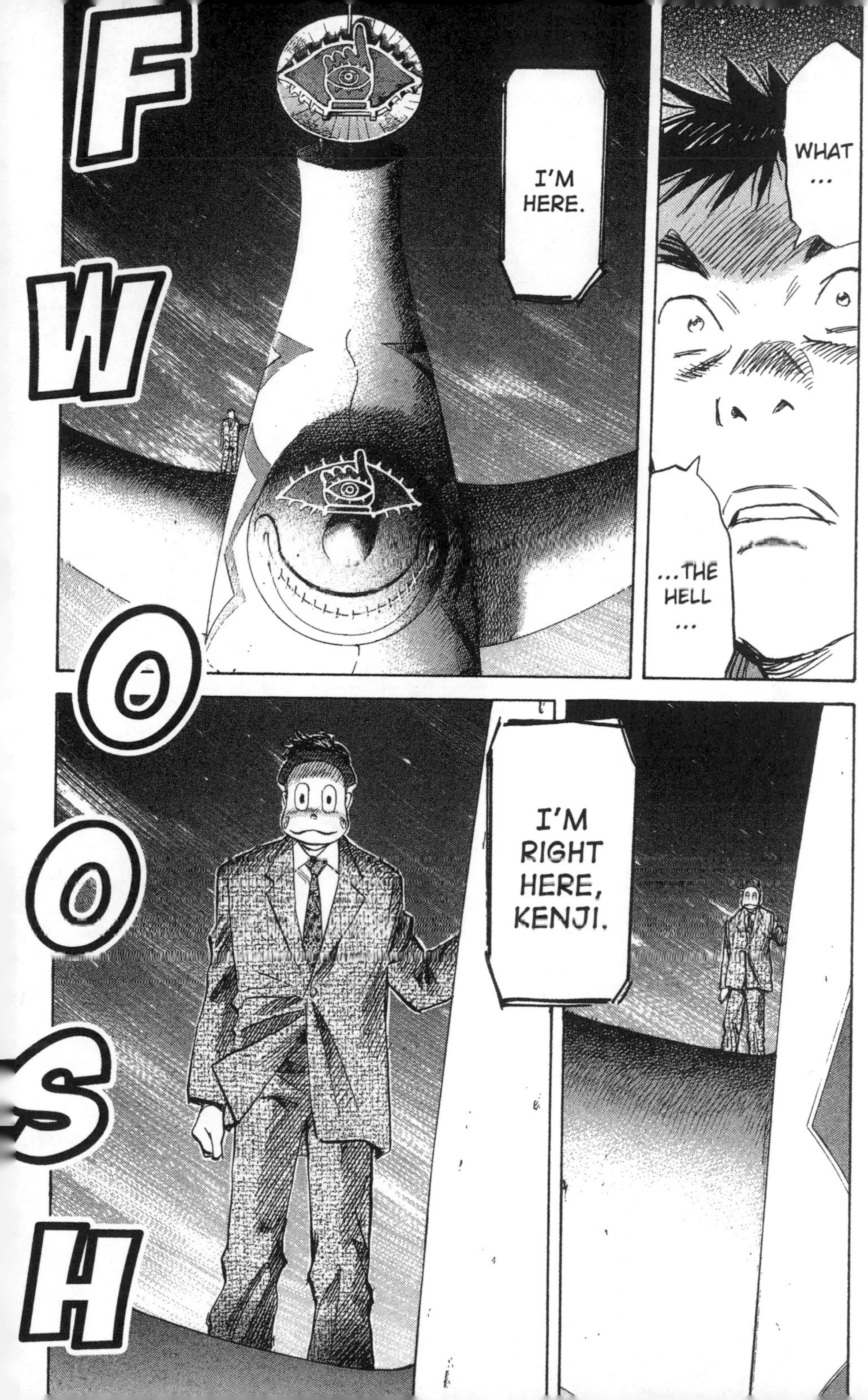
WHAT ...
...THE HELL ...
I'M HERE.
FWOOSH
I'M RIGHT HERE, KENJI.

Chapter 3 Kenji's Song

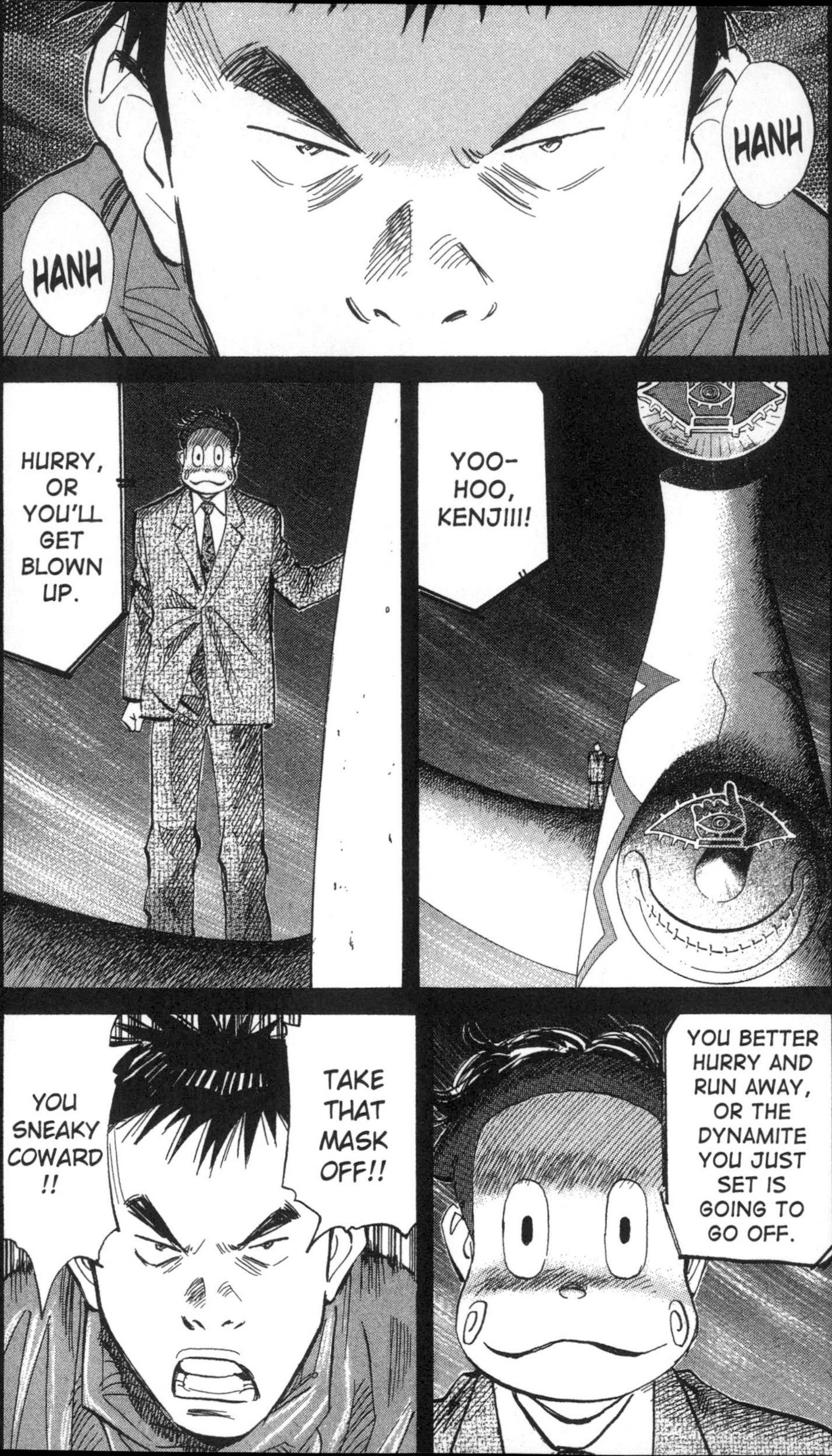
HANH
HANH
YOO-HOO, KENJIII!
HURRY, OR YOU'LL GET BLOWN UP.
YOU BETTER HURRY AND RUN AWAY, OR THE DYNAMITE YOU JUST SET IS GOING TO GO OFF.
TAKE THAT MASK OFF!!
YOU SNEAKY COWARD!!

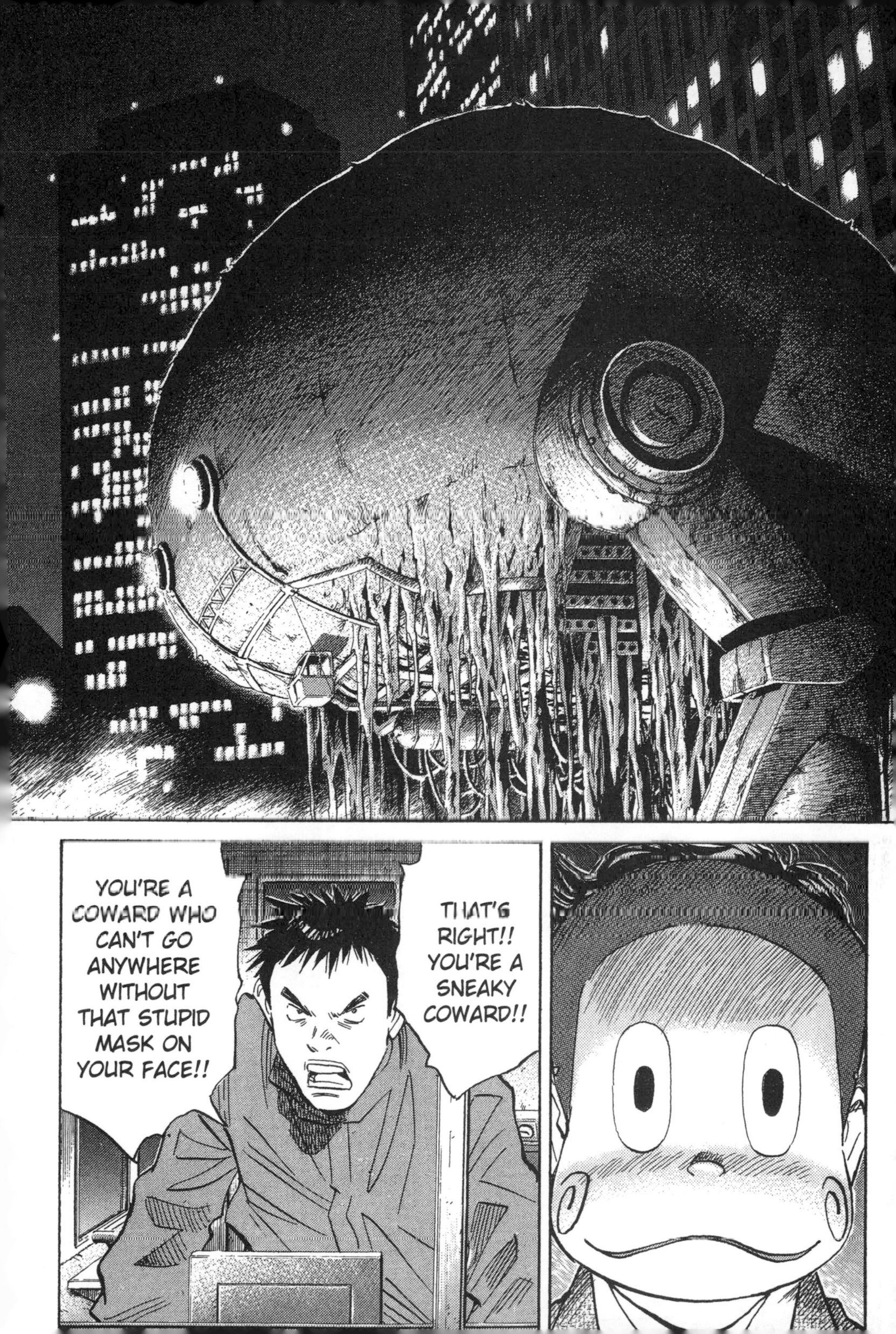
THAT'S RIGHT!! YOU'RE A SNEAKY COWARD!!
YOU'RE A COWARD WHO CAN'T GO ANYWHERE WITHOUT THAT STUPID MASK ON YOUR FACE!!

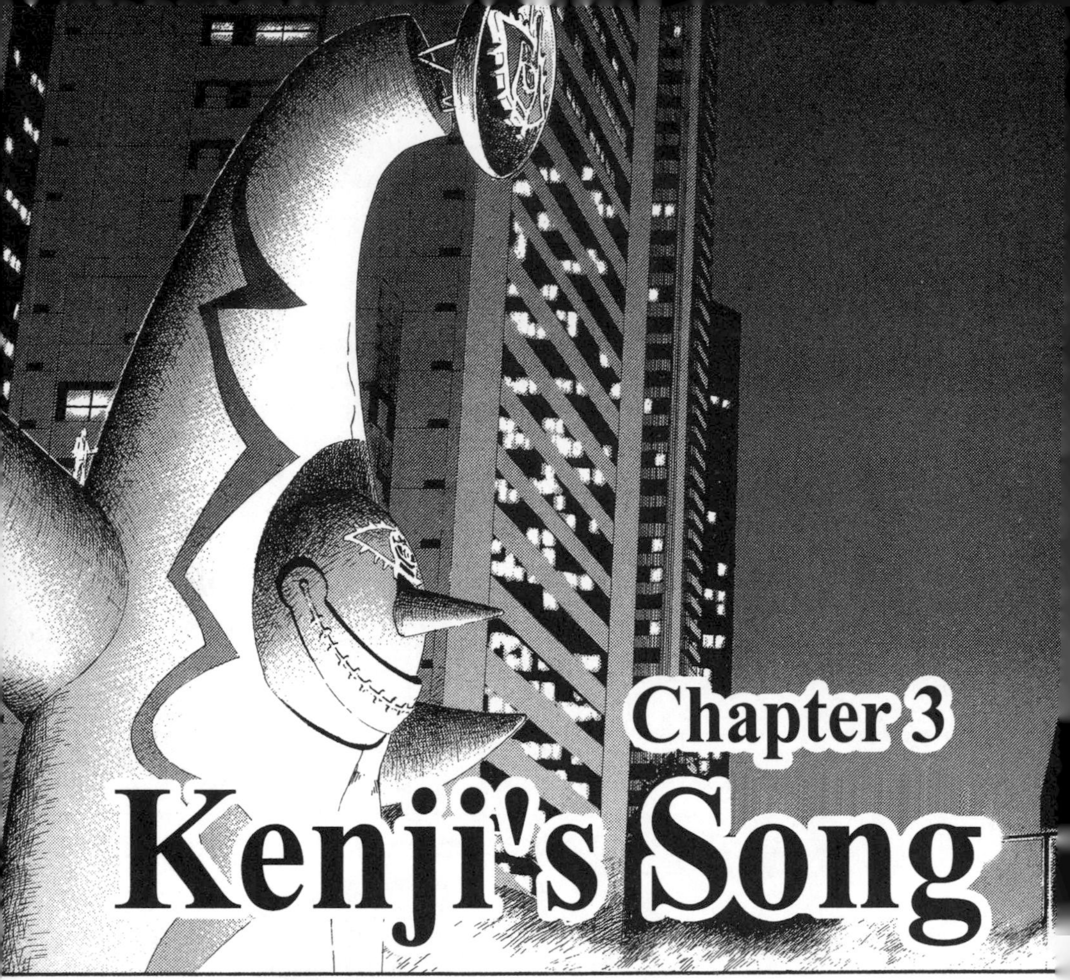
Chapter 3
Kenji's Song

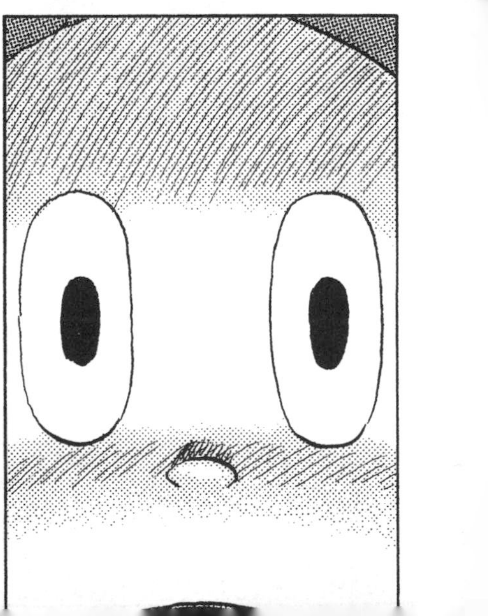

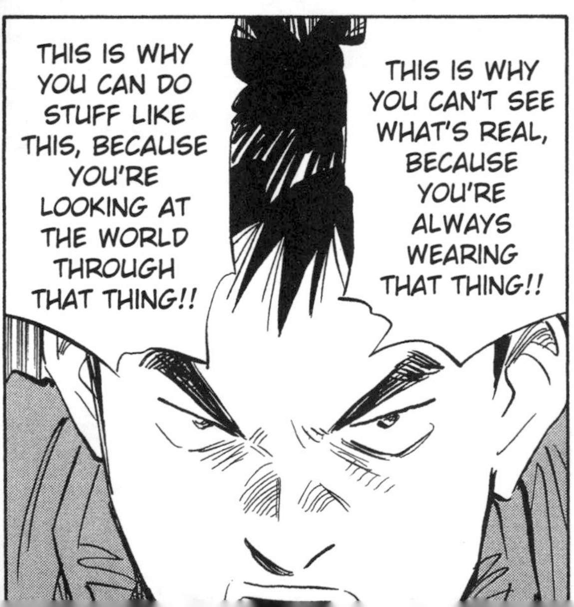
THIS IS WHY YOU CAN'T SEE WHAT'S REAL, BECAUSE YOU'RE ALWAYS WEARING THAT THING!!
THIS IS WHY YOU CAN DO STUFF LIKE THIS, BECAUSE YOU'RE LOOKING AT THE WORLD THROUGH THAT THING!!

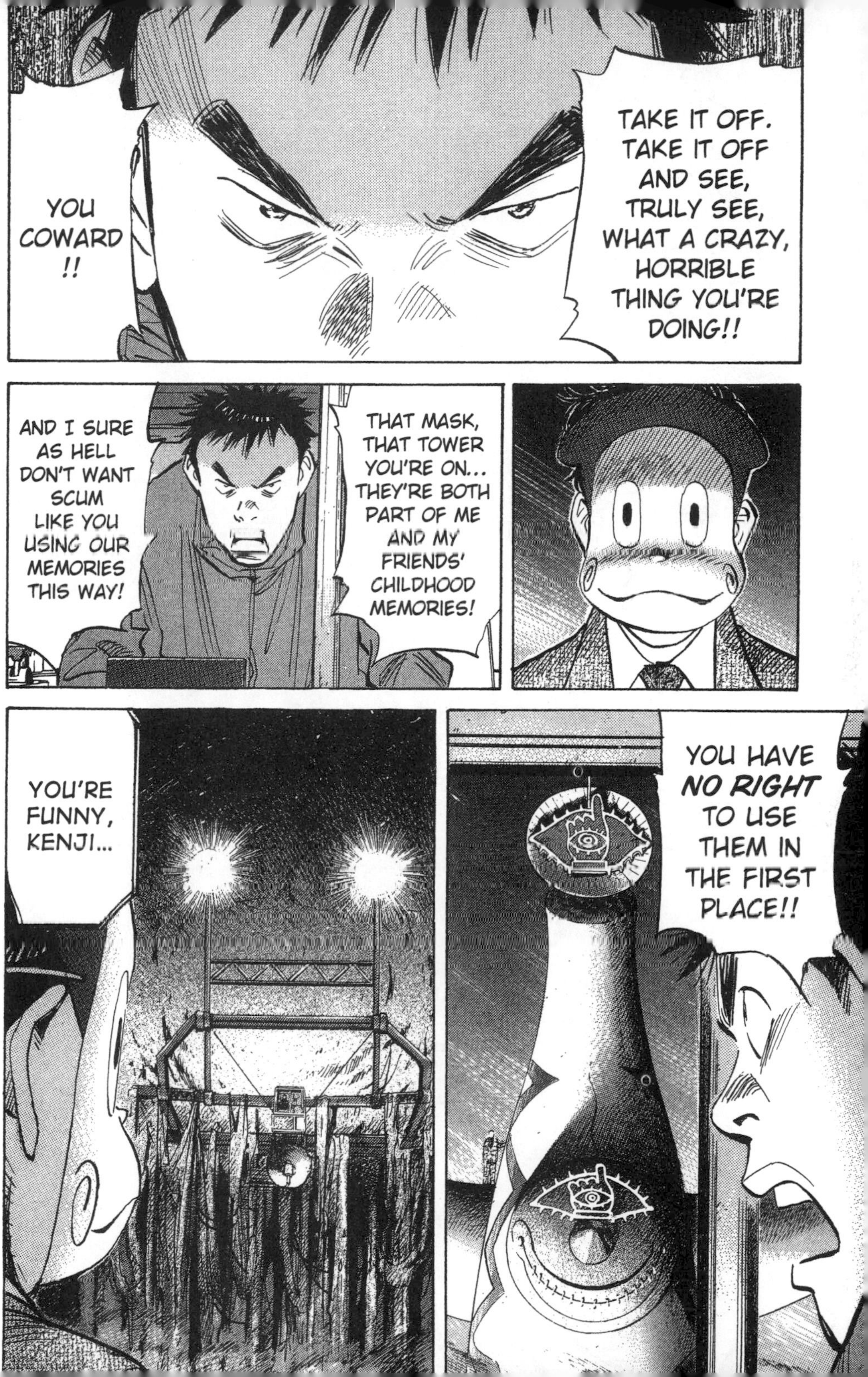
TAKE IT OFF. TAKE IT OFF AND SEE, TRULY SEE, WHAT A CRAZY, HORRIBLE THING YOU'RE DOING!!
YOU COWARD!!
THAT MASK, THAT TOWER YOU'RE ON... THEY'RE BOTH PART OF ME AND MY FRIENDS' CHILDHOOD MEMORIES!
AND I SURE AS HELL DON'T WANT SCUM LIKE YOU USING OUR MEMORIES THIS WAY!
YOU HAVE **NO RIGHT** TO USE THEM IN THE FIRST PLACE!!
YOU'RE FUNNY, KENJI...

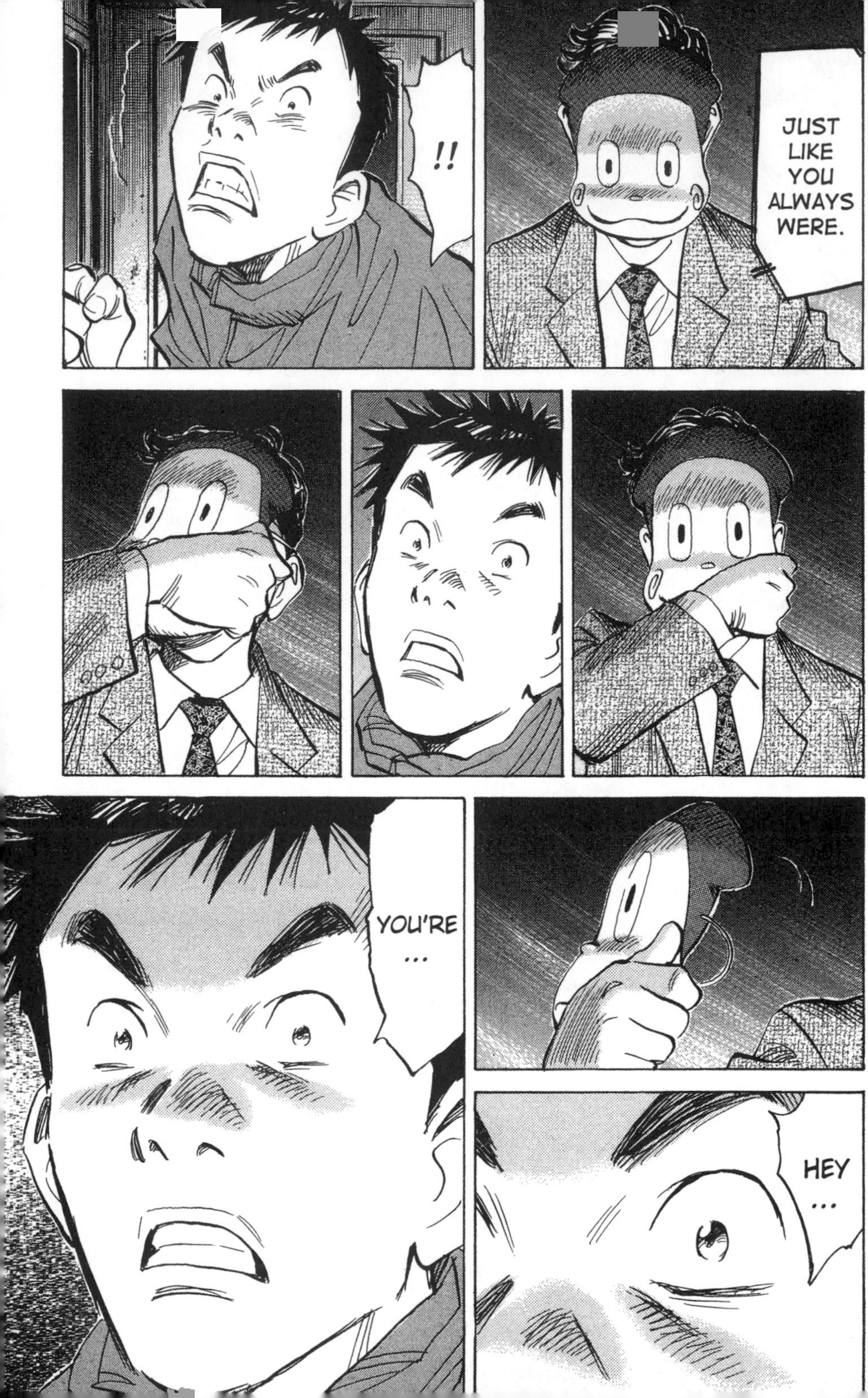
JUST LIKE YOU ALWAYS WERE.
!!
HEY ...
YOU'RE ...

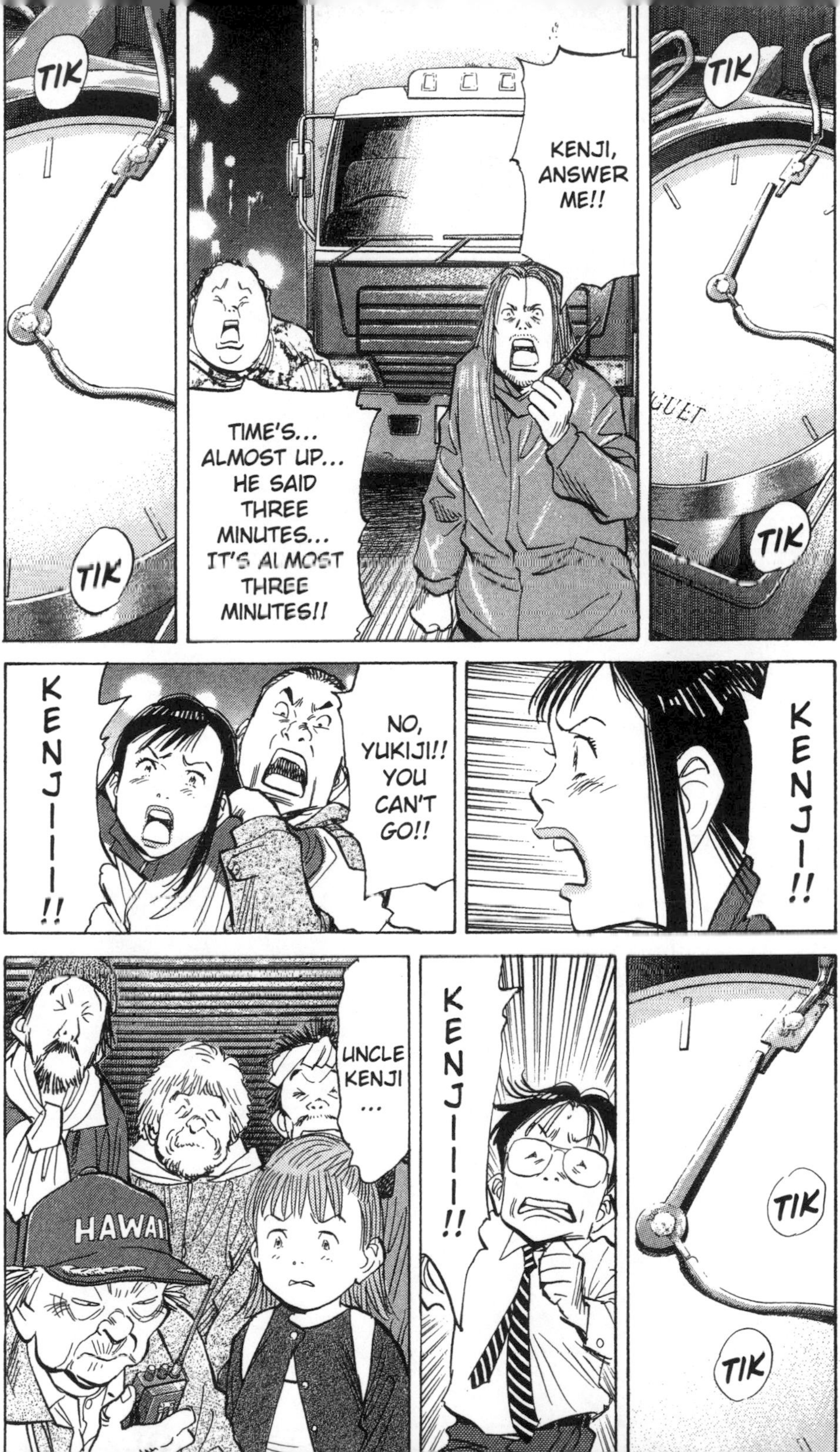
TIK
TIK
KENJI, ANSWER ME!!
TIME'S... ALMOST UP... HE SAID THREE MINUTES... IT'S ALMOST THREE MINUTES!!
TIK
TIK
KENJI!!
NO, YUKIJI!! YOU CAN'T GO!!
KENJI-I-I-I!!
TIK
TIK
KENJI-I-I-I!!
UNCLE KENJI...
HAWAI

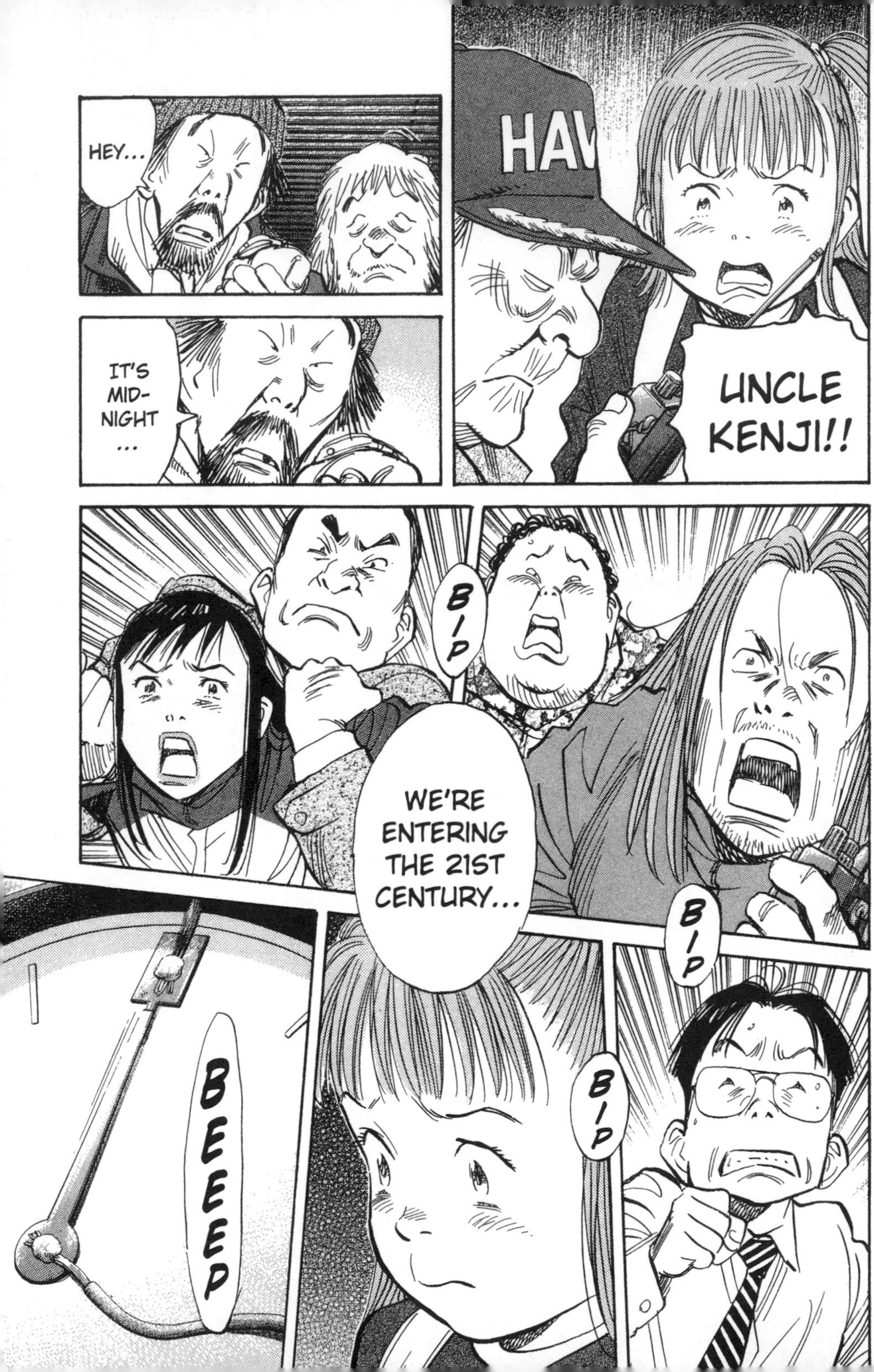
UNCLE KENJI!!
HEY...
IT'S MIDNIGHT...
BIP
WE'RE ENTERING THE 21ST CENTURY...
BIP
BIP
BEEEP

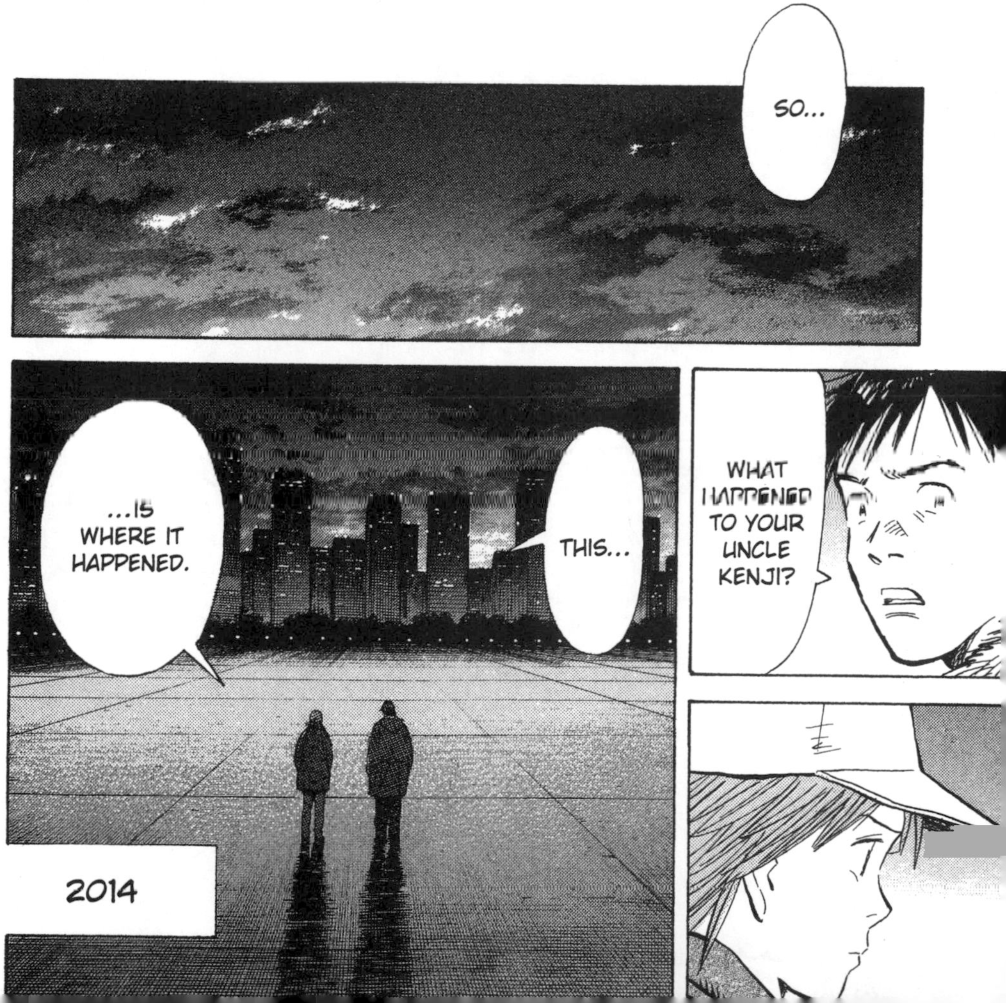
SO...
WHAT HAPPENED TO YOUR UNCLE KENJI?
THIS...
...IS WHERE IT HAPPENED.
2014

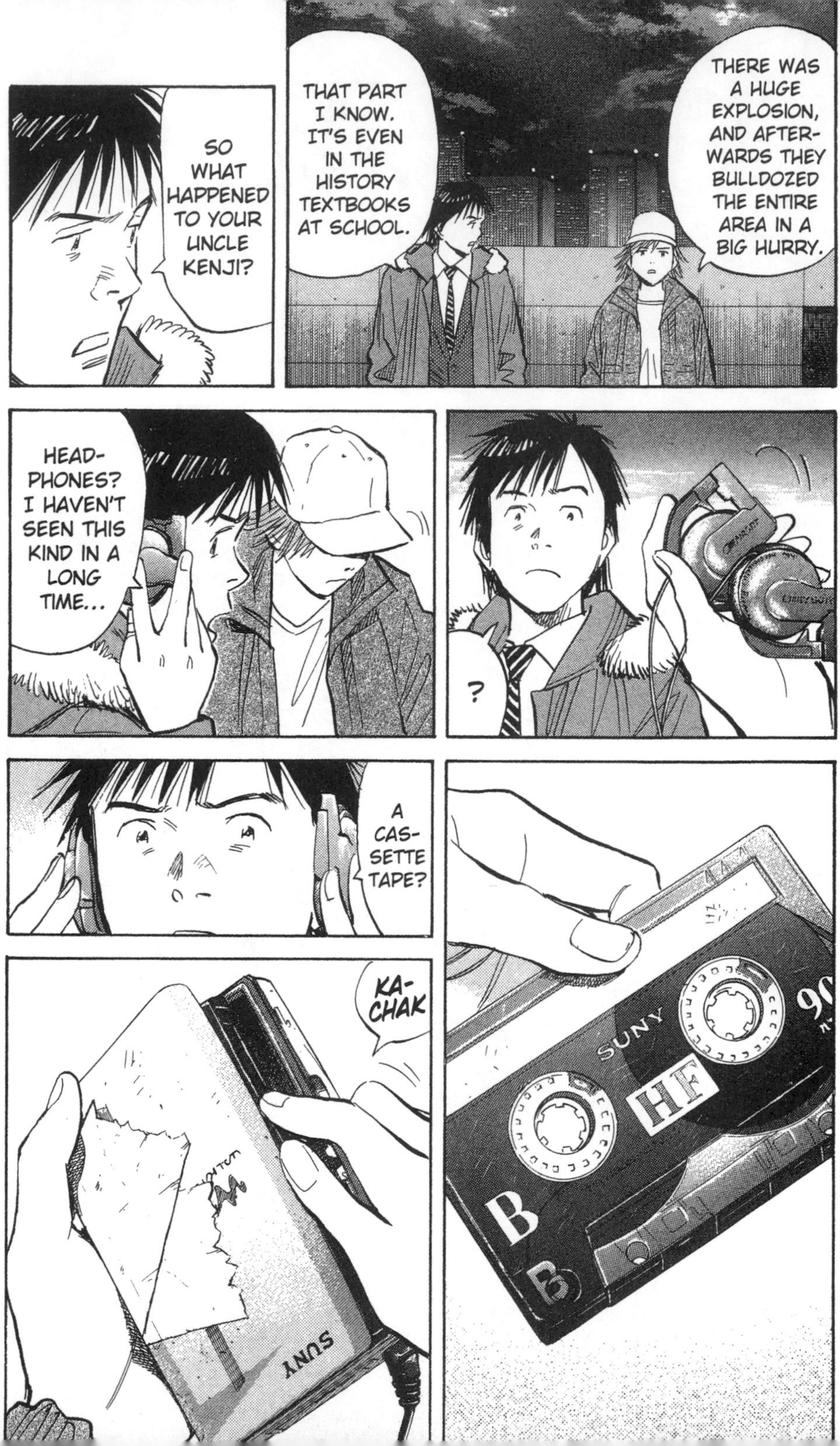
THERE WAS A HUGE EXPLOSION, AND AFTER-WARDS THEY BULLDOZED THE ENTIRE AREA IN A BIG HURRY.
THAT PART I KNOW. IT'S EVEN IN THE HISTORY TEXTBOOKS AT SCHOOL.
SO WHAT HAPPENED TO YOUR UNCLE KENJI?
?
HEAD-PHONES? I HAVEN'T SEEN THIS KIND IN A LONG TIME...
SUNY
HF
90
B
A CAS-SETTE TAPE?
KA-CHAK
SUNY

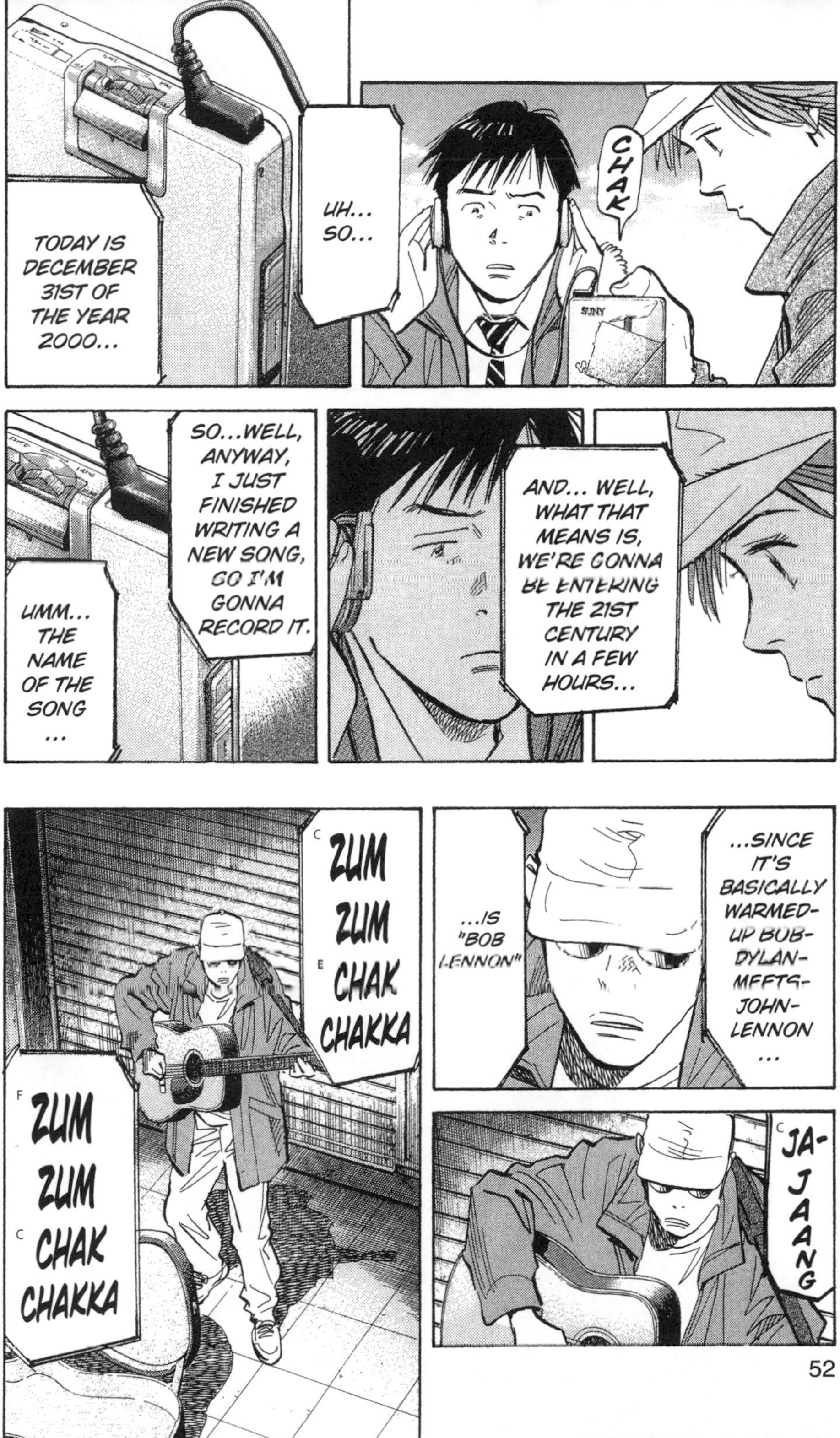
TODAY IS DECEMBER 31ST OF THE YEAR 2000...
UH... SO...
CHAK
SO...WELL, ANYWAY, I JUST FINISHED WRITING A NEW SONG, SO I'M GONNA RECORD IT.
AND... WELL, WHAT THAT MEANS IS, WE'RE GONNA BE ENTERING THE 21ST CENTURY IN A FEW HOURS...
UMM... THE NAME OF THE SONG ...
C
ZUM ZUM
E
CHAK CHAKKA
F
ZUM ZUM
C
CHAK CHAKKA
...IS "BOB LENNON"
...SINCE IT'S BASICALLY WARMED-UP BOB-DYLAN-MEETS-JOHN-LENNON ...
C
JA-JAANG

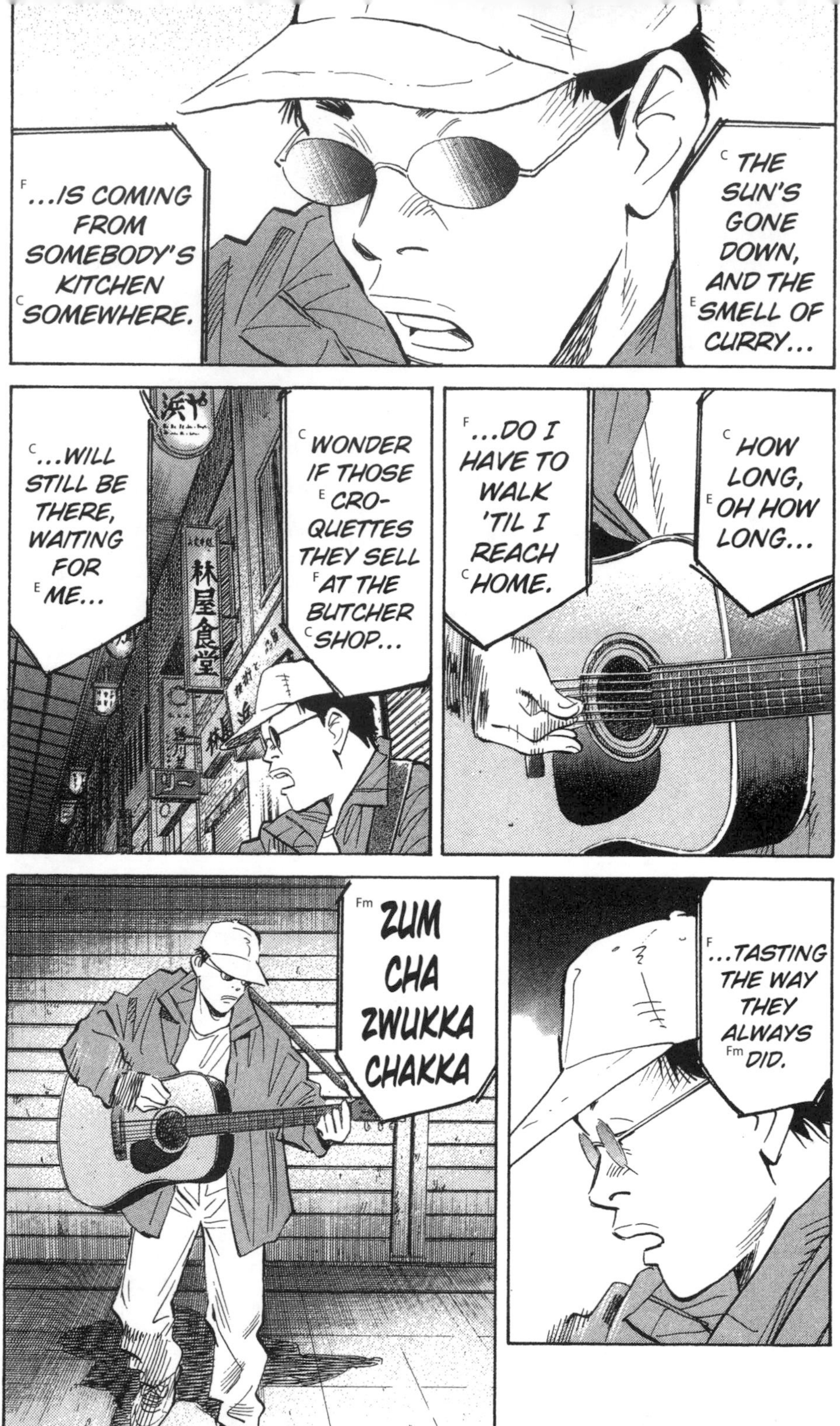
C THE SUN'S GONE DOWN, AND THE E SMELL OF CURRY...
F ...IS COMING FROM SOMEBODY'S KITCHEN C SOMEWHERE.
C HOW LONG, E OH HOW LONG...
F ...DO I HAVE TO WALK 'TIL I REACH C HOME.
C WONDER IF THOSE E CRO-QUETTES THEY SELL F AT THE BUTCHER C SHOP...
C ...WILL STILL BE THERE, WAITING FOR E ME...
林屋食堂
F ...TASTING THE WAY THEY ALWAYS Fm DID.
Fm ZUM CHA ZWUKKA CHAKKA

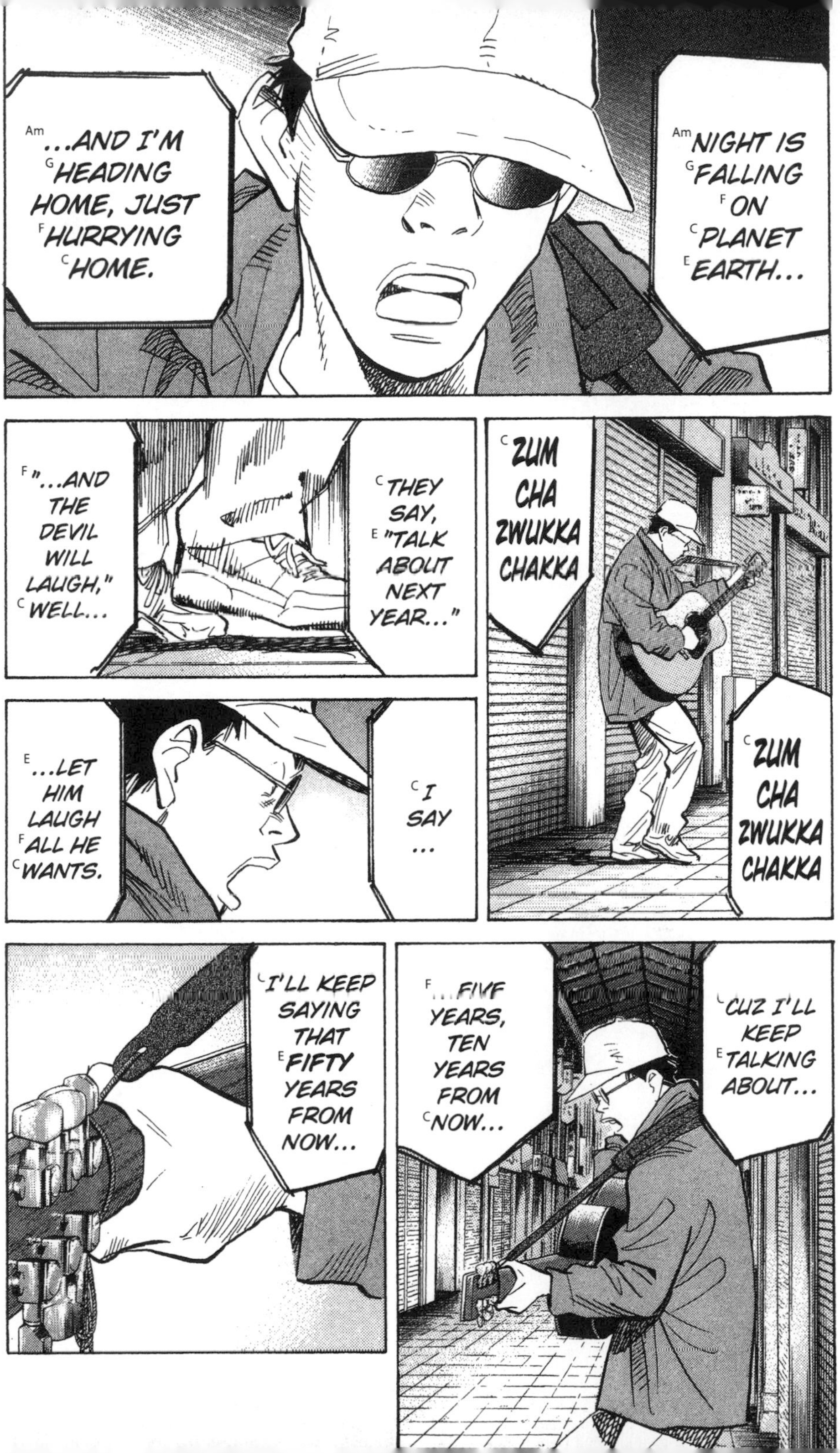
Am NIGHT IS G FALLING F ON C PLANET E EARTH...
Am ...AND I'M G HEADING HOME, JUST F HURRYING C HOME.
C ZUM CHA ZWUKKA CHAKKA
C ZUM CHA ZWUKKA CHAKKA
C THEY SAY, E "TALK ABOUT NEXT YEAR..."
F "...AND THE DEVIL WILL LAUGH," C WELL...
C I SAY ...
E ...LET HIM LAUGH F ALL HE C WANTS.
C CUZ I'LL KEEP E TALKING ABOUT...
F ...FIVE YEARS, TEN YEARS FROM C NOW...
C I'LL KEEP SAYING THAT E FIFTY YEARS FROM NOW...

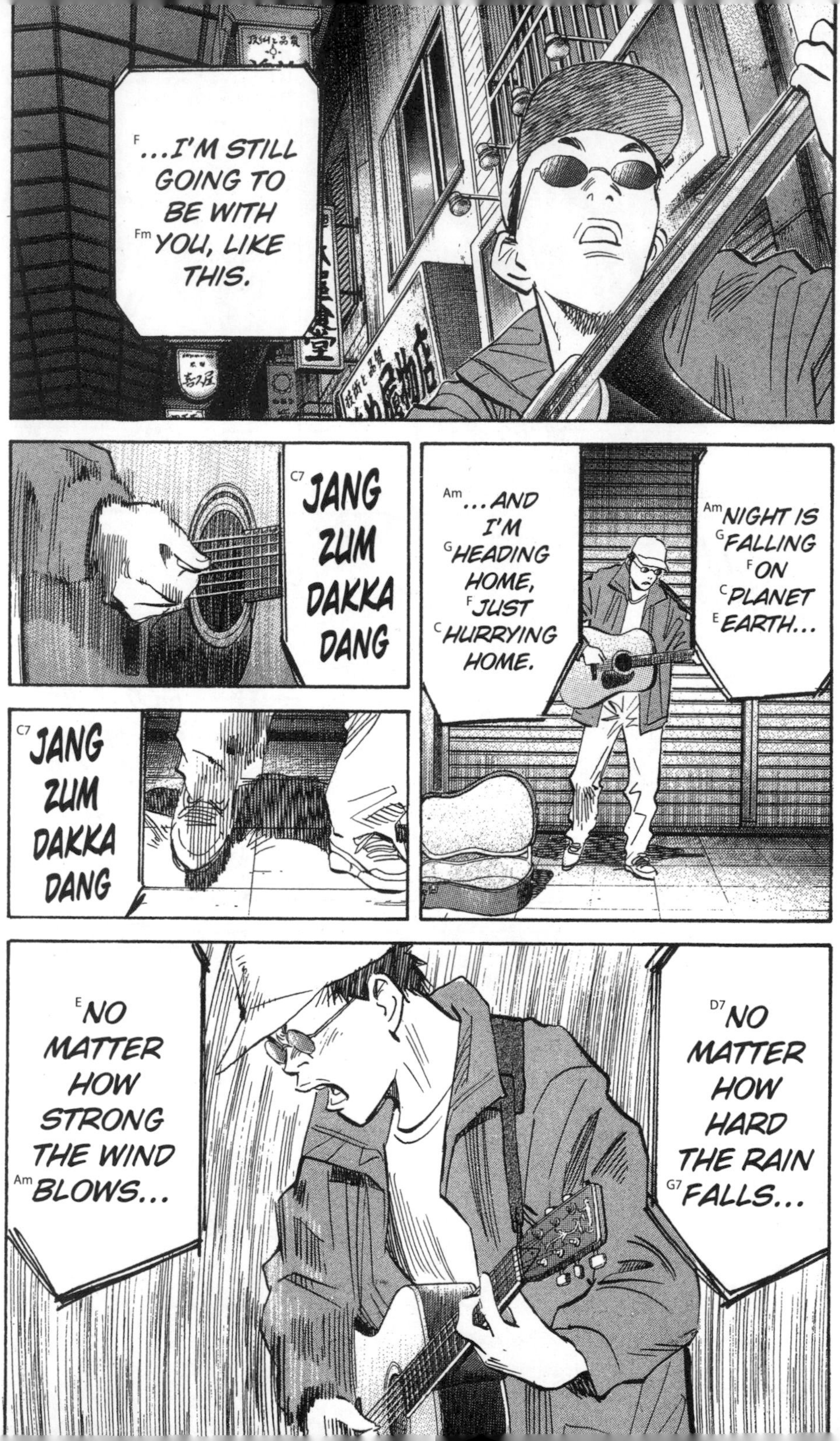
F ...I'M STILL GOING TO BE WITH Fm YOU, LIKE THIS.
Am NIGHT IS G FALLING F ON C PLANET E EARTH...
Am ...AND I'M G HEADING HOME, F JUST C HURRYING HOME.
C7 JANG ZUM DAKKA DANG
C7 JANG ZUM DAKKA DANG
D7 NO MATTER HOW HARD THE RAIN G7 FALLS...
E NO MATTER HOW STRONG THE WIND Am BLOWS...

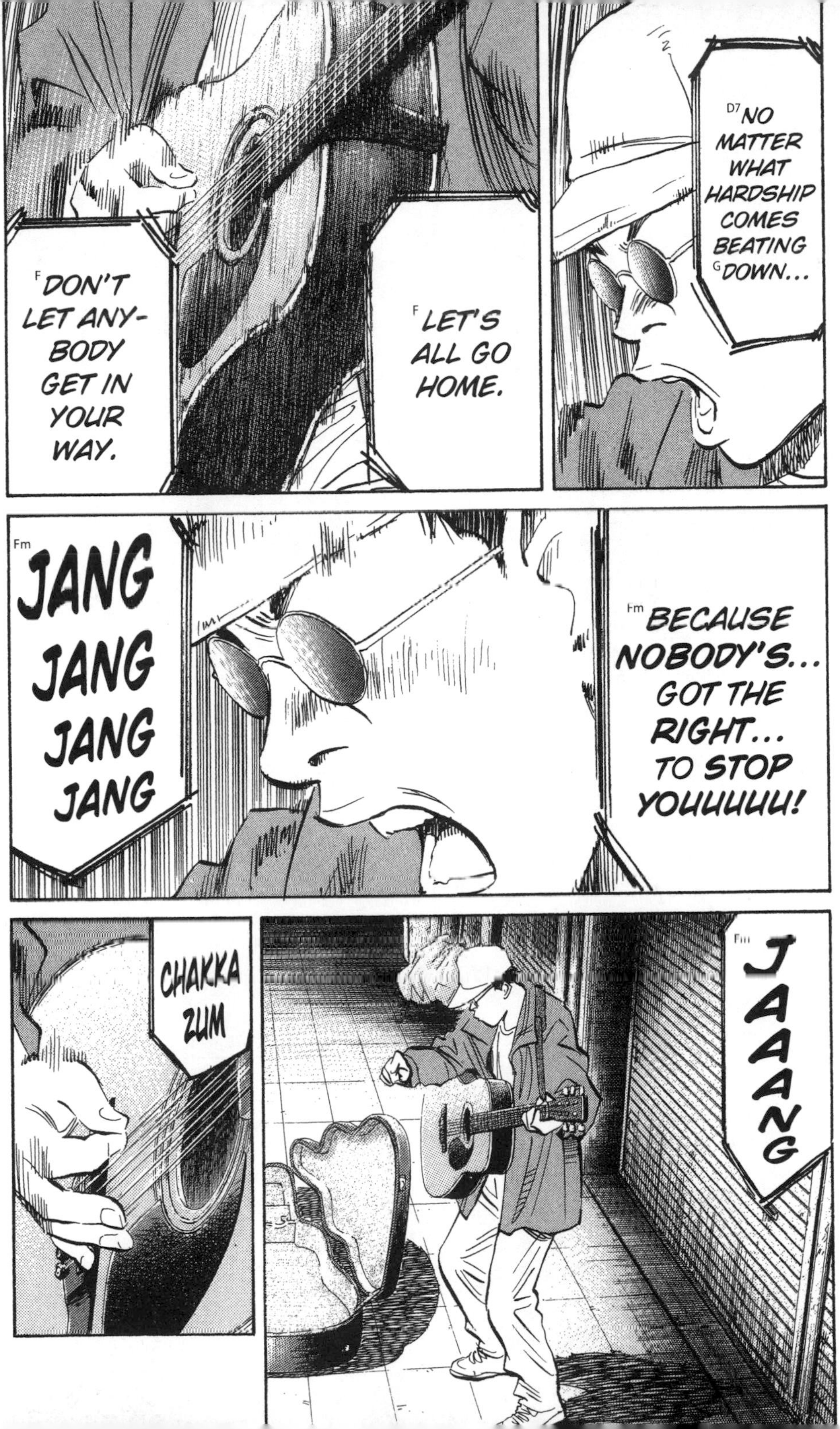
D7 NO MATTER WHAT HARDSHIP COMES BEATING G DOWN...
F LET'S ALL GO HOME.
F DON'T LET ANY-BODY GET IN YOUR WAY.
Fm BECAUSE NOBODY'S... GOT THE RIGHT... TO STOP YOUUUUUU!
Fm JANG JANG JANG JANG
Fm JAAAANG
CHAKKA ZUM

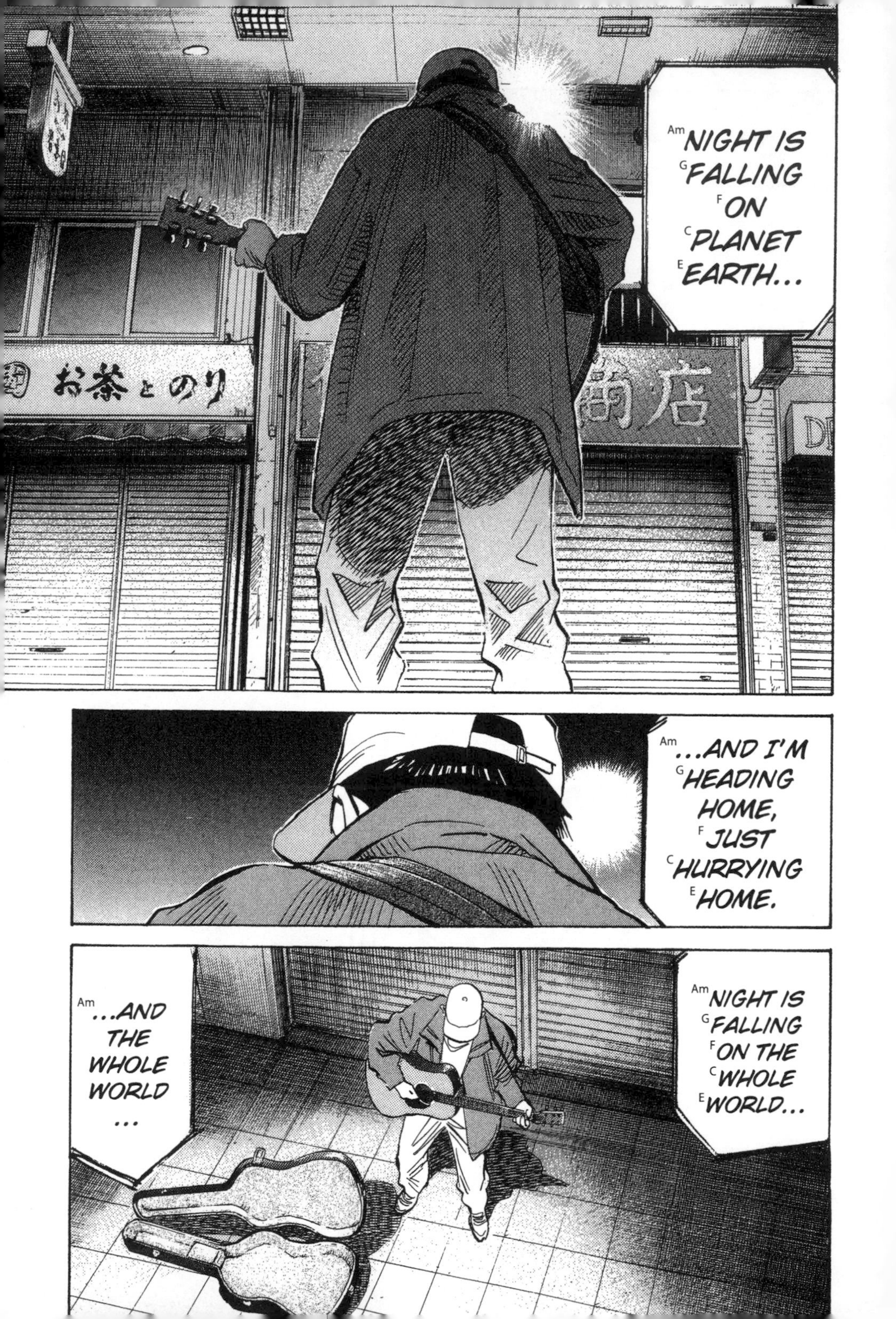
Am NIGHT IS G FALLING F ON C PLANET E EARTH...
お茶とのり
店
Am ...AND I'M G HEADING HOME, F JUST C HURRYING E HOME.
Am NIGHT IS G FALLING F ON THE C WHOLE E WORLD...
Am ...AND THE WHOLE WORLD ...

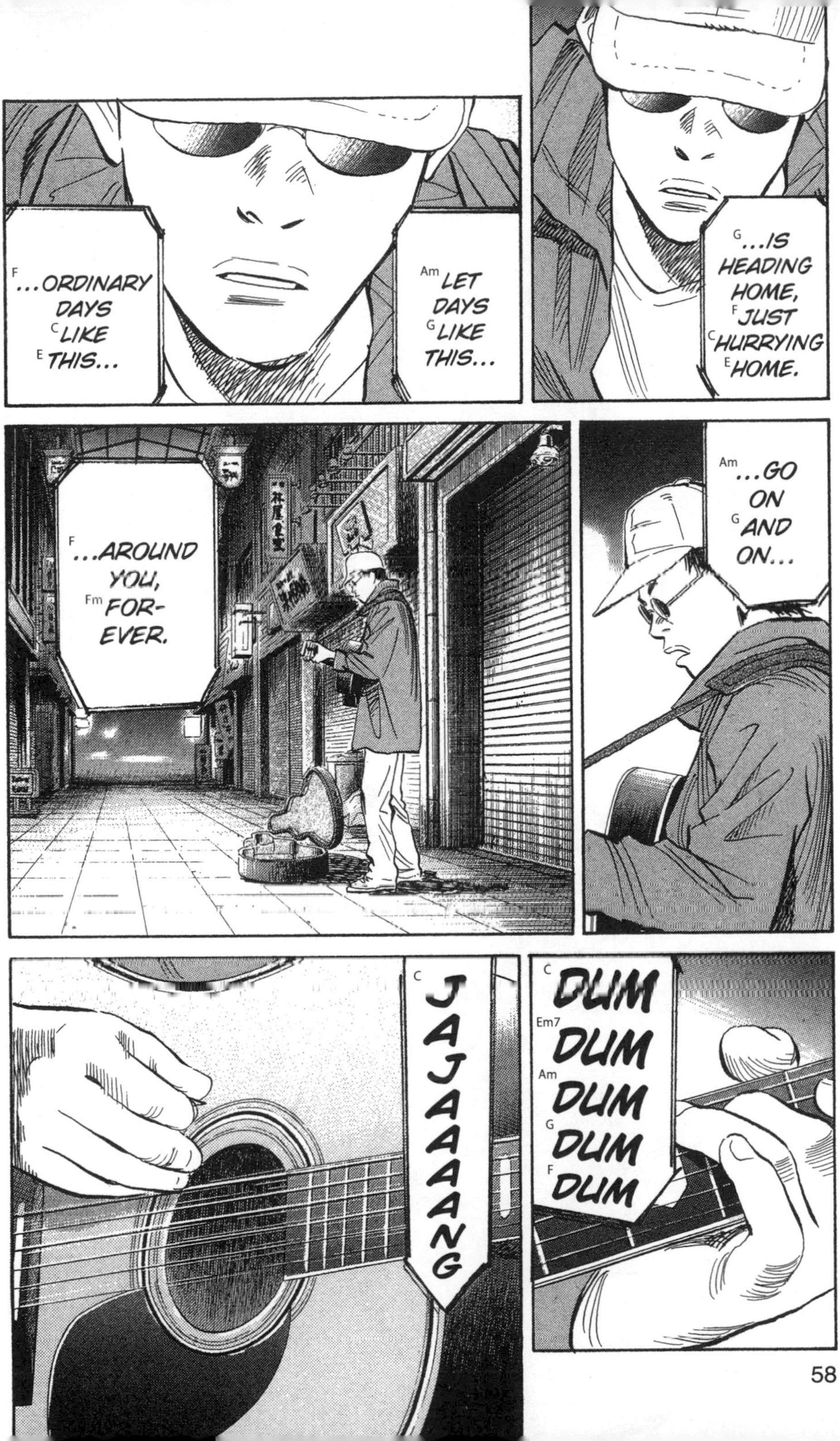
G ...IS HEADING HOME, F JUST C HURRYING E HOME.
Am LET DAYS G LIKE THIS...
F ...ORDINARY DAYS C LIKE E THIS...
Am ...GO ON G AND ON...
F ...AROUND YOU, Fm FOR-EVER.
C DUM Em7 DUM Am DUM G DUM F DUM
C JAJAAAAANG

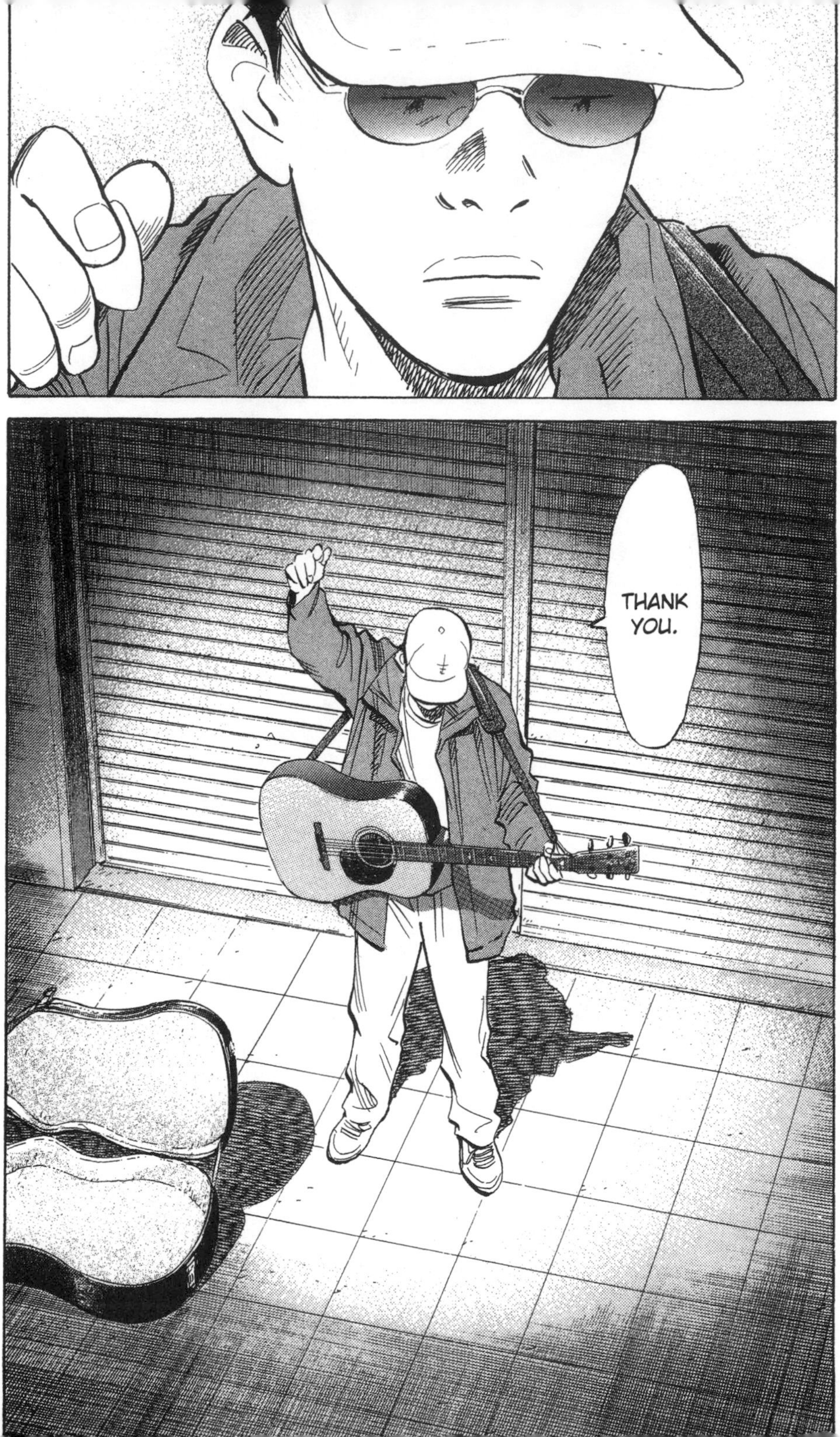
THANK YOU.

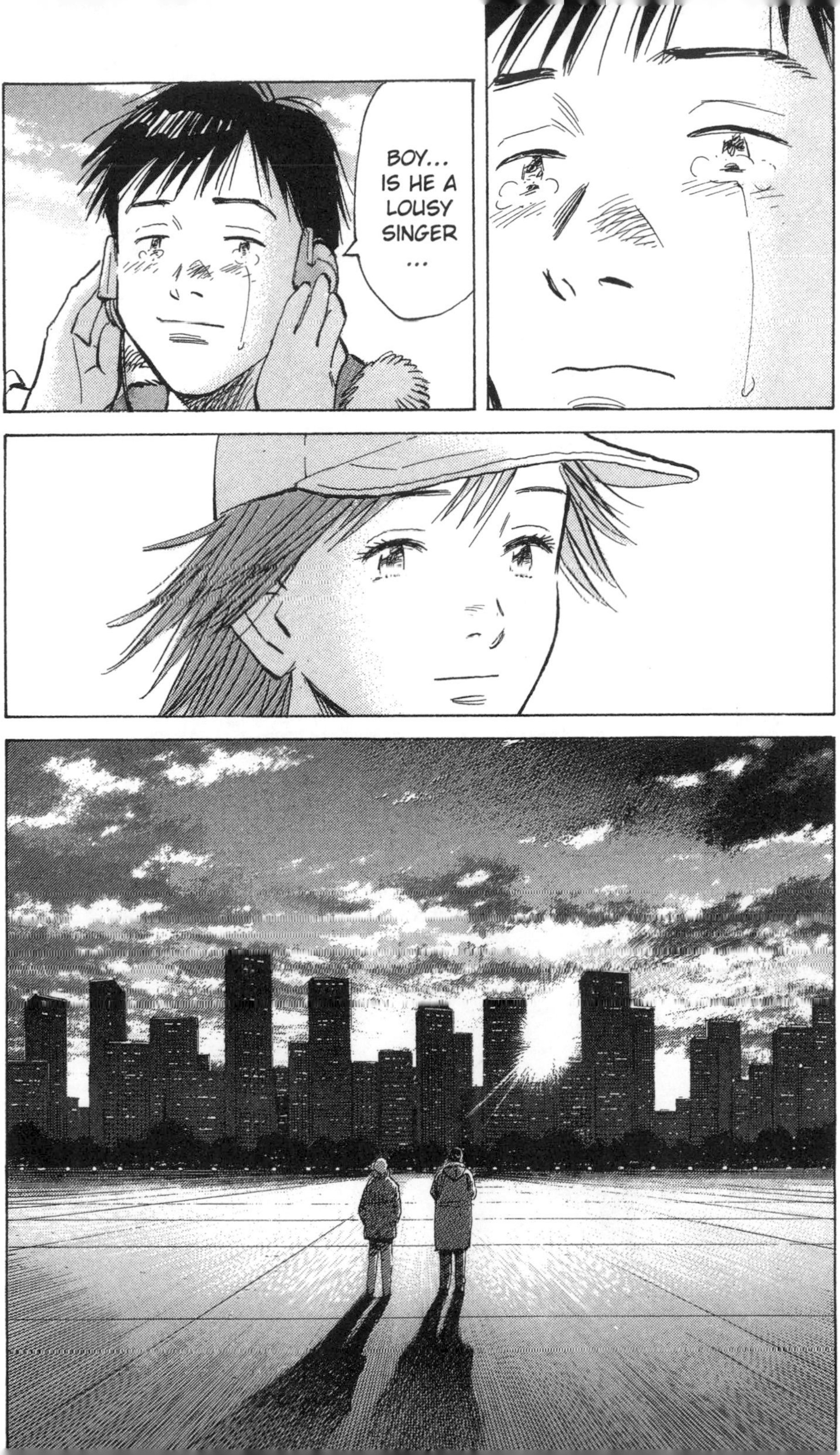
BOY... IS HE A LOUSY SINGER ...

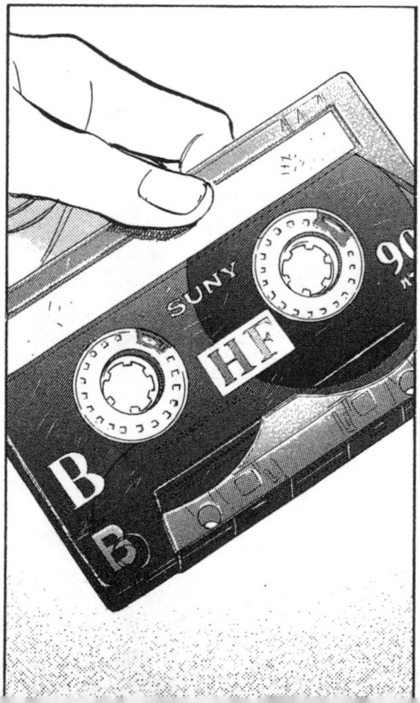
SUNY
HF
90
B
B

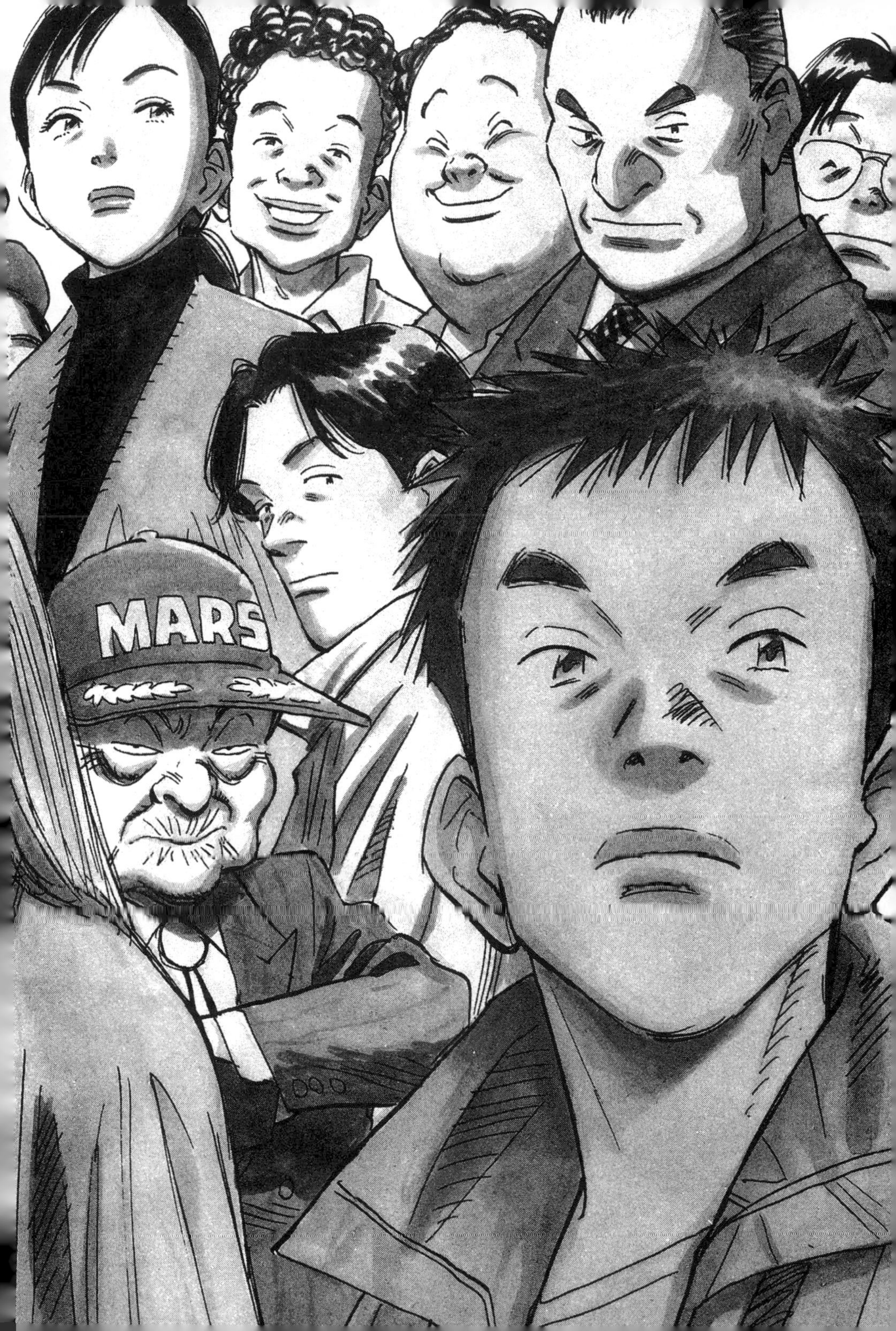
MARS

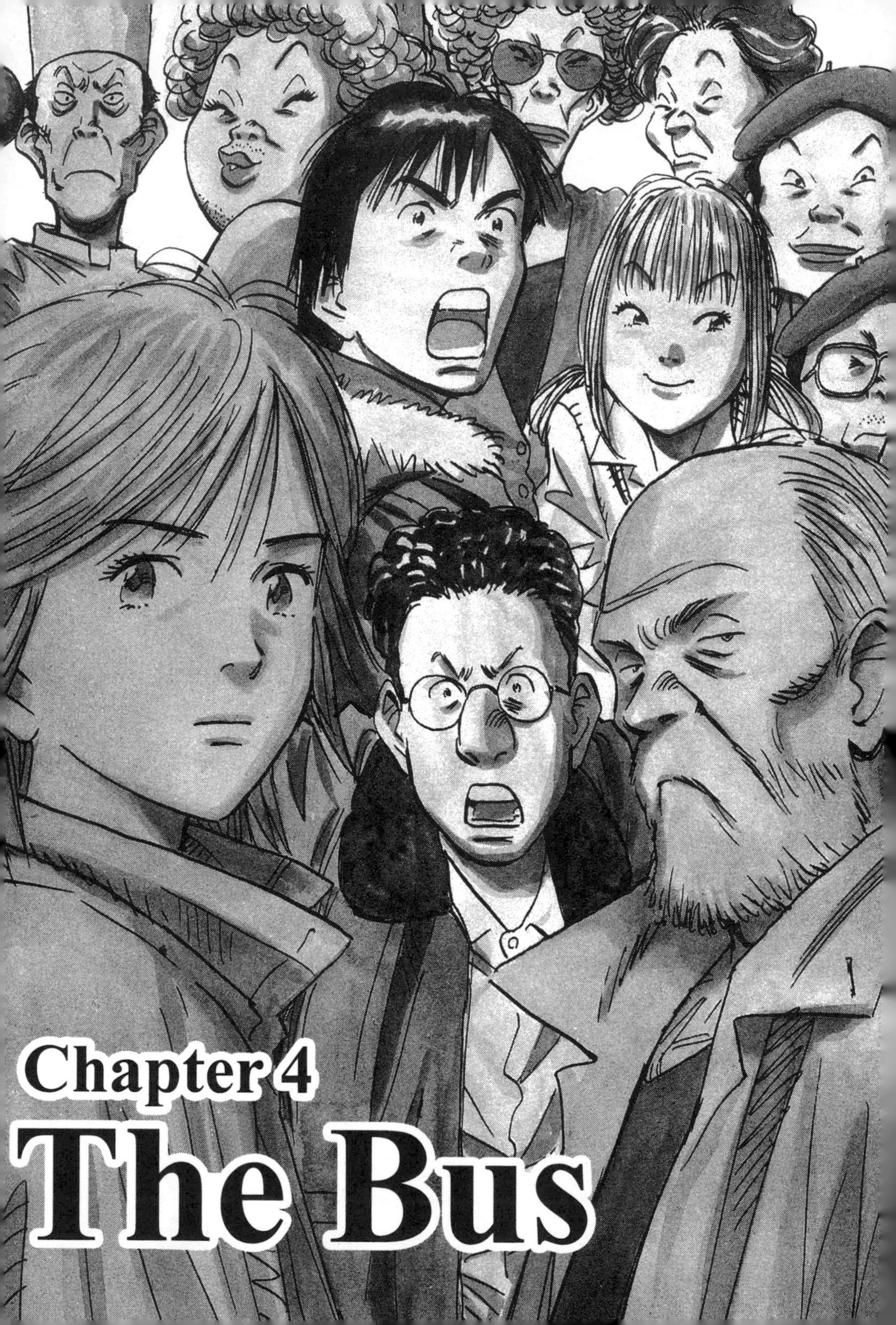
Chapter 4
The Bus

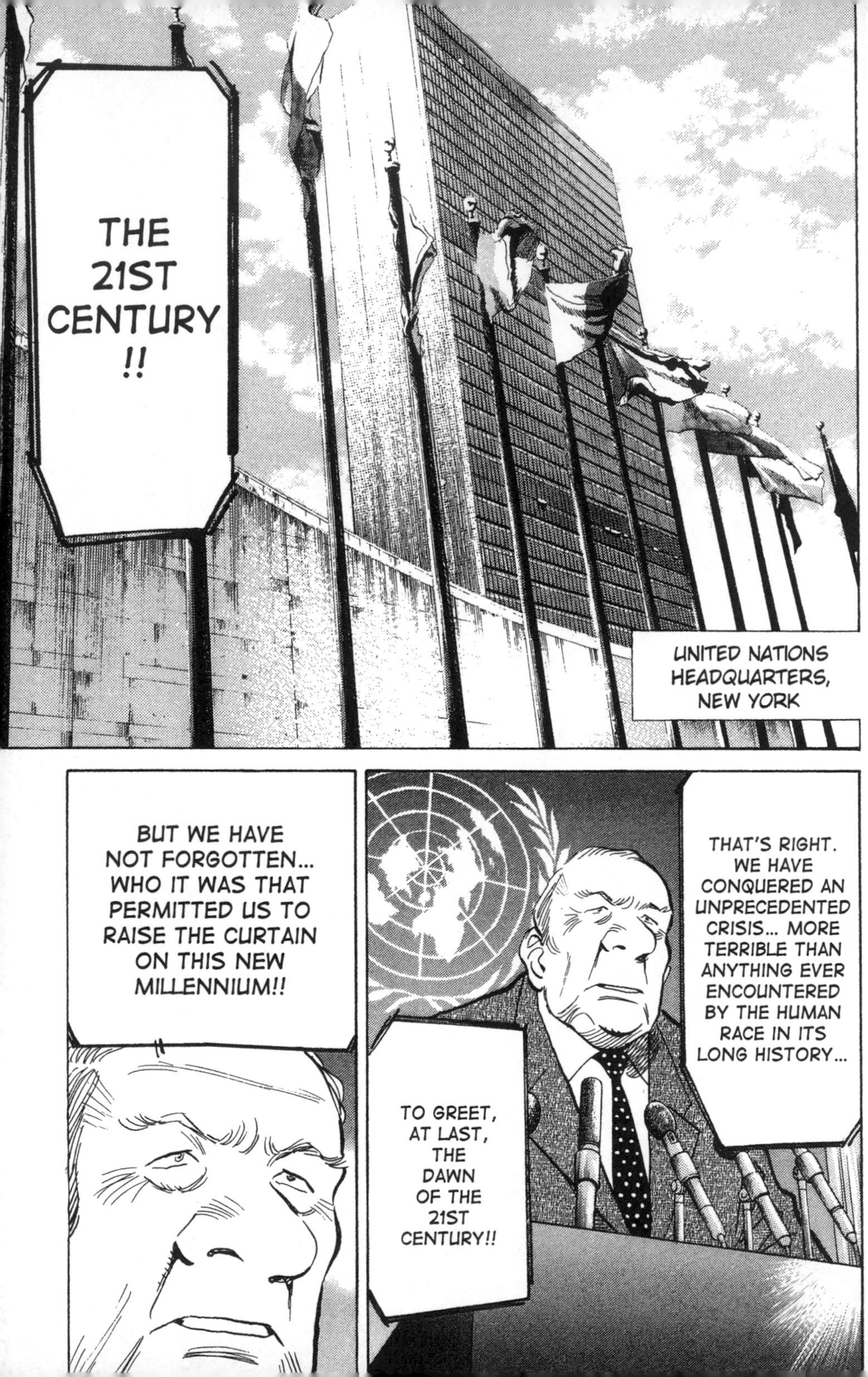
THE 21ST CENTURY!!
UNITED NATIONS HEADQUARTERS, NEW YORK
THAT'S RIGHT. WE HAVE CONQUERED AN UNPRECEDENTED CRISIS... MORE TERRIBLE THAN ANYTHING EVER ENCOUNTERED BY THE HUMAN RACE IN ITS LONG HISTORY...
TO GREET, AT LAST, THE DAWN OF THE 21ST CENTURY!!
BUT WE HAVE NOT FORGOTTEN... WHO IT WAS THAT PERMITTED US TO RAISE THE CURTAIN ON THIS NEW MILLENNIUM!!

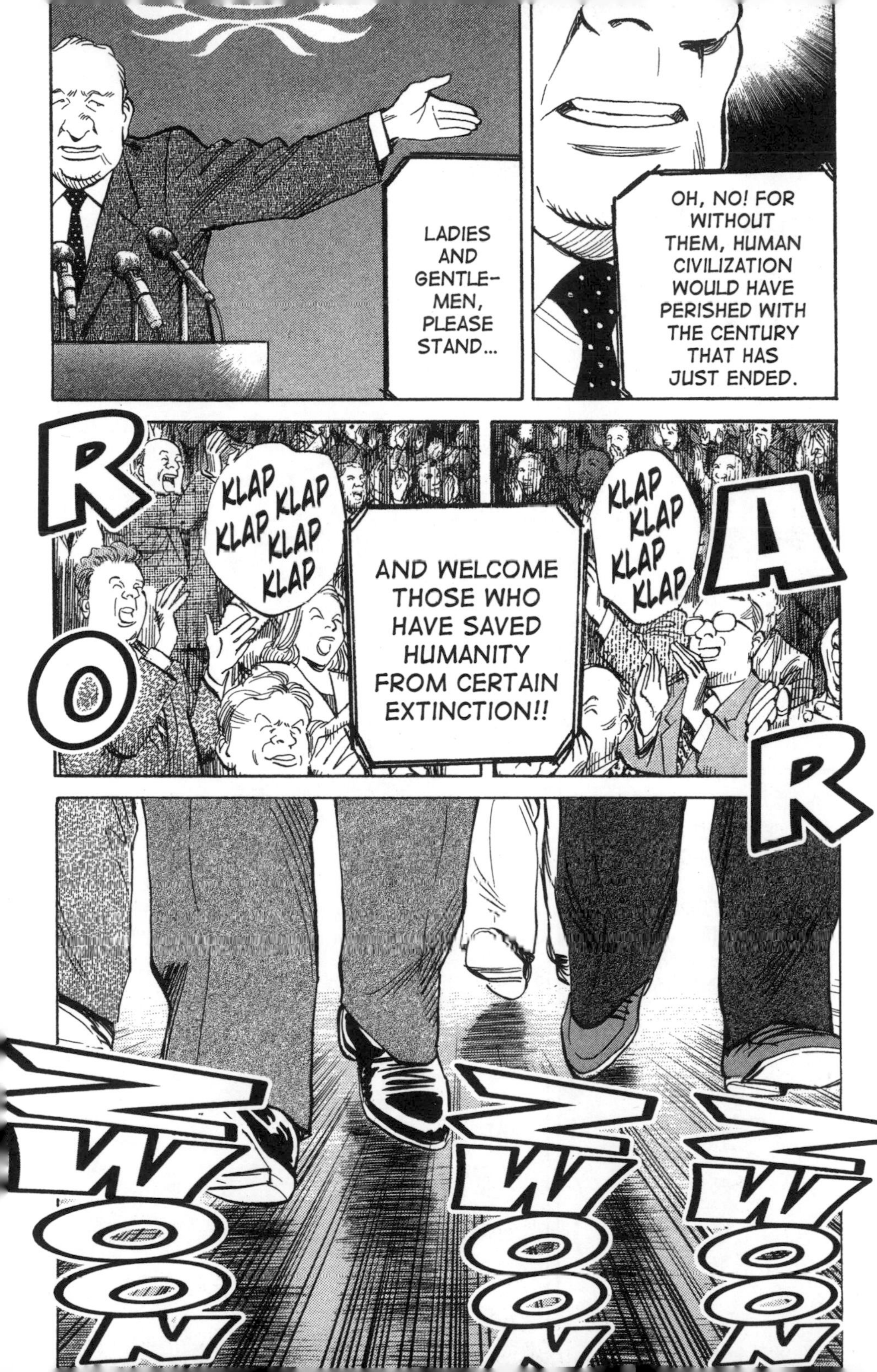
OH, NO! FOR WITHOUT THEM, HUMAN CIVILIZATION WOULD HAVE PERISHED WITH THE CENTURY THAT HAS JUST ENDED.
LADIES AND GENTLE-MEN, PLEASE STAND...
ROAR
KLAP KLAP KLAP KLAP
AND WELCOME THOSE WHO HAVE SAVED HUMANITY FROM CERTAIN EXTINCTION!!
KLAP KLAP KLAP KLAP KLAP
ZWOON
ZWOON
ZWOON

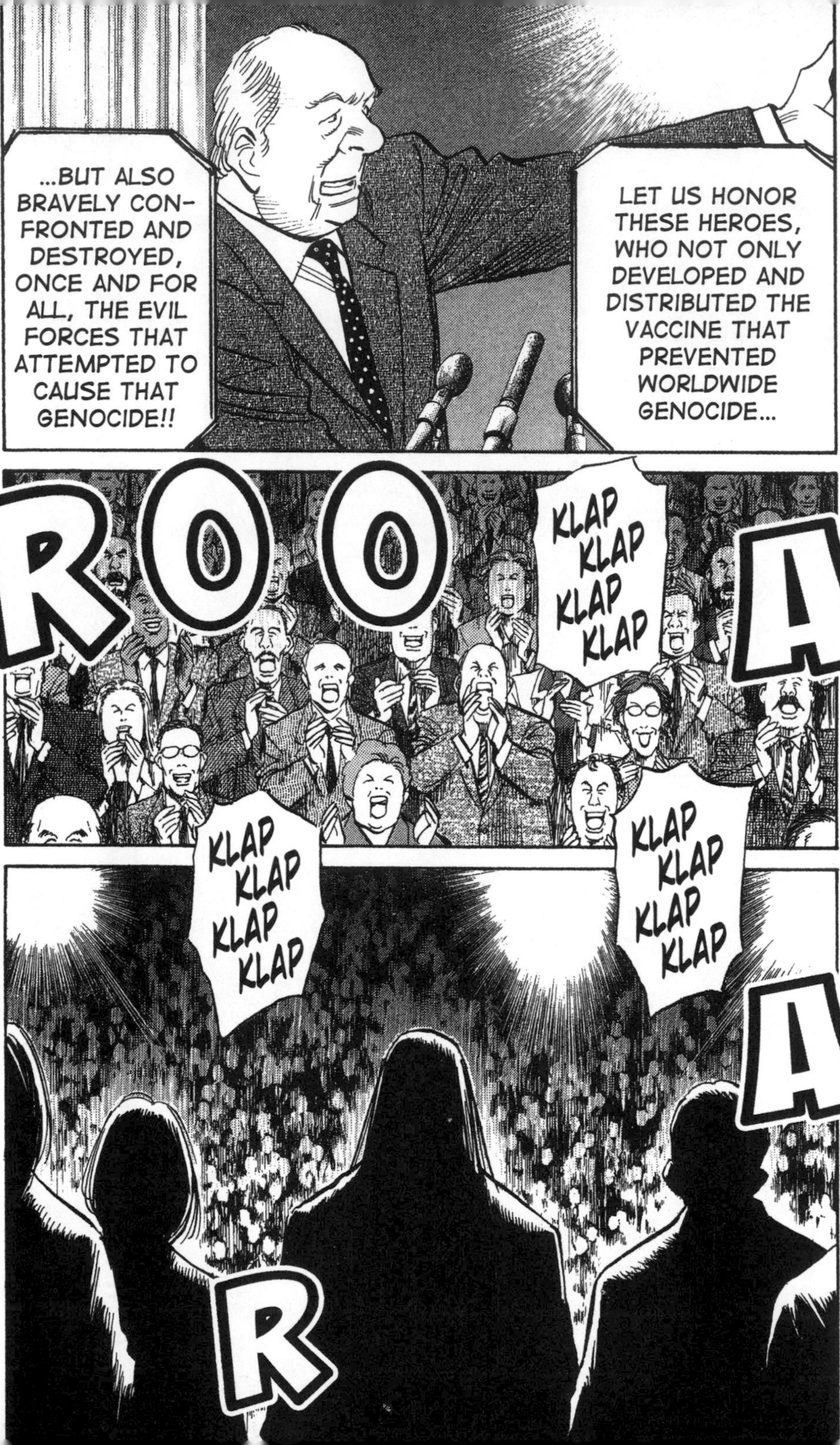
LET US HONOR THESE HEROES, WHO NOT ONLY DEVELOPED AND DISTRIBUTED THE VACCINE THAT PREVENTED WORLDWIDE GENOCIDE...
...BUT ALSO BRAVELY CON-FRONTED AND DESTROYED, ONCE AND FOR ALL, THE EVIL FORCES THAT ATTEMPTED TO CAUSE THAT GENOCIDE!!
KLAP KLAP KLAP KLAP
ROO
A
KLAP KLAP KLAP KLAP
KLAP KLAP KLAP KLAP
A
R

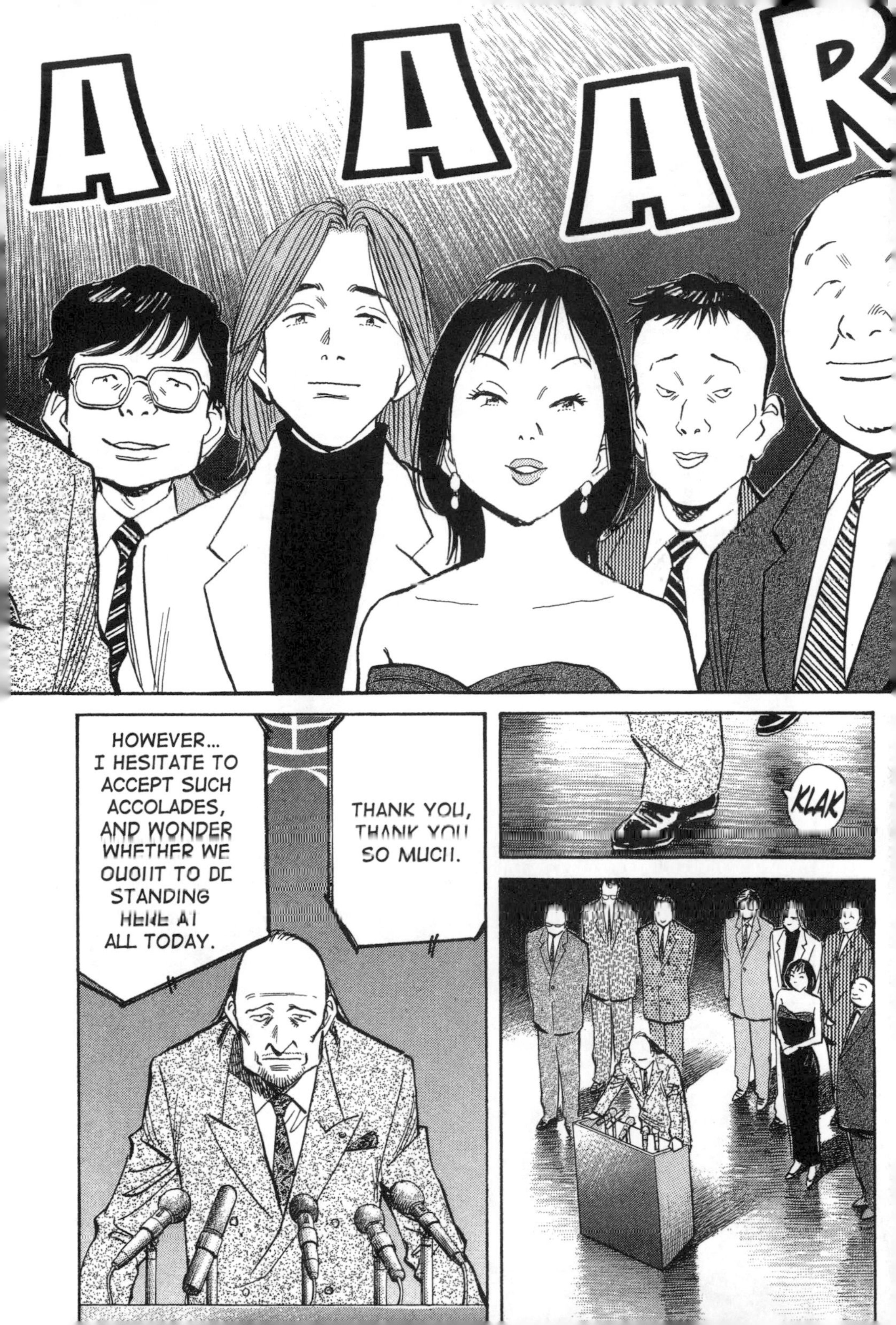
AAAR
KLAK
THANK YOU, THANK YOU SO MUCH.
HOWEVER... I HESITATE TO ACCEPT SUCH ACCOLADES, AND WONDER WHETHER WE OUGHT TO BE STANDING HERE AT ALL TODAY.

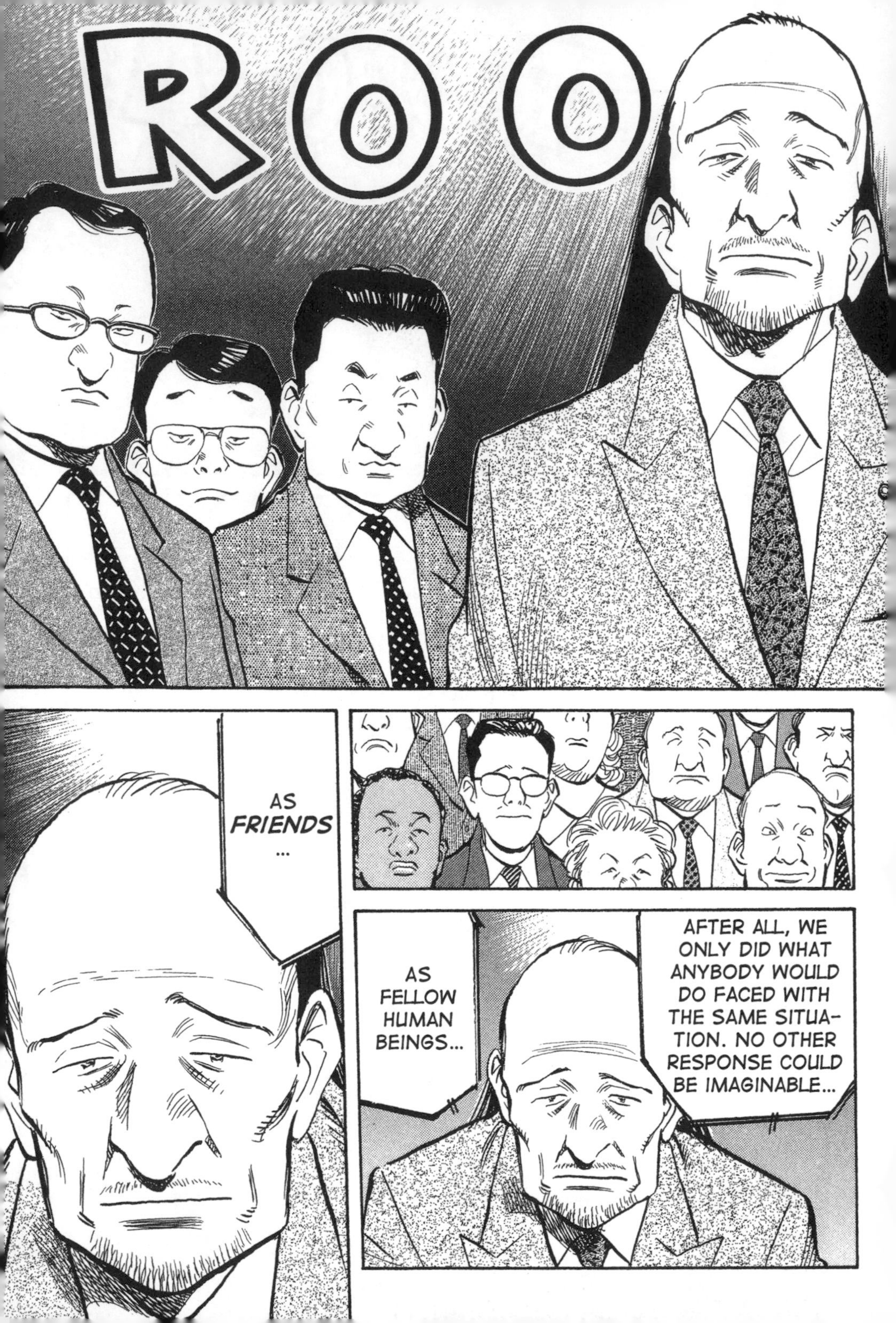
ROO
AFTER ALL, WE ONLY DID WHAT ANYBODY WOULD DO FACED WITH THE SAME SITUATION. NO OTHER RESPONSE COULD BE IMAGINABLE...
AS FELLOW HUMAN BEINGS...
AS *FRIENDS* ...

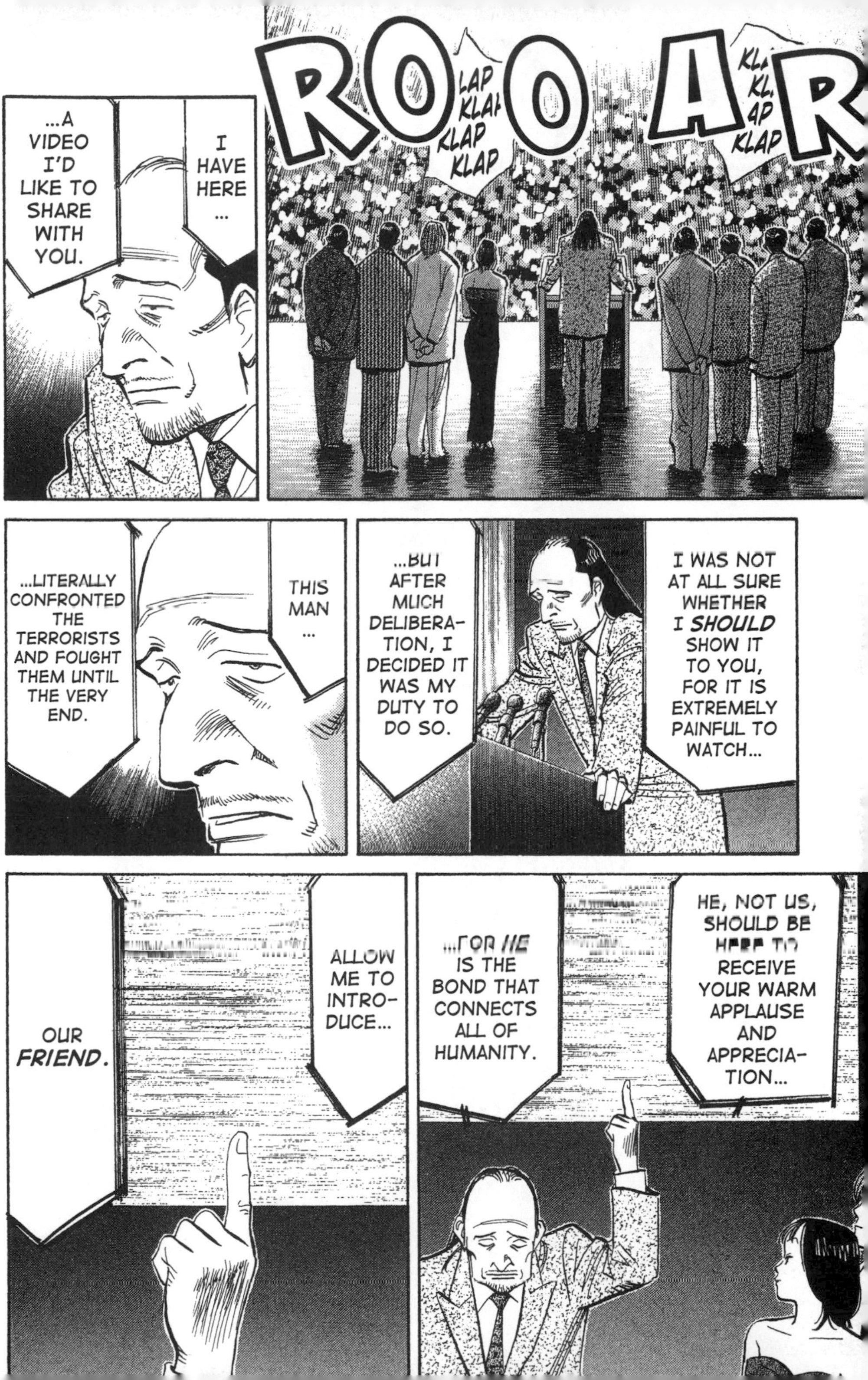
ROOAR
KLAP KLAP KLAP KLAP
KLAP
I HAVE HERE…
…A VIDEO I'D LIKE TO SHARE WITH YOU.
I WAS NOT AT ALL SURE WHETHER I *SHOULD* SHOW IT TO YOU, FOR IT IS EXTREMELY PAINFUL TO WATCH…
…BUT AFTER MUCH DELIBERATION, I DECIDED IT WAS MY DUTY TO DO SO.
THIS MAN…
…LITERALLY CONFRONTED THE TERRORISTS AND FOUGHT THEM UNTIL THE VERY END.
HE, NOT US, SHOULD BE HERE TO RECEIVE YOUR WARM APPLAUSE AND APPRECIATION…
…FOR *HE* IS THE BOND THAT CONNECTS ALL OF HUMANITY.
ALLOW ME TO INTRODUCE…
OUR *FRIEND*.

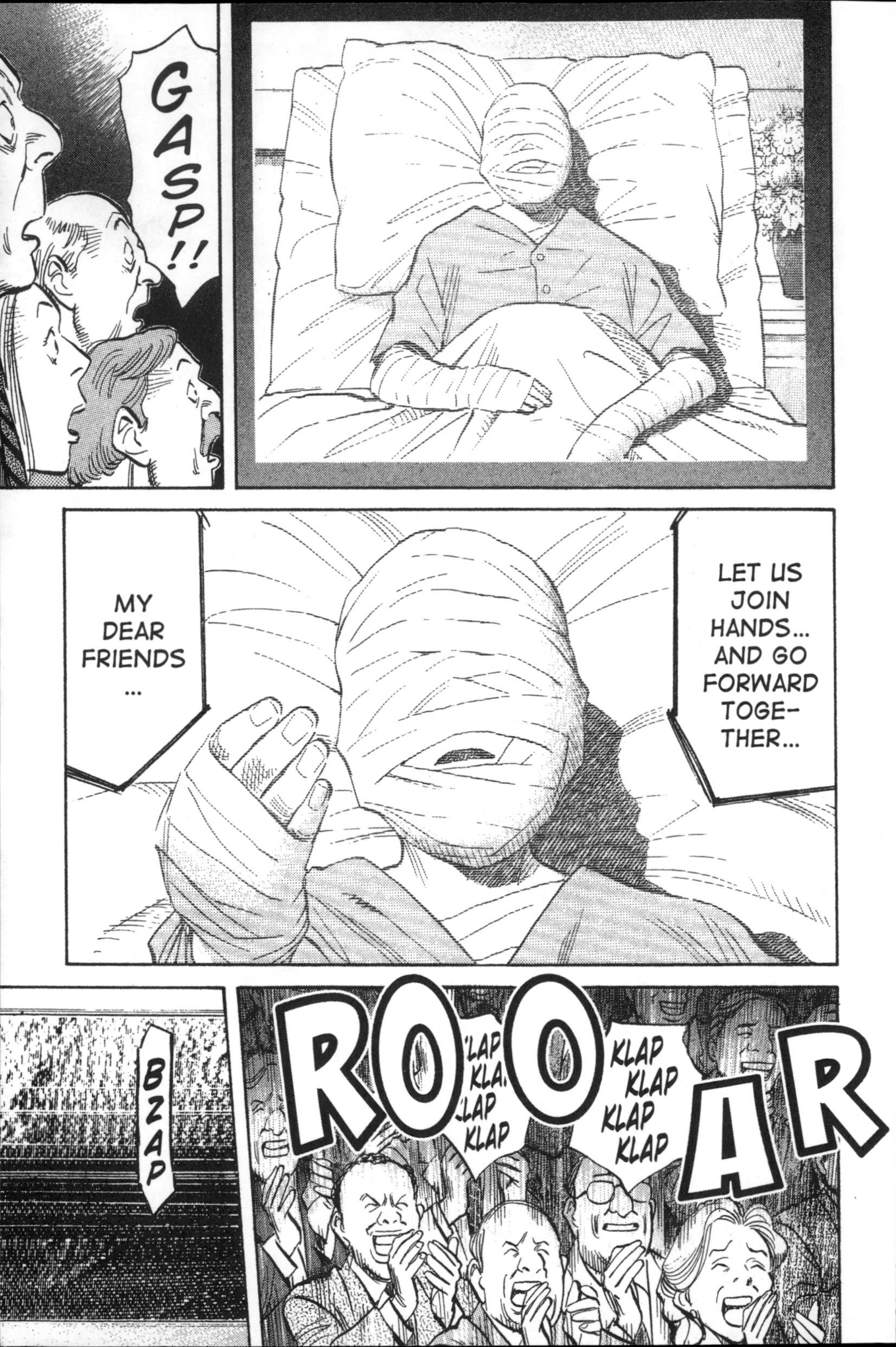
GASP!!
LET US JOIN HANDS... AND GO FORWARD TOGE-THER...
MY DEAR FRIENDS ...
ROOOAR
KLAP KLAP KLAP KLAP
KLAP KLA. KLAP KLAP
BZAP

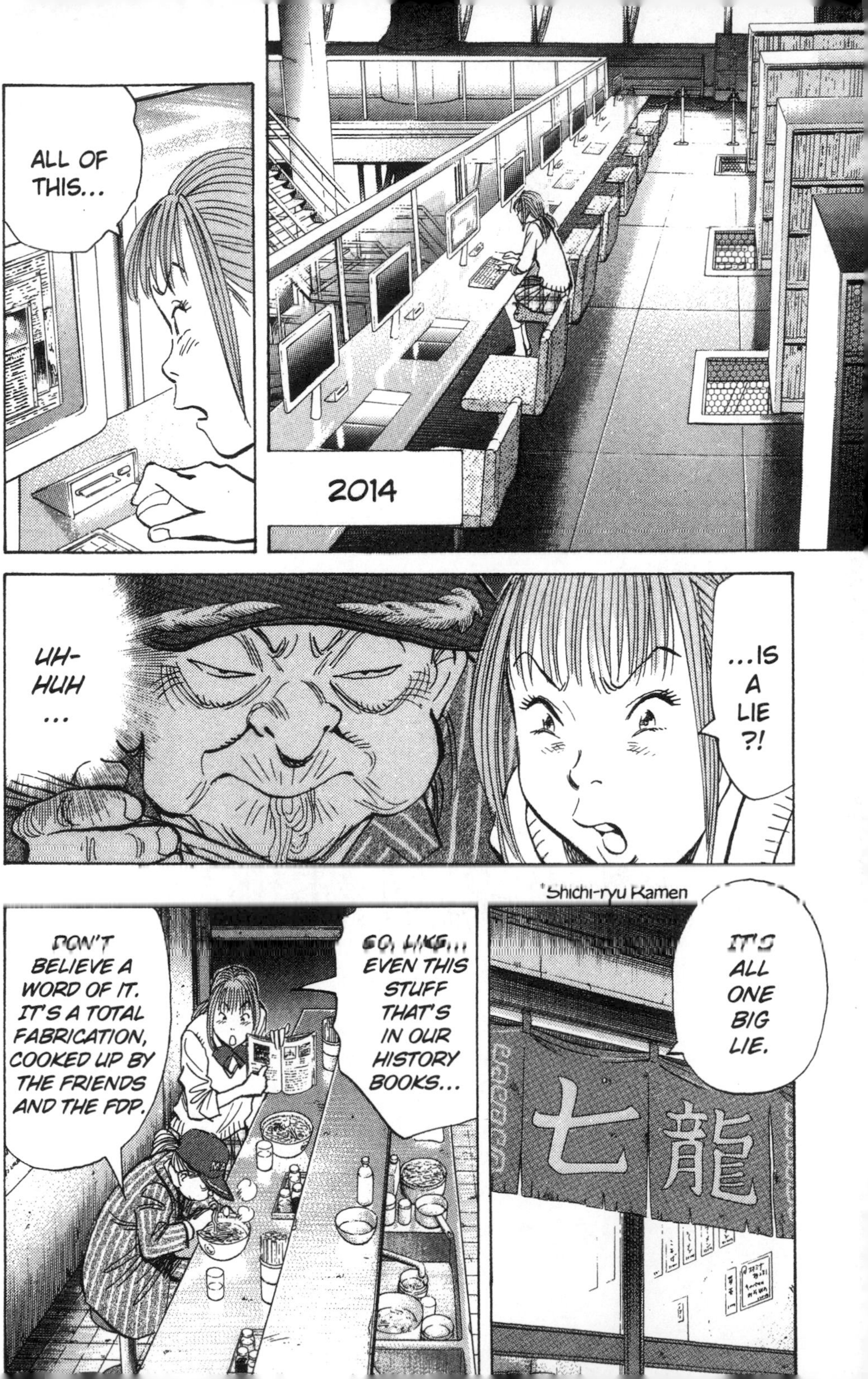

2014
ALL OF THIS...
...IS A LIE?!
UH-HUH...
IT'S ALL ONE BIG LIE.
七龍
*Shichi-ryu Ramen
SO, LIKE... EVEN THIS STUFF THAT'S IN OUR HISTORY BOOKS...
DON'T BELIEVE A WORD OF IT. IT'S A TOTAL FABRICATION, COOKED UP BY THE FRIENDS AND THE FDP.

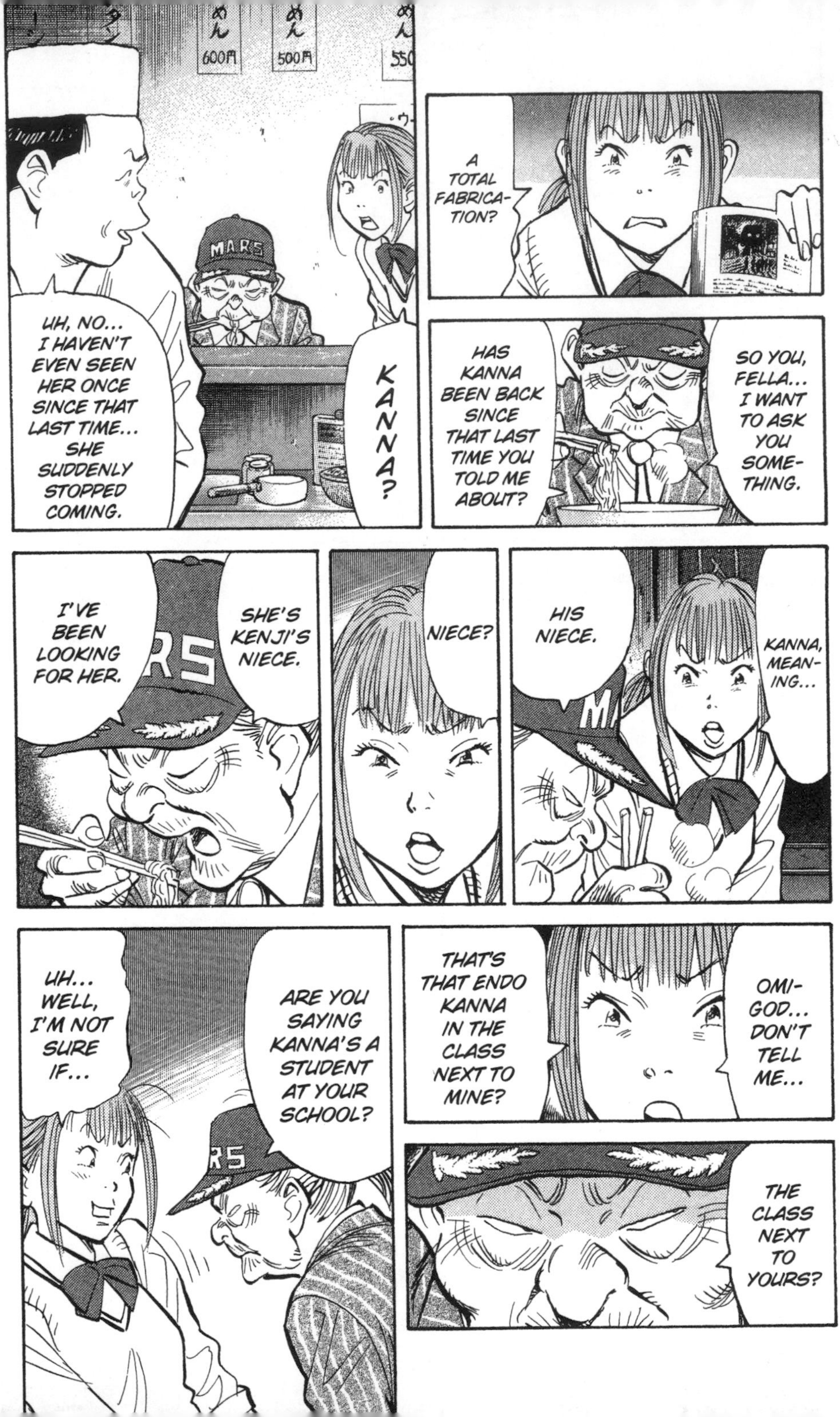
A TOTAL FABRICATION?
SO YOU, FELLA... I WANT TO ASK YOU SOMETHING.
HAS KANNA BEEN BACK SINCE THAT LAST TIME YOU TOLD ME ABOUT?
めん 600円
めん 500円
KANNA?
UH, NO... I HAVEN'T EVEN SEEN HER ONCE SINCE THAT LAST TIME... SHE SUDDENLY STOPPED COMING.
KANNA, MEANING...
HIS NIECE.
NIECE?
SHE'S KENJI'S NIECE.
I'VE BEEN LOOKING FOR HER.
OMIGOD... DON'T TELL ME...
THAT'S THAT ENDO KANNA IN THE CLASS NEXT TO MINE?
THE CLASS NEXT TO YOURS?
ARE YOU SAYING KANNA'S A STUDENT AT YOUR SCHOOL?
UH... WELL, I'M NOT SURE IF...

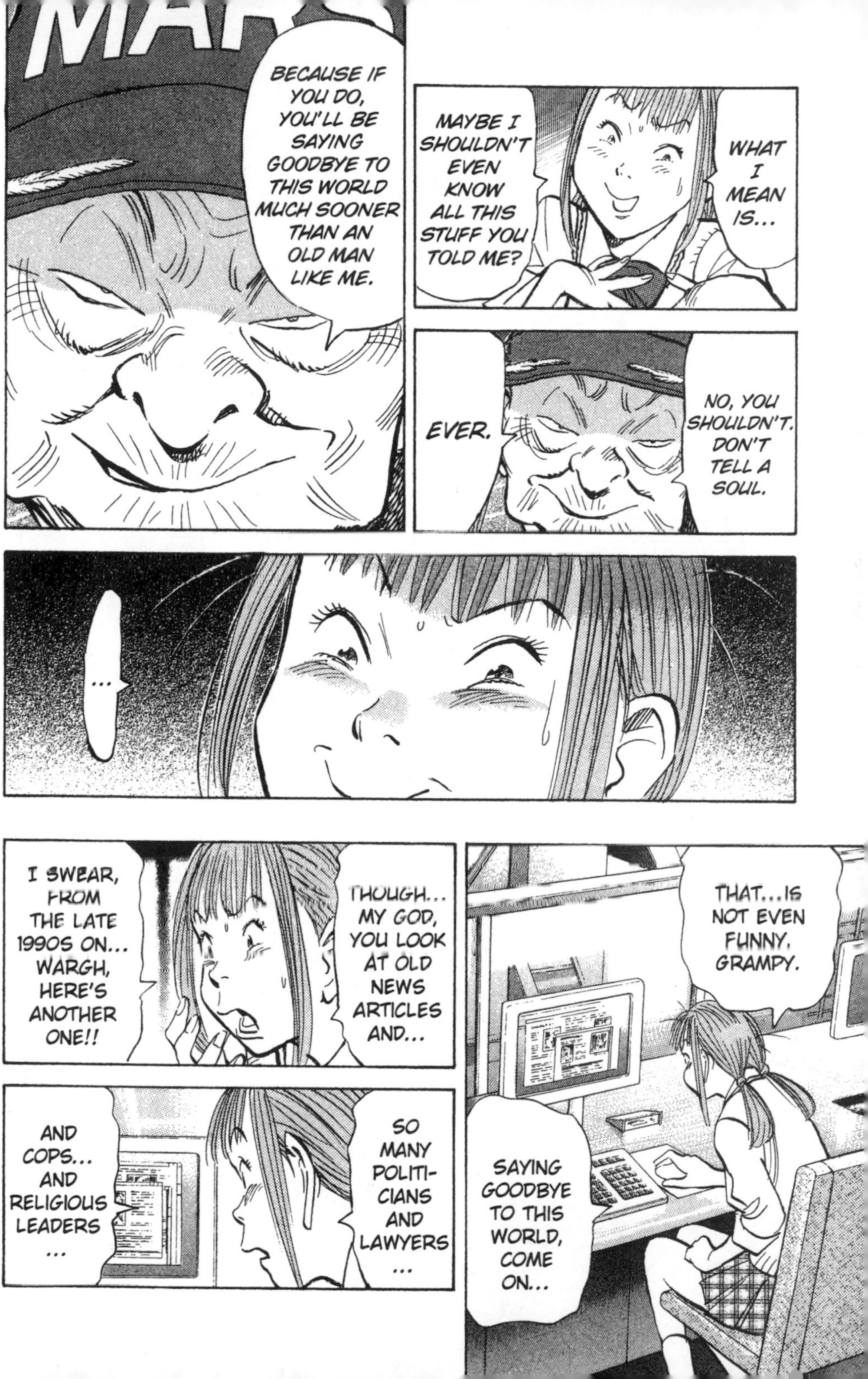
WHAT I MEAN IS...
MAYBE I SHOULDN'T EVEN KNOW ALL THIS STUFF YOU TOLD ME?
NO, YOU SHOULDN'T. DON'T TELL A SOUL.
EVER.
BECAUSE IF YOU DO, YOU'LL BE SAYING GOODBYE TO THIS WORLD MUCH SOONER THAN AN OLD MAN LIKE ME.
...
THAT...IS NOT EVEN FUNNY, GRAMPY.
SAYING GOODBYE TO THIS WORLD, COME ON...
THOUGH... MY GOD, YOU LOOK AT OLD NEWS ARTICLES AND...
I SWEAR, FROM THE LATE 1990S ON... WARGH, HERE'S ANOTHER ONE!!
SO MANY POLITI-CIANS AND LAWYERS...
AND COPS... AND RELIGIOUS LEADERS...

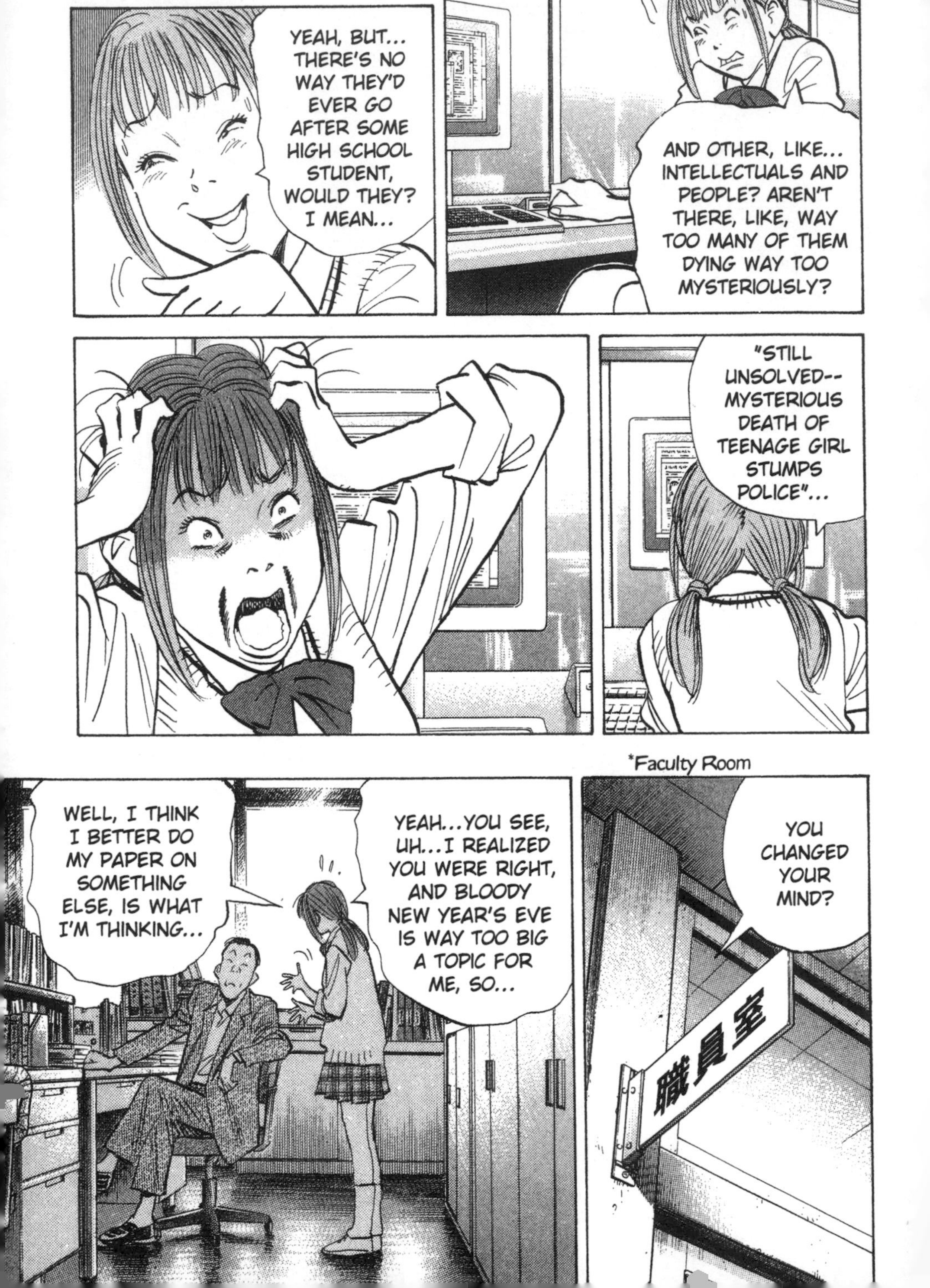
AND OTHER, LIKE... INTELLECTUALS AND PEOPLE? AREN'T THERE, LIKE, WAY TOO MANY OF THEM DYING WAY TOO MYSTERIOUSLY?
YEAH, BUT... THERE'S NO WAY THEY'D EVER GO AFTER SOME HIGH SCHOOL STUDENT, WOULD THEY? I MEAN...
"STILL UNSOLVED--MYSTERIOUS DEATH OF TEENAGE GIRL STUMPS POLICE"...
*Faculty Room
YOU CHANGED YOUR MIND?
職員室
YEAH...YOU SEE, UH...I REALIZED YOU WERE RIGHT, AND BLOODY NEW YEAR'S EVE IS WAY TOO BIG A TOPIC FOR ME, SO...
WELL, I THINK I BETTER DO MY PAPER ON SOMETHING ELSE, IS WHAT I'M THINKING...

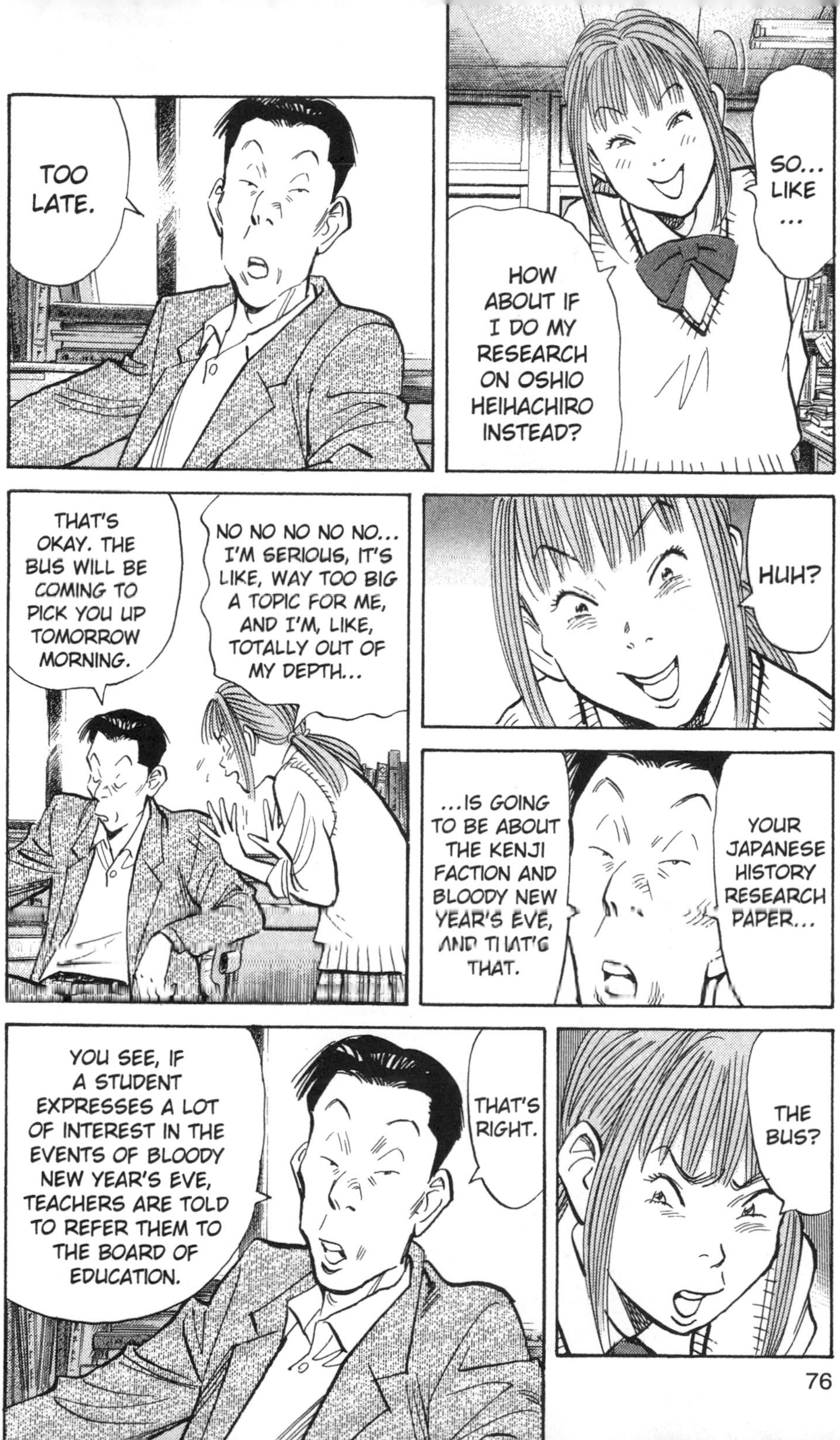
SO... LIKE ...
HOW ABOUT IF I DO MY RESEARCH ON OSHIO HEIHACHIRO INSTEAD?
TOO LATE.
HUH?
YOUR JAPANESE HISTORY RESEARCH PAPER...
...IS GOING TO BE ABOUT THE KENJI FACTION AND BLOODY NEW YEAR'S EVE, AND THAT'S THAT.
NO NO NO NO NO... I'M SERIOUS, IT'S LIKE, WAY TOO BIG A TOPIC FOR ME, AND I'M, LIKE, TOTALLY OUT OF MY DEPTH...
THAT'S OKAY. THE BUS WILL BE COMING TO PICK YOU UP TOMORROW MORNING.
THE BUS?
THAT'S RIGHT.
YOU SEE, IF A STUDENT EXPRESSES A LOT OF INTEREST IN THE EVENTS OF BLOODY NEW YEAR'S EVE, TEACHERS ARE TOLD TO REFER THEM TO THE BOARD OF EDUCATION.

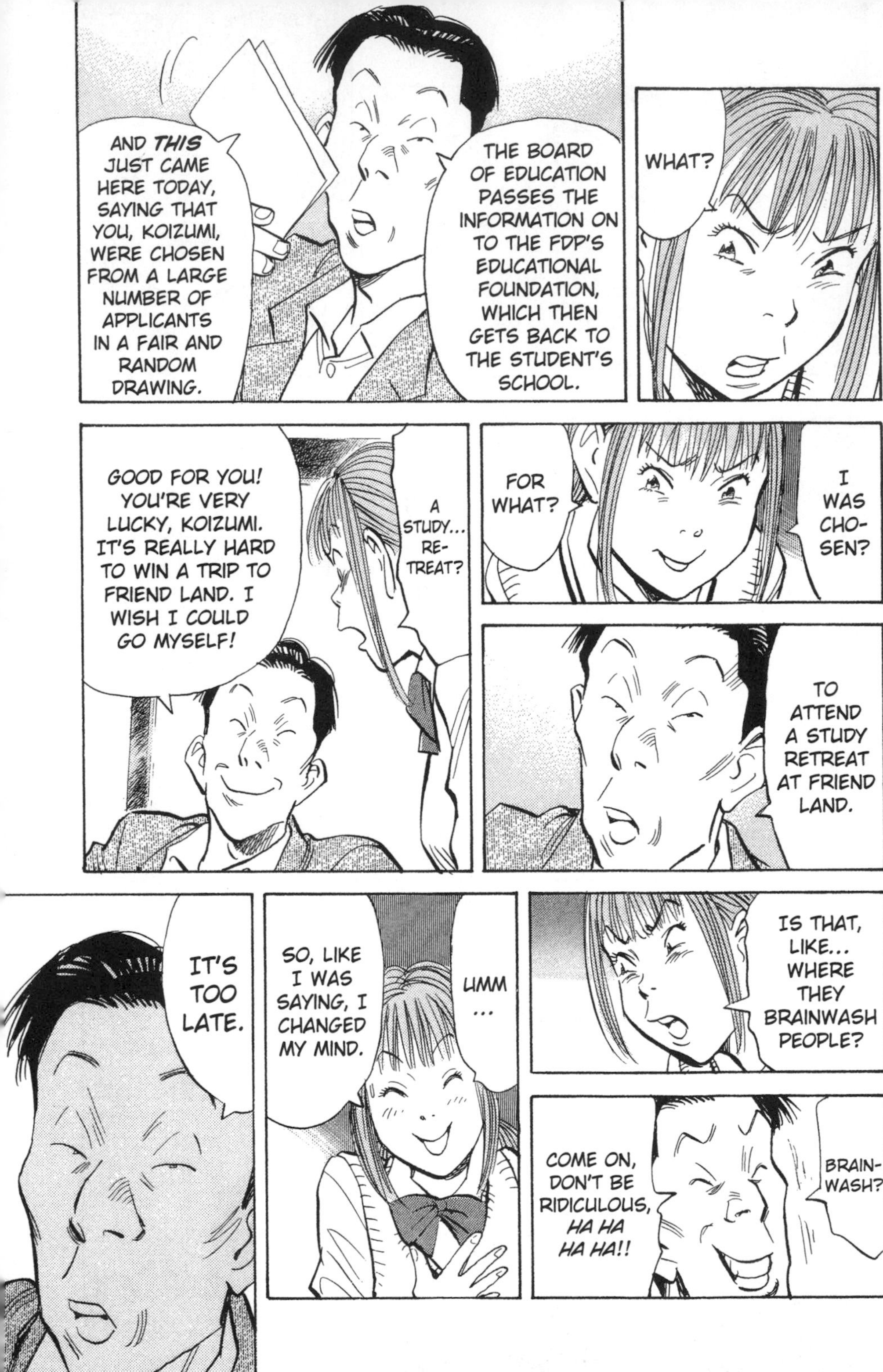
WHAT?
THE BOARD OF EDUCATION PASSES THE INFORMATION ON TO THE FDP'S EDUCATIONAL FOUNDATION, WHICH THEN GETS BACK TO THE STUDENT'S SCHOOL.
AND *THIS* JUST CAME HERE TODAY, SAYING THAT YOU, KOIZUMI, WERE CHOSEN FROM A LARGE NUMBER OF APPLICANTS IN A FAIR AND RANDOM DRAWING.
I WAS CHO-SEN?
FOR WHAT?
TO ATTEND A STUDY RETREAT AT FRIEND LAND.
A STUDY... RE-TREAT?
GOOD FOR YOU! YOU'RE VERY LUCKY, KOIZUMI. IT'S REALLY HARD TO WIN A TRIP TO FRIEND LAND. I WISH I COULD GO MYSELF!
IS THAT, LIKE... WHERE THEY BRAINWASH PEOPLE?
BRAIN-WASH?
COME ON, DON'T BE RIDICULOUS, *HA HA HA HA!!*
UMM ...
SO, LIKE I WAS SAYING, I CHANGED MY MIND.
IT'S TOO LATE.

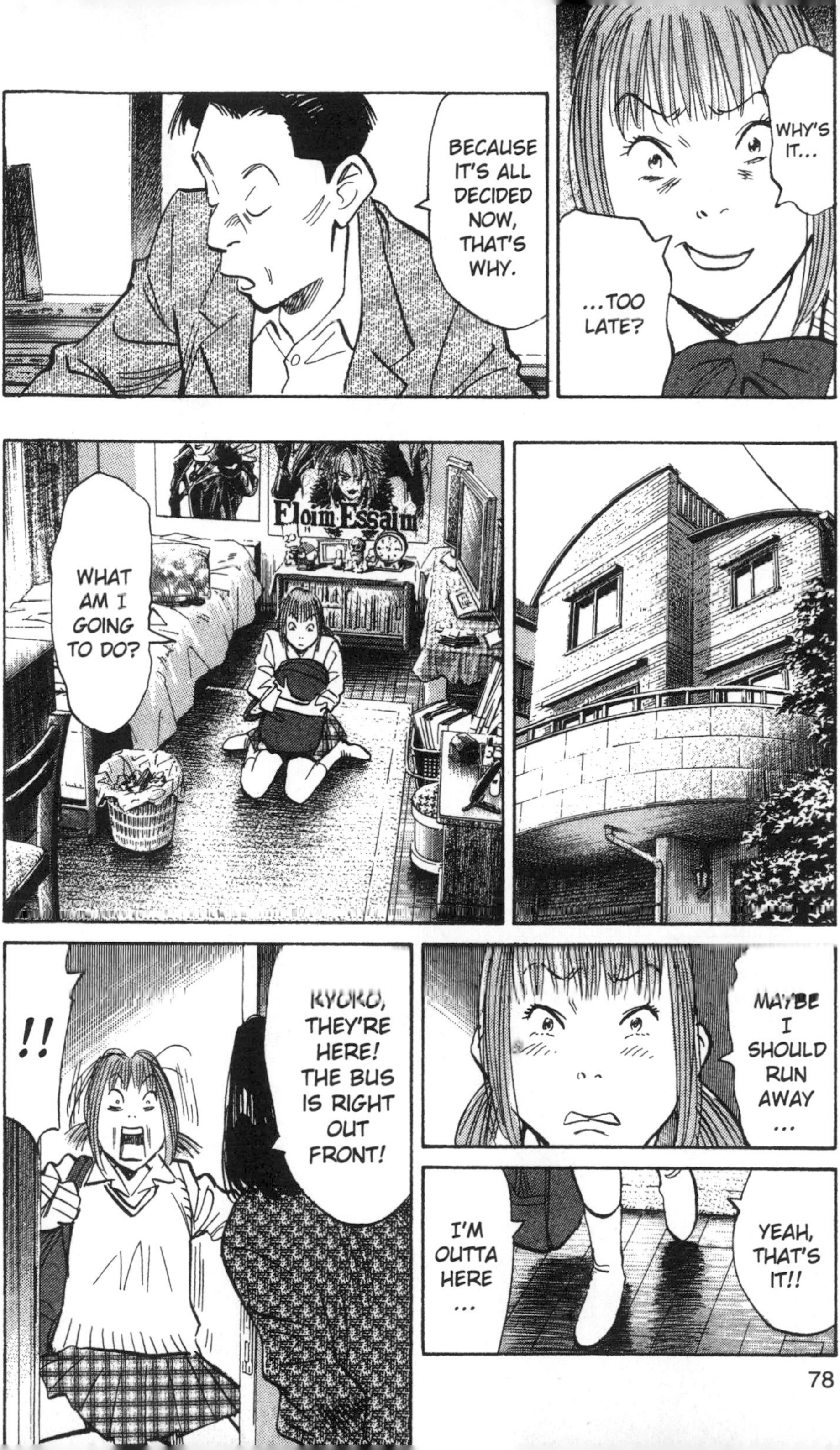
WHY'S IT...
...TOO LATE?
BECAUSE IT'S ALL DECIDED NOW, THAT'S WHY.
WHAT AM I GOING TO DO?
MAYBE I SHOULD RUN AWAY...
YEAH, THAT'S IT!!
I'M OUTTA HERE...
KYOKO, THEY'RE HERE! THE BUS IS RIGHT OUT FRONT!
!!

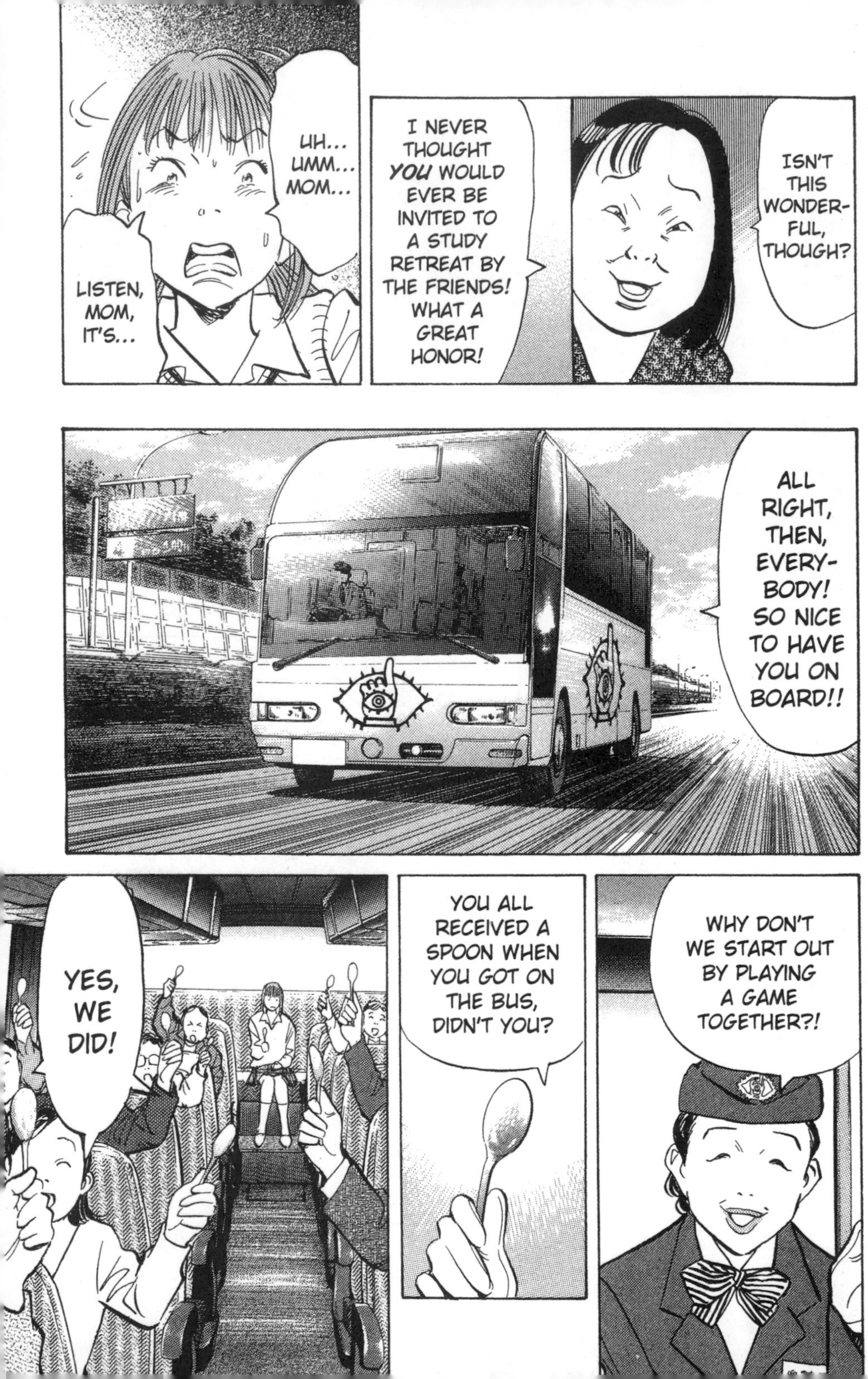
ISN'T THIS WONDERFUL, THOUGH?
I NEVER THOUGHT *YOU* WOULD EVER BE INVITED TO A STUDY RETREAT BY THE FRIENDS! WHAT A GREAT HONOR!
UH... UMM... MOM...
LISTEN, MOM, IT'S...
ALL RIGHT, THEN, EVERYBODY! SO NICE TO HAVE YOU ON BOARD!!
WHY DON'T WE START OUT BY PLAYING A GAME TOGETHER?!
YOU ALL RECEIVED A SPOON WHEN YOU GOT ON THE BUS, DIDN'T YOU?
YES, WE DID!

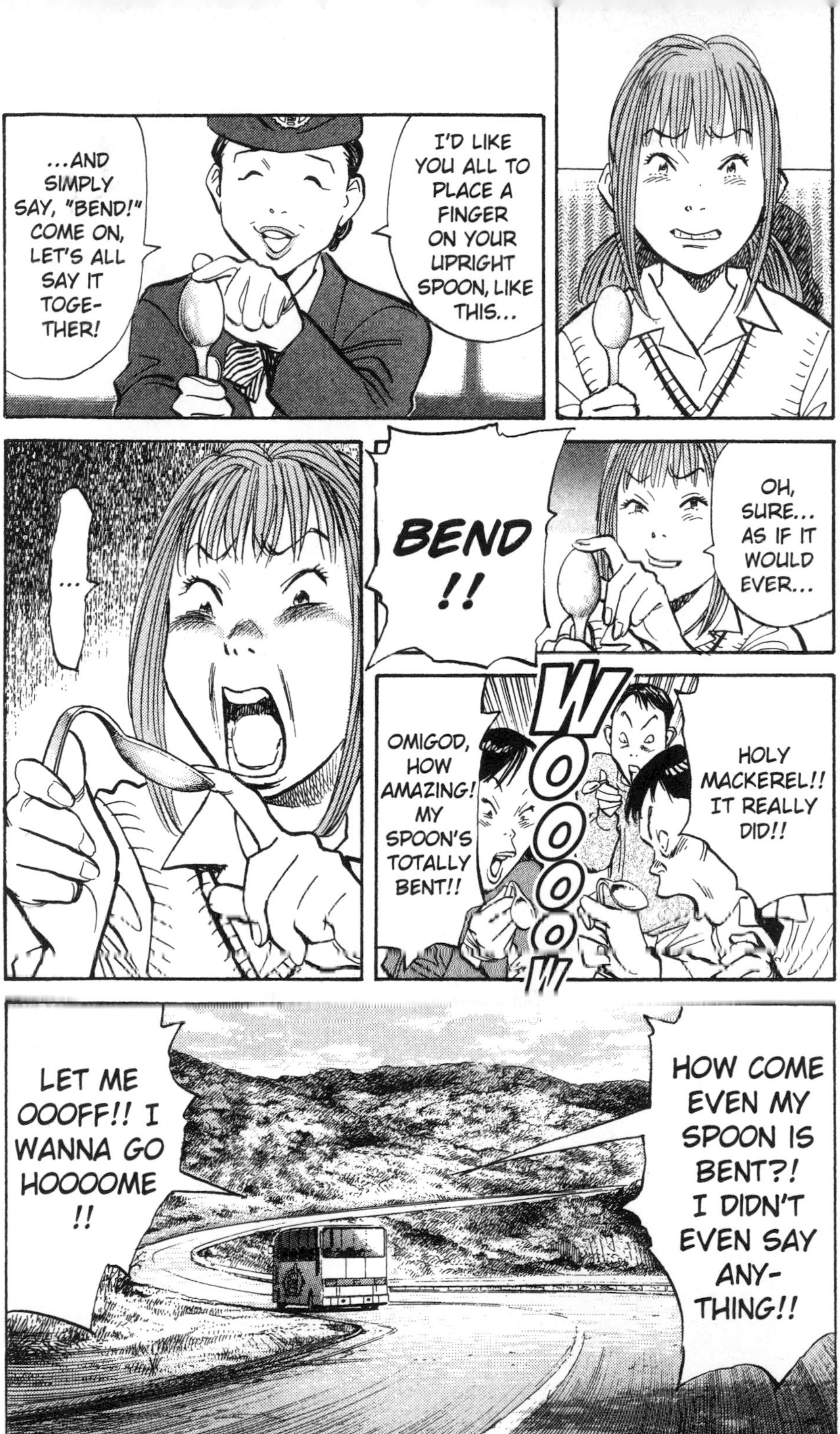
I'D LIKE YOU ALL TO PLACE A FINGER ON YOUR UPRIGHT SPOON, LIKE THIS...
...AND SIMPLY SAY, "BEND!" COME ON, LET'S ALL SAY IT TOGE-THER!
OH, SURE... AS IF IT WOULD EVER...
WOOOOOW
HOLY MACKEREL!! IT REALLY DID!!
OMIGOD, HOW AMAZING! MY SPOON'S TOTALLY BENT!!
BEND !!
...
HOW COME EVEN MY SPOON IS BENT?! I DIDN'T EVEN SAY ANY-THING!!
LET ME OOOFF!! I WANNA GO HOOOOME !!

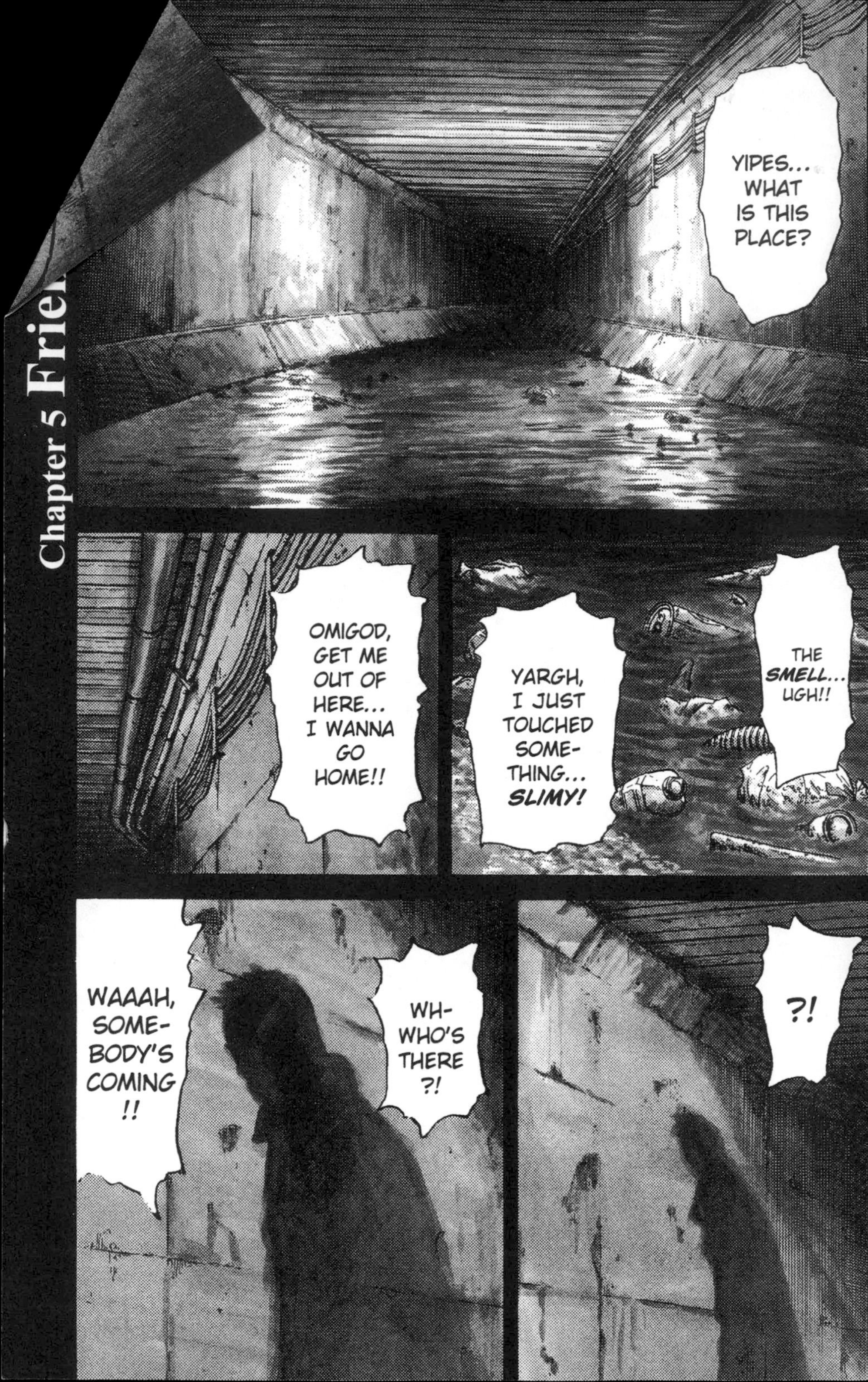
Chapter 5 Frie
YIPES... WHAT IS THIS PLACE?
THE *SMELL*... UGH!!
YARGH, I JUST TOUCHED SOME-THING... ***SLIMY!***
OMIGOD, GET ME OUT OF HERE... I WANNA GO HOME!!
?!
WH-WHO'S THERE ?!
WAAAH, SOME-BODY'S COMING !!

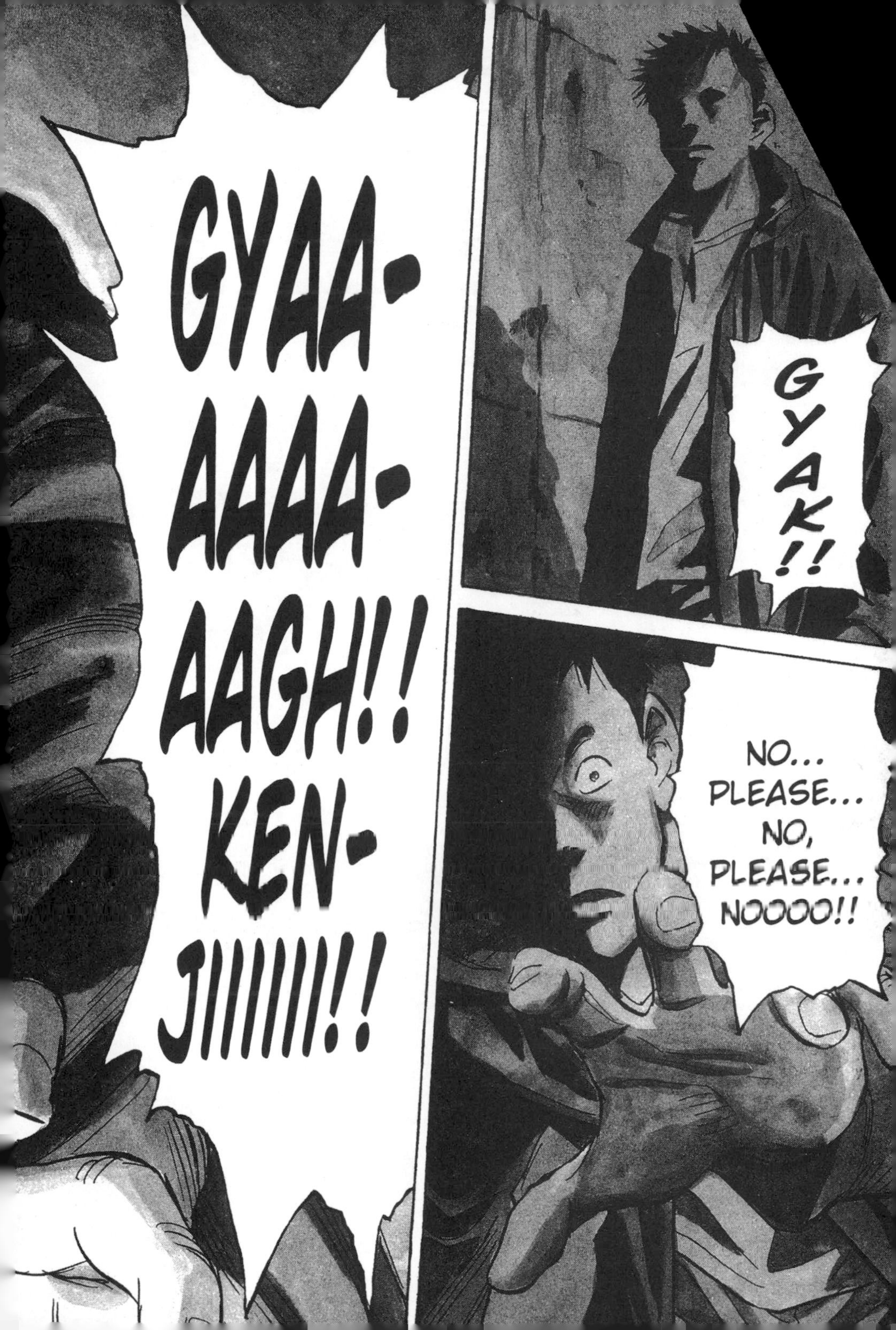
GYAK!!
NO... PLEASE... NO, PLEASE... NOOOO!!
GYAA-AAAA-AAGH!! KEN-JIIIIII!!

Chapter 5
Friend Land

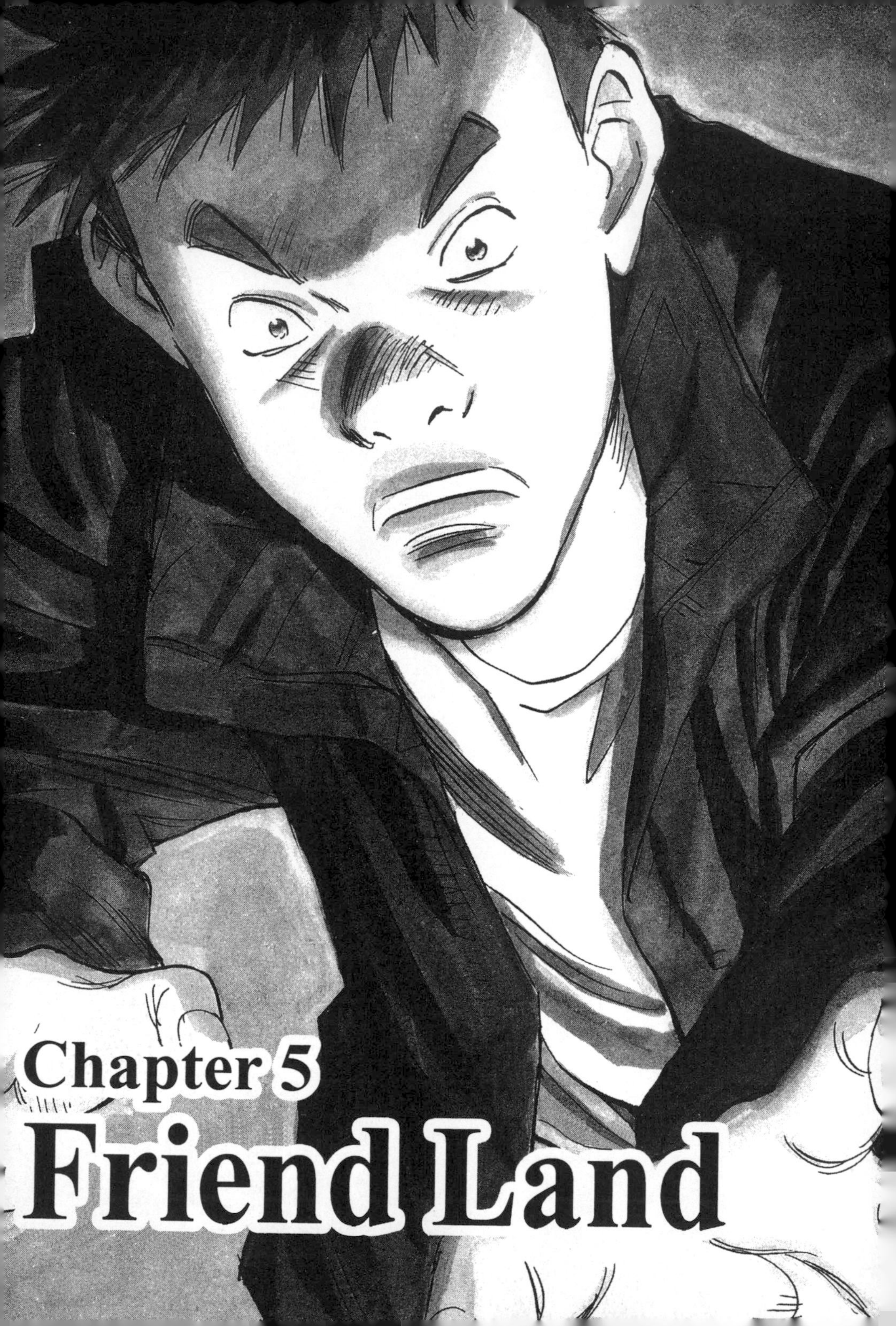

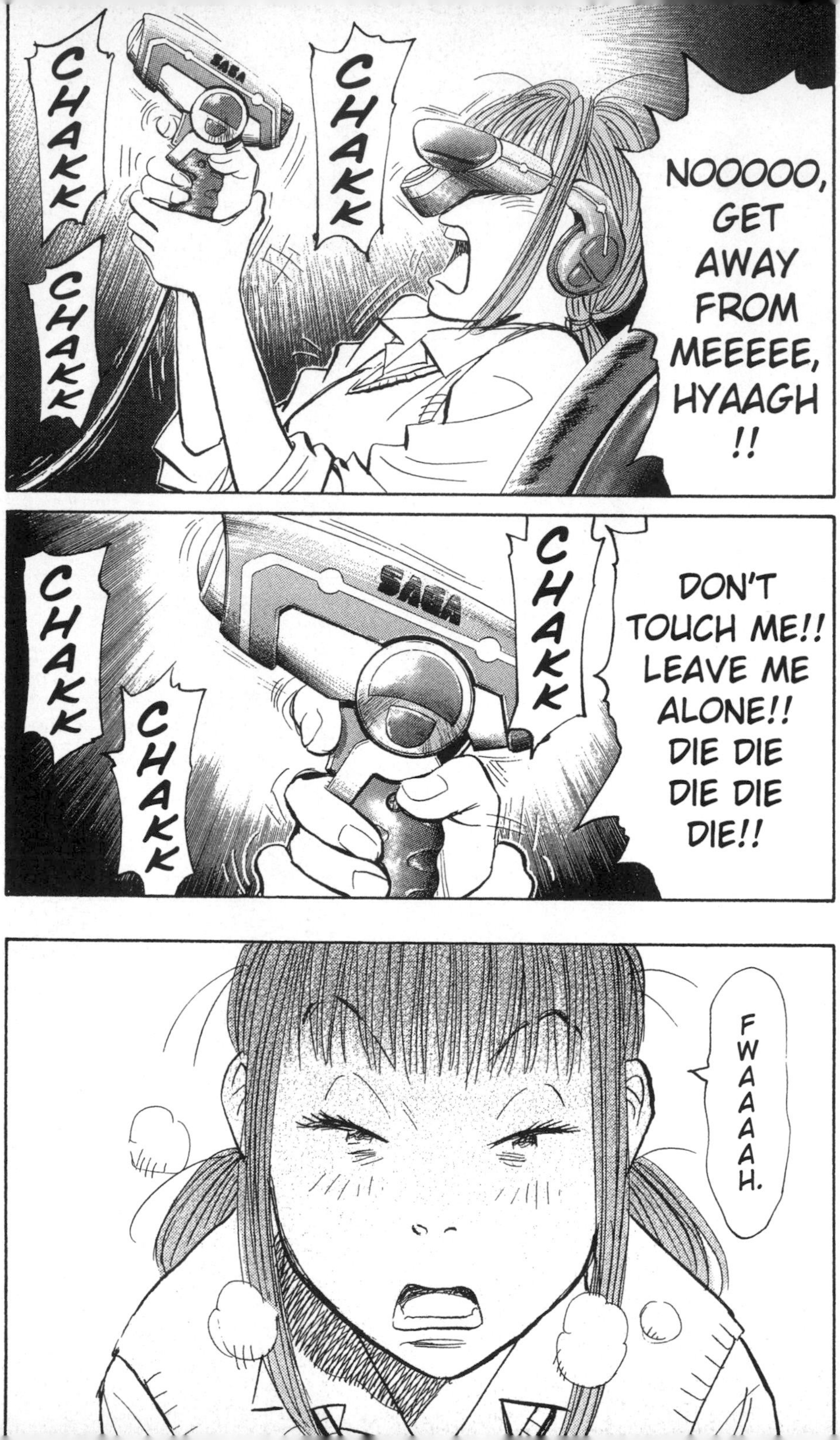
NOOOOO, GET AWAY FROM MEEEEE, HYAAGH!!
CHAKK
CHAKK
CHAKK
DON'T TOUCH ME!! LEAVE ME ALONE!! DIE DIE DIE DIE DIE!!
CHAKK
CHAKK
CHAKK
FWAAAAAH.

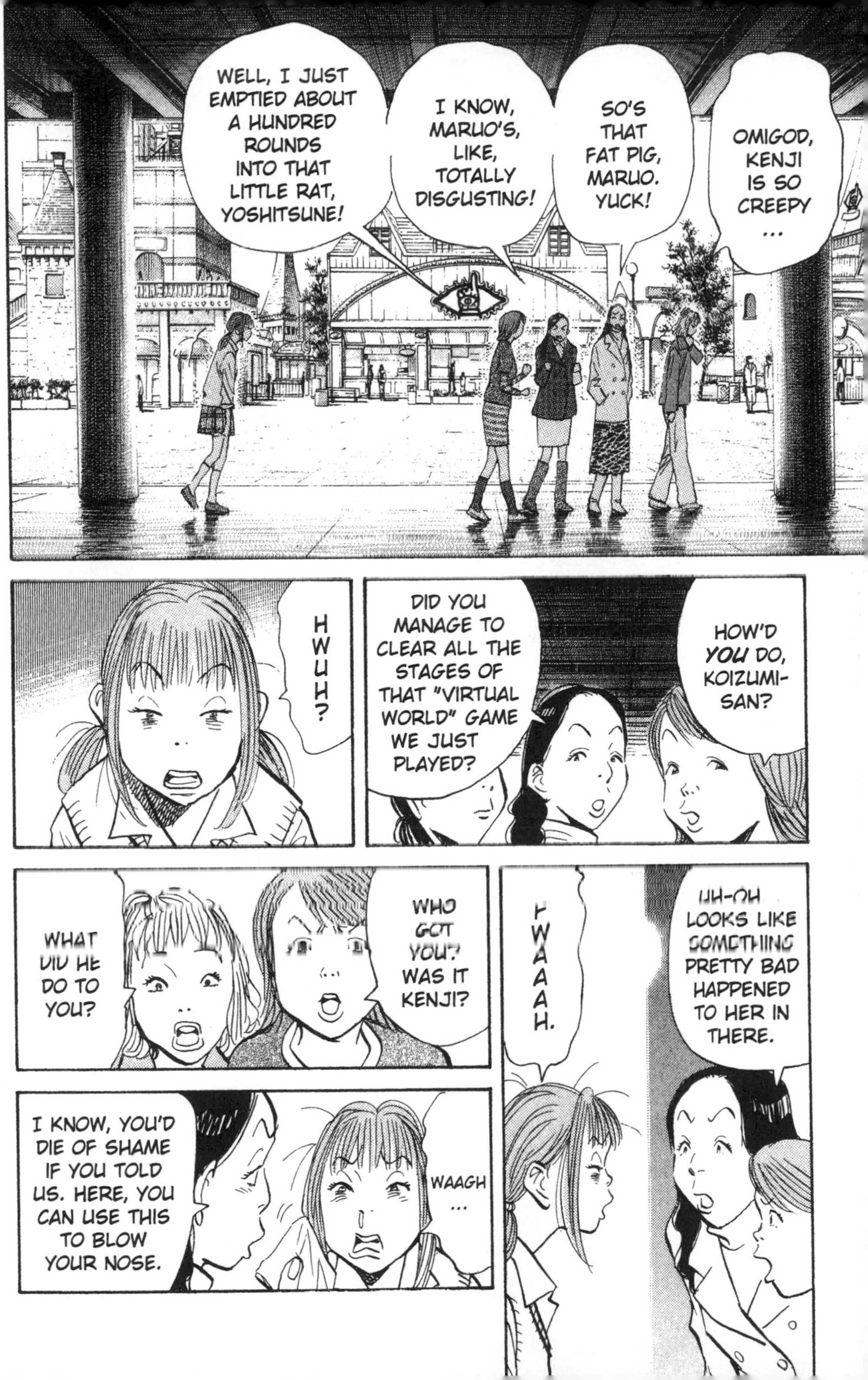
OMIGOD, KENJI IS SO CREEPY ...
SO'S THAT FAT PIG, MARUO. YUCK!
I KNOW, MARUO'S, LIKE, TOTALLY DISGUSTING!
WELL, I JUST EMPTIED ABOUT A HUNDRED ROUNDS INTO THAT LITTLE RAT, YOSHITSUNE!
HOW'D *YOU* DO, KOIZUMI-SAN?
DID YOU MANAGE TO CLEAR ALL THE STAGES OF THAT "VIRTUAL WORLD" GAME WE JUST PLAYED?
HWUH?
UH-OH... LOOKS LIKE SOMETHING PRETTY BAD HAPPENED TO HER IN THERE.
FWAAAAH.
WHO GOT YOU? WAS IT KENJI?
WHAT DID HE DO TO YOU?
WAAGH ...
I KNOW, YOU'D DIE OF SHAME IF YOU TOLD US. HERE, YOU CAN USE THIS TO BLOW YOUR NOSE.

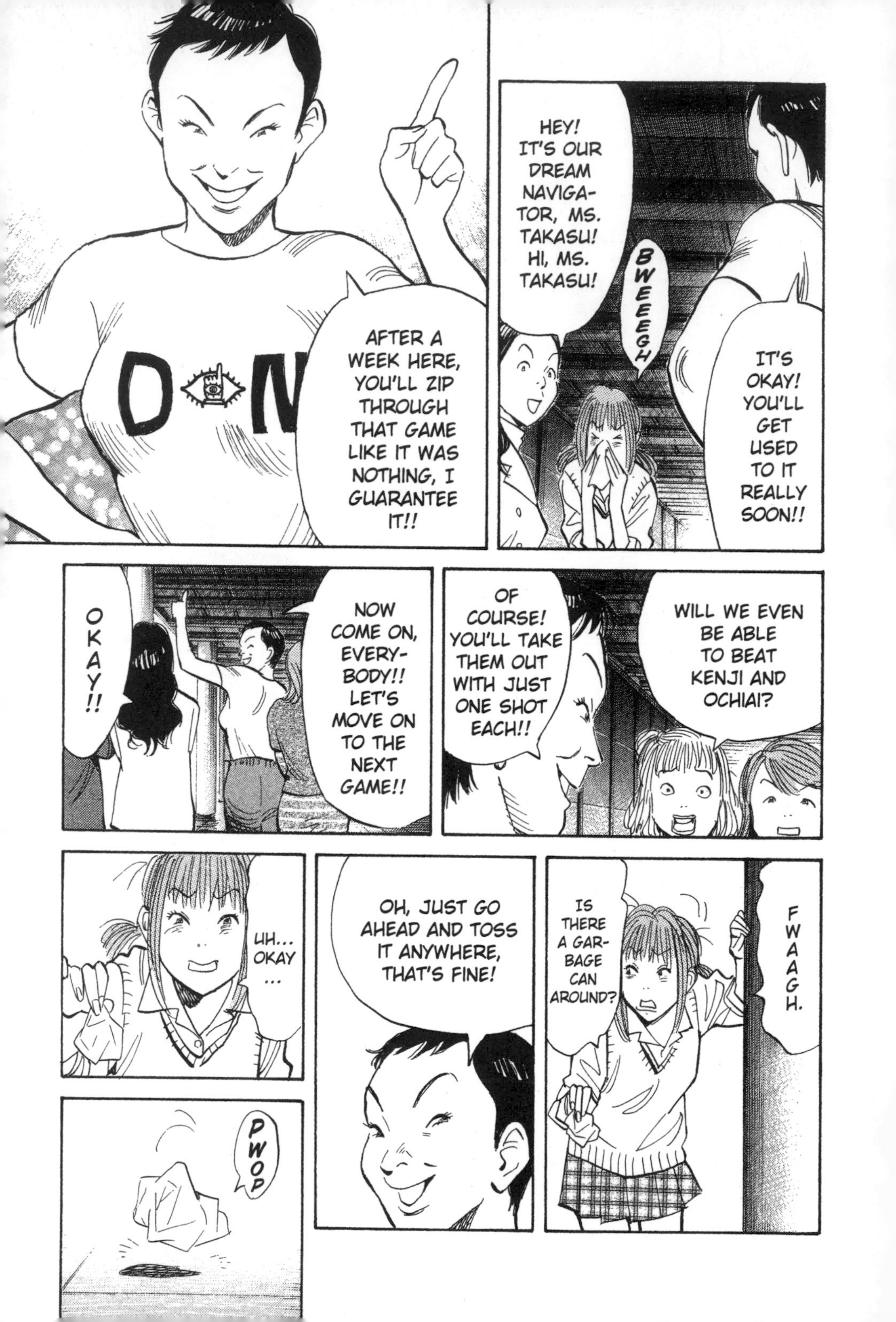
HEY! IT'S OUR DREAM NAVIGATOR, MS. TAKASU! HI, MS. TAKASU!
BWEEEEGH
IT'S OKAY! YOU'LL GET USED TO IT REALLY SOON!!
AFTER A WEEK HERE, YOU'LL ZIP THROUGH THAT GAME LIKE IT WAS NOTHING, I GUARANTEE IT!!
WILL WE EVEN BE ABLE TO BEAT KENJI AND OCHIAI?
OF COURSE! YOU'LL TAKE THEM OUT WITH JUST ONE SHOT EACH!!
NOW COME ON, EVERYBODY!! LET'S MOVE ON TO THE NEXT GAME!!
OKAY!!
FWAAAGH.
IS THERE A GARBAGE CAN AROUND?
OH, JUST GO AHEAD AND TOSS IT ANYWHERE, THAT'S FINE!
UH... OKAY ...
PWOP

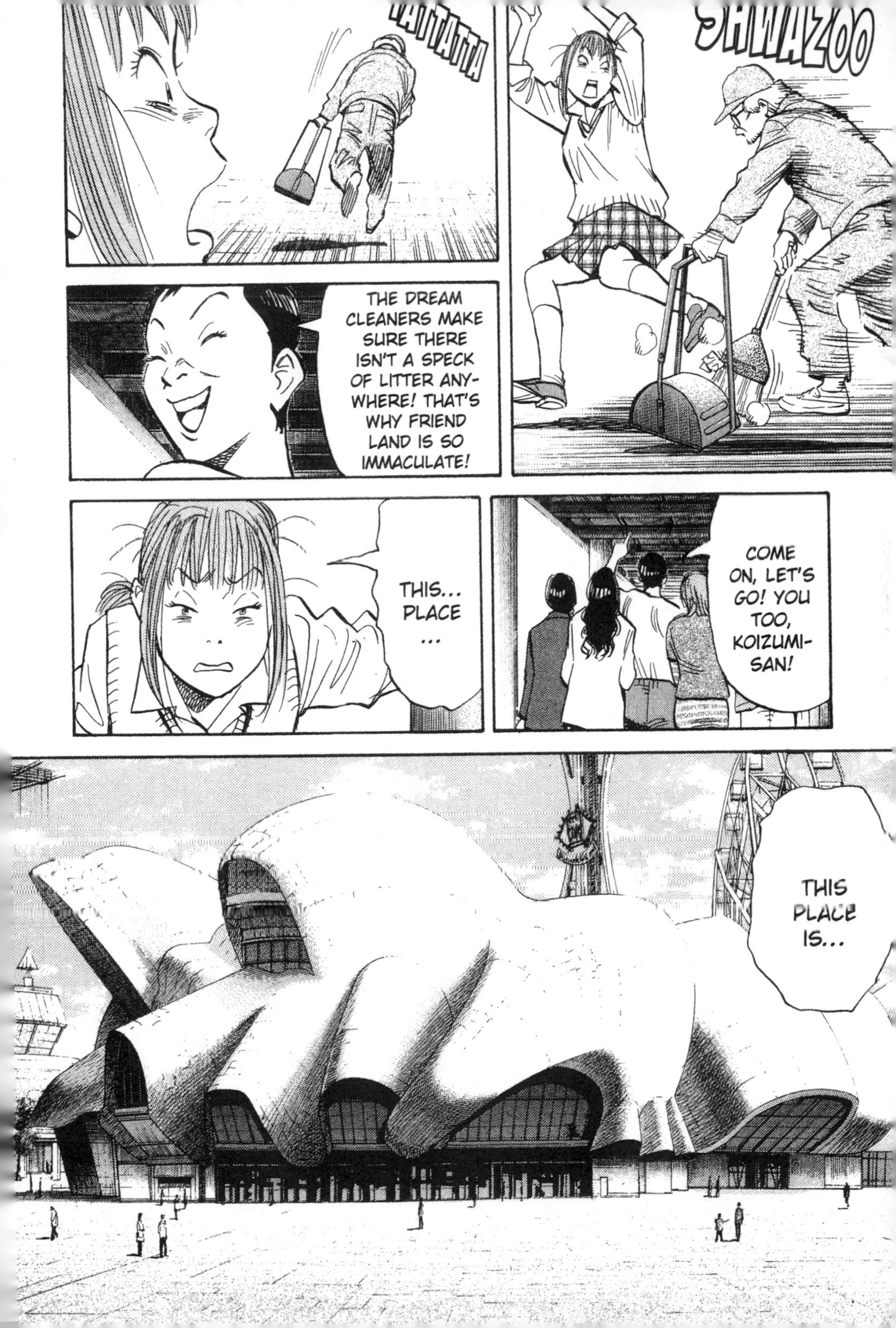
SHWAZOO
TATTATTA
THE DREAM CLEANERS MAKE SURE THERE ISN'T A SPECK OF LITTER ANYWHERE! THAT'S WHY FRIEND LAND IS SO IMMACULATE!
COME ON, LET'S GO! YOU TOO, KOIZUMI-SAN!
THIS... PLACE ...
THIS PLACE IS...

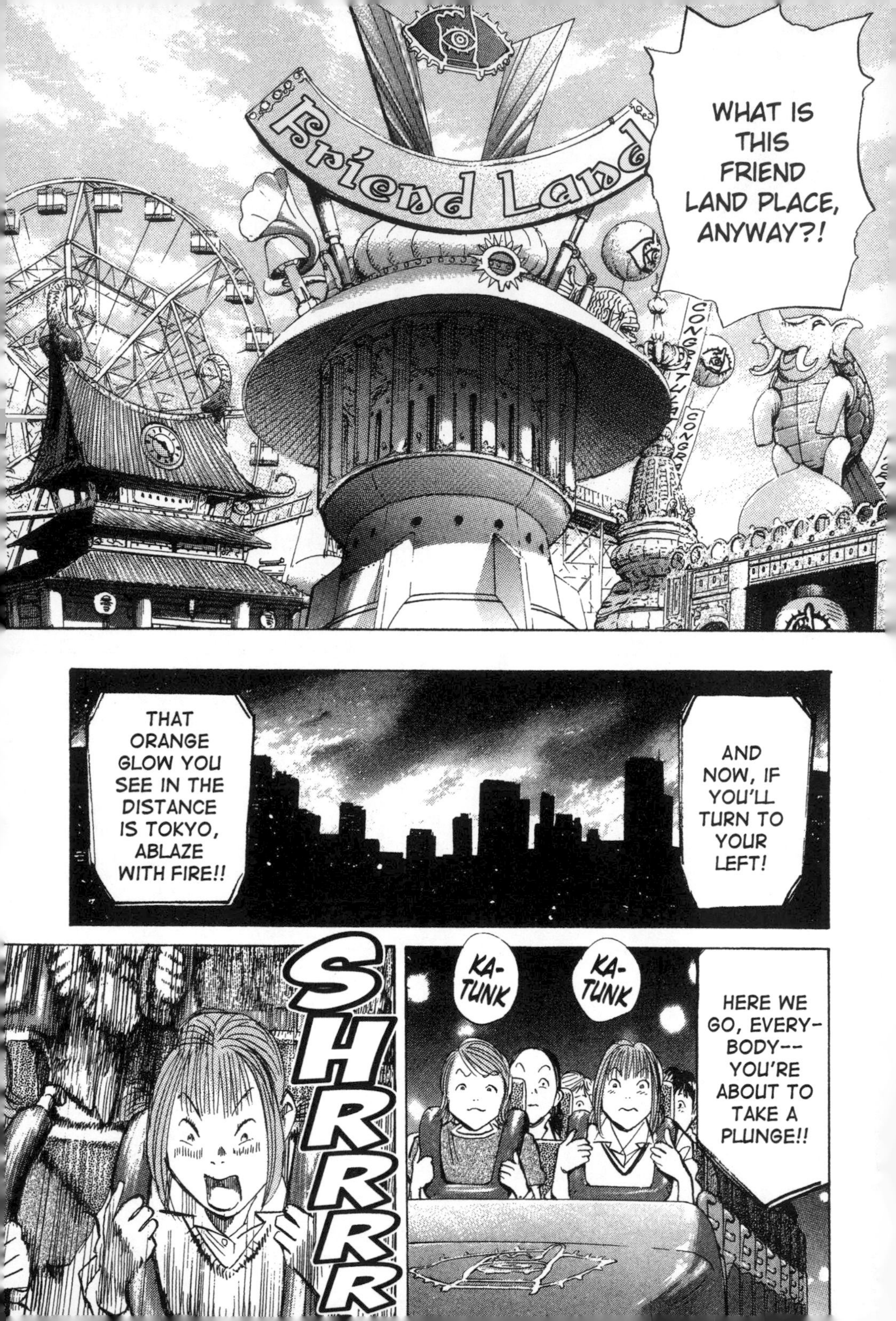
Friend Land
WHAT IS THIS FRIEND LAND PLACE, ANYWAY?!
AND NOW, IF YOU'LL TURN TO YOUR LEFT!
THAT ORANGE GLOW YOU SEE IN THE DISTANCE IS TOKYO, ABLAZE WITH FIRE!!
HERE WE GO, EVERY-BODY-- YOU'RE ABOUT TO TAKE A PLUNGE!!
KA-TUNK
KA-TUNK
SHRRRR

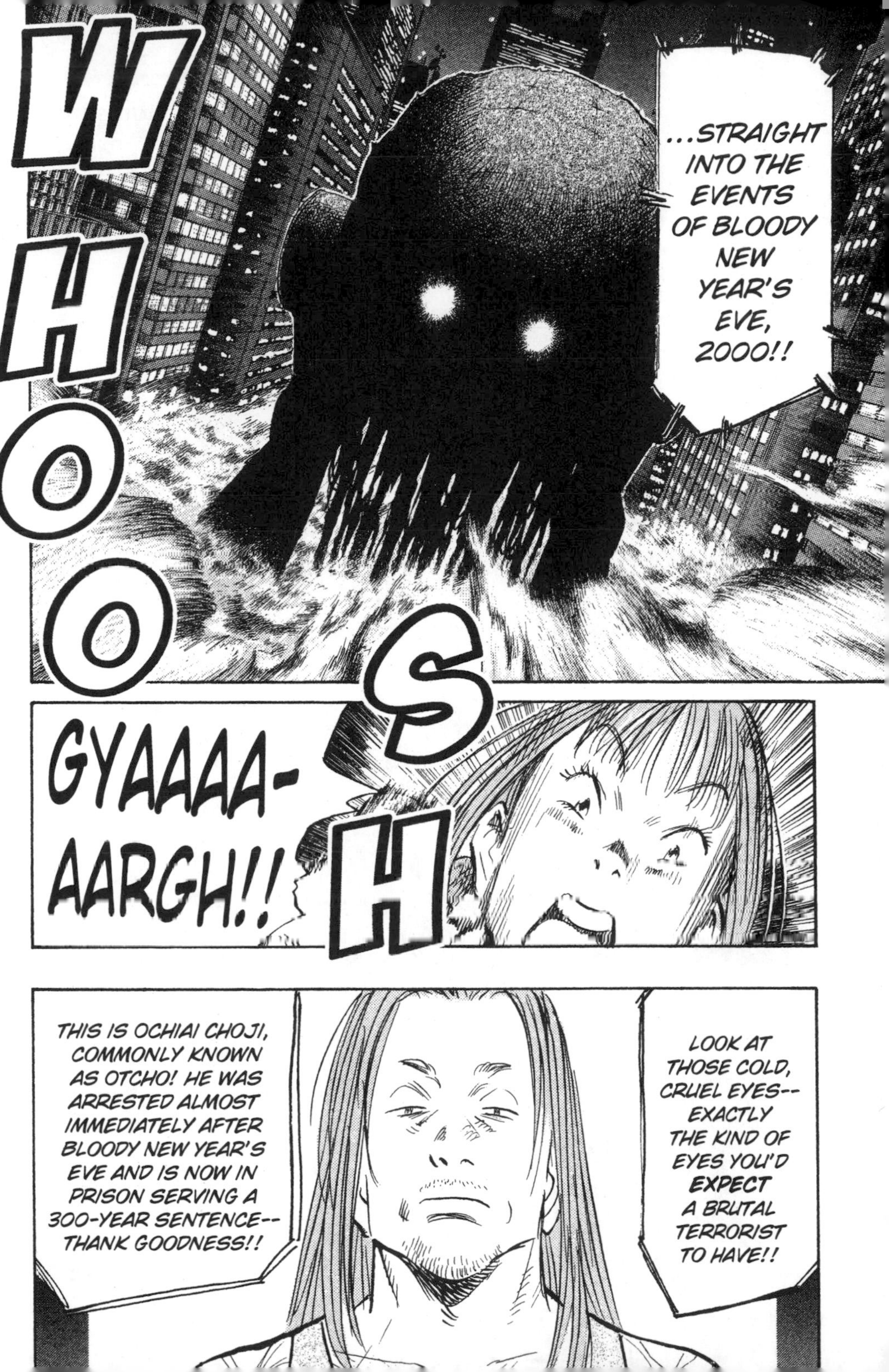
...STRAIGHT INTO THE EVENTS OF BLOODY NEW YEAR'S EVE, 2000!!
WHOOSH
GYAAAA-AARGH!!
LOOK AT THOSE COLD, CRUEL EYES--EXACTLY THE KIND OF EYES YOU'D **EXPECT** A BRUTAL TERRORIST TO HAVE!!
THIS IS OCHIAI CHOJI, COMMONLY KNOWN AS OTCHO! HE WAS ARRESTED ALMOST IMMEDIATELY AFTER BLOODY NEW YEAR'S EVE AND IS NOW IN PRISON SERVING A 300-YEAR SENTENCE--THANK GOODNESS!!

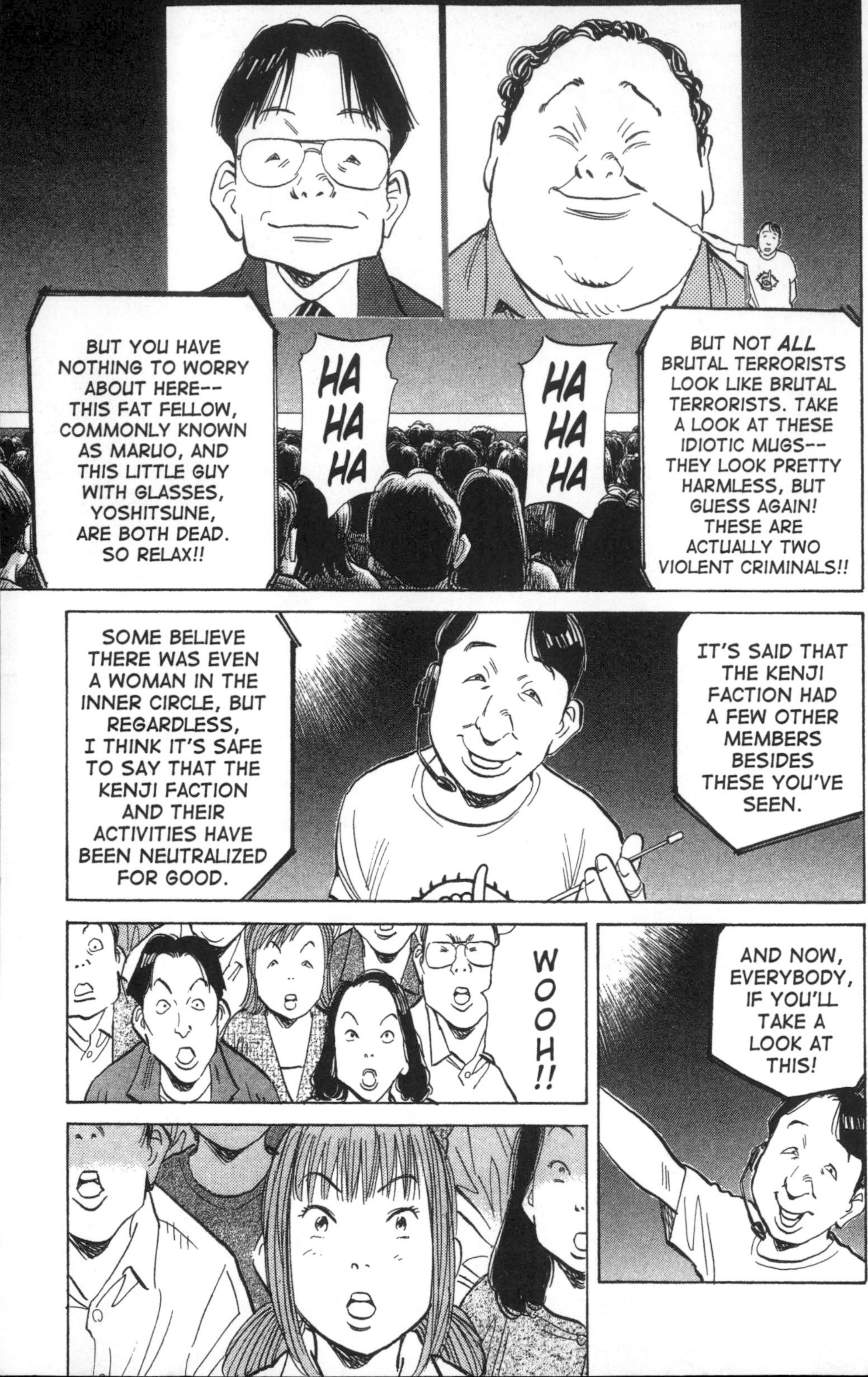
BUT NOT ALL BRUTAL TERRORISTS LOOK LIKE BRUTAL TERRORISTS. TAKE A LOOK AT THESE IDIOTIC MUGS-- THEY LOOK PRETTY HARMLESS, BUT GUESS AGAIN! THESE ARE ACTUALLY TWO VIOLENT CRIMINALS!!
HA HA HA
HA HA HA
BUT YOU HAVE NOTHING TO WORRY ABOUT HERE-- THIS FAT FELLOW, COMMONLY KNOWN AS MARUO, AND THIS LITTLE GUY WITH GLASSES, YOSHITSUNE, ARE BOTH DEAD. SO RELAX!!
IT'S SAID THAT THE KENJI FACTION HAD A FEW OTHER MEMBERS BESIDES THESE YOU'VE SEEN.
SOME BELIEVE THERE WAS EVEN A WOMAN IN THE INNER CIRCLE, BUT REGARDLESS, I THINK IT'S SAFE TO SAY THAT THE KENJI FACTION AND THEIR ACTIVITIES HAVE BEEN NEUTRALIZED FOR GOOD.
AND NOW, EVERYBODY, IF YOU'LL TAKE A LOOK AT THIS!
WOOOH!!

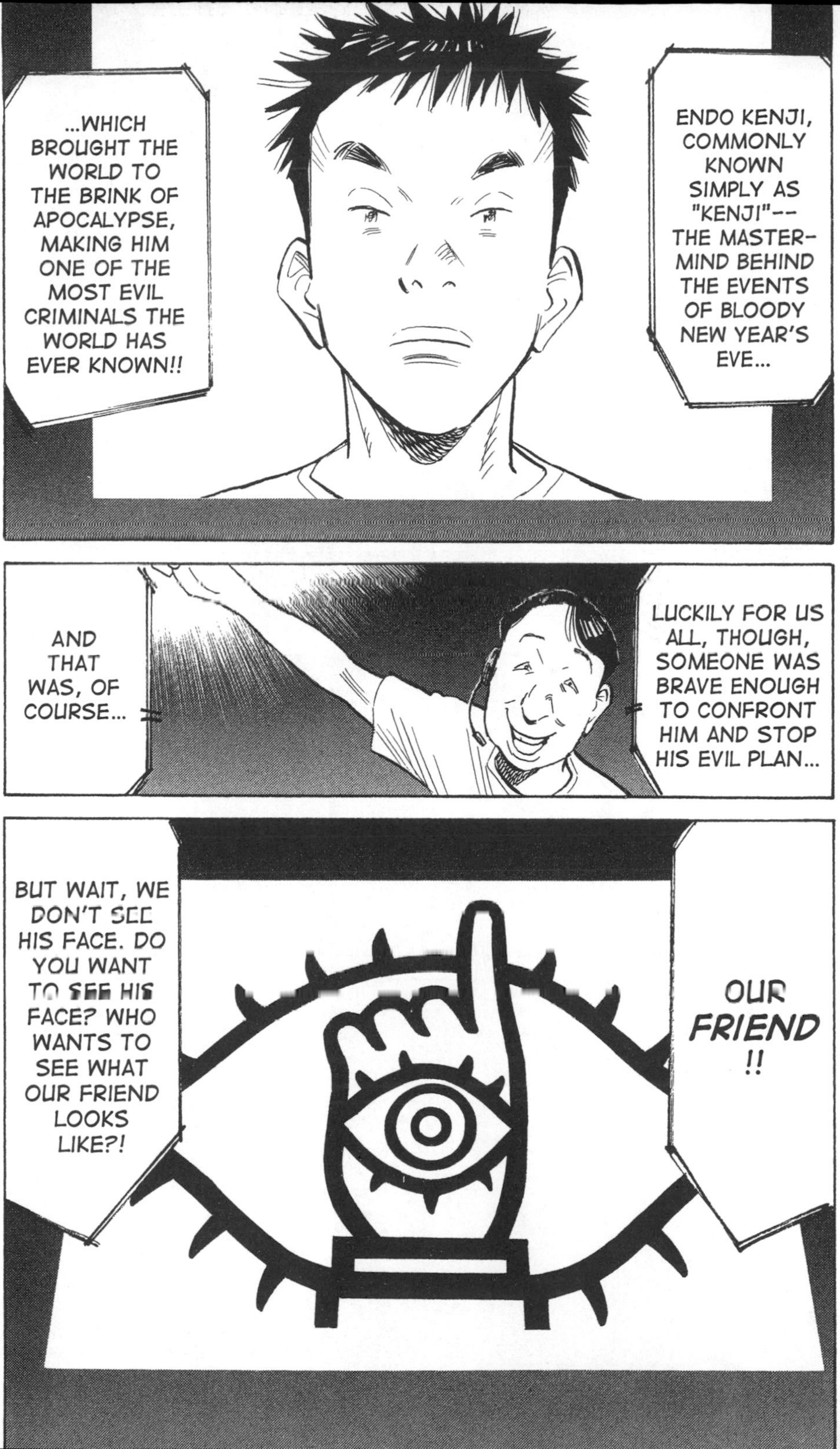

ENDO KENJI, COMMONLY KNOWN SIMPLY AS "KENJI"-- THE MASTER-MIND BEHIND THE EVENTS OF BLOODY NEW YEAR'S EVE...
...WHICH BROUGHT THE WORLD TO THE BRINK OF APOCALYPSE, MAKING HIM ONE OF THE MOST EVIL CRIMINALS THE WORLD HAS EVER KNOWN!!
LUCKILY FOR US ALL, THOUGH, SOMEONE WAS BRAVE ENOUGH TO CONFRONT HIM AND STOP HIS EVIL PLAN...
AND THAT WAS, OF COURSE...
OUR FRIEND !!
BUT WAIT, WE DON'T SEE HIS FACE. DO YOU WANT TO SEE HIS FACE? WHO WANTS TO SEE WHAT OUR FRIEND LOOKS LIKE?!

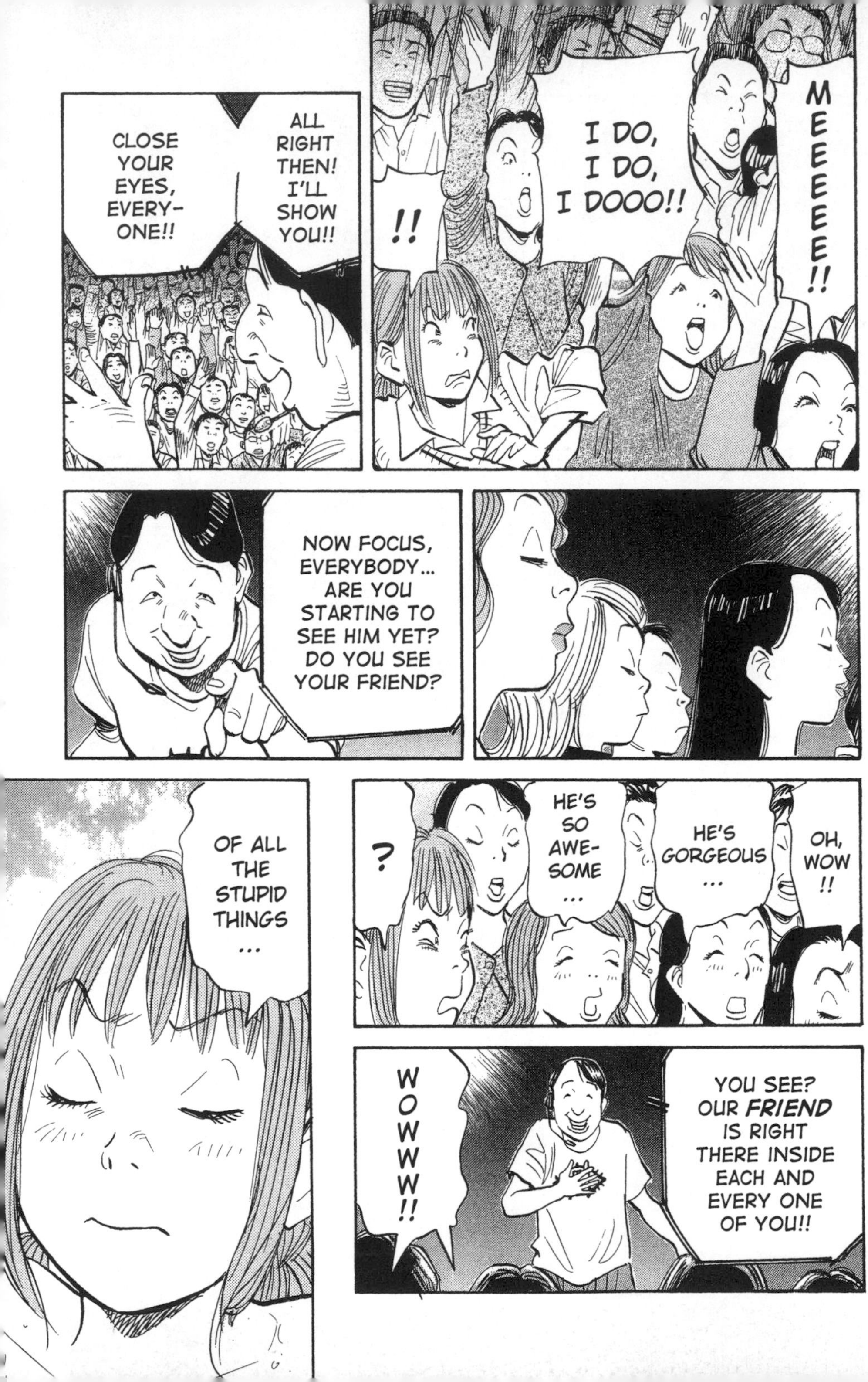
MEEEEEE!!
I DO, I DO, I DOOO!!
!!
ALL RIGHT THEN! I'LL SHOW YOU!!
CLOSE YOUR EYES, EVERY-ONE!!
NOW FOCUS, EVERYBODY... ARE YOU STARTING TO SEE HIM YET? DO YOU SEE YOUR FRIEND?
OH, WOW!!
HE'S GORGEOUS...
HE'S SO AWE-SOME...
?
YOU SEE? OUR FRIEND IS RIGHT THERE INSIDE EACH AND EVERY ONE OF YOU!!
WOWWWW!!
OF ALL THE STUPID THINGS...

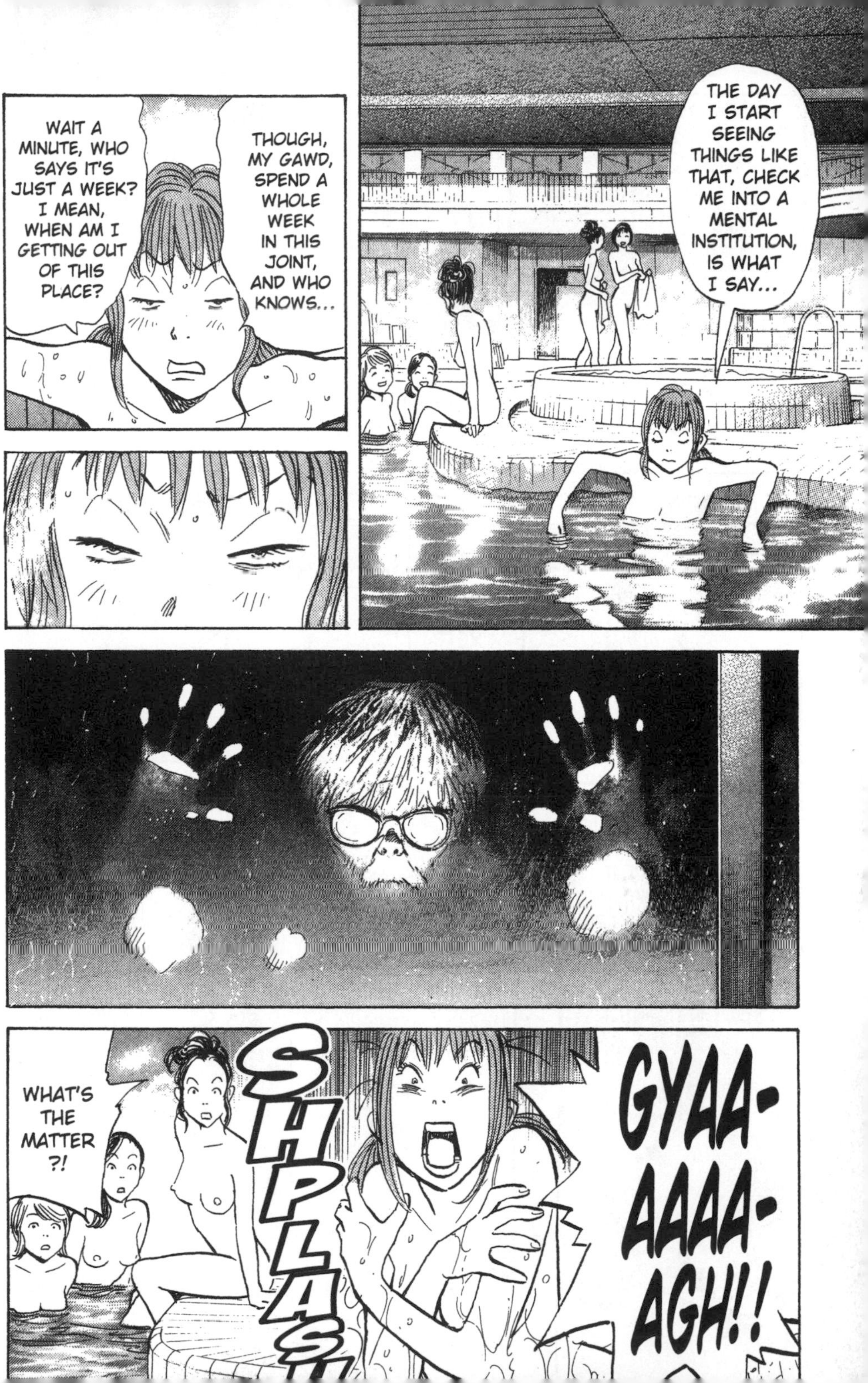
THE DAY I START SEEING THINGS LIKE THAT, CHECK ME INTO A MENTAL INSTITUTION, IS WHAT I SAY...
THOUGH, MY GAWD, SPEND A WHOLE WEEK IN THIS JOINT, AND WHO KNOWS...
WAIT A MINUTE, WHO SAYS IT'S JUST A WEEK? I MEAN, WHEN AM I GETTING OUT OF THIS PLACE?
GYAA-AAAA-AGH!!
SHPLASH
WHAT'S THE MATTER ?!

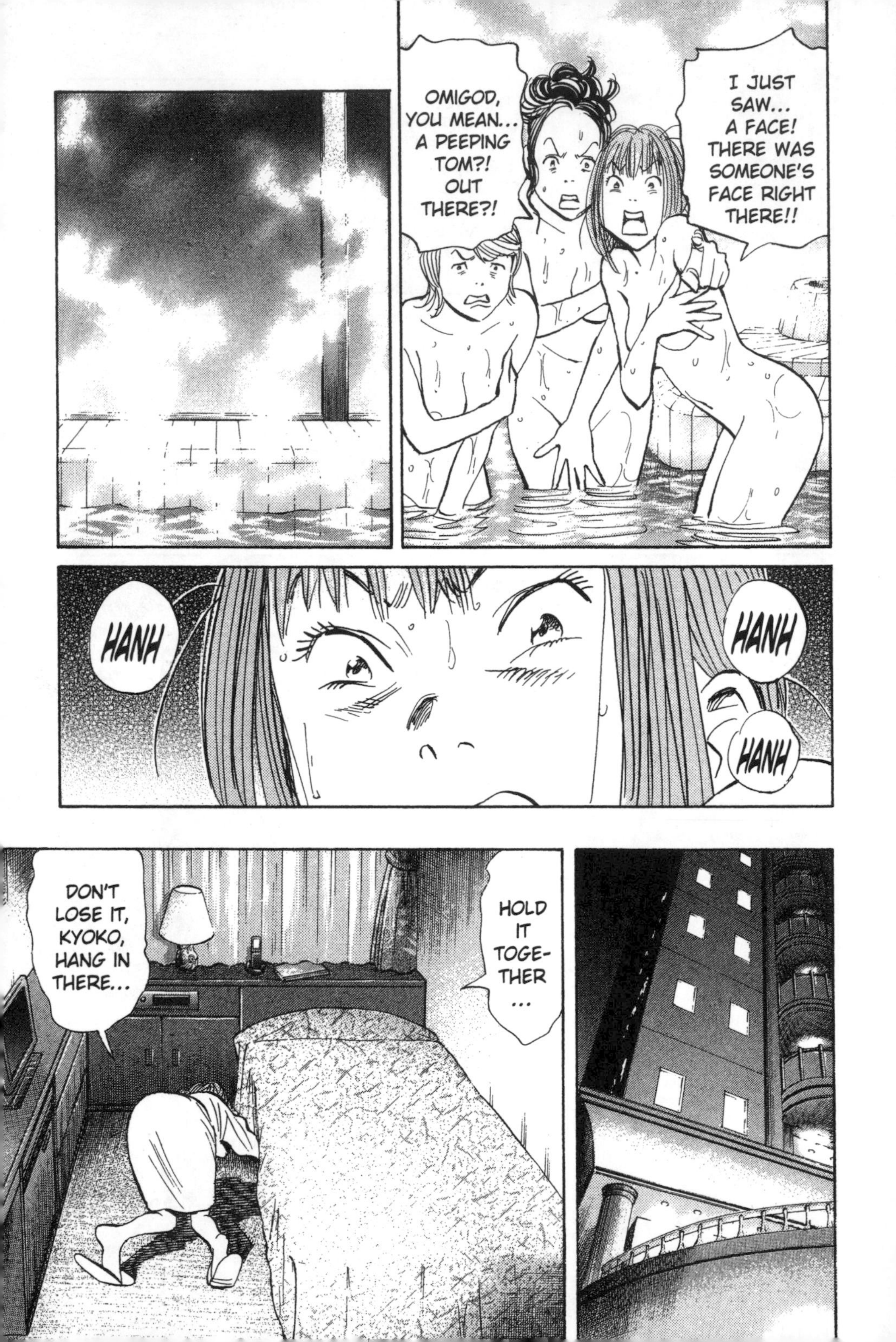
I JUST SAW... A FACE! THERE WAS SOMEONE'S FACE RIGHT THERE!!
OMIGOD, YOU MEAN... A PEEPING TOM?! OUT THERE?!
HANH
HANH
HANH
HOLD IT TOGE-THER...
DON'T LOSE IT, KYOKO, HANG IN THERE...

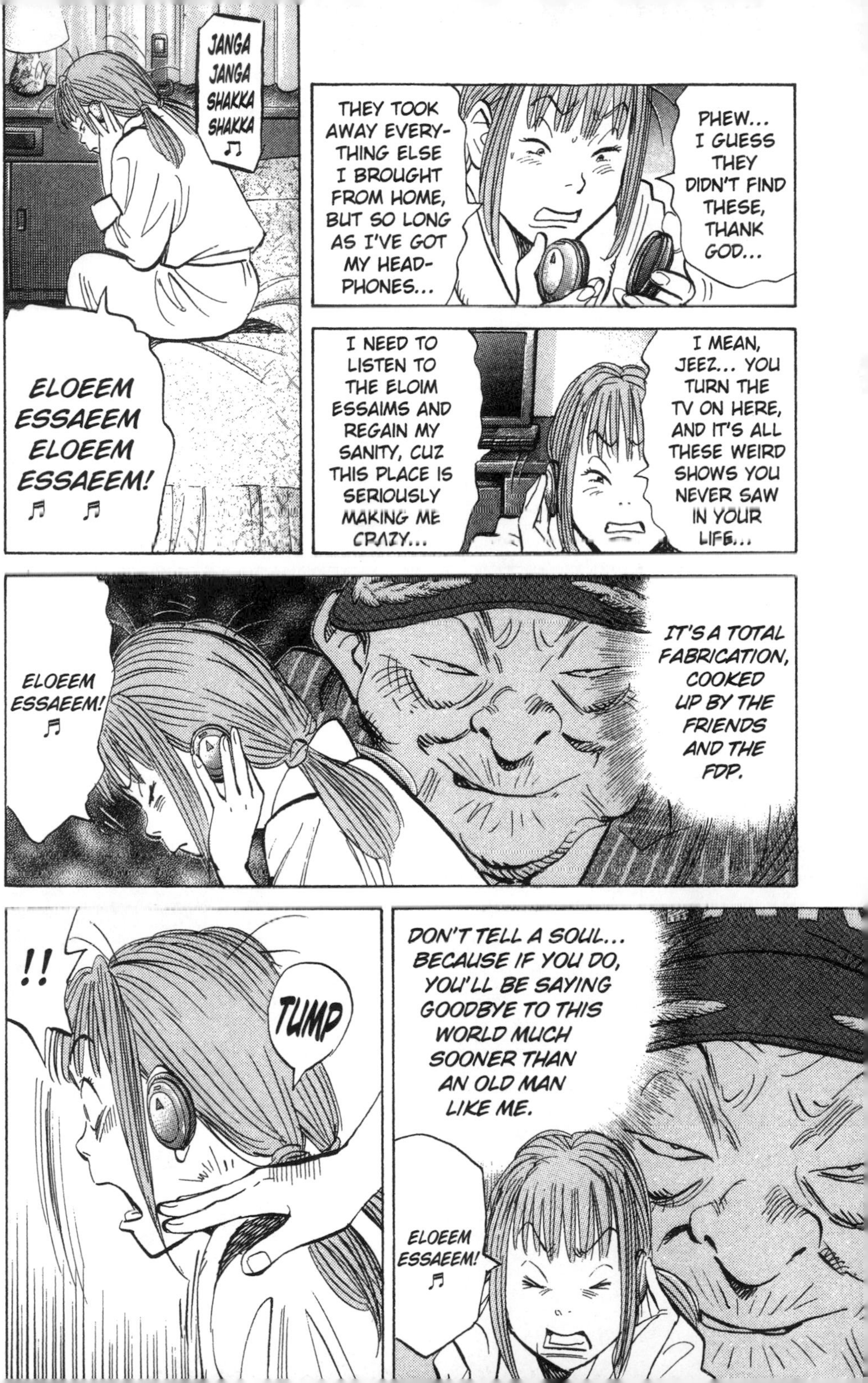
PHEW... I GUESS THEY DIDN'T FIND THESE, THANK GOD...
THEY TOOK AWAY EVERY-THING ELSE I BROUGHT FROM HOME, BUT SO LONG AS I'VE GOT MY HEAD-PHONES...
I MEAN, JEEZ... YOU TURN THE TV ON HERE, AND IT'S ALL THESE WEIRD SHOWS YOU NEVER SAW IN YOUR LIFE...
I NEED TO LISTEN TO THE ELOIM ESSAIMS AND REGAIN MY SANITY, CUZ THIS PLACE IS SERIOUSLY MAKING ME CRAZY...
JANGA JANGA SHAKKA SHAKKA ♫
ELOEEM ESSAEEM ELOEEM ESSAEEM! ♬ ♬
IT'S A TOTAL FABRICATION, COOKED UP BY THE FRIENDS AND THE FDP.
ELOEEM ESSAEEM! ♬
DON'T TELL A SOUL... BECAUSE IF YOU DO, YOU'LL BE SAYING GOODBYE TO THIS WORLD MUCH SOONER THAN AN OLD MAN LIKE ME.
ELOEEM ESSAEEM! ♬
TUMP
!!

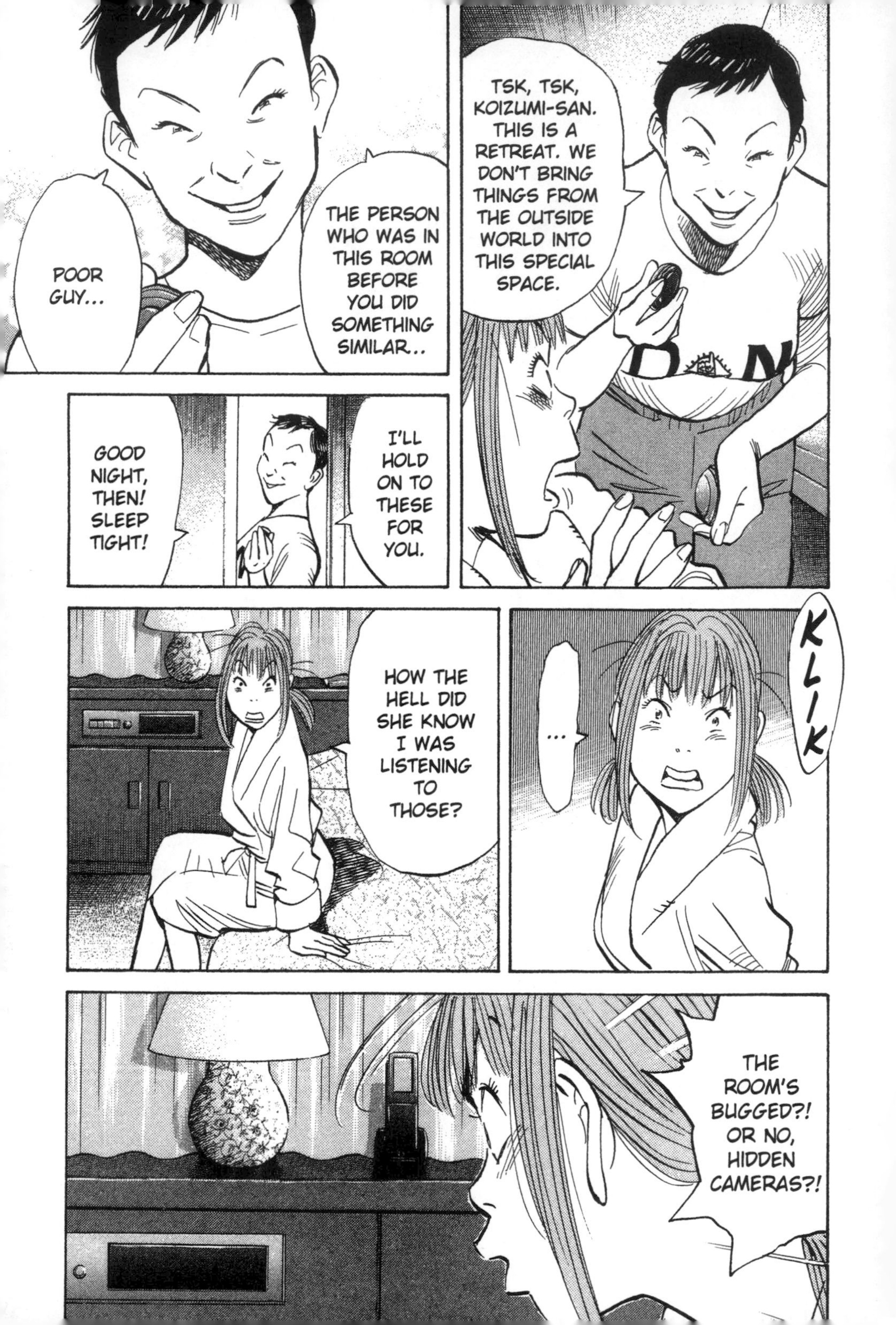
TSK, TSK, KOIZUMI-SAN. THIS IS A RETREAT. WE DON'T BRING THINGS FROM THE OUTSIDE WORLD INTO THIS SPECIAL SPACE.
THE PERSON WHO WAS IN THIS ROOM BEFORE YOU DID SOMETHING SIMILAR...
POOR GUY...
I'LL HOLD ON TO THESE FOR YOU.
GOOD NIGHT, THEN! SLEEP TIGHT!
KLIK
...
HOW THE HELL DID SHE KNOW I WAS LISTENING TO THOSE?
THE ROOM'S BUGGED?! OR NO, HIDDEN CAMERAS?!

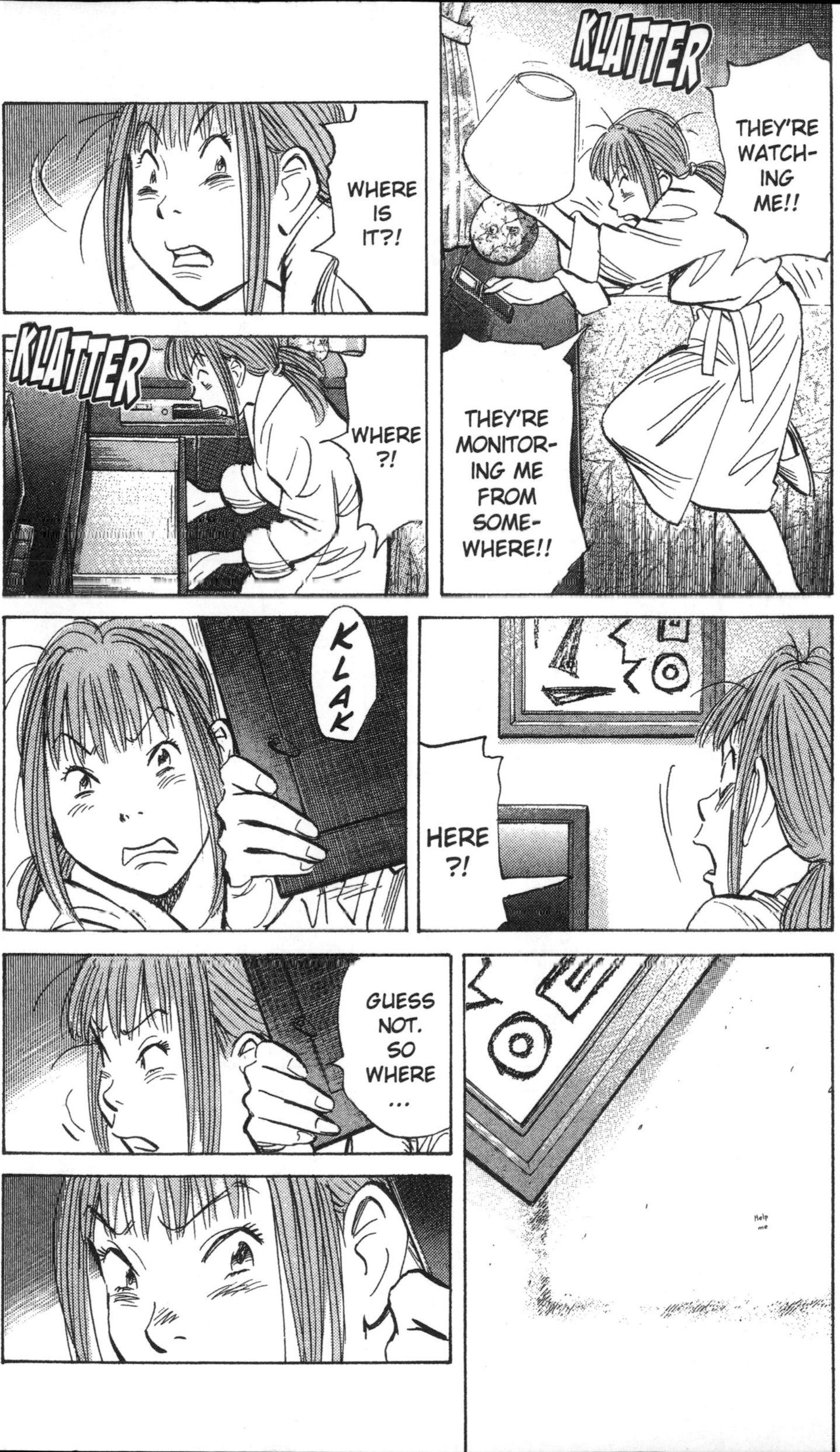
KLATTER
THEY'RE WATCH-ING ME!!
THEY'RE MONITOR-ING ME FROM SOME-WHERE!!
WHERE IS IT?!
KLATTER
WHERE ?!
HERE ?!
KLAK
Help me
GUESS NOT. SO WHERE ...

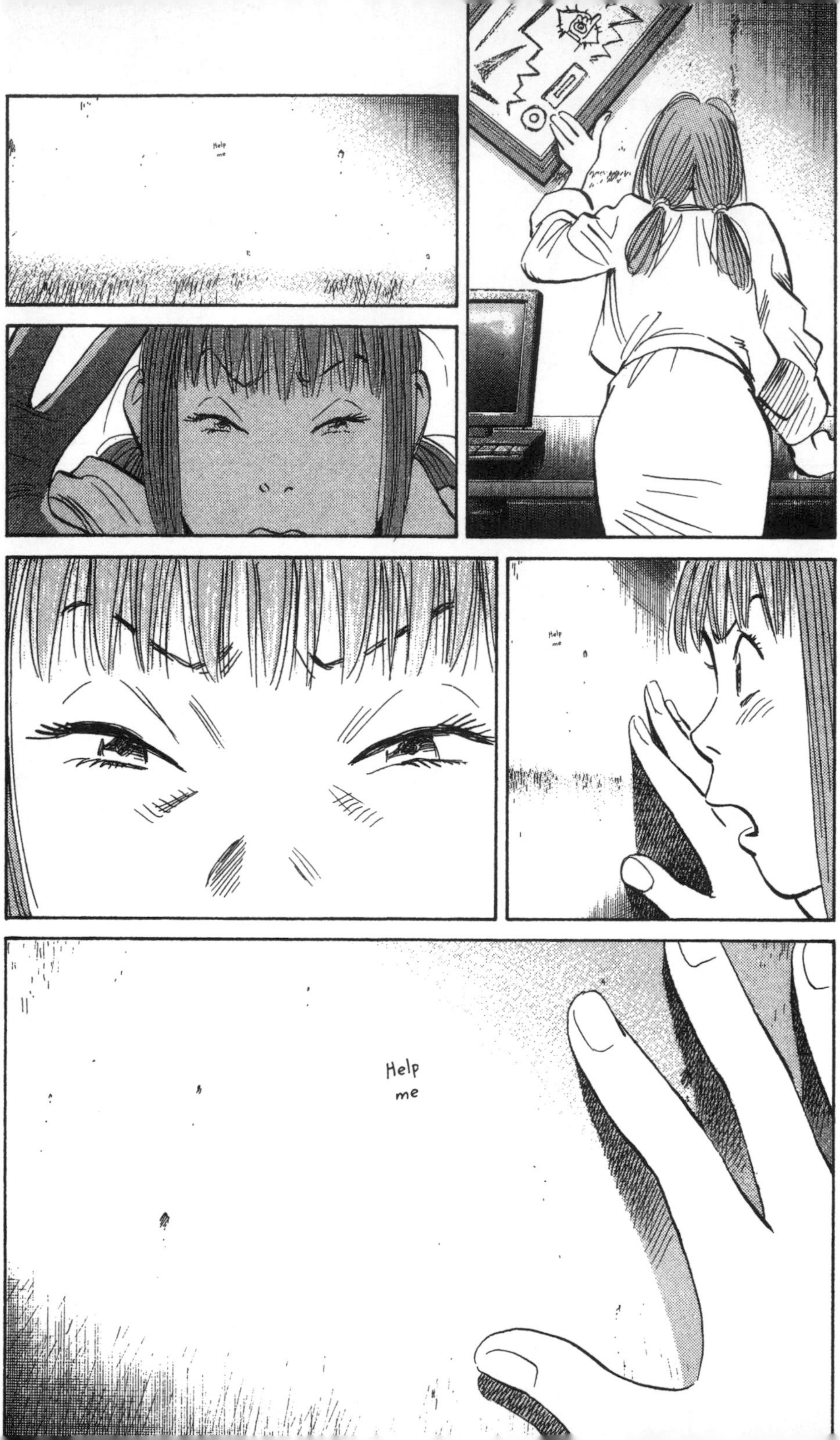
Help me
Help me
Help me

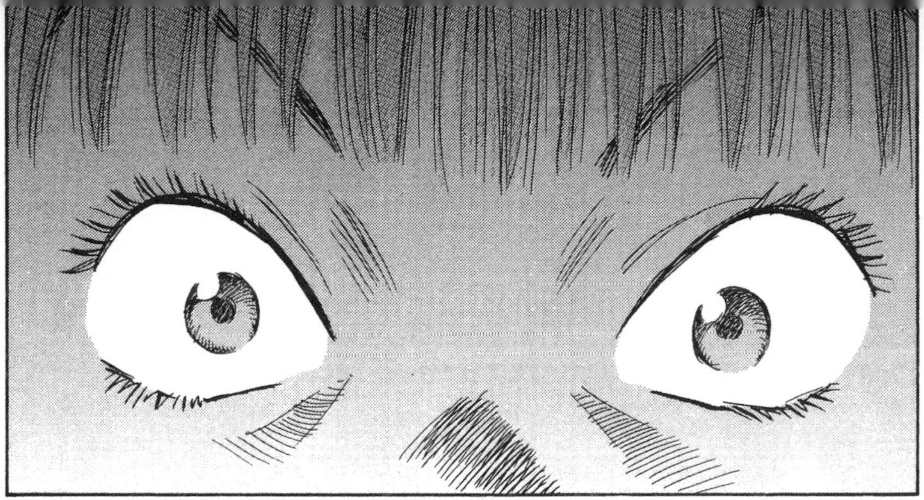

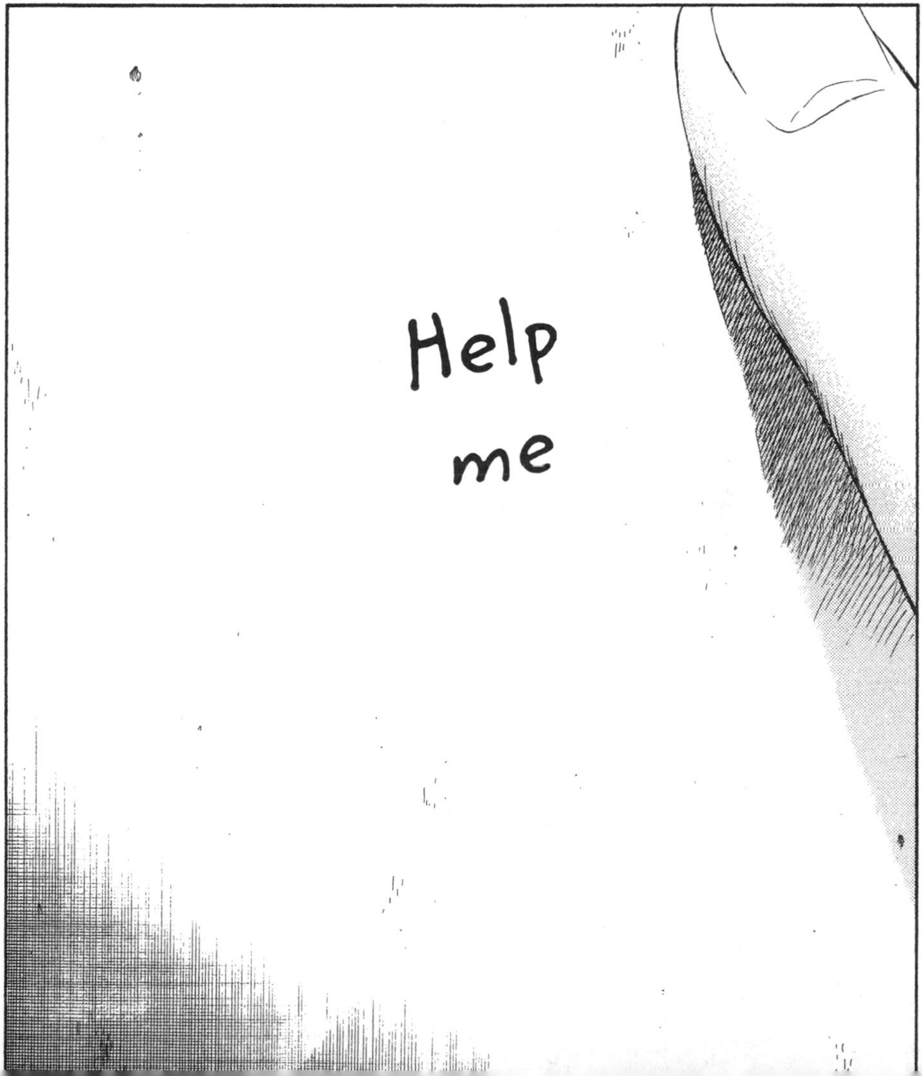
Help me

Chapter 6 Escape

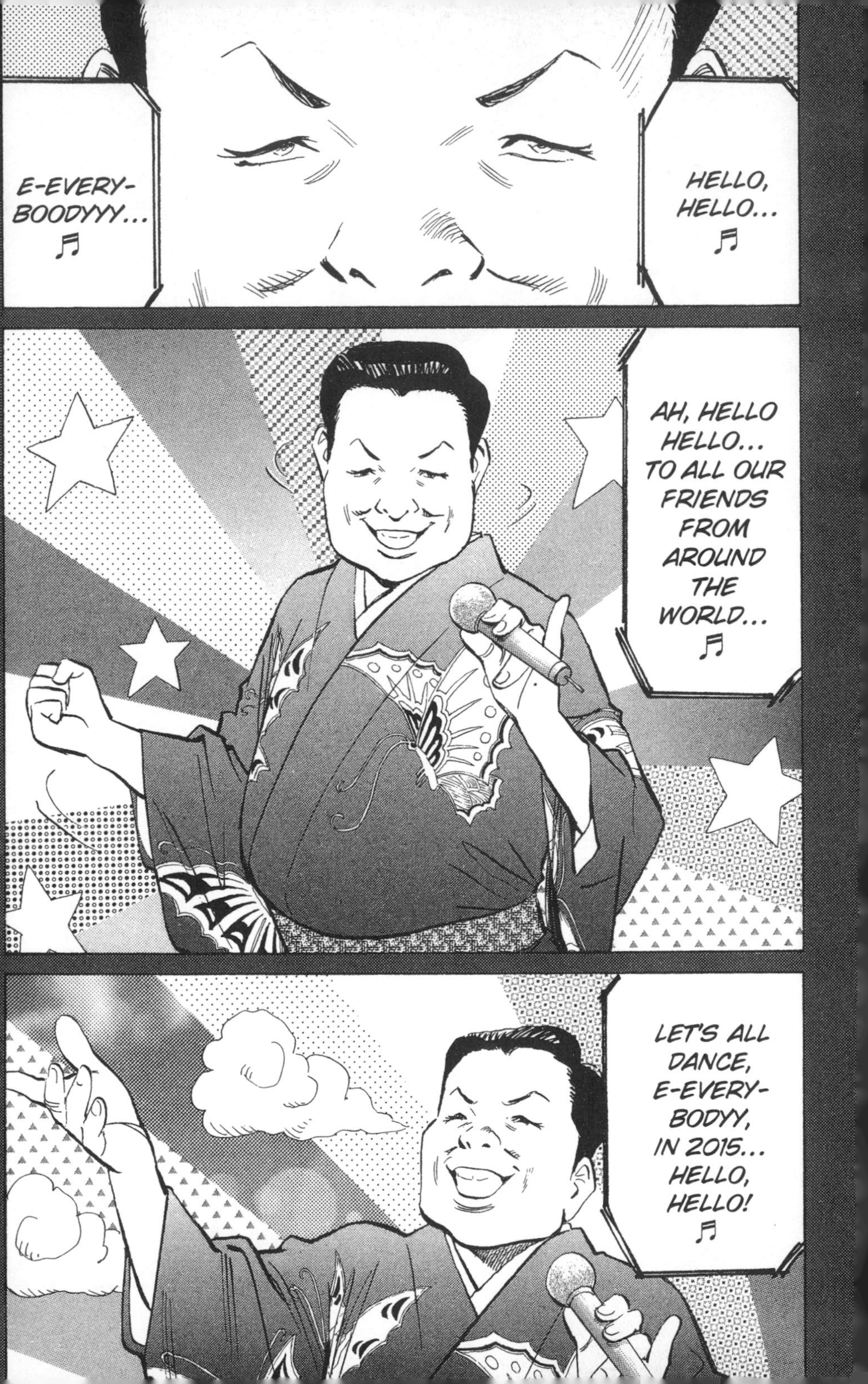
HELLO, HELLO... ♬
E-EVERY-BOODYYY... ♬
AH, HELLO HELLO... TO ALL OUR FRIENDS FROM AROUND THE WORLD... ♬
LET'S ALL DANCE, E-EVERY-BODYY, IN 2015... HELLO, HELLO! ♬

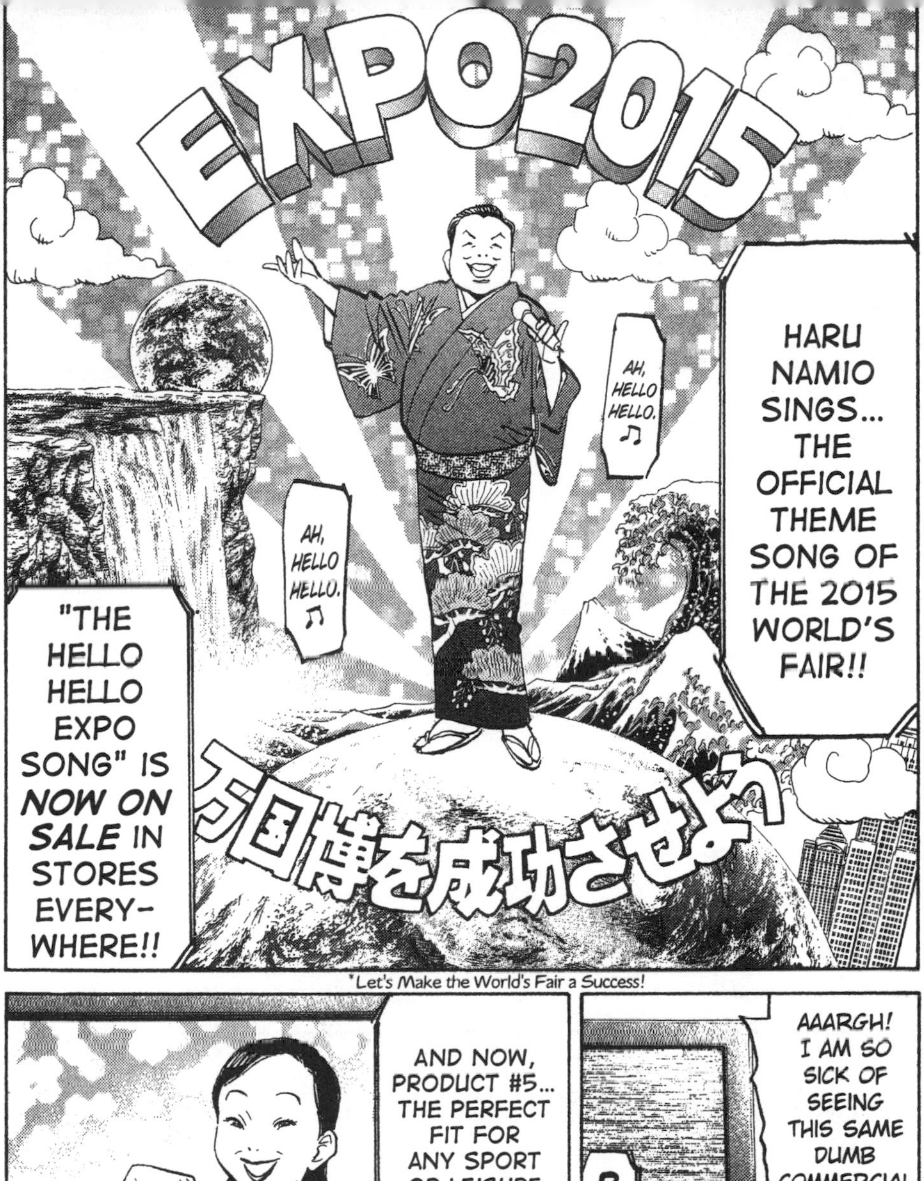
EXPO 2015
HARU NAMIO SINGS... THE OFFICIAL THEME SONG OF THE 2015 WORLD'S FAIR!!
AH, HELLO HELLO. ♫
AH, HELLO HELLO. ♫
万国博を成功させよう
"THE HELLO HELLO EXPO SONG" IS *NOW ON SALE* IN STORES EVERY-WHERE!!

*Let's Make the World's Fair a Success!

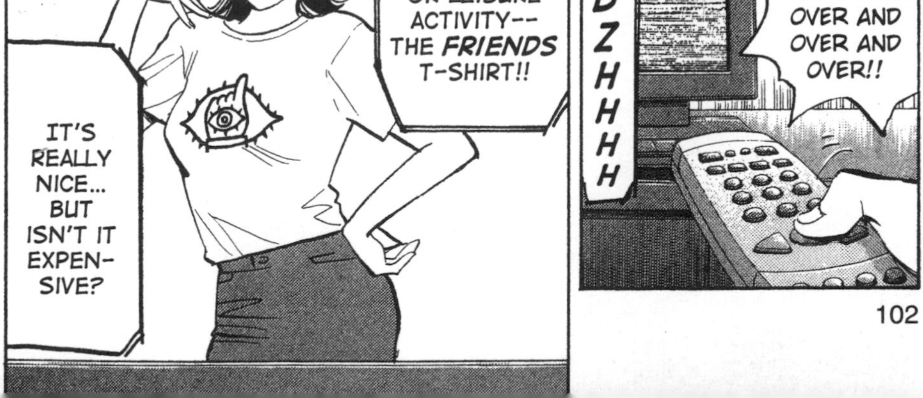
AAARGH! I AM SO SICK OF SEEING THIS SAME DUMB COMMERCIAL OVER AND OVER AND OVER!!
BZHHHHH
AND NOW, PRODUCT #5... THE PERFECT FIT FOR ANY SPORT OR LEISURE ACTIVITY-- THE *FRIENDS* T-SHIRT!!
IT'S REALLY NICE... BUT ISN'T IT EXPEN-SIVE?

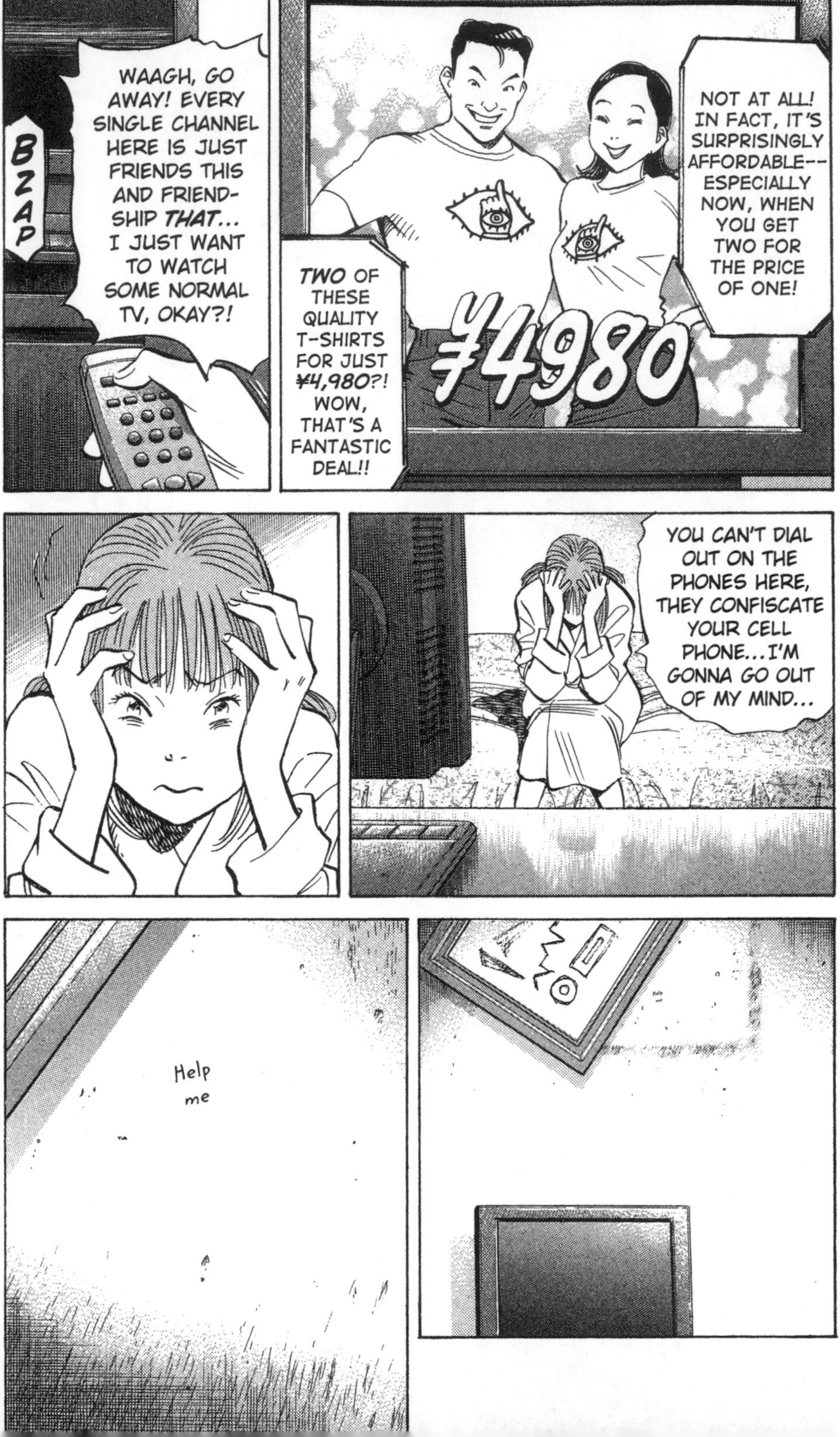
NOT AT ALL! IN FACT, IT'S SURPRISINGLY AFFORDABLE-- ESPECIALLY NOW, WHEN YOU GET TWO FOR THE PRICE OF ONE!
¥4980
TWO OF THESE QUALITY T-SHIRTS FOR JUST ¥4,980?! WOW, THAT'S A FANTASTIC DEAL!!
WAAGH, GO AWAY! EVERY SINGLE CHANNEL HERE IS JUST FRIENDS THIS AND FRIENDSHIP THAT... I JUST WANT TO WATCH SOME NORMAL TV, OKAY?!
BZAP
YOU CAN'T DIAL OUT ON THE PHONES HERE, THEY CONFISCATE YOUR CELL PHONE...I'M GONNA GO OUT OF MY MIND...
Help me
Help me

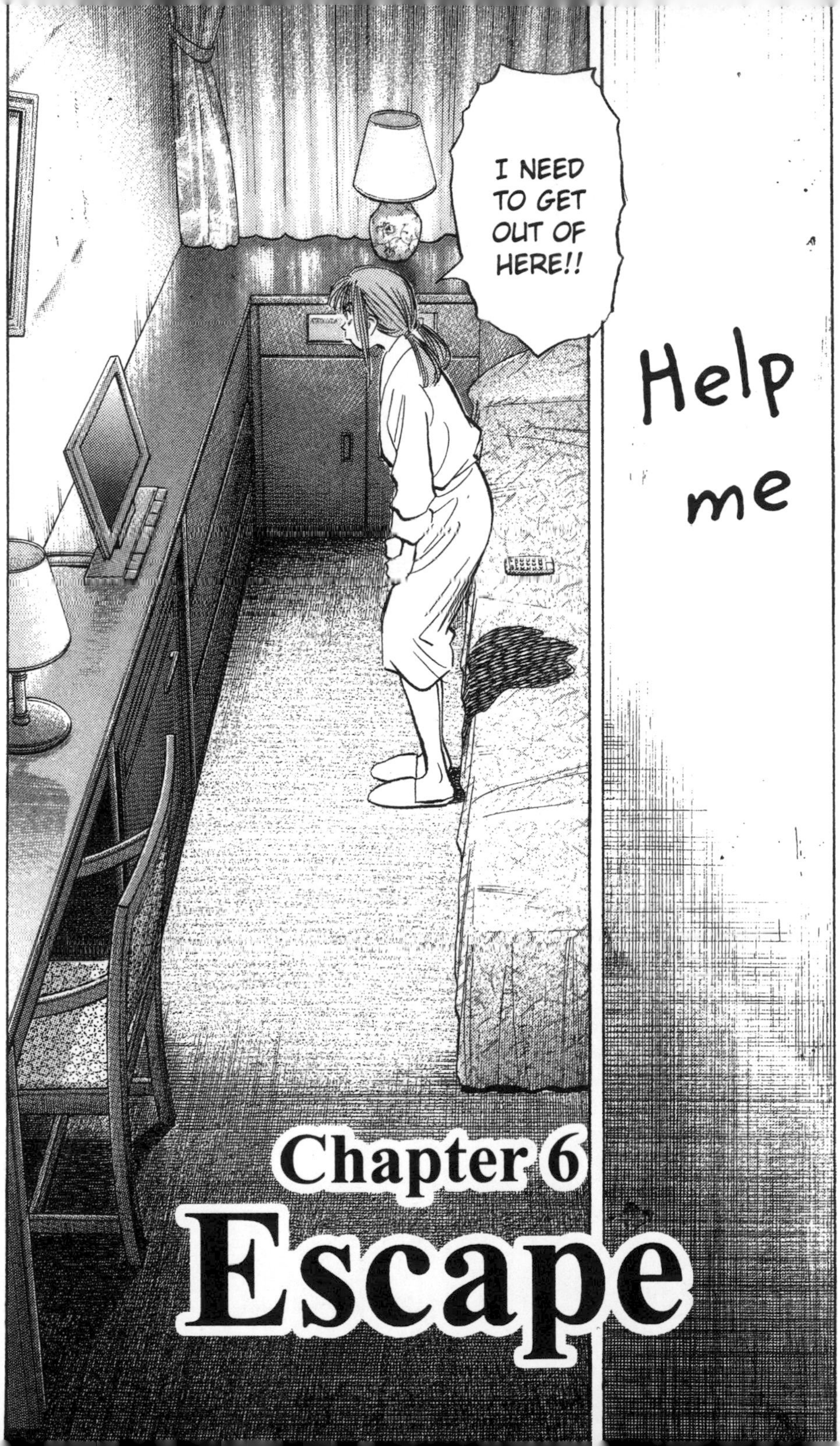
Help me
I NEED TO GET OUT OF HERE!!

Chapter 6
Escape

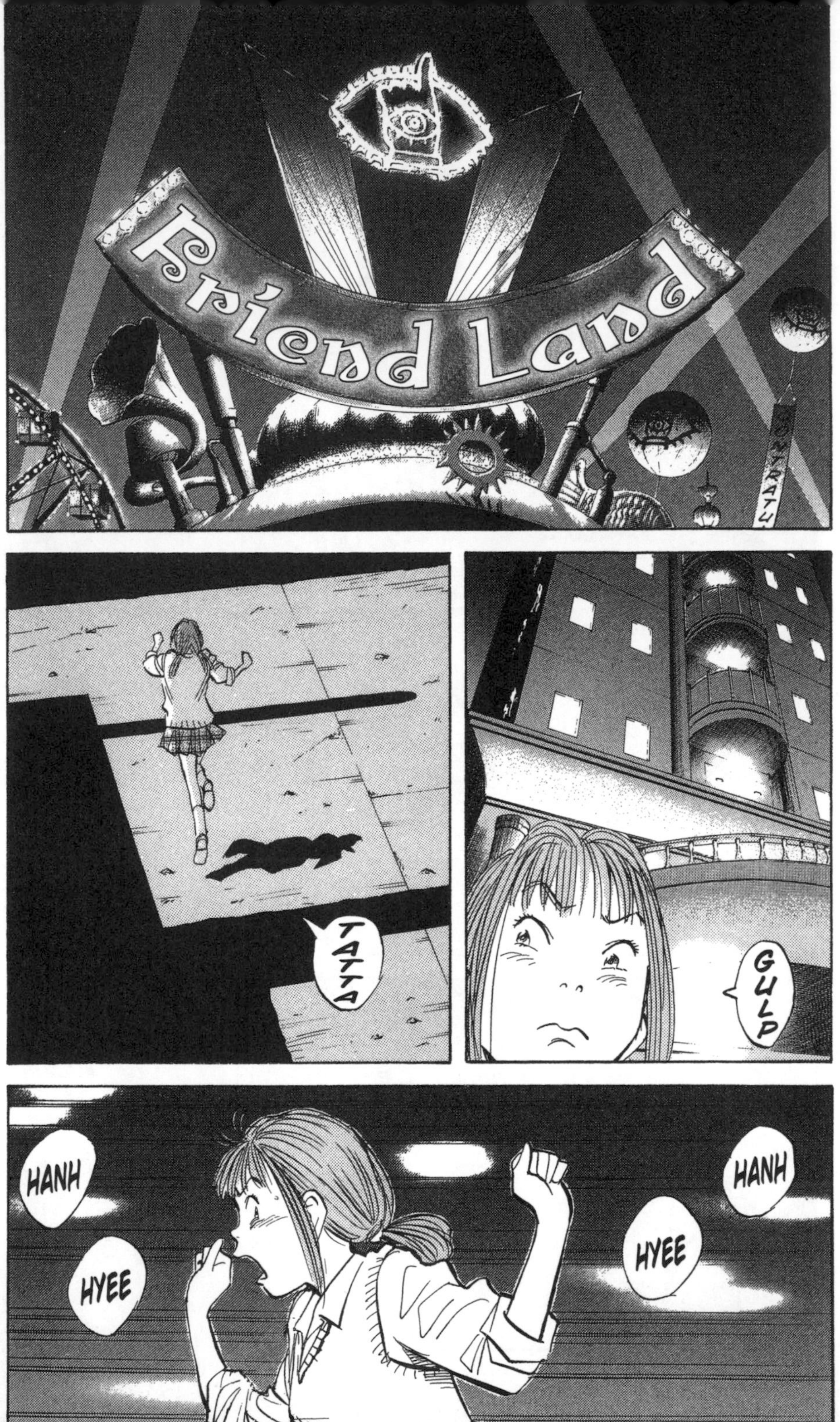
Friend Land
GULP
TATTA
HANH
HANH
HYEE
HYEE

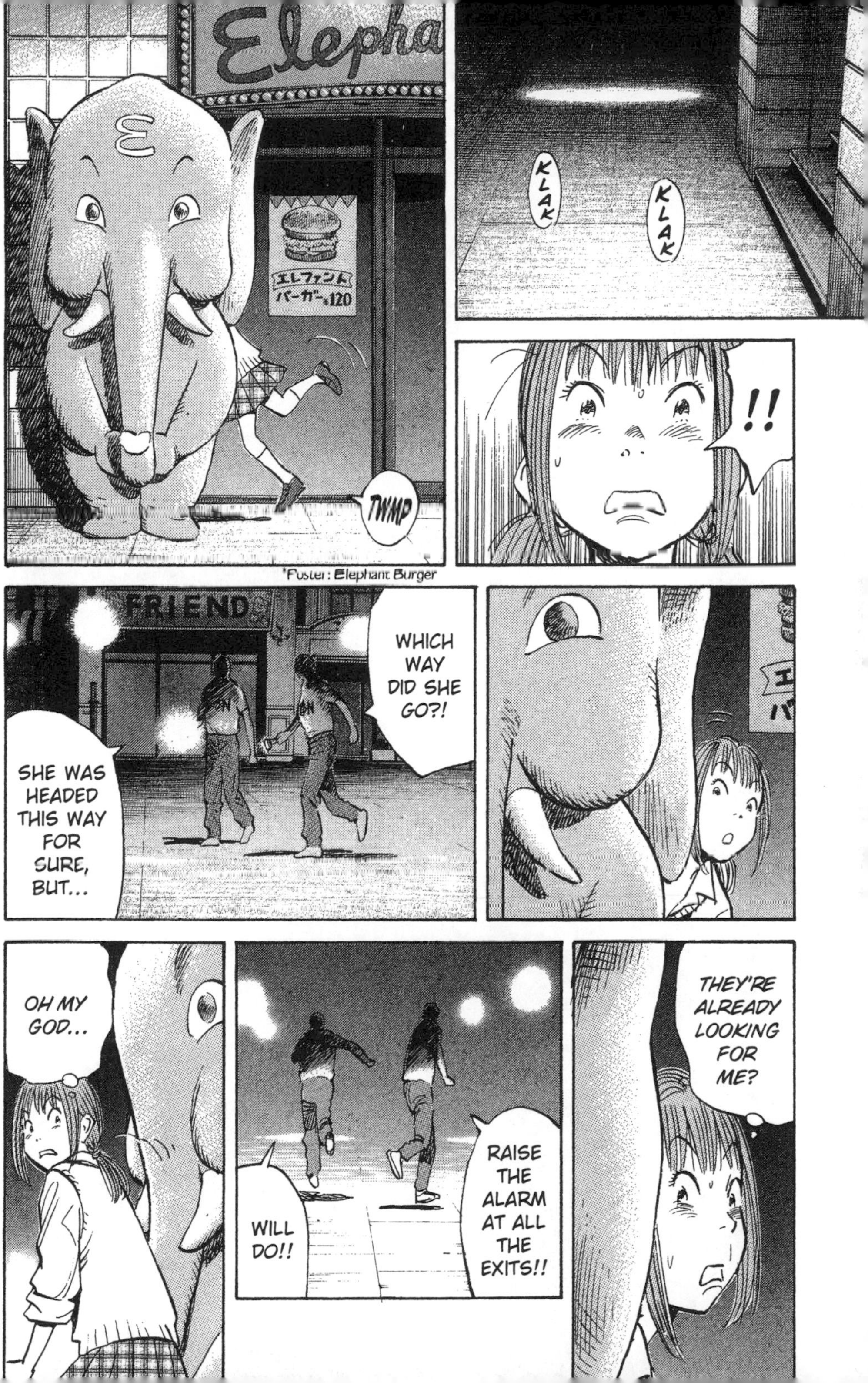
KLAK
KLAK
!!
Elepha
エレファント
バーガー ¥120
TWMP
FRIEND
WHICH WAY DID SHE GO?!
SHE WAS HEADED THIS WAY FOR SURE, BUT...
THEY'RE ALREADY LOOKING FOR ME?
RAISE THE ALARM AT ALL THE EXITS!!
WILL DO!!
OH MY GOD...

*Poster: Elephant Burger

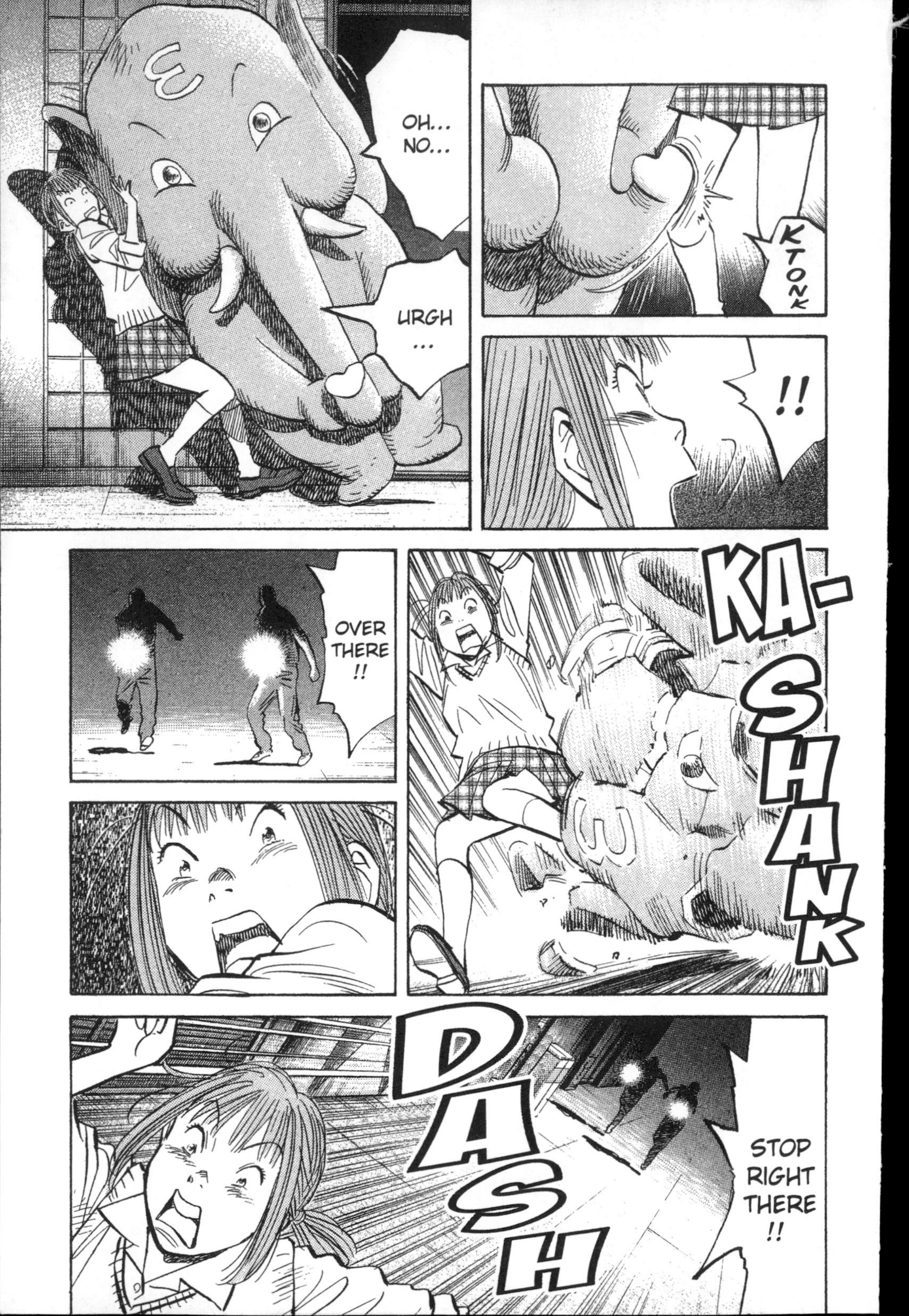
KTONK
!!
OH... NO...
URGH ...
KA-SHANK
OVER THERE !!
STOP RIGHT THERE !!
DASH

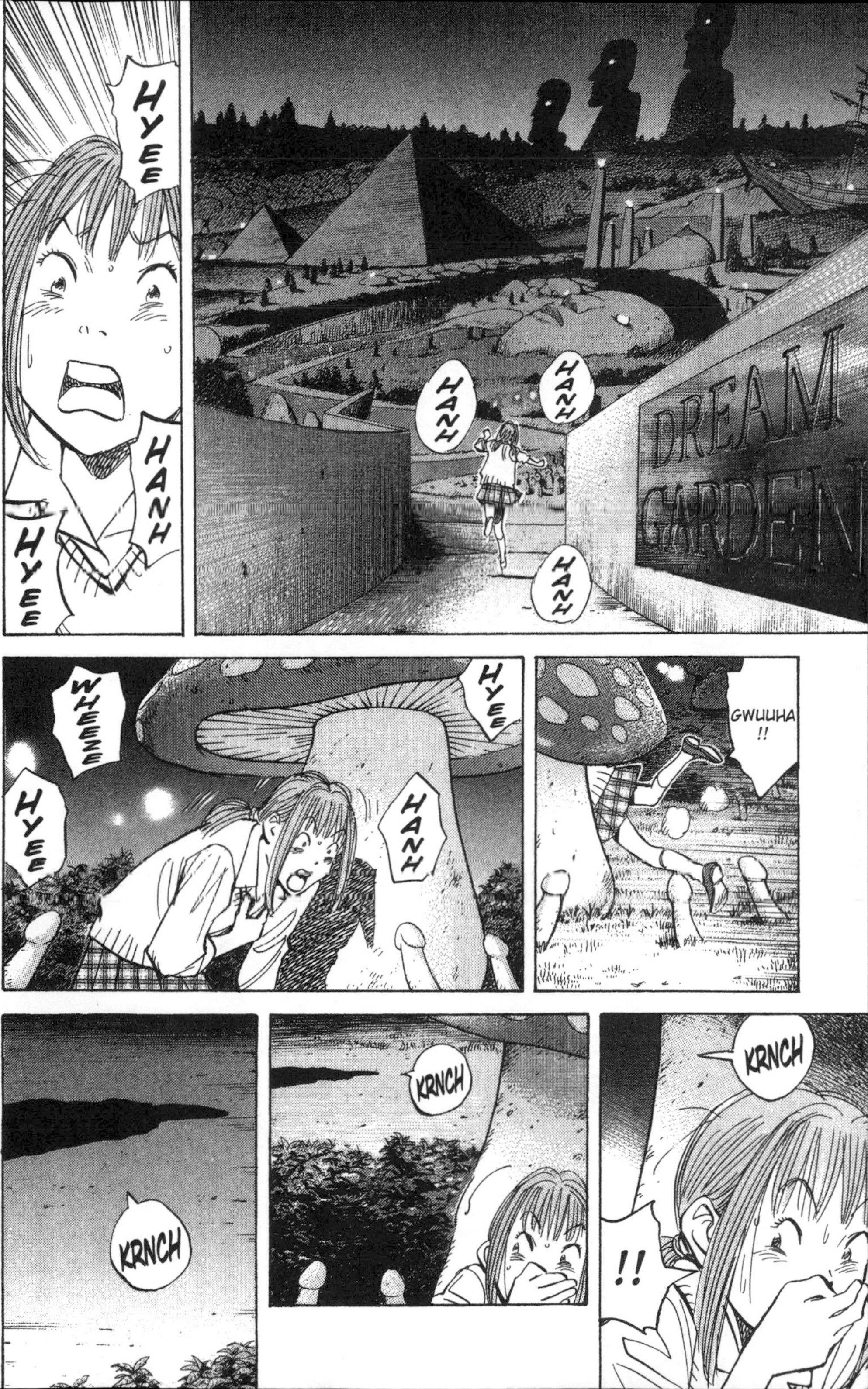
DREAM GARDEN
HANH
HANH
HANH
HYEE
HANH
HYEE
GWUUHA !!
HYEE
HANH
WHEEZE
HYEE
KRNCH
!!
KRNCH
KRNCH

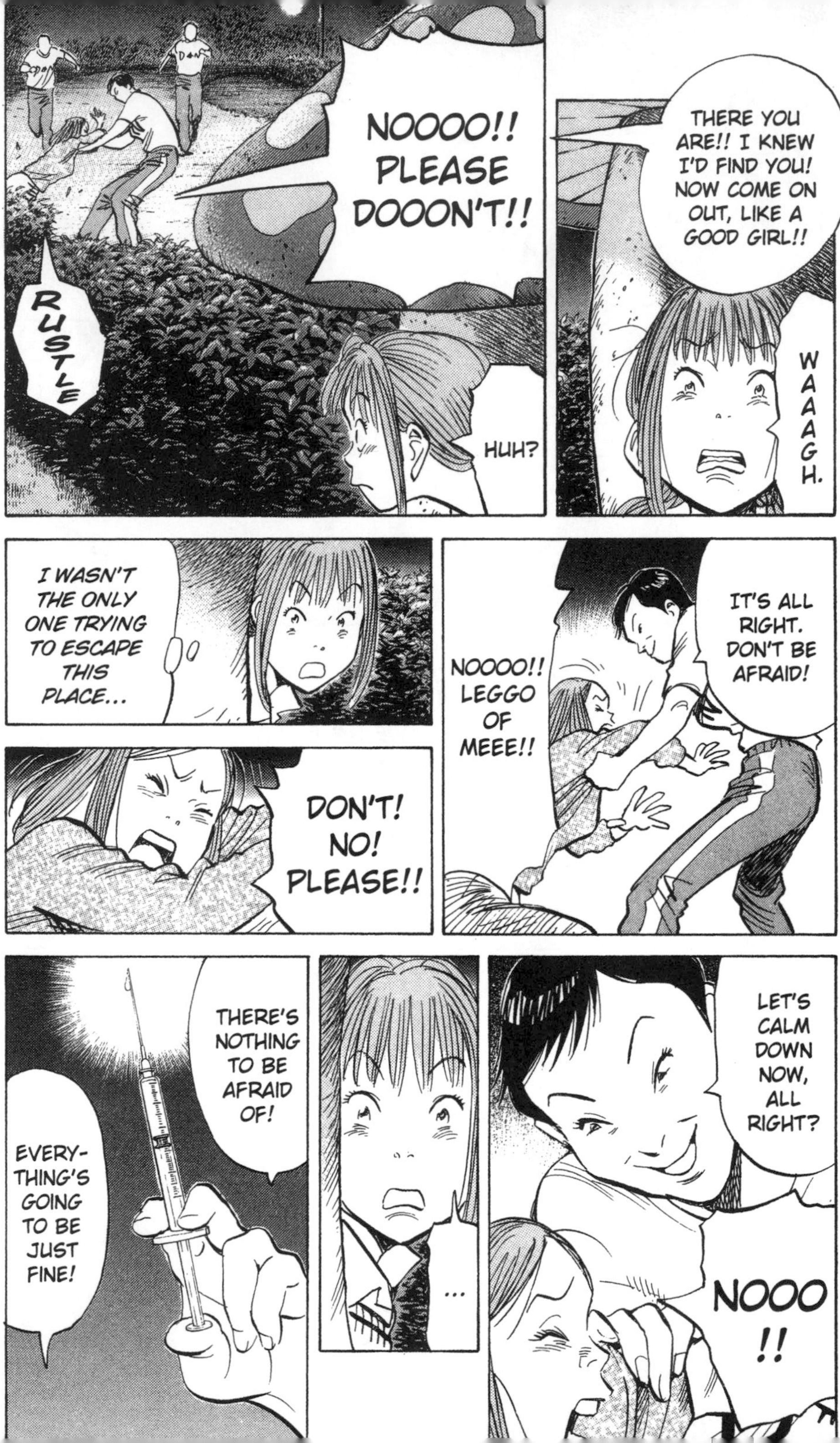
THERE YOU ARE!! I KNEW I'D FIND YOU! NOW COME ON OUT, LIKE A GOOD GIRL!!
WAAAAGH.
NOOOO!! PLEASE DOOOON'T!!
RUSTLE
HUH?
IT'S ALL RIGHT. DON'T BE AFRAID!
NOOOO!! LEGGO OF MEEE!!
I WASN'T THE ONLY ONE TRYING TO ESCAPE THIS PLACE...
DON'T! NO! PLEASE!!
LET'S CALM DOWN NOW, ALL RIGHT?
NOOO !!
...
THERE'S NOTHING TO BE AFRAID OF!
EVERY-THING'S GOING TO BE JUST FINE!

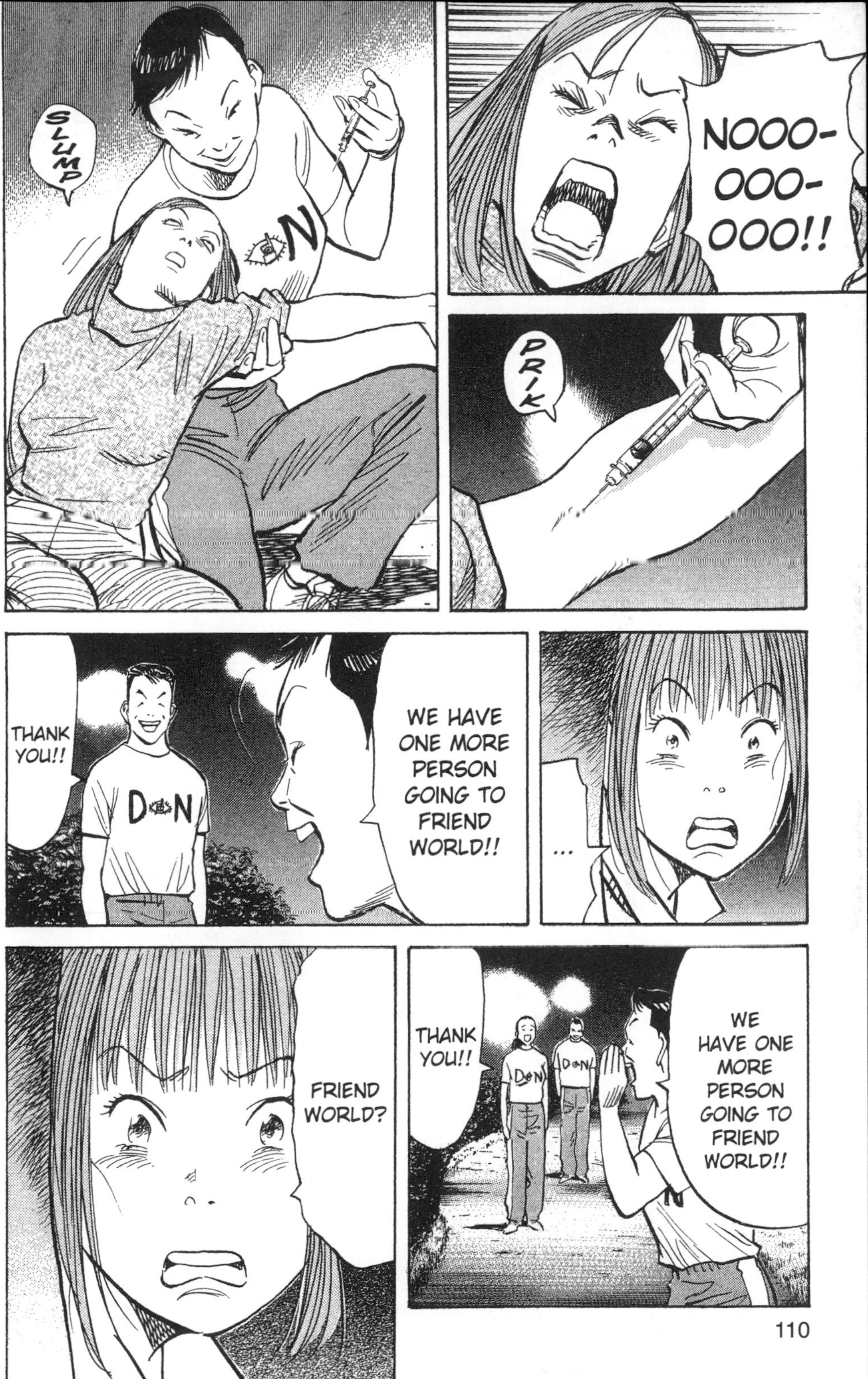
NOOO-OOO-OOO!!
PRIK
SLUMP
...
WE HAVE ONE MORE PERSON GOING TO FRIEND WORLD!!
THANK YOU!!
WE HAVE ONE MORE PERSON GOING TO FRIEND WORLD!!
THANK YOU!!
FRIEND WORLD?

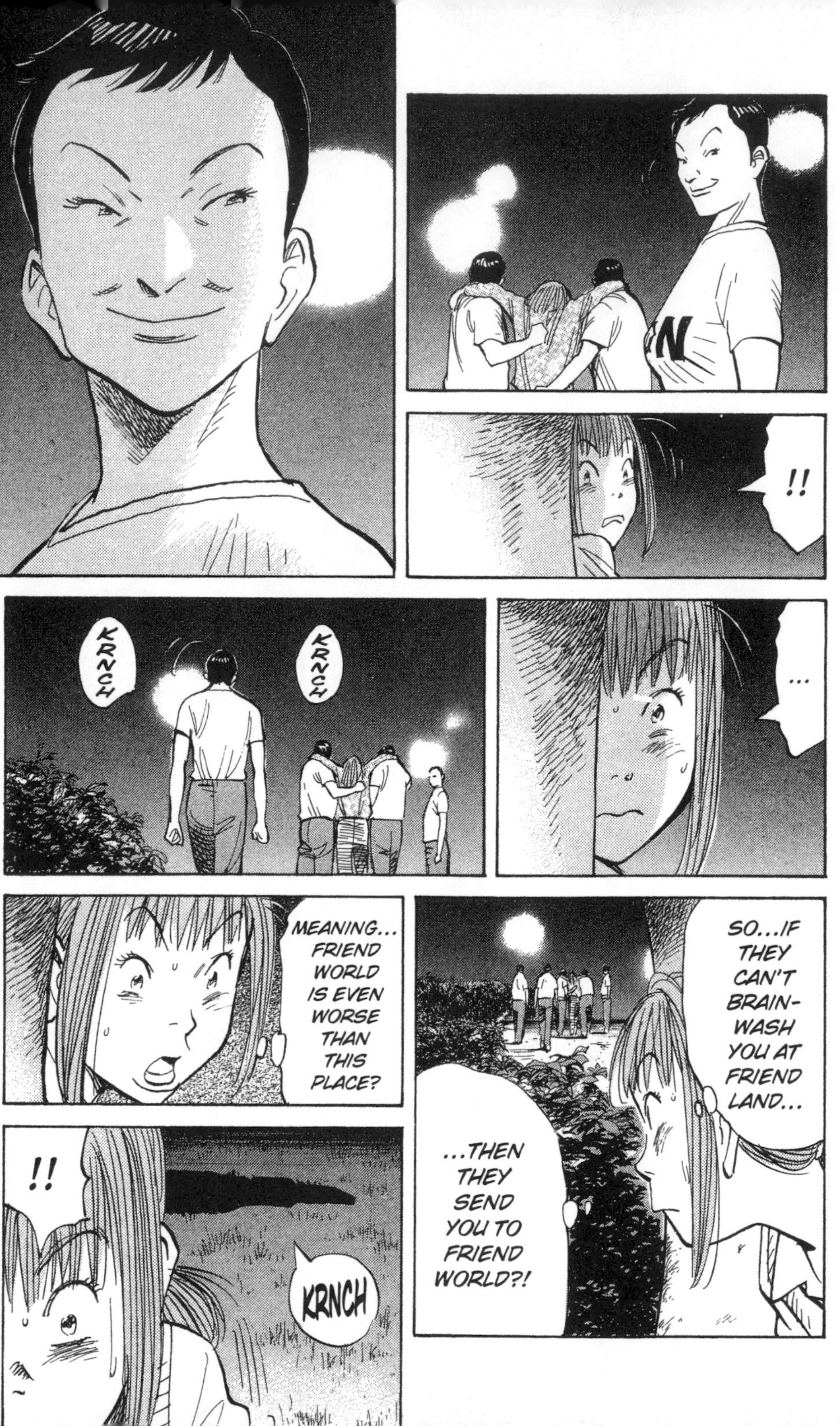
!!
...
KRNCH
KRNCH
SO...IF THEY CAN'T BRAIN-WASH YOU AT FRIEND LAND...
...THEN THEY SEND YOU TO FRIEND WORLD?!
MEANING... FRIEND WORLD IS EVEN WORSE THAN THIS PLACE?
!!
KRNCH

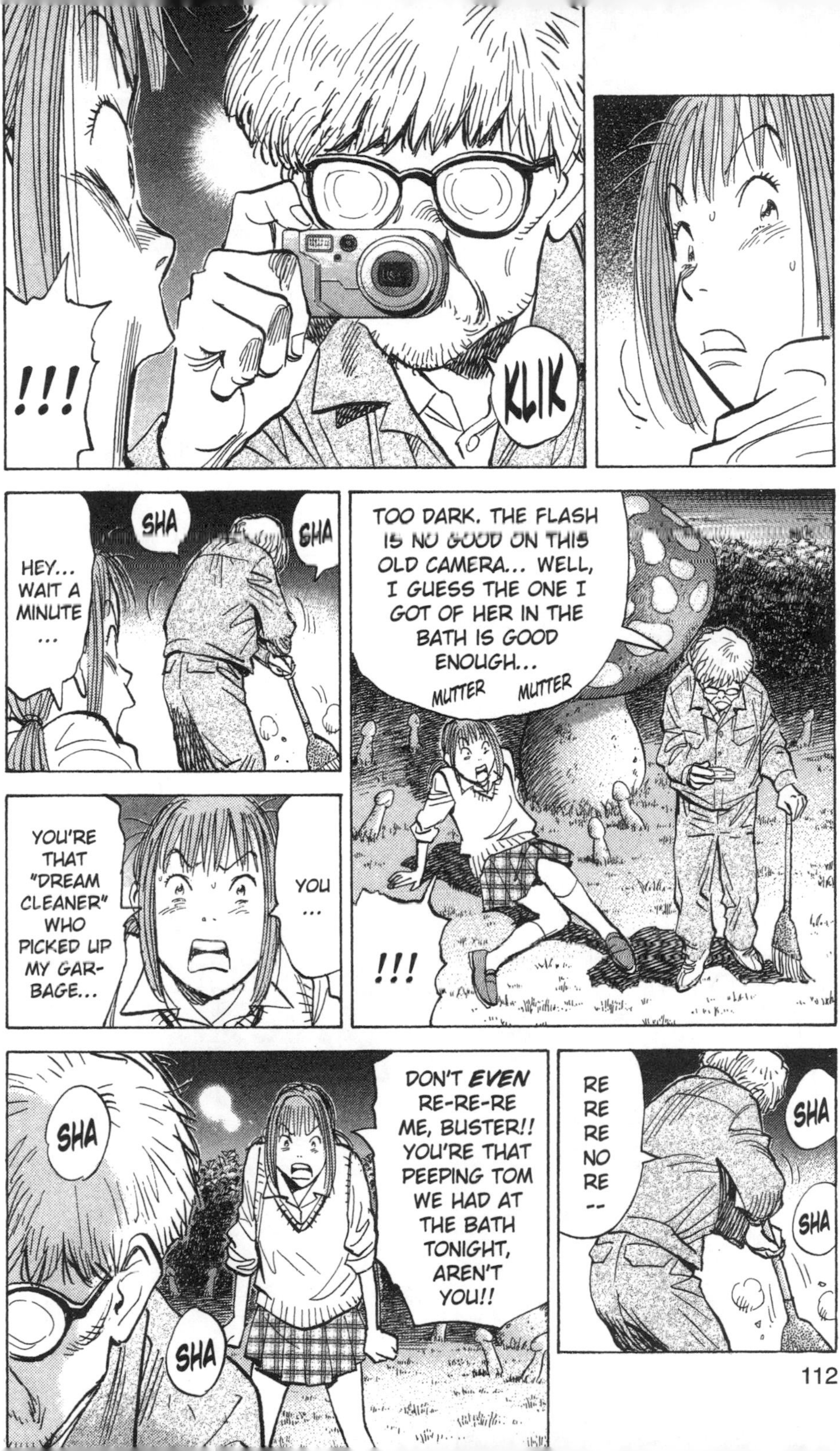
KLIK
!!!
TOO DARK. THE FLASH IS NO GOOD ON THIS OLD CAMERA... WELL, I GUESS THE ONE I GOT OF HER IN THE BATH IS GOOD ENOUGH...
MUTTER MUTTER
!!!
SHA
SHA
HEY... WAIT A MINUTE ...
YOU ...
YOU'RE THAT "DREAM CLEANER" WHO PICKED UP MY GAR-BAGE...
SHA
RE RE RE NO RE --
SHA
DON'T *EVEN* RE-RE-RE ME, BUSTER!! YOU'RE THAT PEEPING TOM WE HAD AT THE BATH TONIGHT, AREN'T YOU!!
SHA
SHA

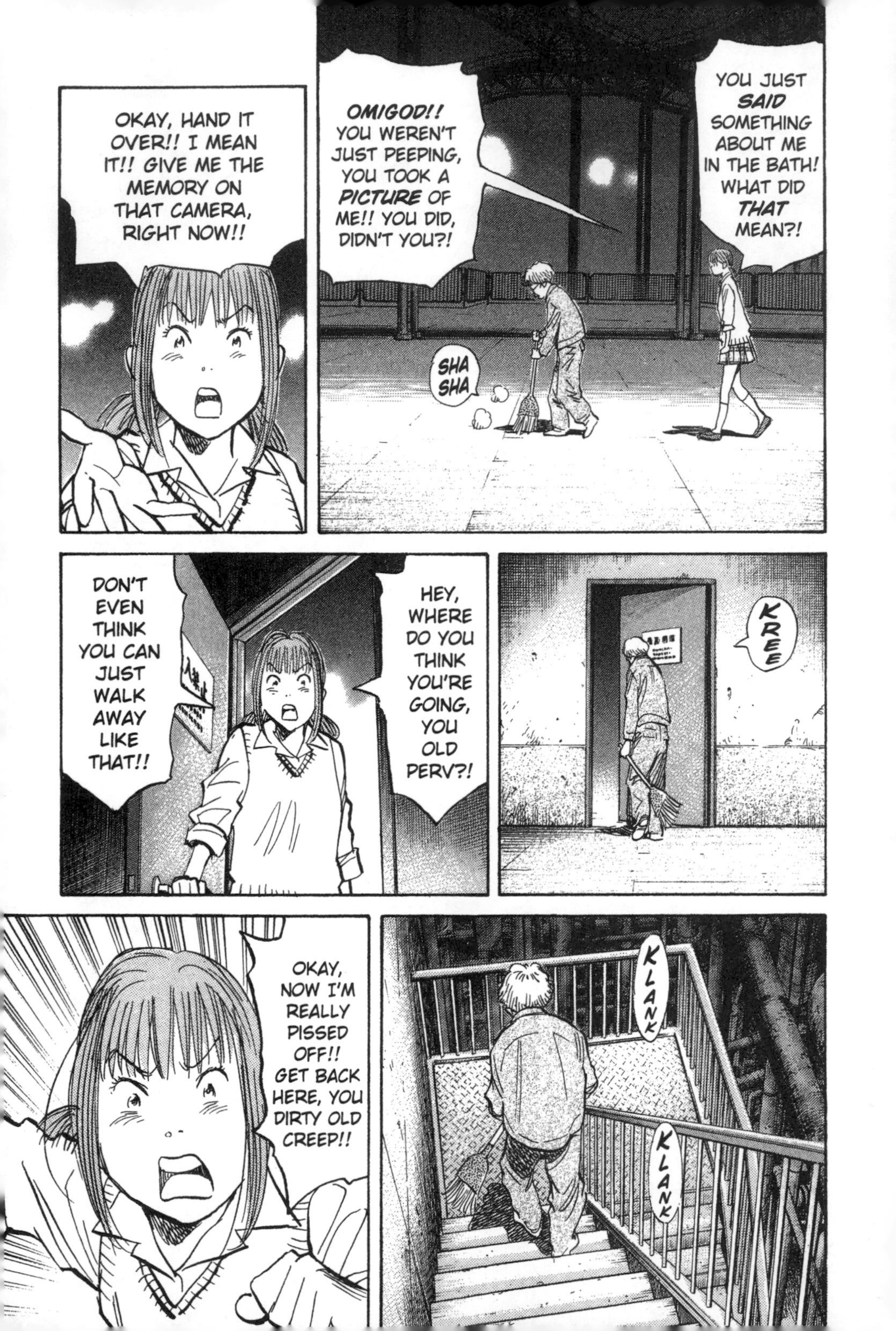
YOU JUST SAID SOMETHING ABOUT ME IN THE BATH! WHAT DID THAT MEAN?!
OMIGOD!! YOU WEREN'T JUST PEEPING, YOU TOOK A PICTURE OF ME!! YOU DID, DIDN'T YOU?!
SHA SHA
OKAY, HAND IT OVER!! I MEAN IT!! GIVE ME THE MEMORY ON THAT CAMERA, RIGHT NOW!!
KREE
HEY, WHERE DO YOU THINK YOU'RE GOING, YOU OLD PERV?!
DON'T EVEN THINK YOU CAN JUST WALK AWAY LIKE THAT!!
KLANK
KLANK
OKAY, NOW I'M REALLY PISSED OFF!! GET BACK HERE, YOU DIRTY OLD CREEP!!

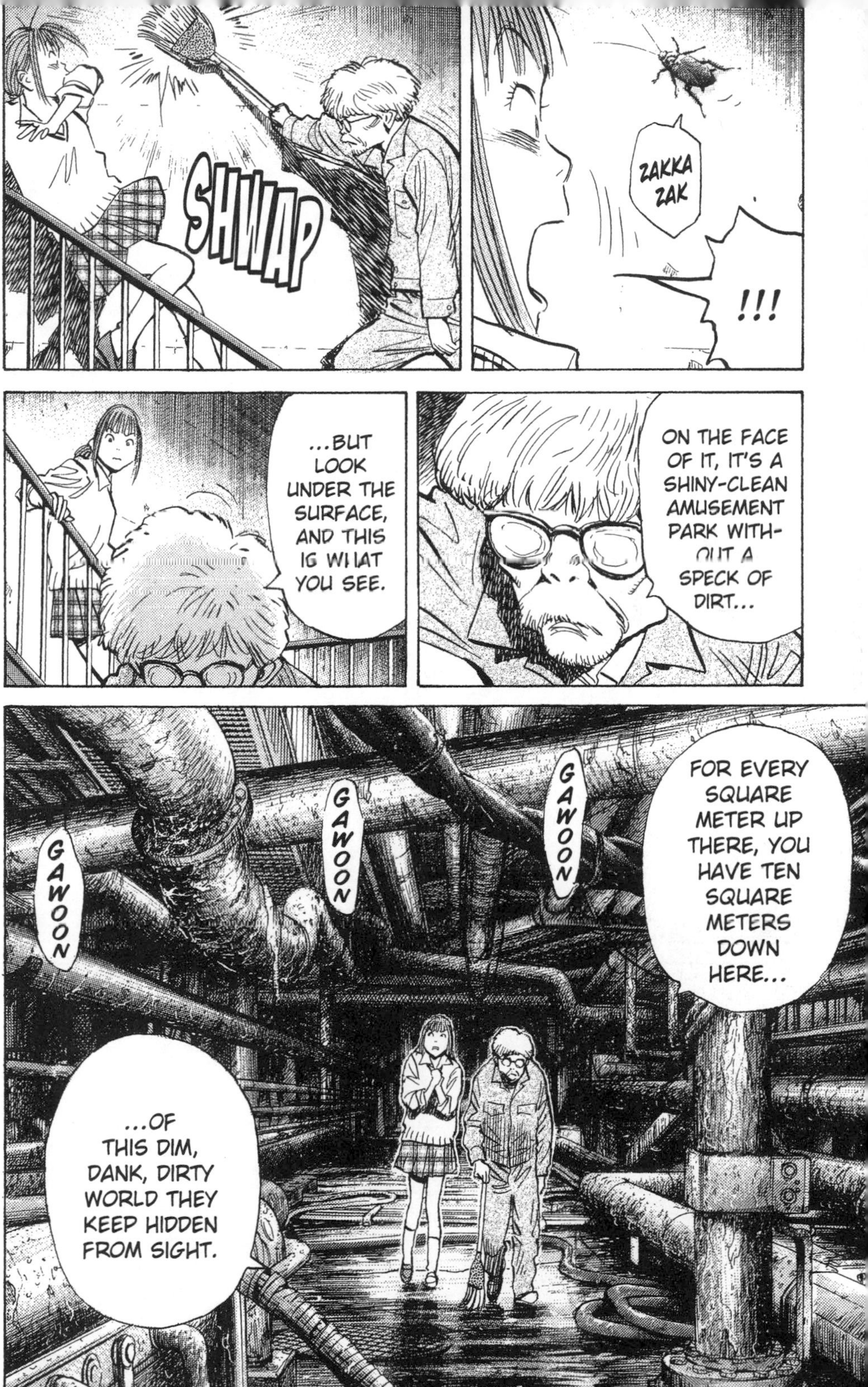
ZAKKA ZAK
!!!
SHWAP
ON THE FACE OF IT, IT'S A SHINY-CLEAN AMUSEMENT PARK WITH-OUT A SPECK OF DIRT...
...BUT LOOK UNDER THE SURFACE, AND THIS IS WHAT YOU SEE.
FOR EVERY SQUARE METER UP THERE, YOU HAVE TEN SQUARE METERS DOWN HERE...
GAWOON
GAWOON
GAWOON
...OF THIS DIM, DANK, DIRTY WORLD THEY KEEP HIDDEN FROM SIGHT.

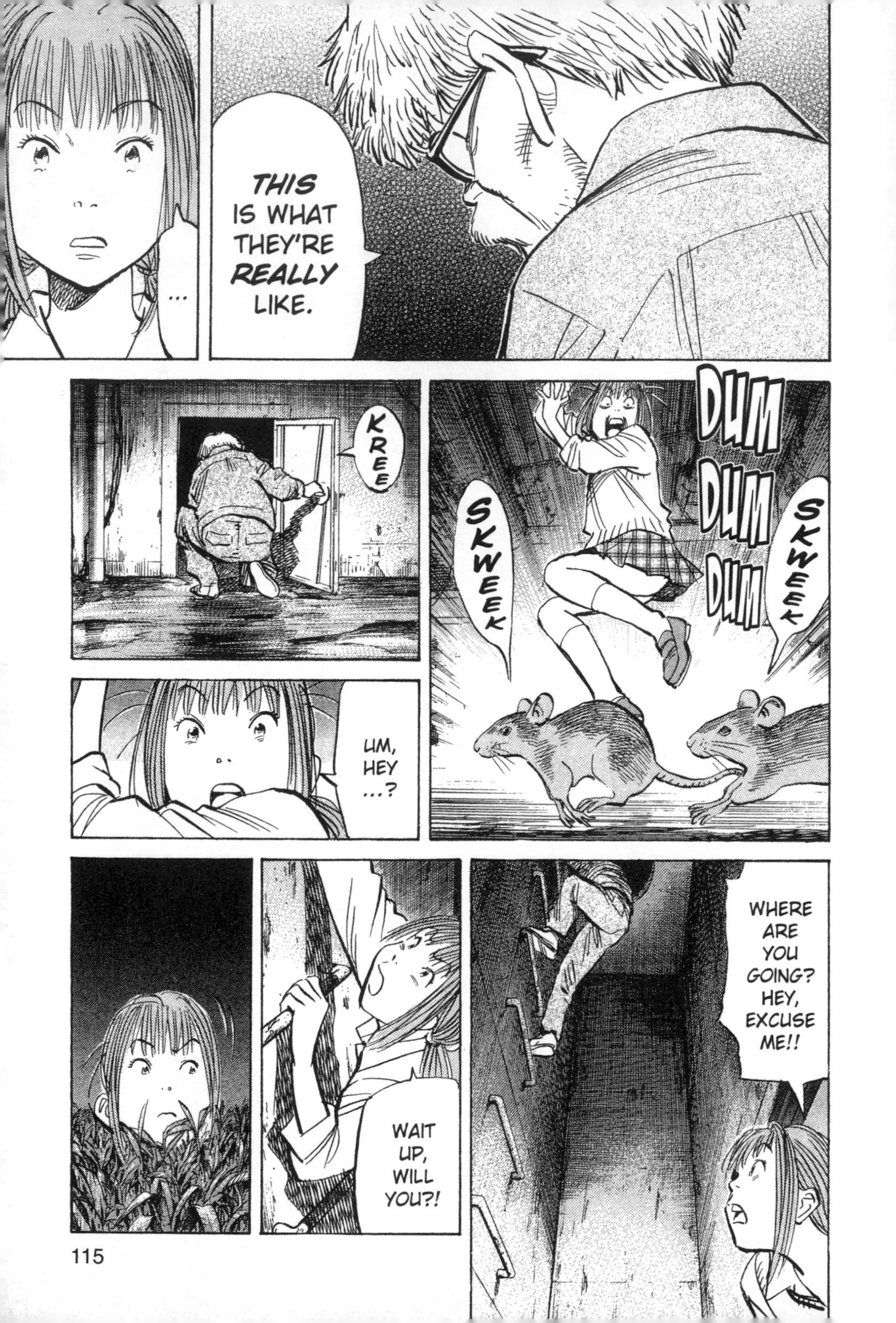
THIS IS WHAT THEY'RE REALLY LIKE.
...
DUM DUM DUM
SKWEEK
SKWEEK
KREE
UM, HEY ...?
WHERE ARE YOU GOING? HEY, EXCUSE ME!!
WAIT UP, WILL YOU?!

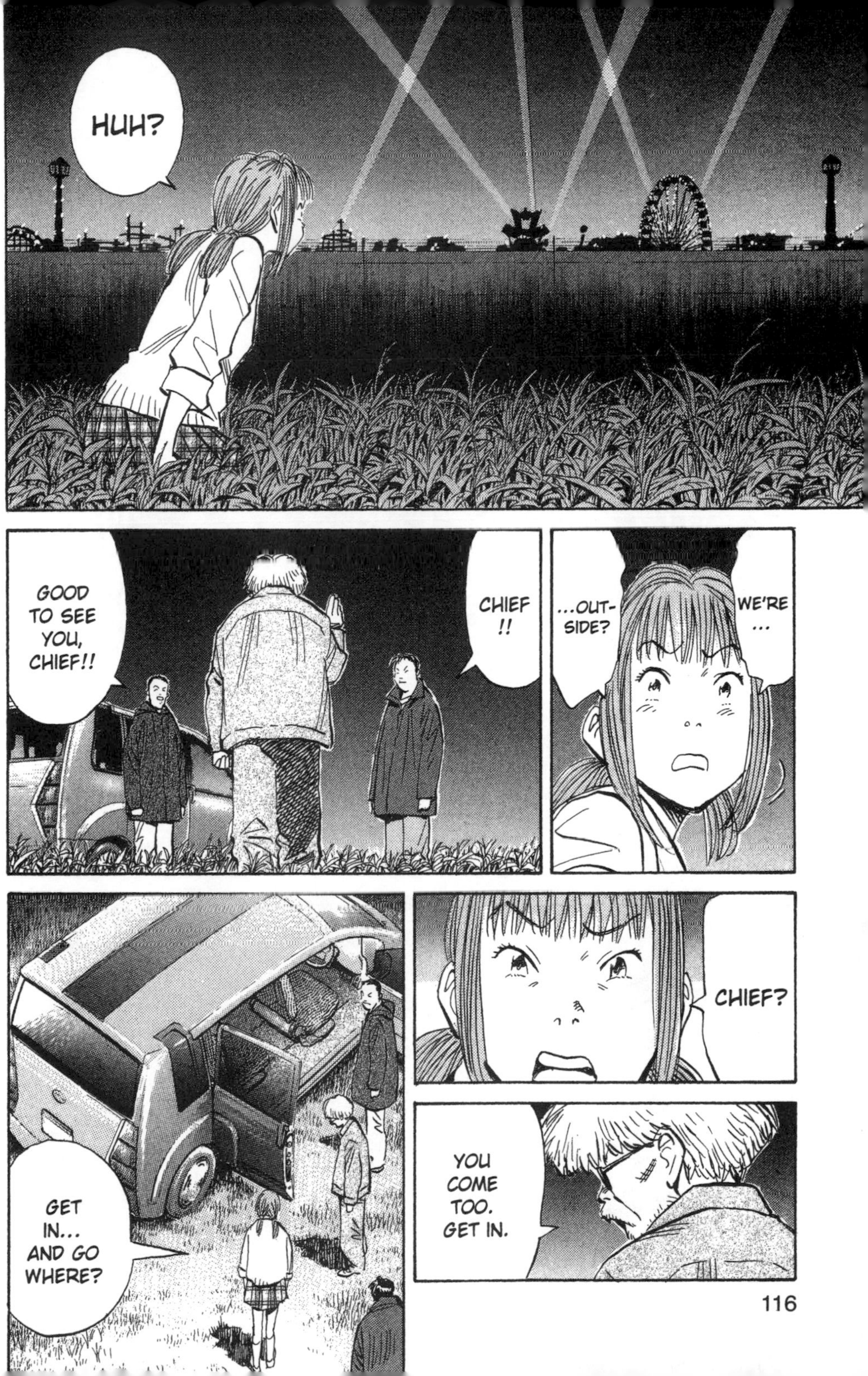
HUH?
WE'RE ...
...OUT-SIDE?
CHIEF !!
GOOD TO SEE YOU, CHIEF!!
CHIEF?
YOU COME TOO. GET IN.
GET IN... AND GO WHERE?

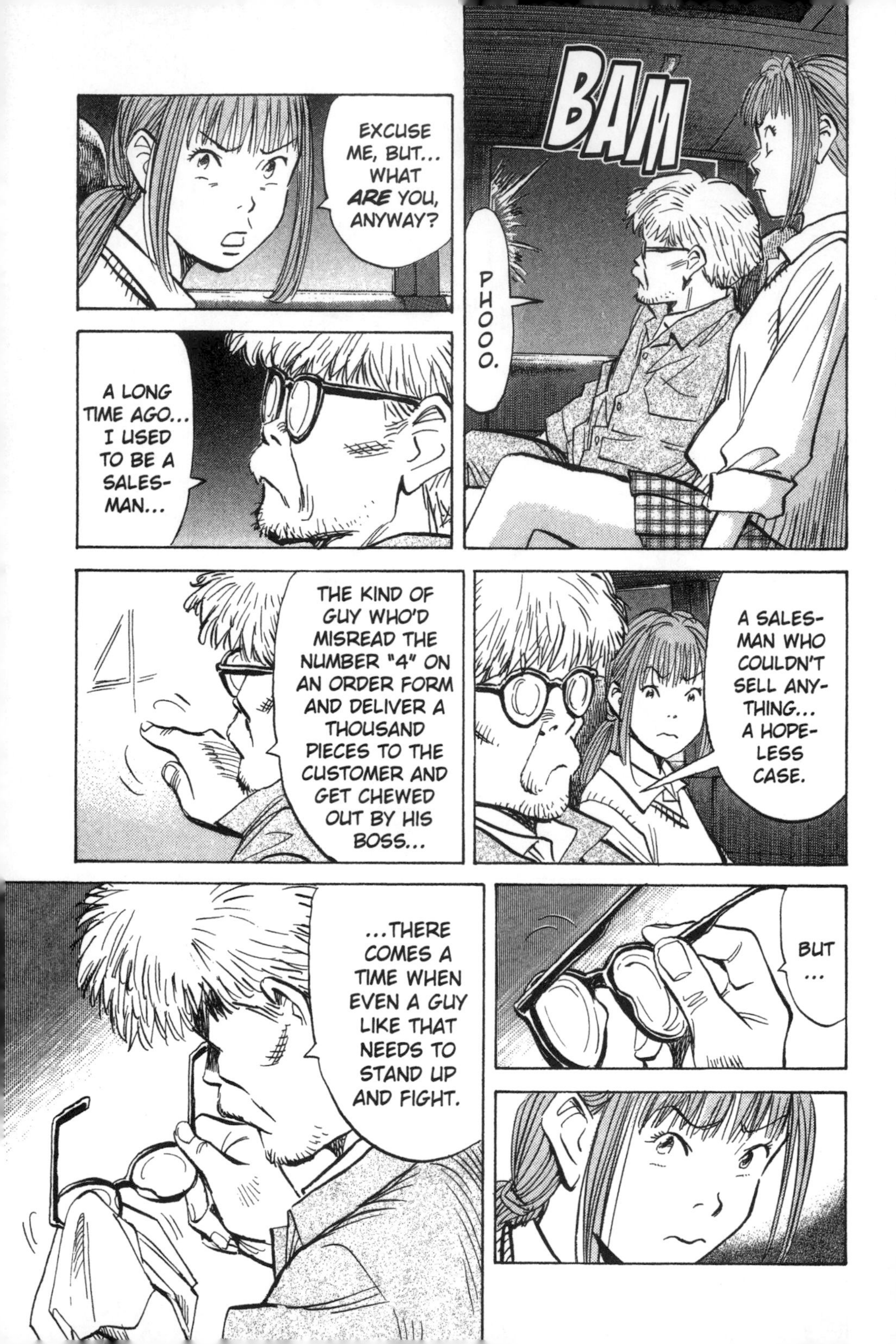
BAM
PHOOO.
EXCUSE ME, BUT... WHAT ARE YOU, ANYWAY?
A LONG TIME AGO... I USED TO BE A SALES-MAN...
A SALES-MAN WHO COULDN'T SELL ANY-THING... A HOPE-LESS CASE.
THE KIND OF GUY WHO'D MISREAD THE NUMBER "4" ON AN ORDER FORM AND DELIVER A THOUSAND PIECES TO THE CUSTOMER AND GET CHEWED OUT BY HIS BOSS...
BUT...
...THERE COMES A TIME WHEN EVEN A GUY LIKE THAT NEEDS TO STAND UP AND FIGHT.

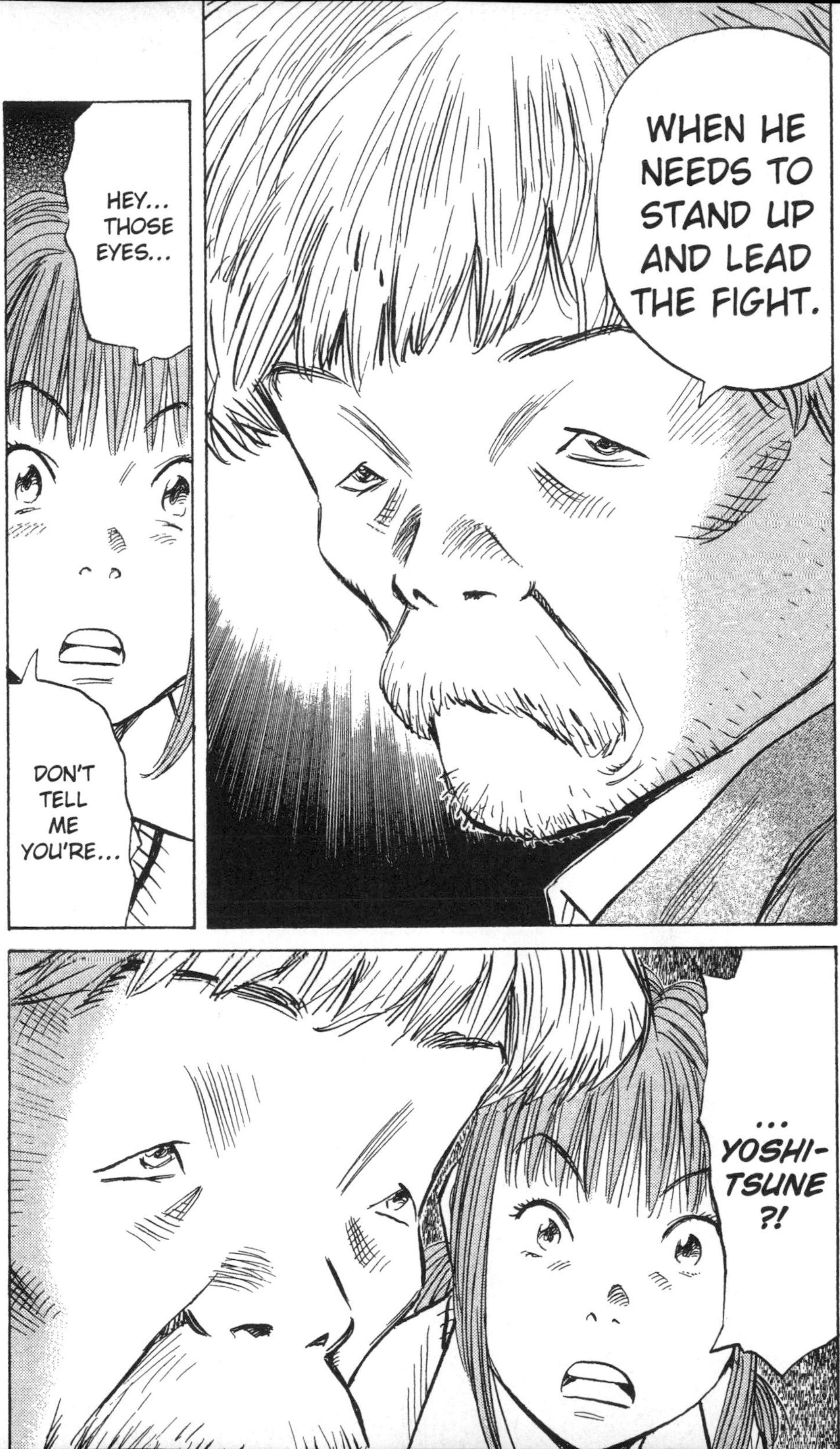
WHEN HE NEEDS TO STAND UP AND LEAD THE FIGHT.
HEY... THOSE EYES...
DON'T TELL ME YOU'RE...
...YOSHI-TSUNE?!

Chapter 7 Request

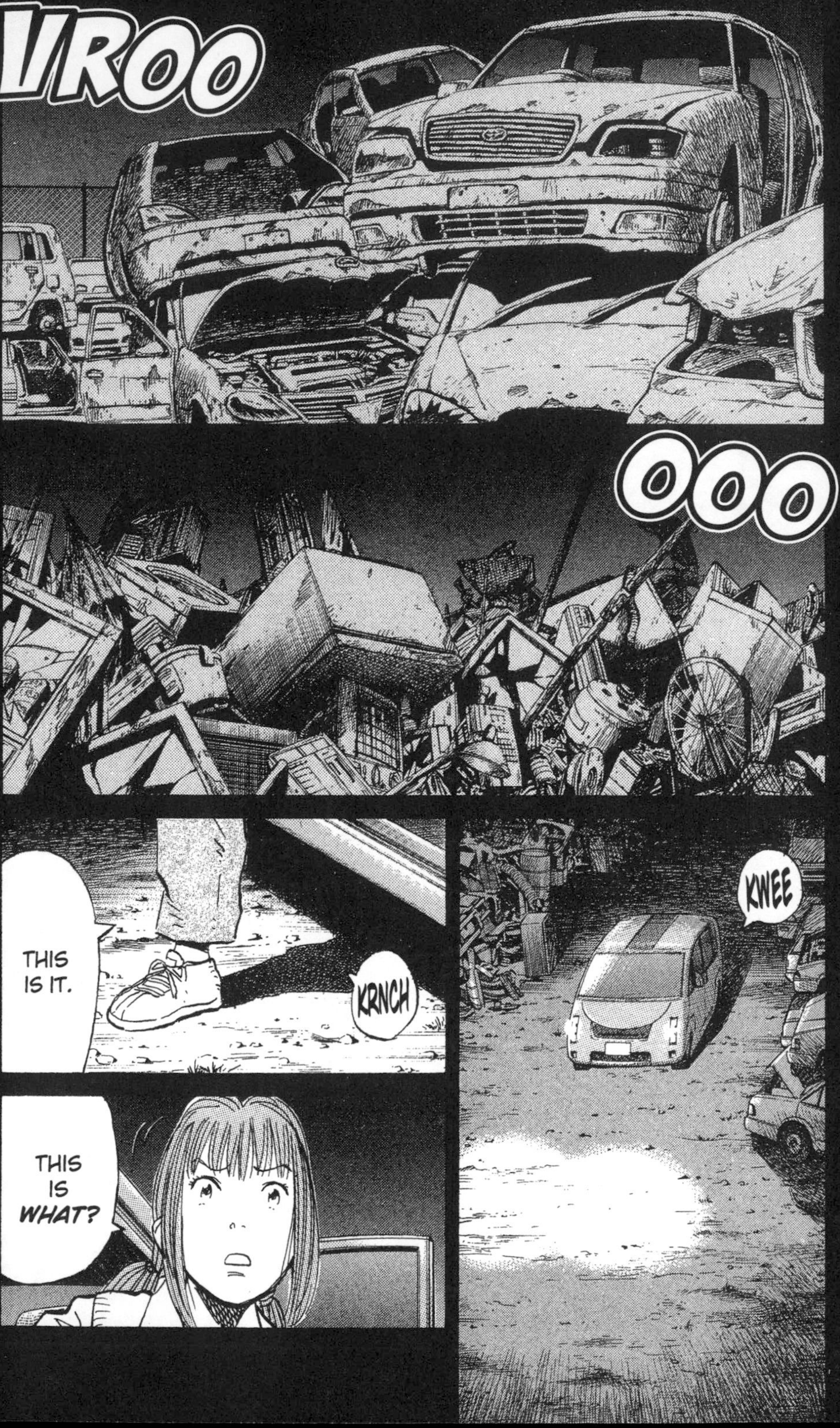
VROO
OOO
KWEE
THIS IS IT.
KRNCH
THIS IS WHAT?

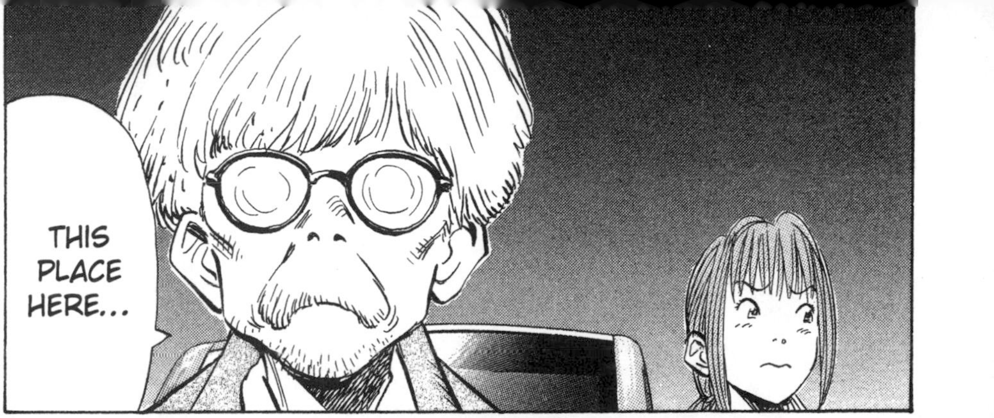
THIS PLACE HERE...

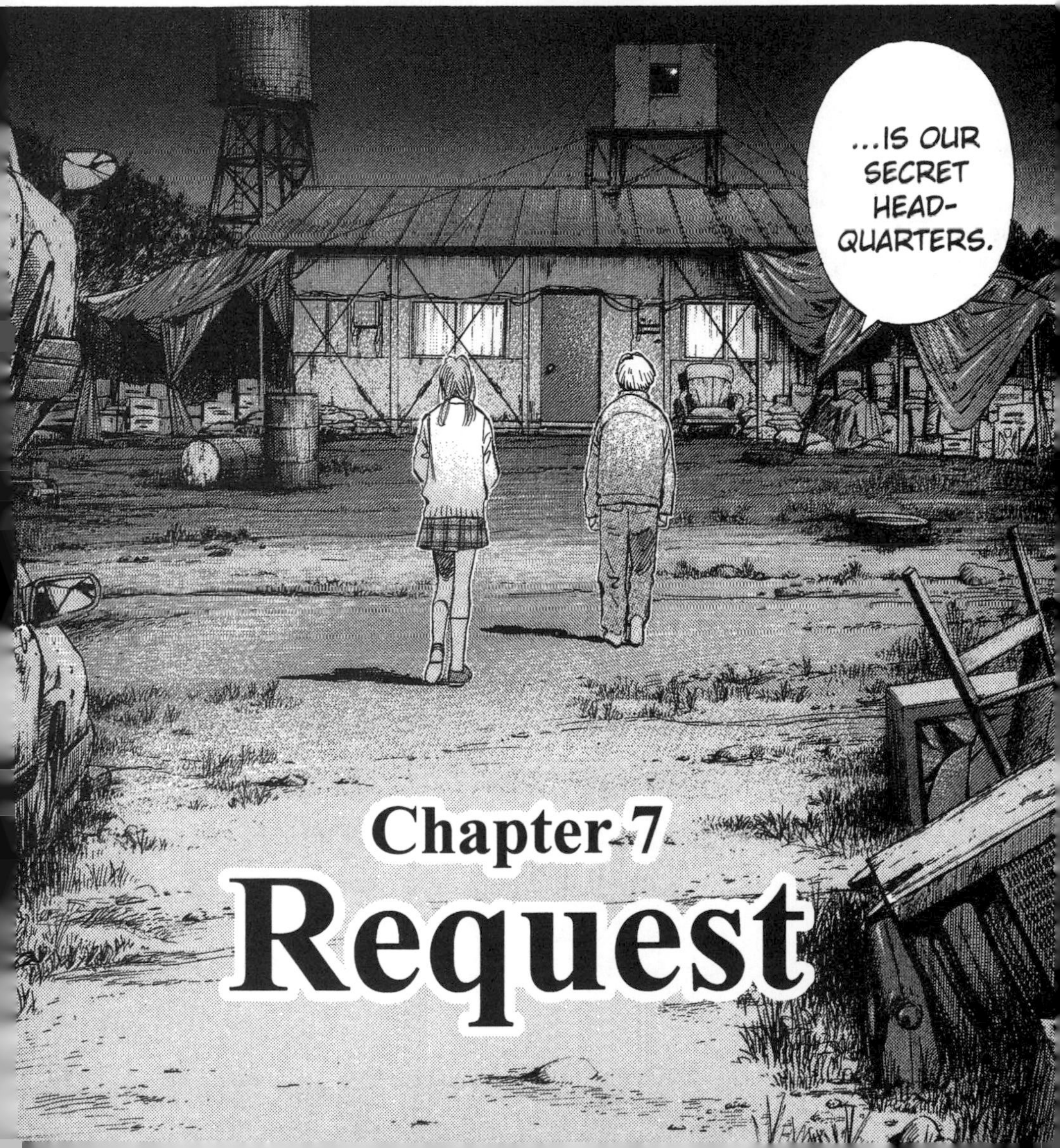
...IS OUR SECRET HEAD-QUARTERS.

Chapter 7
Request

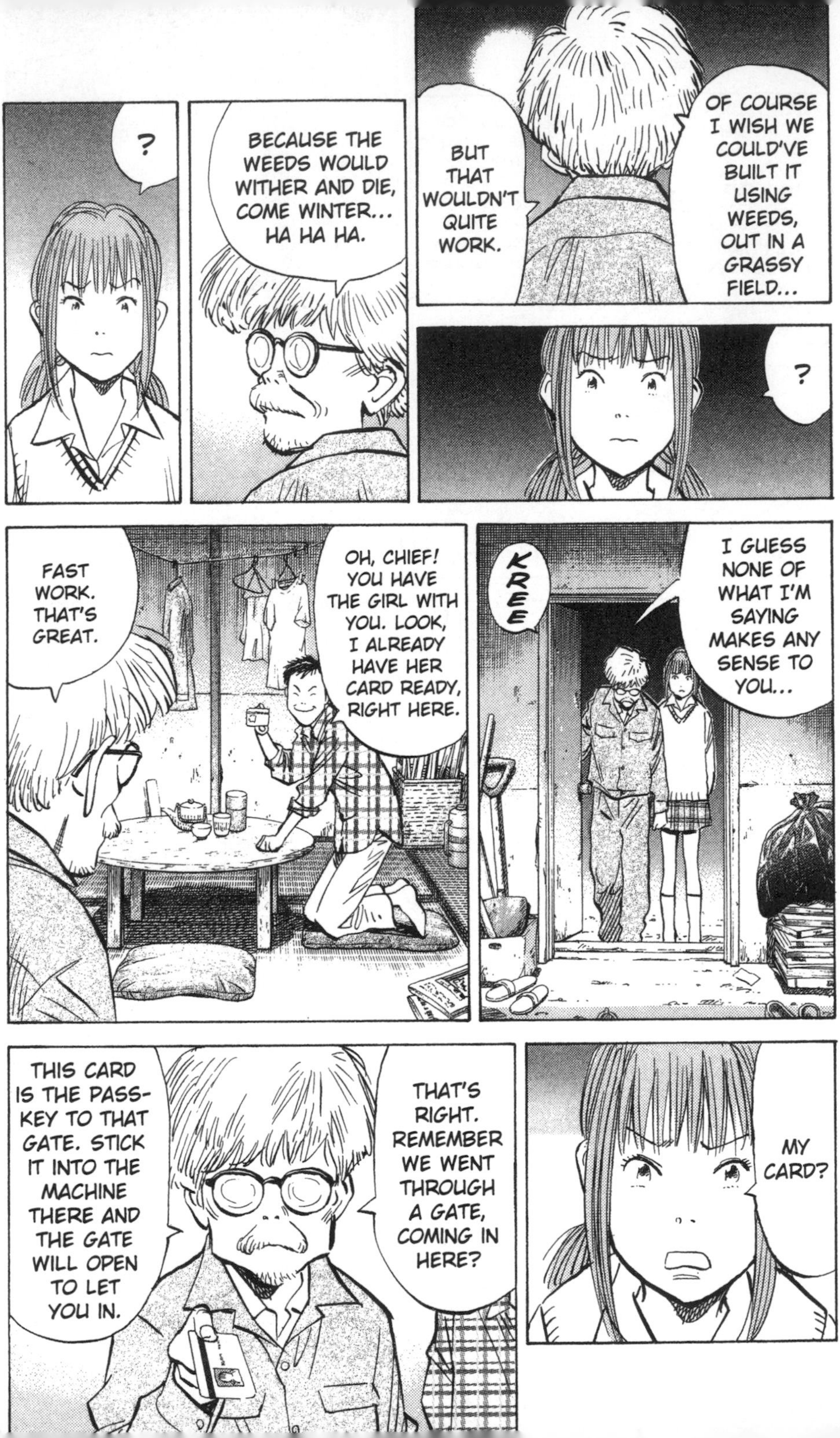
OF COURSE I WISH WE COULD'VE BUILT IT USING WEEDS, OUT IN A GRASSY FIELD...
BUT THAT WOULDN'T QUITE WORK.
?
BECAUSE THE WEEDS WOULD WITHER AND DIE, COME WINTER... HA HA HA.
?
I GUESS NONE OF WHAT I'M SAYING MAKES ANY SENSE TO YOU...
KREE
OH, CHIEF! YOU HAVE THE GIRL WITH YOU. LOOK, I ALREADY HAVE HER CARD READY, RIGHT HERE.
FAST WORK. THAT'S GREAT.
MY CARD?
THAT'S RIGHT. REMEMBER WE WENT THROUGH A GATE, COMING IN HERE?
THIS CARD IS THE PASS-KEY TO THAT GATE. STICK IT INTO THE MACHINE THERE AND THE GATE WILL OPEN TO LET YOU IN.

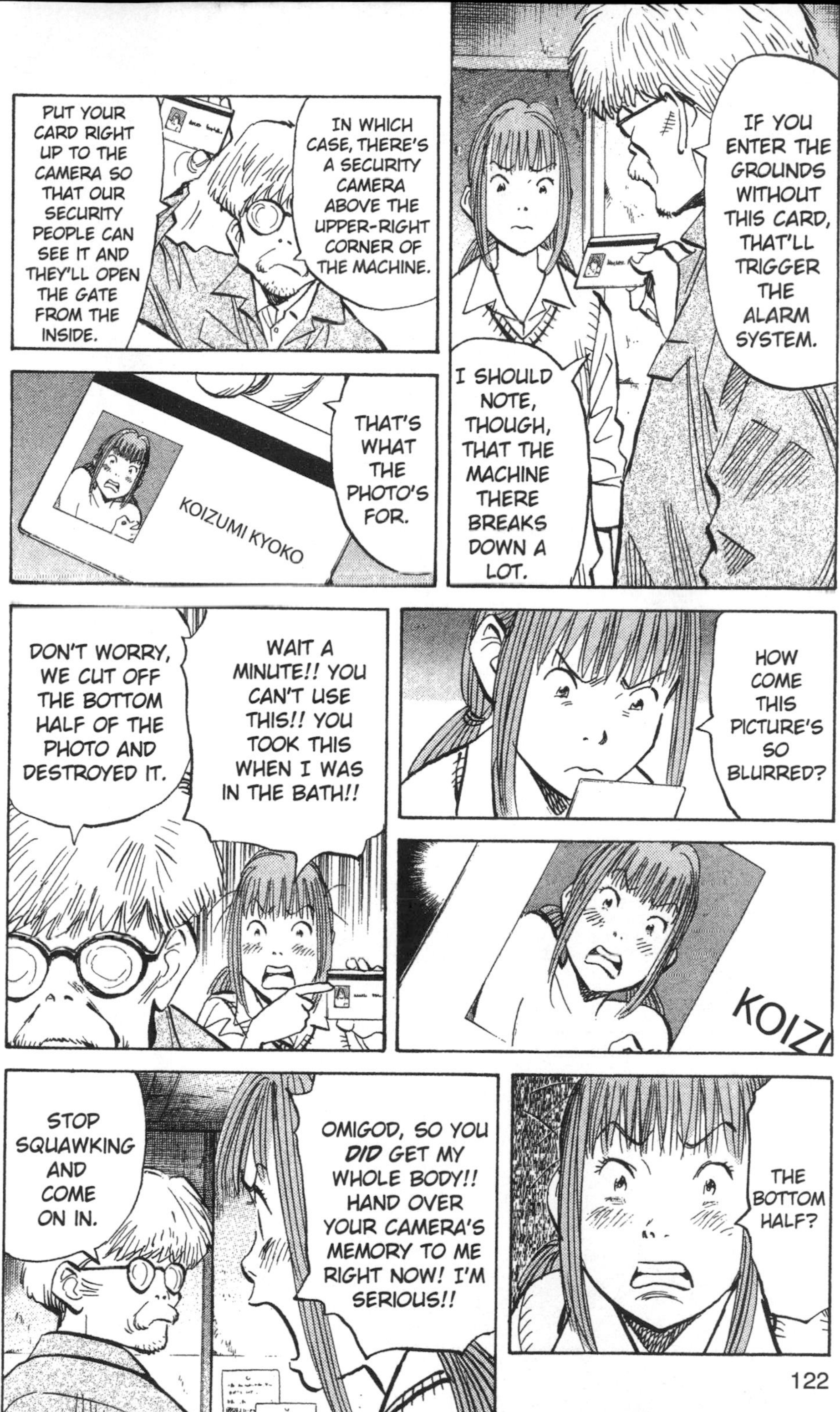
IF YOU ENTER THE GROUNDS WITHOUT THIS CARD, THAT'LL TRIGGER THE ALARM SYSTEM.
I SHOULD NOTE, THOUGH, THAT THE MACHINE THERE BREAKS DOWN A LOT.
IN WHICH CASE, THERE'S A SECURITY CAMERA ABOVE THE UPPER-RIGHT CORNER OF THE MACHINE.
PUT YOUR CARD RIGHT UP TO THE CAMERA SO THAT OUR SECURITY PEOPLE CAN SEE IT AND THEY'LL OPEN THE GATE FROM THE INSIDE.
THAT'S WHAT THE PHOTO'S FOR.
KOIZUMI KYOKO
HOW COME THIS PICTURE'S SO BLURRED?
KOIZ
WAIT A MINUTE!! YOU CAN'T USE THIS!! YOU TOOK THIS WHEN I WAS IN THE BATH!!
DON'T WORRY, WE CUT OFF THE BOTTOM HALF OF THE PHOTO AND DESTROYED IT.
THE BOTTOM HALF?
OMIGOD, SO YOU *DID* GET MY WHOLE BODY!! HAND OVER YOUR CAMERA'S MEMORY TO ME RIGHT NOW! I'M SERIOUS!!
STOP SQUAWKING AND COME ON IN.

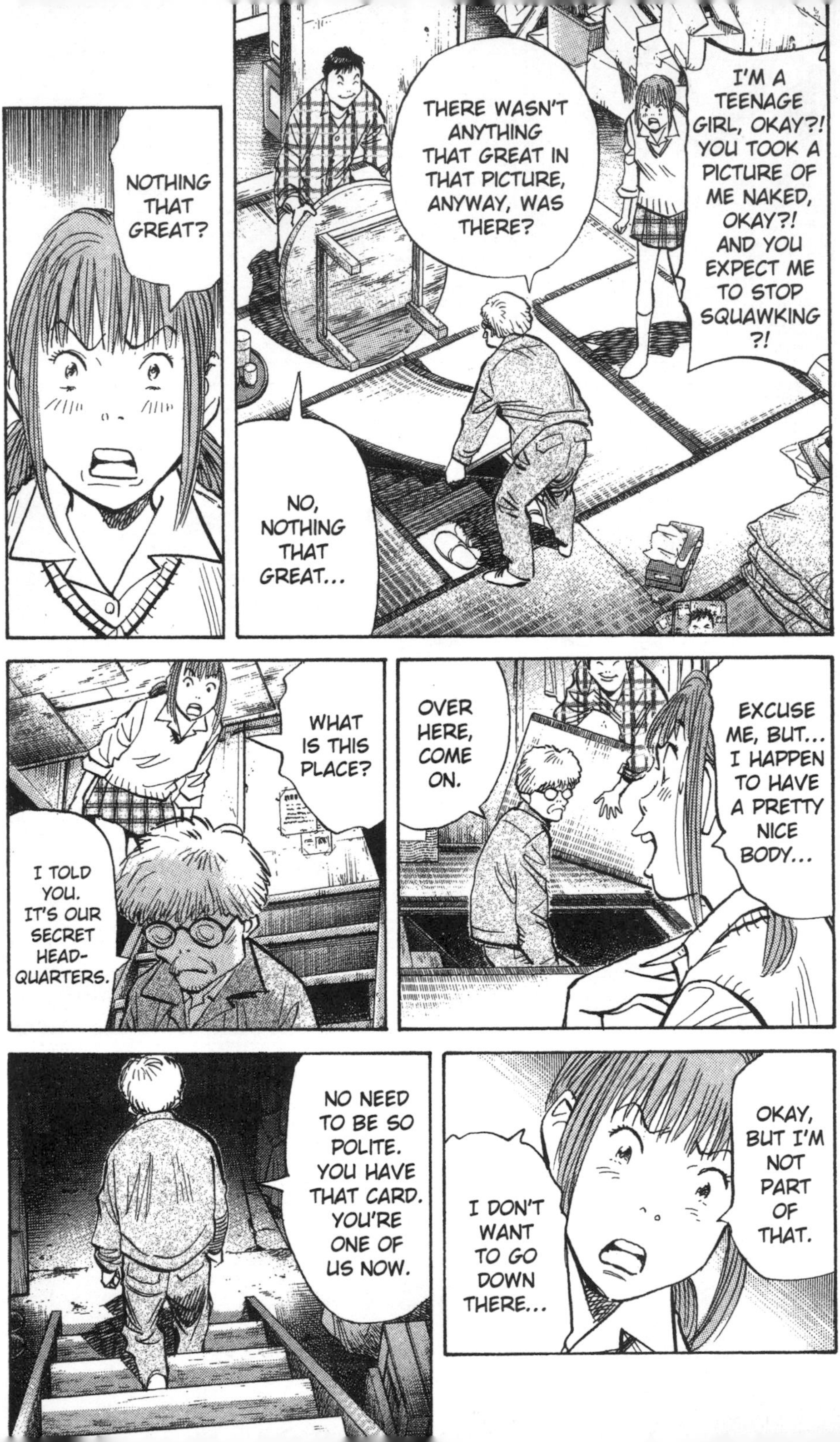
I'M A TEENAGE GIRL, OKAY?! YOU TOOK A PICTURE OF ME NAKED, OKAY?! AND YOU EXPECT ME TO STOP SQUAWKING?!
THERE WASN'T ANYTHING THAT GREAT IN THAT PICTURE, ANYWAY, WAS THERE?
NO, NOTHING THAT GREAT...
NOTHING THAT GREAT?
EXCUSE ME, BUT... I HAPPEN TO HAVE A PRETTY NICE BODY...
OVER HERE, COME ON.
WHAT IS THIS PLACE?
I TOLD YOU. IT'S OUR SECRET HEAD-QUARTERS.
OKAY, BUT I'M NOT PART OF THAT.
I DON'T WANT TO GO DOWN THERE...
NO NEED TO BE SO POLITE. YOU HAVE THAT CARD. YOU'RE ONE OF US NOW.

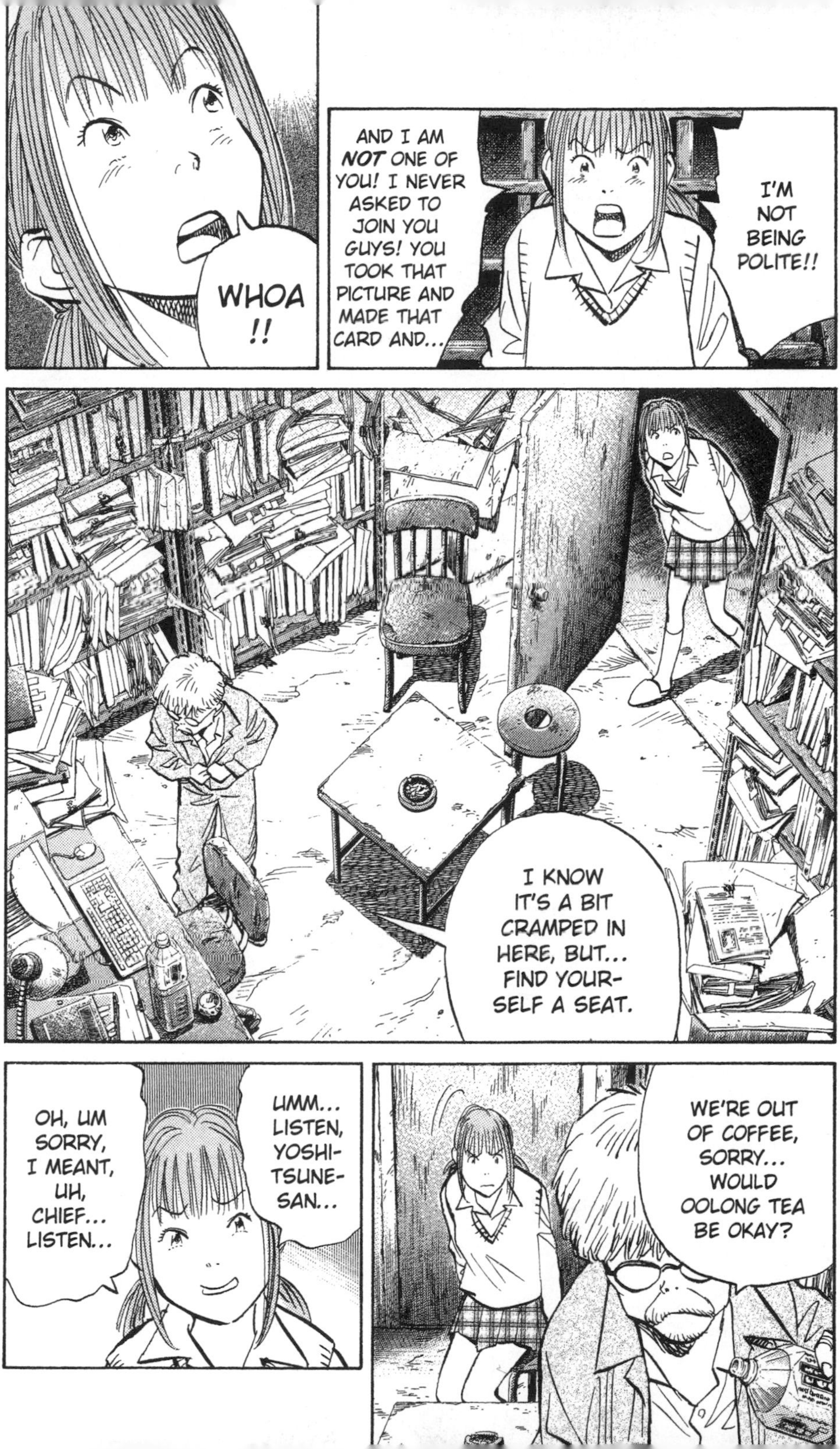
I'M NOT BEING POLITE!!
AND I AM NOT ONE OF YOU! I NEVER ASKED TO JOIN YOU GUYS! YOU TOOK THAT PICTURE AND MADE THAT CARD AND...
WHOA !!
I KNOW IT'S A BIT CRAMPED IN HERE, BUT... FIND YOUR-SELF A SEAT.
WE'RE OUT OF COFFEE, SORRY... WOULD OOLONG TEA BE OKAY?
UMM... LISTEN, YOSHI-TSUNE-SAN...
OH, UM SORRY, I MEANT, UH, CHIEF... LISTEN...

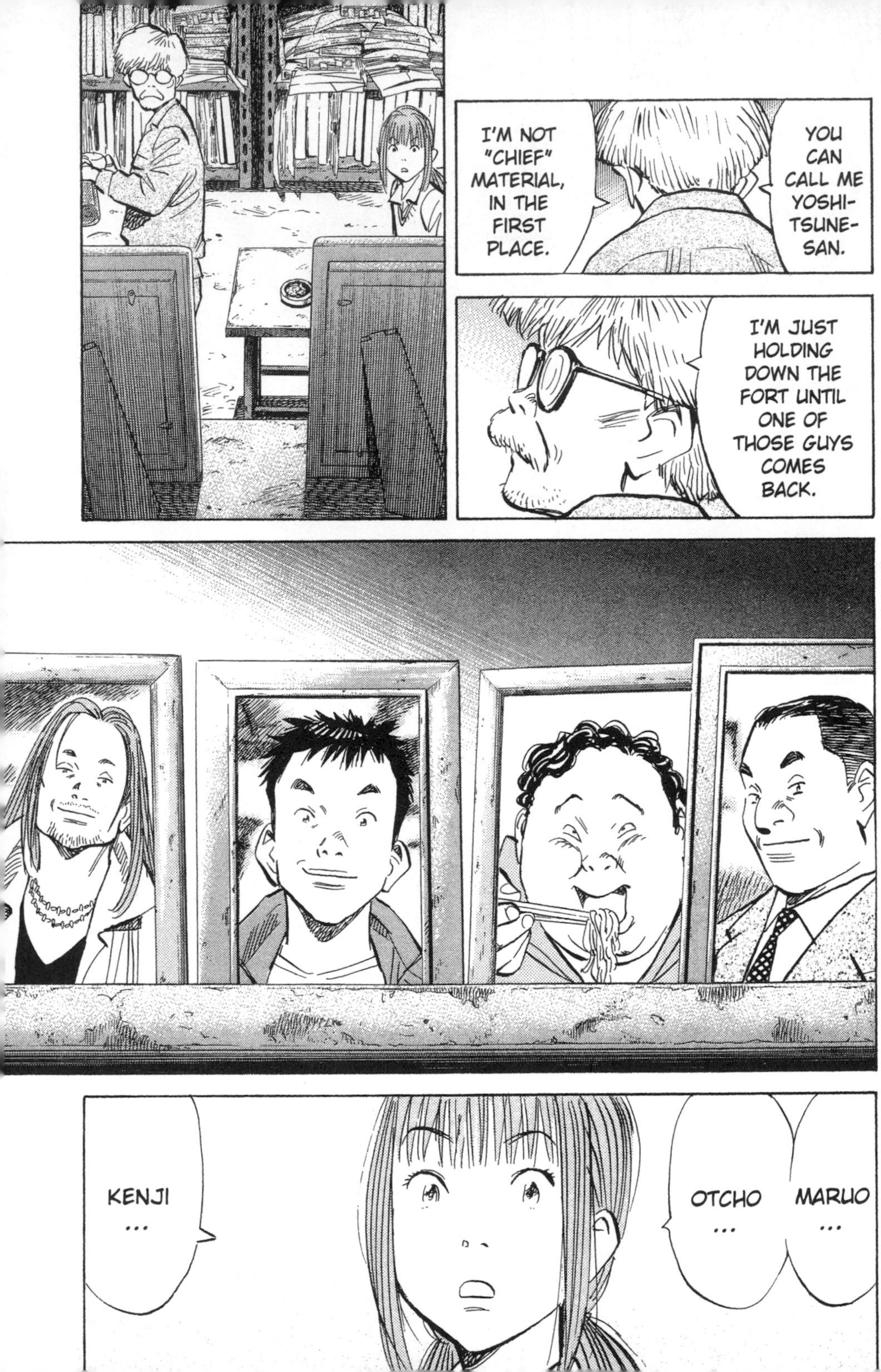
YOU CAN CALL ME YOSHI-TSUNE-SAN.
I'M NOT "CHIEF" MATERIAL, IN THE FIRST PLACE.
I'M JUST HOLDING DOWN THE FORT UNTIL ONE OF THOSE GUYS COMES BACK.
MARUO ...
OTCHO ...
KENJI ...

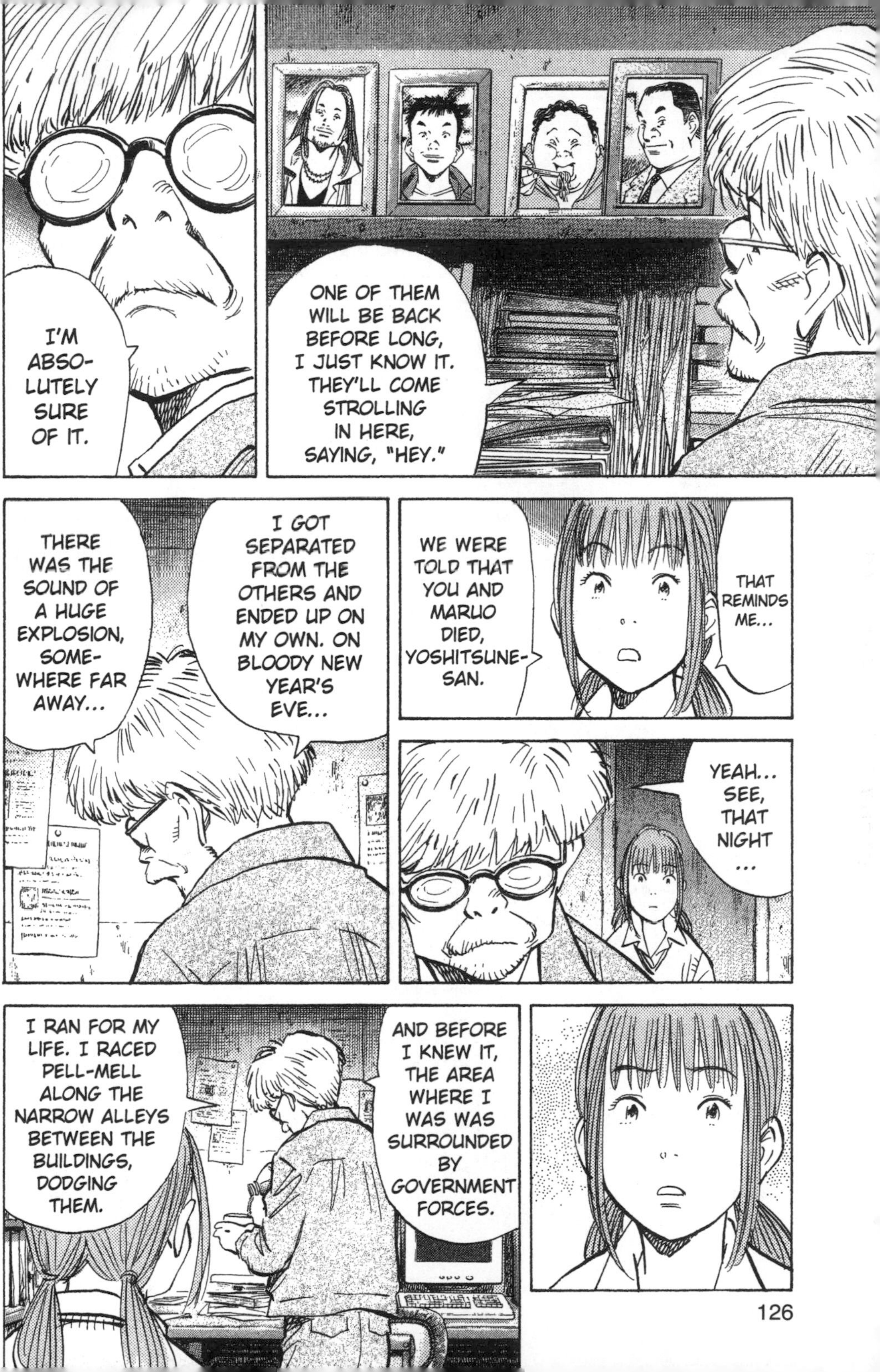
ONE OF THEM WILL BE BACK BEFORE LONG, I JUST KNOW IT. THEY'LL COME STROLLING IN HERE, SAYING, "HEY."
I'M ABSO-LUTELY SURE OF IT.
THAT REMINDS ME...
WE WERE TOLD THAT YOU AND MARUO DIED, YOSHITSUNE-SAN.
YEAH... SEE, THAT NIGHT...
I GOT SEPARATED FROM THE OTHERS AND ENDED UP ON MY OWN. ON BLOODY NEW YEAR'S EVE...
THERE WAS THE SOUND OF A HUGE EXPLOSION, SOME-WHERE FAR AWAY...
AND BEFORE I KNEW IT, THE AREA WHERE I WAS WAS SURROUNDED BY GOVERNMENT FORCES.
I RAN FOR MY LIFE. I RACED PELL-MELL ALONG THE NARROW ALLEYS BETWEEN THE BUILDINGS, DODGING THEM.

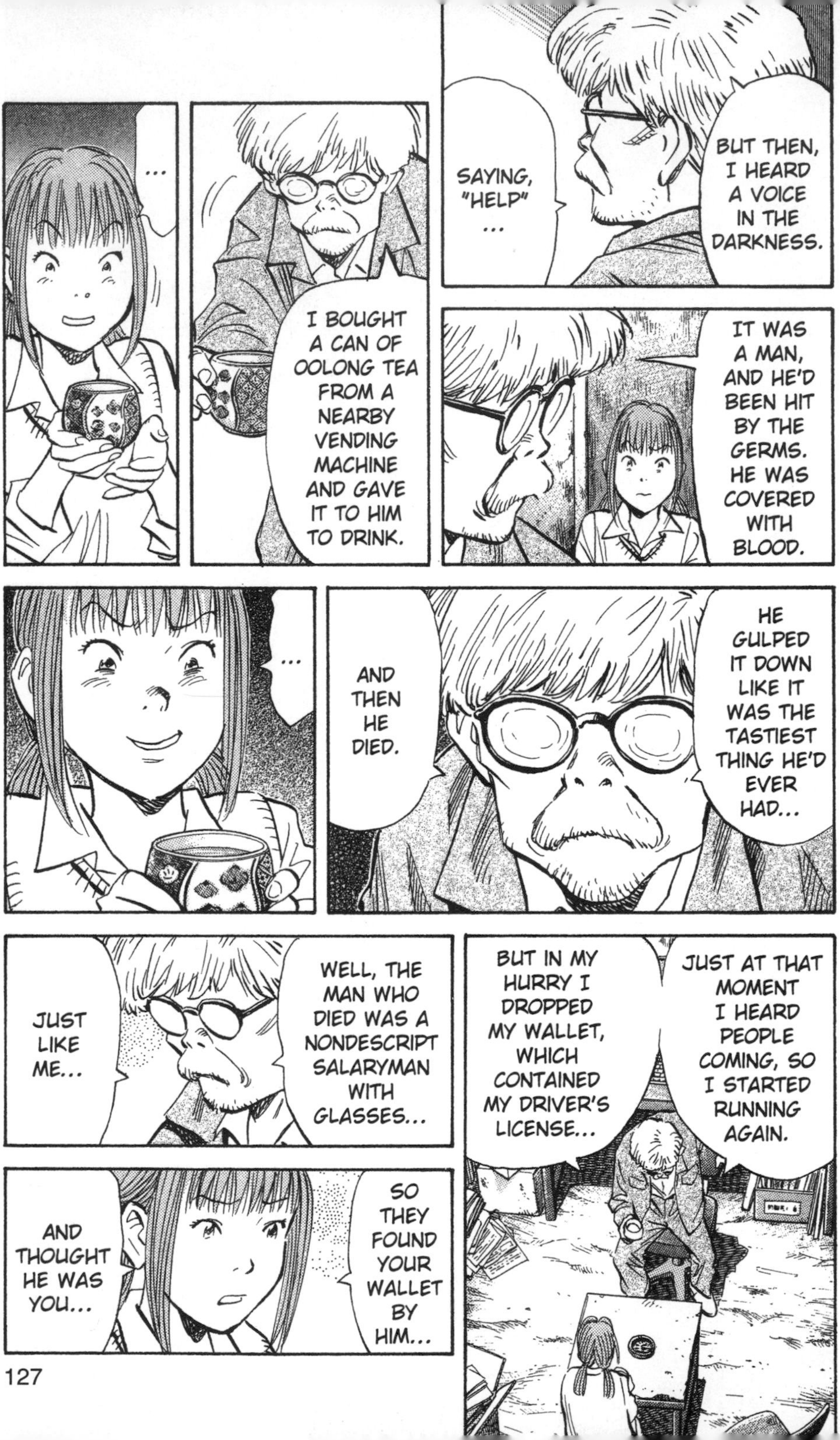
BUT THEN, I HEARD A VOICE IN THE DARKNESS.
SAYING, "HELP" ...
IT WAS A MAN, AND HE'D BEEN HIT BY THE GERMS. HE WAS COVERED WITH BLOOD.
I BOUGHT A CAN OF OOLONG TEA FROM A NEARBY VENDING MACHINE AND GAVE IT TO HIM TO DRINK.
...
HE GULPED IT DOWN LIKE IT WAS THE TASTIEST THING HE'D EVER HAD...
AND THEN HE DIED.
...
JUST AT THAT MOMENT I HEARD PEOPLE COMING, SO I STARTED RUNNING AGAIN.
BUT IN MY HURRY I DROPPED MY WALLET, WHICH CONTAINED MY DRIVER'S LICENSE...
WELL, THE MAN WHO DIED WAS A NONDESCRIPT SALARYMAN WITH GLASSES...
JUST LIKE ME...
SO THEY FOUND YOUR WALLET BY HIM...
AND THOUGHT HE WAS YOU...

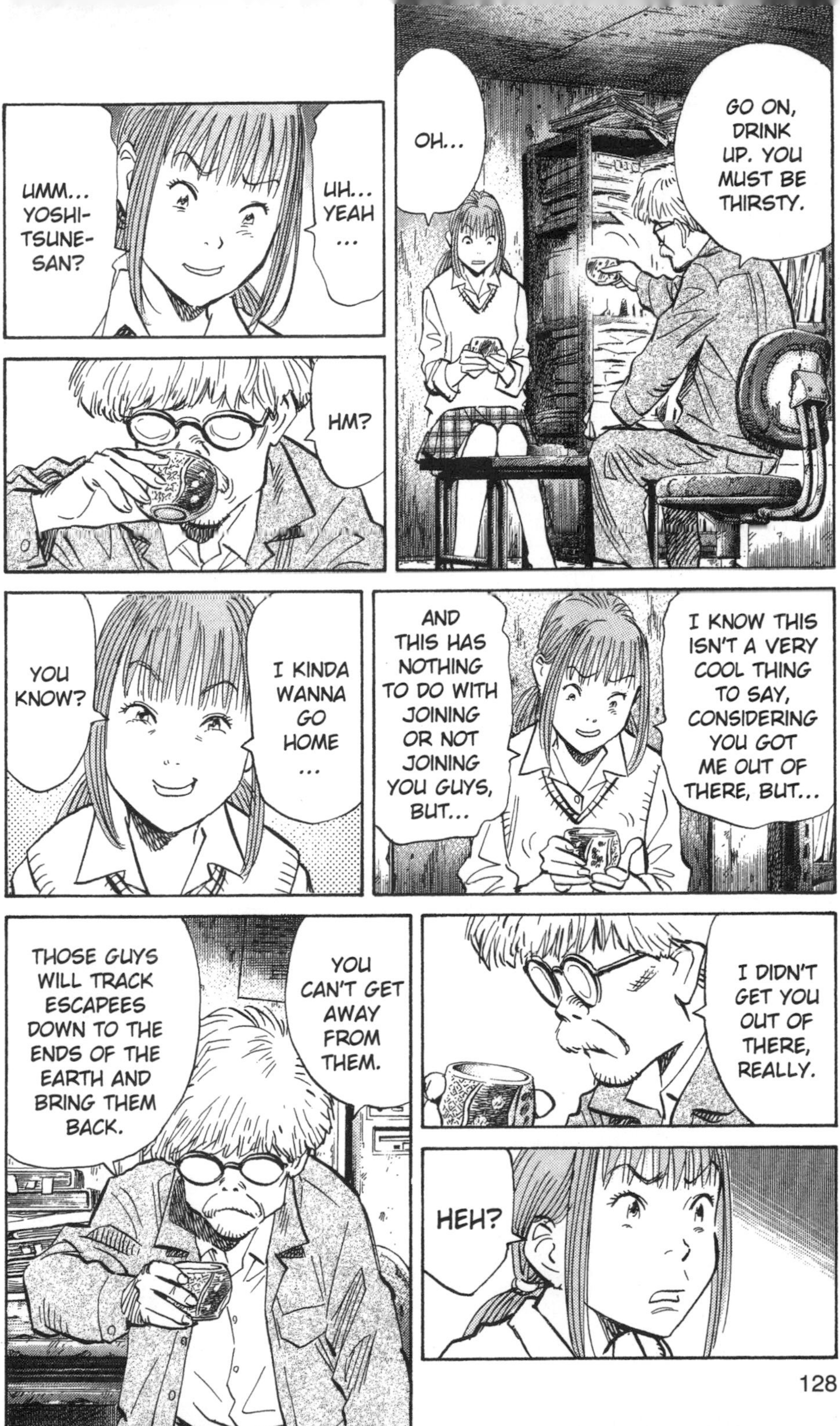
GO ON, DRINK UP. YOU MUST BE THIRSTY.
OH...
UH... YEAH ...
UMM... YOSHI-TSUNE-SAN?
HM?
I KNOW THIS ISN'T A VERY COOL THING TO SAY, CONSIDERING YOU GOT ME OUT OF THERE, BUT...
AND THIS HAS NOTHING TO DO WITH JOINING OR NOT JOINING YOU GUYS, BUT...
I KINDA WANNA GO HOME ...
YOU KNOW?
I DIDN'T GET YOU OUT OF THERE, REALLY.
HEH?
YOU CAN'T GET AWAY FROM THEM.
THOSE GUYS WILL TRACK ESCAPEES DOWN TO THE ENDS OF THE EARTH AND BRING THEM BACK.

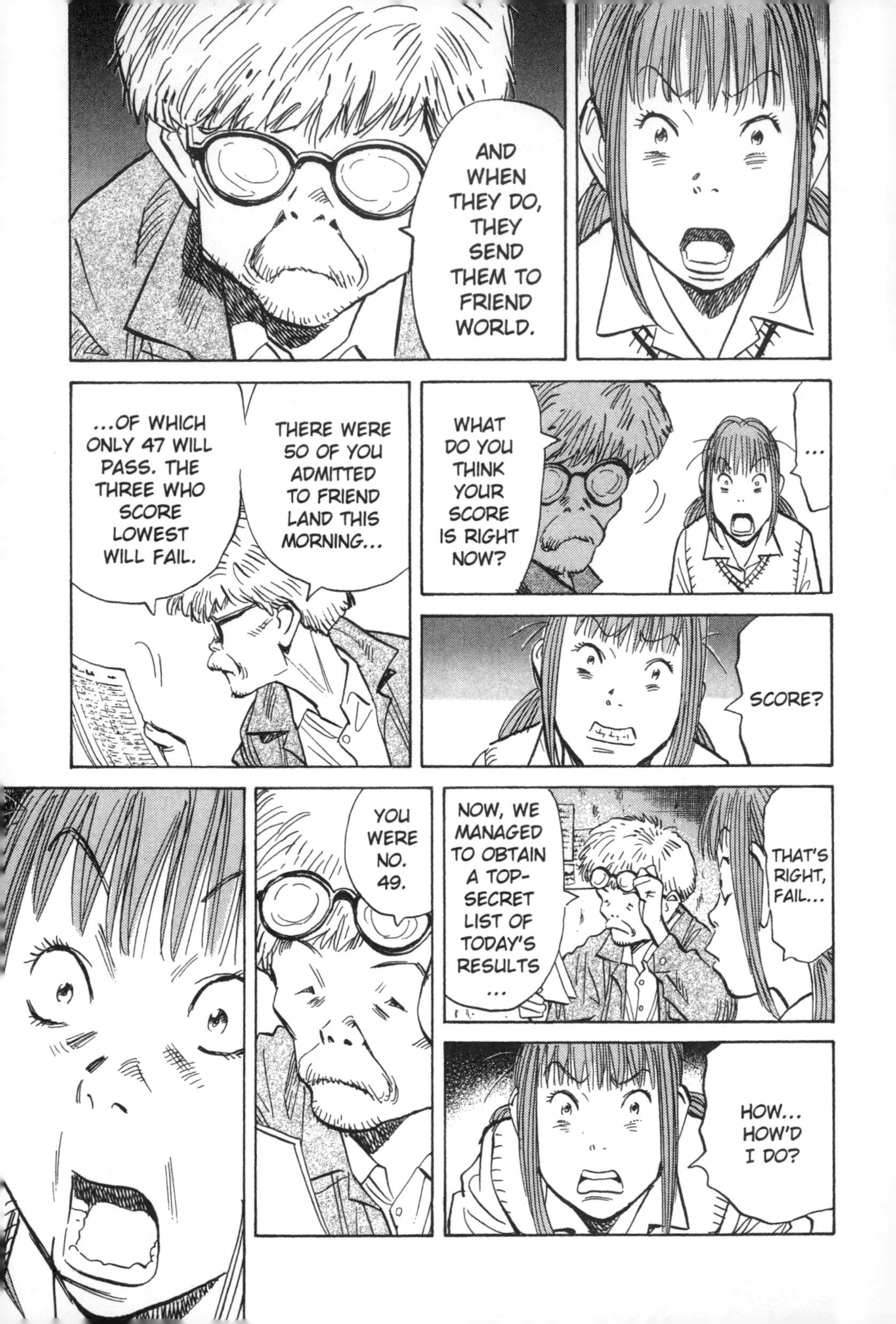
AND WHEN THEY DO, THEY SEND THEM TO FRIEND WORLD.
...
WHAT DO YOU THINK YOUR SCORE IS RIGHT NOW?
SCORE?
THERE WERE 50 OF YOU ADMITTED TO FRIEND LAND THIS MORNING...
...OF WHICH ONLY 47 WILL PASS. THE THREE WHO SCORE LOWEST WILL FAIL.
THAT'S RIGHT, FAIL...
NOW, WE MANAGED TO OBTAIN A TOP-SECRET LIST OF TODAY'S RESULTS ...
HOW... HOW'D I DO?
YOU WERE NO. 49.

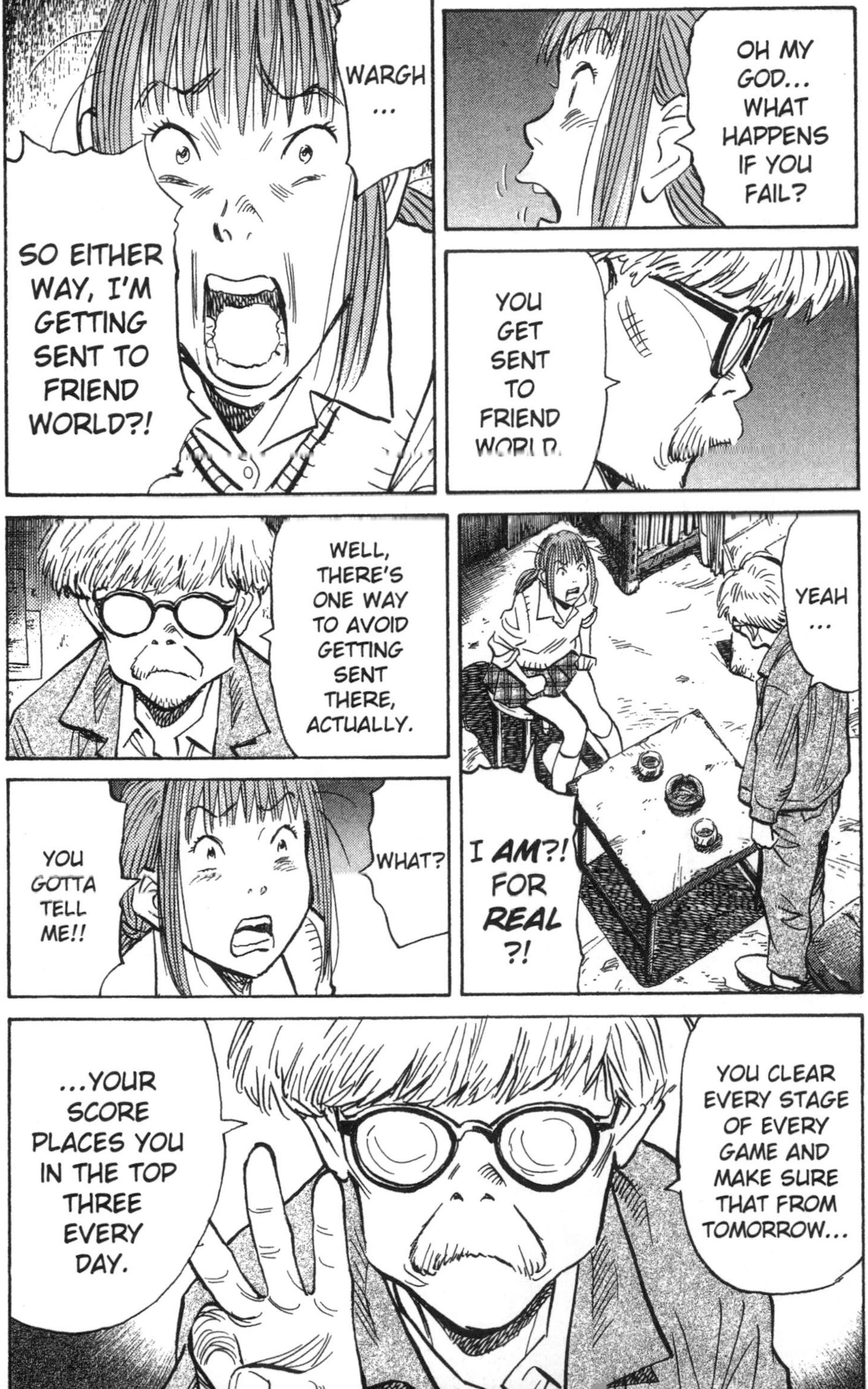
OH MY GOD... WHAT HAPPENS IF YOU FAIL?
YOU GET SENT TO FRIEND WORLD.
WARGH...
SO EITHER WAY, I'M GETTING SENT TO FRIEND WORLD?!
YEAH...
I AM?! FOR REAL?!
WELL, THERE'S ONE WAY TO AVOID GETTING SENT THERE, ACTUALLY.
WHAT?
YOU GOTTA TELL ME!!
YOU CLEAR EVERY STAGE OF EVERY GAME AND MAKE SURE THAT FROM TOMORROW...
...YOUR SCORE PLACES YOU IN THE TOP THREE EVERY DAY.

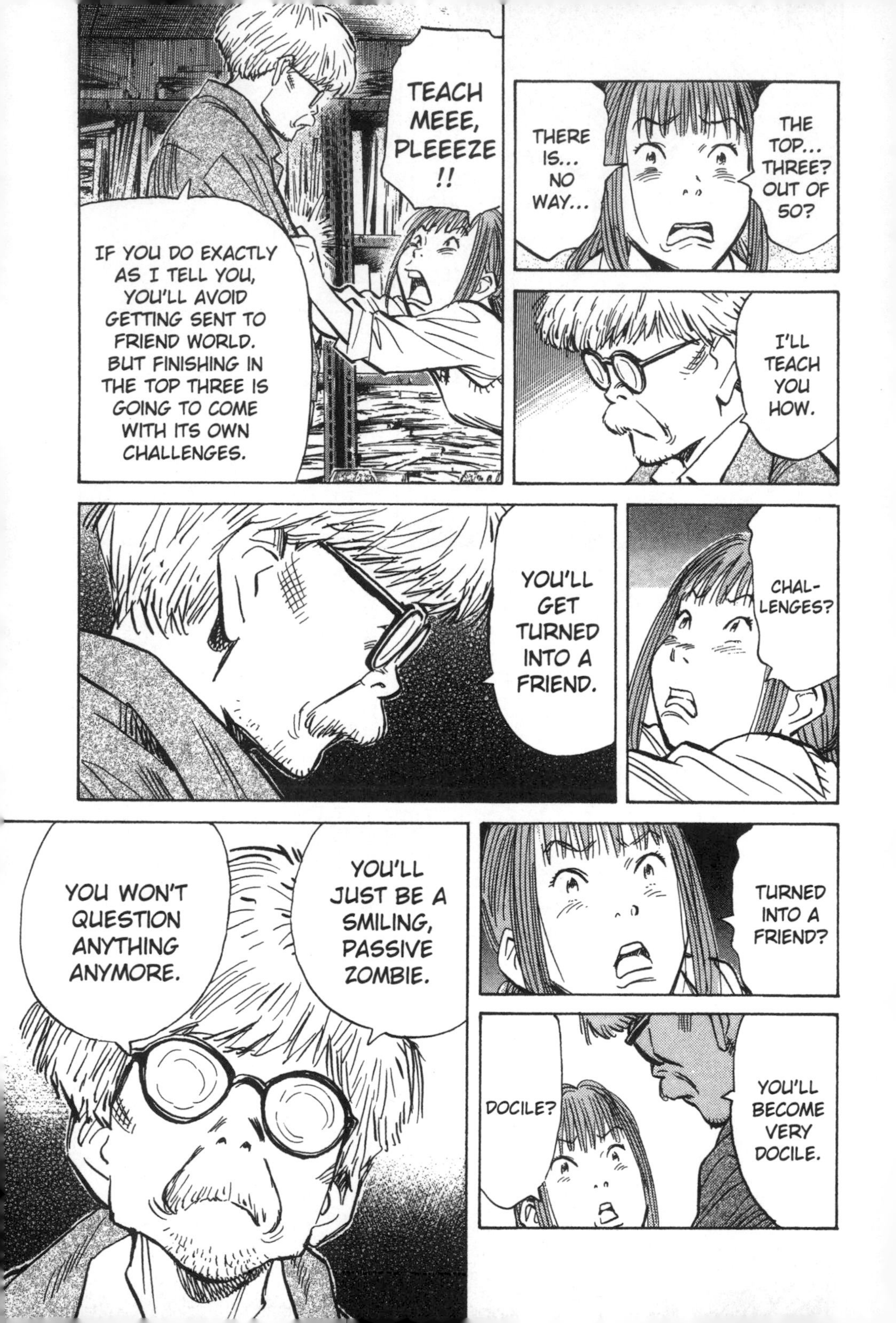
THE TOP... THREE? OUT OF 50?
THERE IS... NO WAY...
I'LL TEACH YOU HOW.
TEACH MEEE, PLEEEZE!!
IF YOU DO EXACTLY AS I TELL YOU, YOU'LL AVOID GETTING SENT TO FRIEND WORLD. BUT FINISHING IN THE TOP THREE IS GOING TO COME WITH ITS OWN CHALLENGES.
CHAL-LENGES?
YOU'LL GET TURNED INTO A FRIEND.
TURNED INTO A FRIEND?
YOU'LL BECOME VERY DOCILE.
DOCILE?
YOU'LL JUST BE A SMILING, PASSIVE ZOMBIE.
YOU WON'T QUESTION ANYTHING ANYMORE.

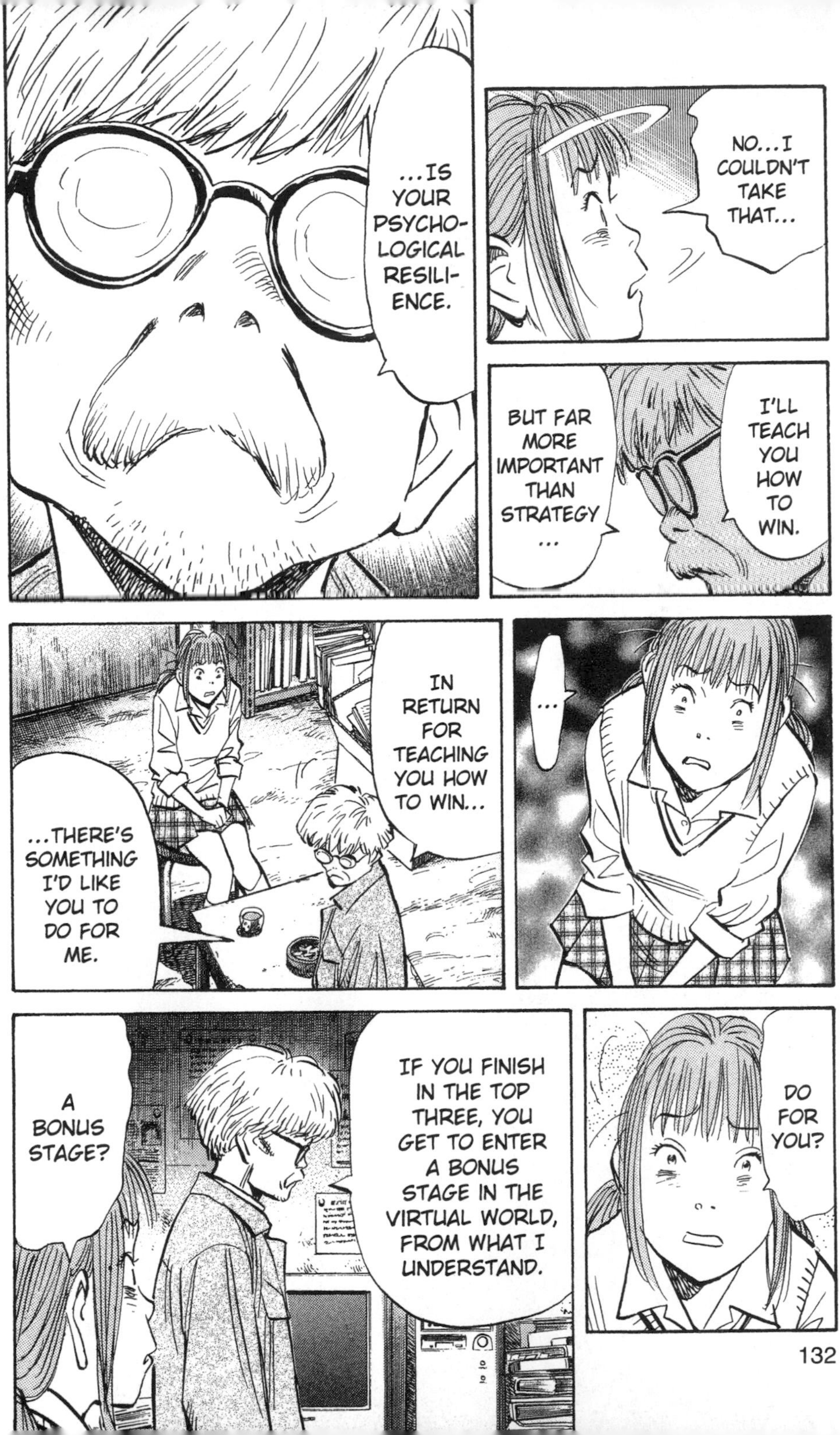

NO...I COULDN'T TAKE THAT...
I'LL TEACH YOU HOW TO WIN.
BUT FAR MORE IMPORTANT THAN STRATEGY...
...IS YOUR PSYCHOLOGICAL RESILIENCE.
...
IN RETURN FOR TEACHING YOU HOW TO WIN...
...THERE'S SOMETHING I'D LIKE YOU TO DO FOR ME.
DO FOR YOU?
IF YOU FINISH IN THE TOP THREE, YOU GET TO ENTER A BONUS STAGE IN THE VIRTUAL WORLD, FROM WHAT I UNDERSTAND.
A BONUS STAGE?

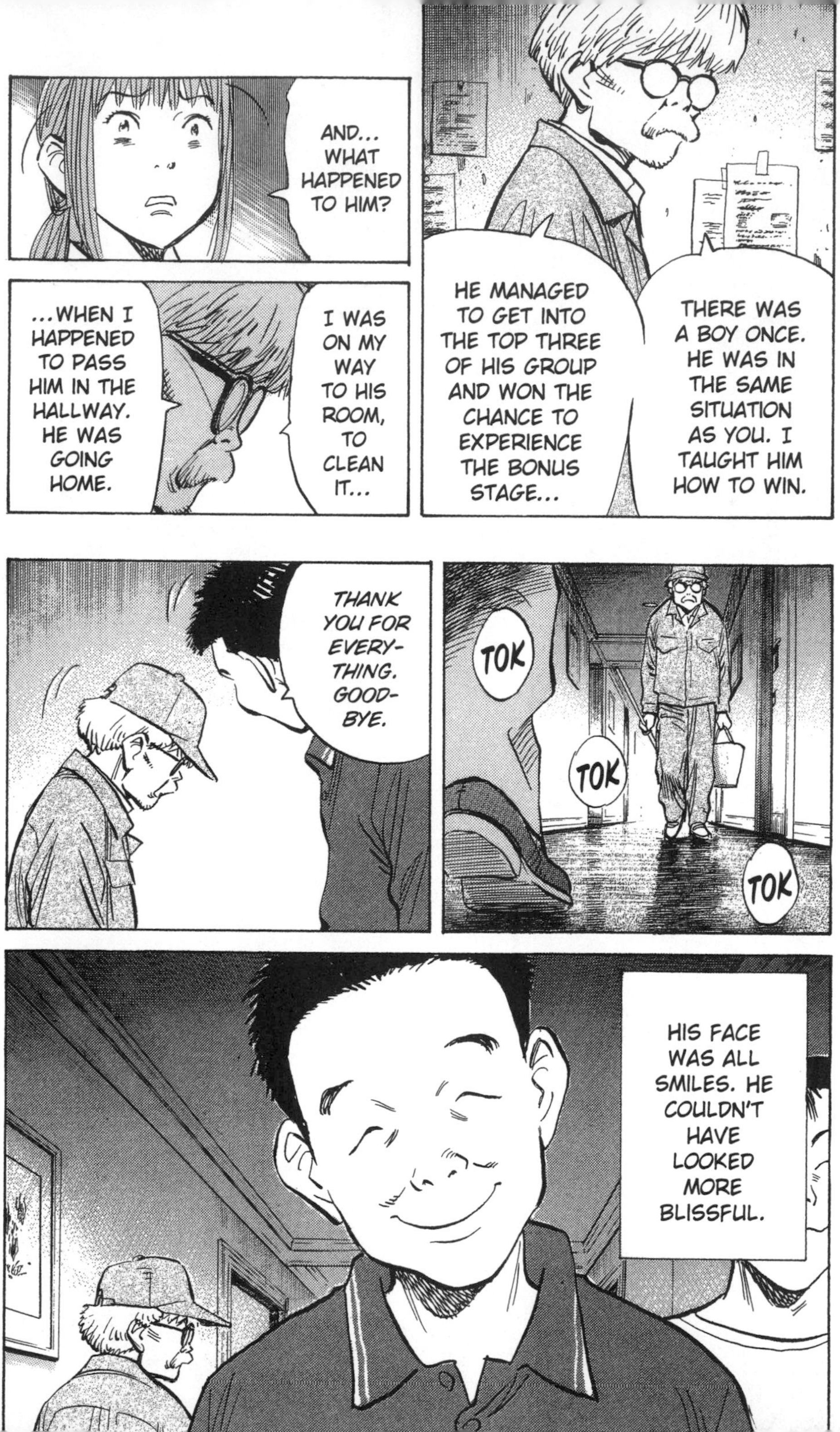
THERE WAS A BOY ONCE. HE WAS IN THE SAME SITUATION AS YOU. I TAUGHT HIM HOW TO WIN.
HE MANAGED TO GET INTO THE TOP THREE OF HIS GROUP AND WON THE CHANCE TO EXPERIENCE THE BONUS STAGE...
AND... WHAT HAPPENED TO HIM?
I WAS ON MY WAY TO HIS ROOM, TO CLEAN IT...
...WHEN I HAPPENED TO PASS HIM IN THE HALLWAY. HE WAS GOING HOME.
TOK
TOK
TOK
THANK YOU FOR EVERY-THING. GOOD-BYE.
HIS FACE WAS ALL SMILES. HE COULDN'T HAVE LOOKED MORE BLISSFUL.

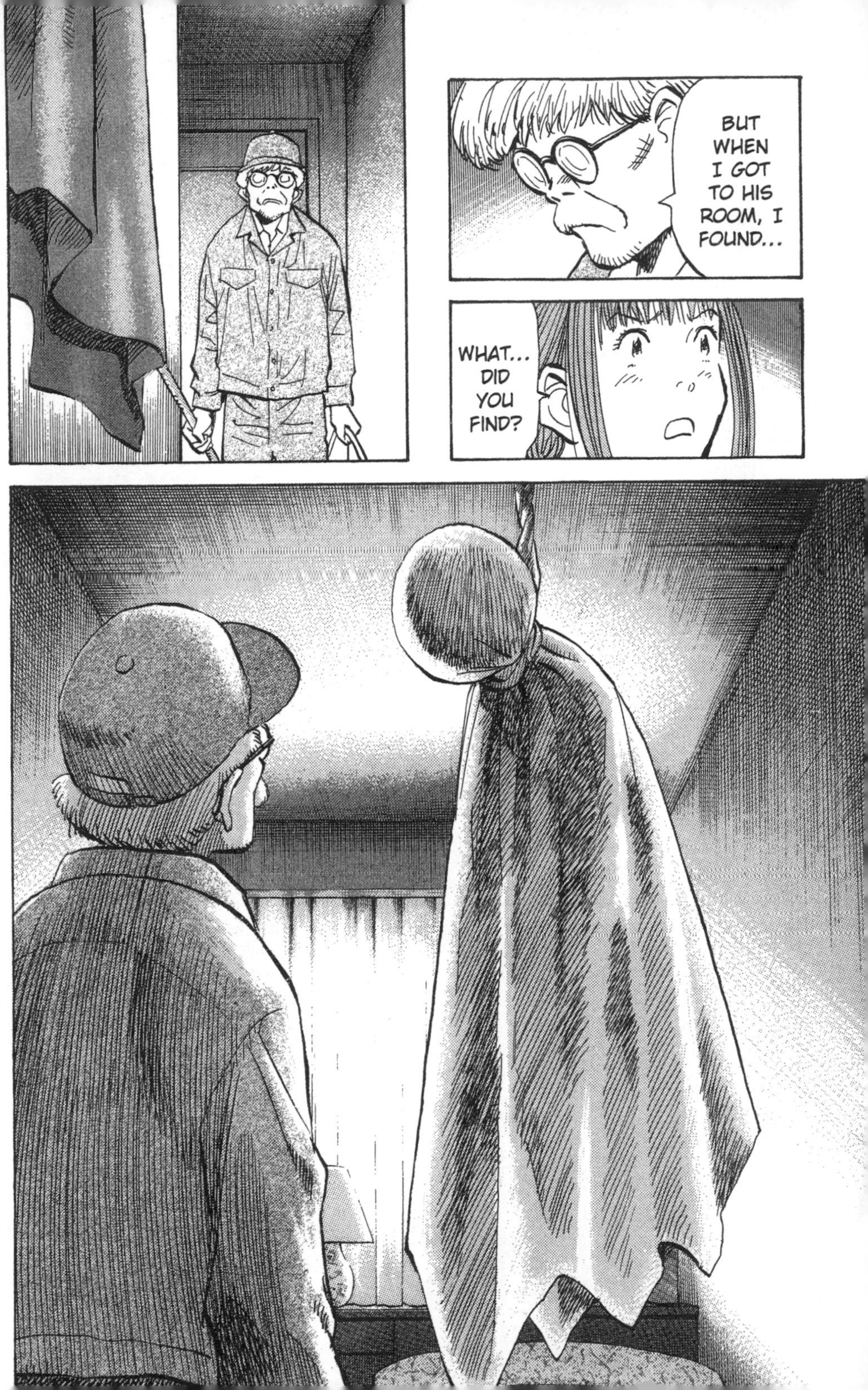
BUT WHEN I GOT TO HIS ROOM, I FOUND...
WHAT... DID YOU FIND?

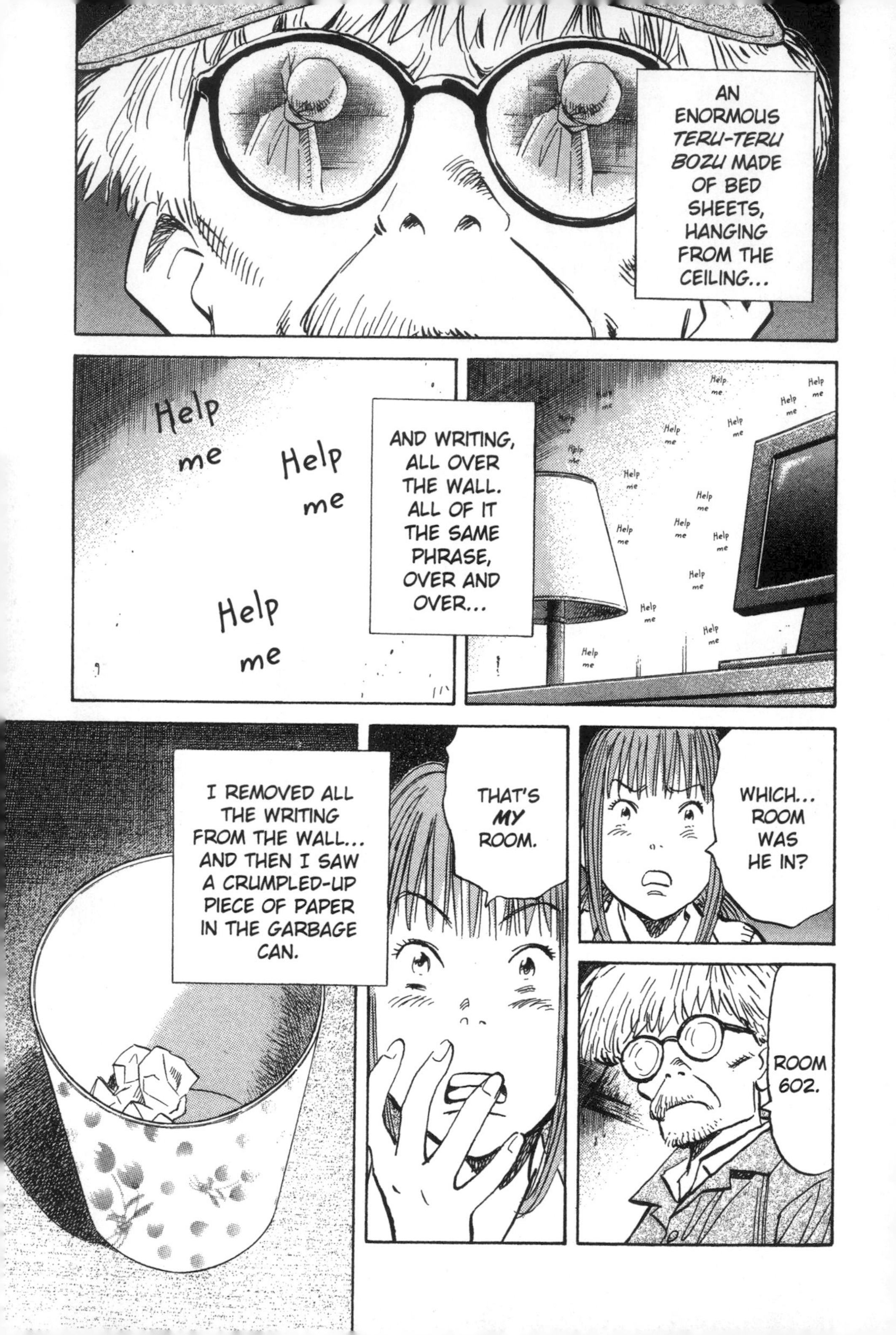
AN ENORMOUS *TERU-TERU BOZU* MADE OF BED SHEETS, HANGING FROM THE CEILING...
AND WRITING, ALL OVER THE WALL. ALL OF IT THE SAME PHRASE, OVER AND OVER...
Help me
Help me
Help me
WHICH... ROOM WAS HE IN?
ROOM 602.
THAT'S *MY* ROOM.
I REMOVED ALL THE WRITING FROM THE WALL... AND THEN I SAW A CRUMPLED-UP PIECE OF PAPER IN THE GARBAGE CAN.

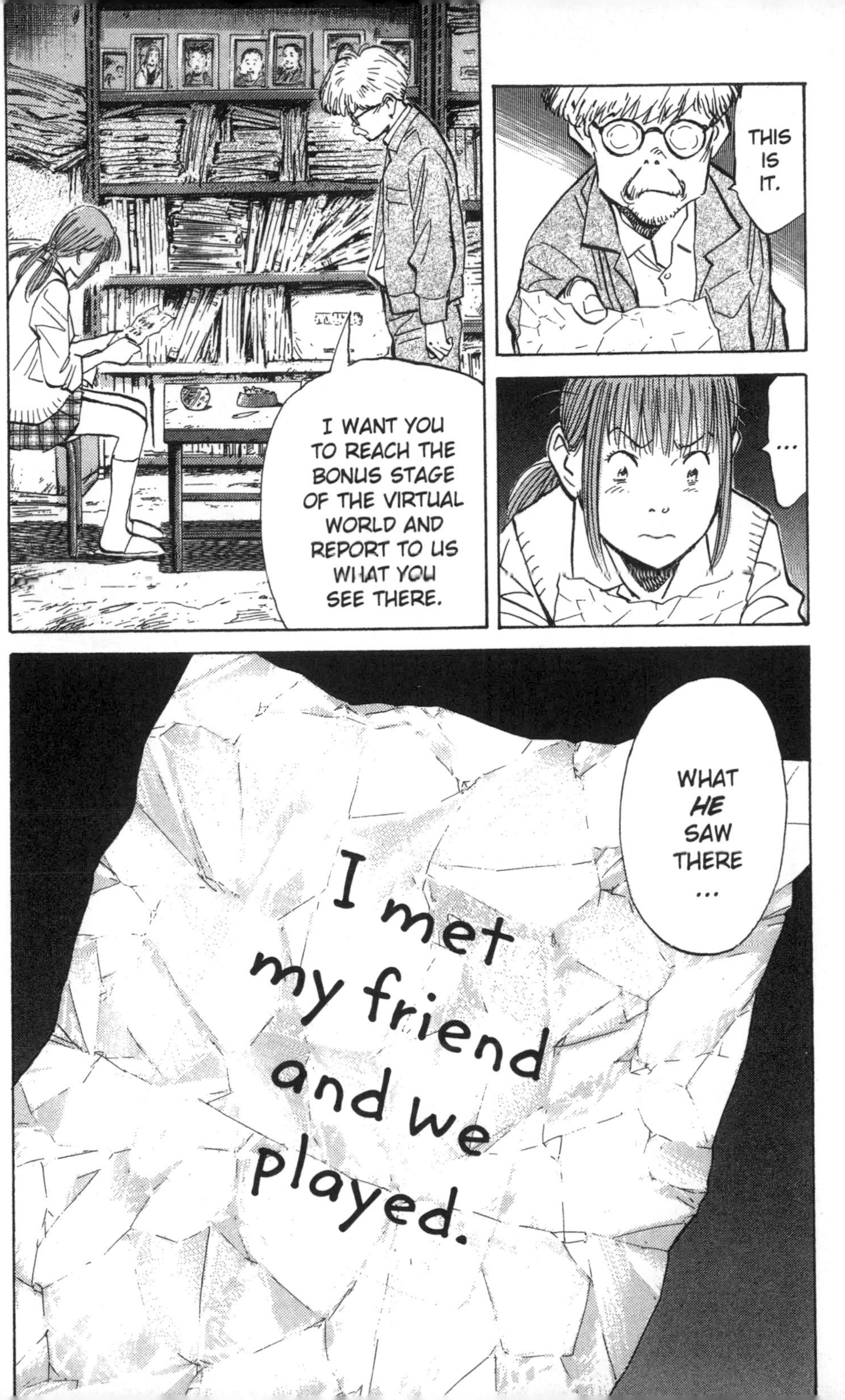
THIS IS IT.
...
I WANT YOU TO REACH THE BONUS STAGE OF THE VIRTUAL WORLD AND REPORT TO US WHAT YOU SEE THERE.
WHAT *HE* SAW THERE ...
I met my friend and we played.

Chapter 8 Score

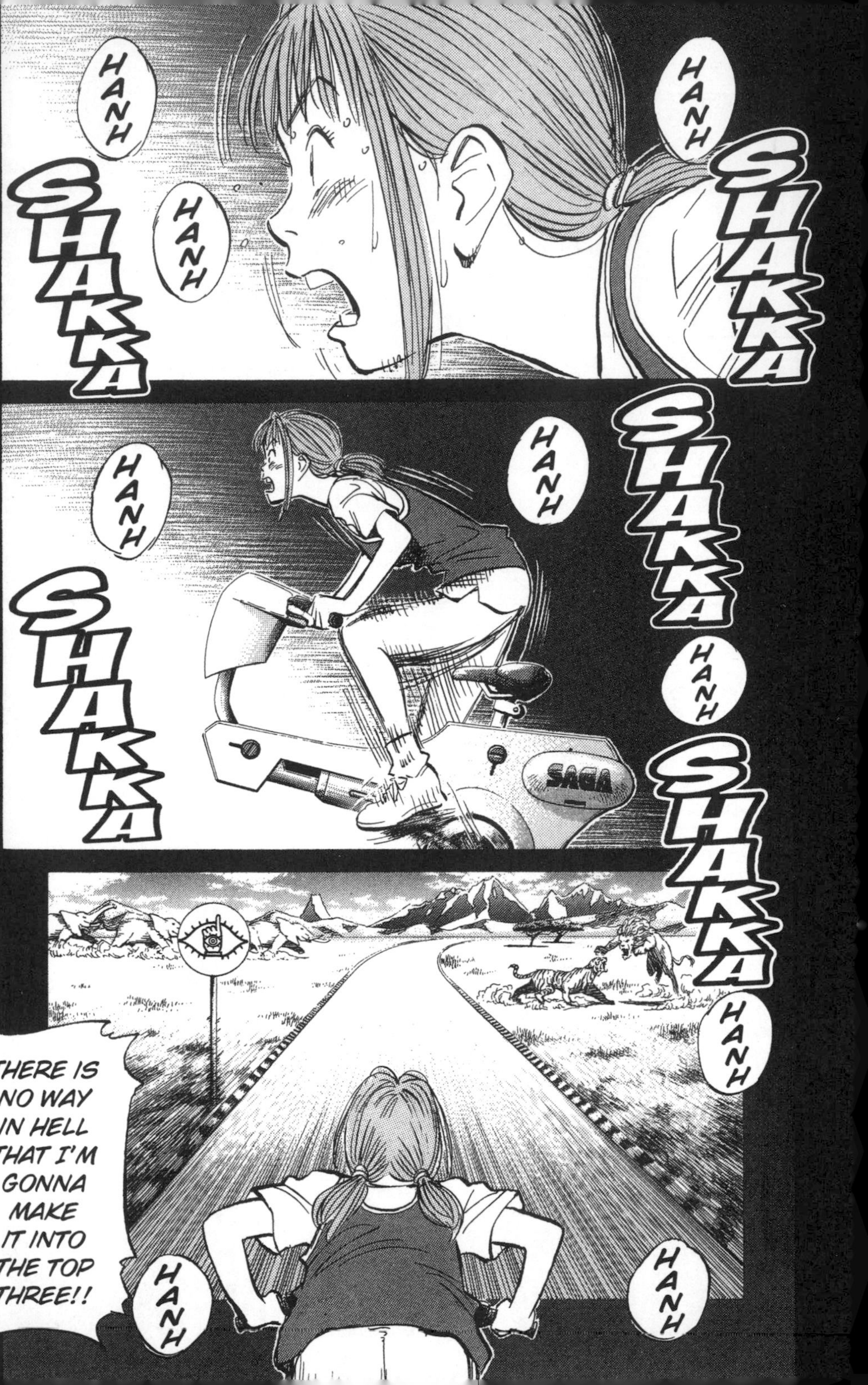
HANH
SHAKA
HANH
HANH
SHAKA
SHAKA
HANH
HANH
SHAKA
HANH
SHAKA
HANH
THERE IS NO WAY IN HELL THAT I'M GONNA MAKE IT INTO THE TOP THREE!!
HANH
HANH
SAGA

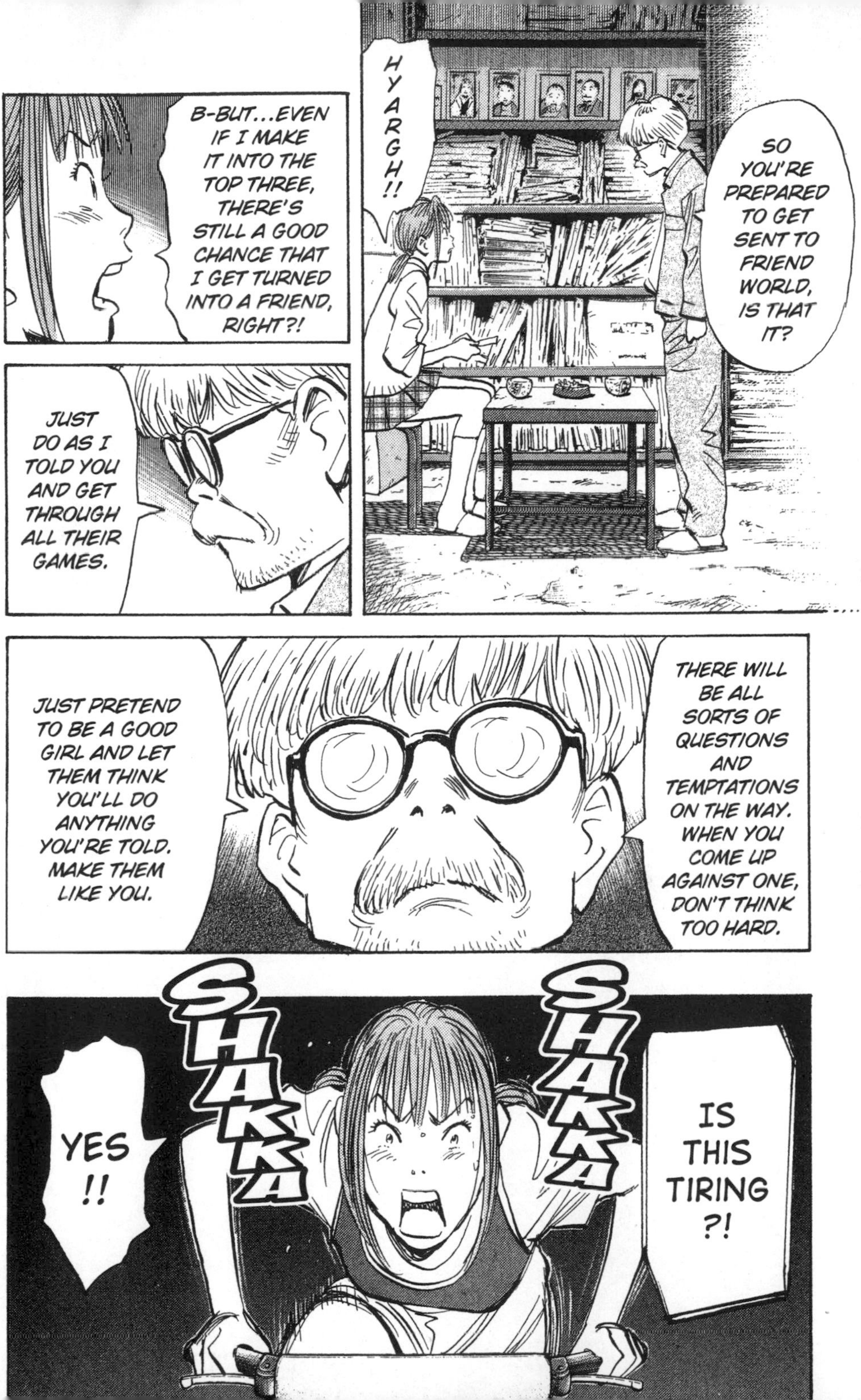
SO YOU'RE PREPARED TO GET SENT TO FRIEND WORLD, IS THAT IT?
HYARGH!!
B-BUT...EVEN IF I MAKE IT INTO THE TOP THREE, THERE'S STILL A GOOD CHANCE THAT I GET TURNED INTO A FRIEND, RIGHT?!
JUST DO AS I TOLD YOU AND GET THROUGH ALL THEIR GAMES.
THERE WILL BE ALL SORTS OF QUESTIONS AND TEMPTATIONS ON THE WAY. WHEN YOU COME UP AGAINST ONE, DON'T THINK TOO HARD.
JUST PRETEND TO BE A GOOD GIRL AND LET THEM THINK YOU'LL DO ANYTHING YOU'RE TOLD. MAKE THEM LIKE YOU.
IS THIS TIRING?!
SHAKA
SHAKA
YES!!

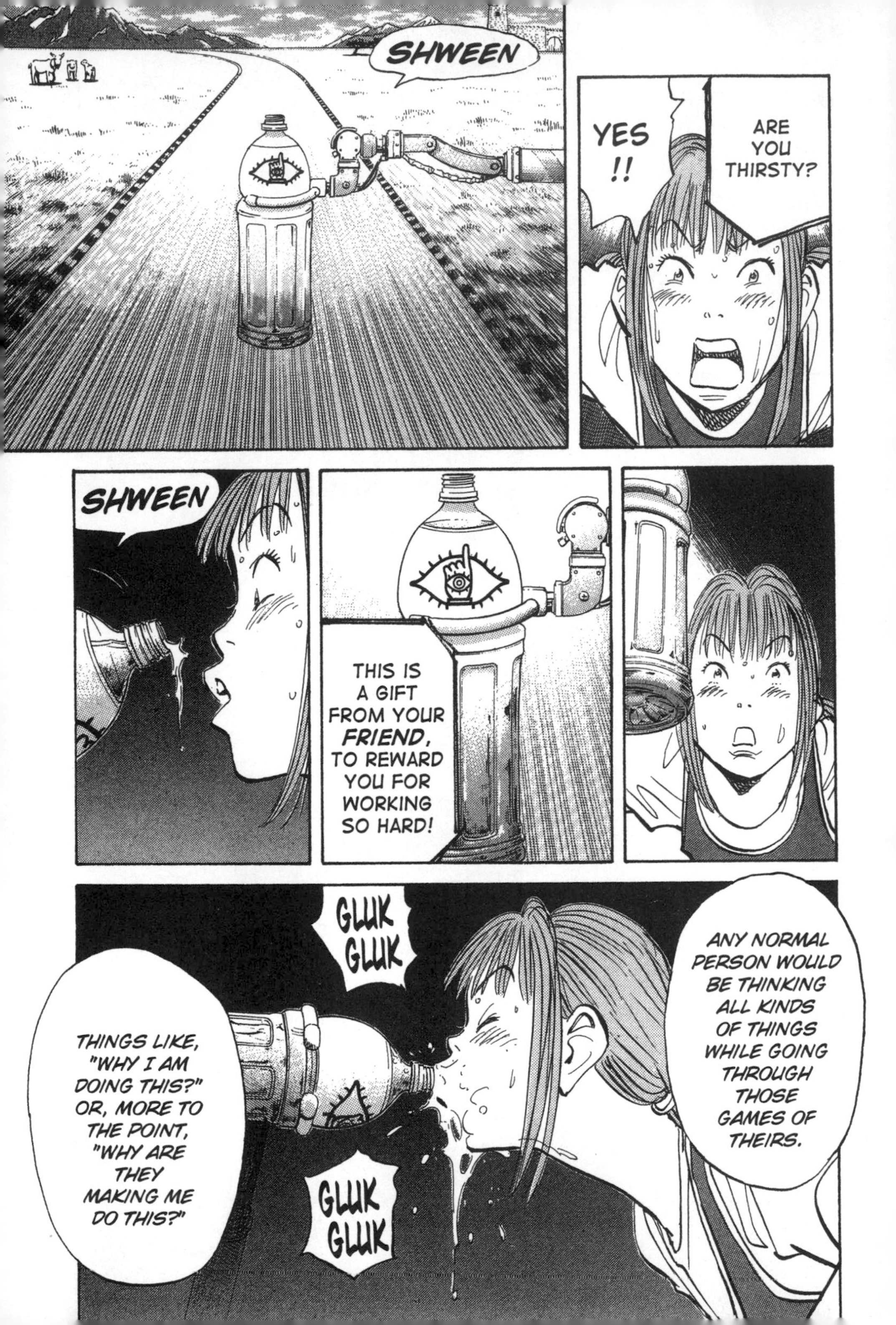
ARE YOU THIRSTY?
YES !!
SHWEEN
THIS IS A GIFT FROM YOUR FRIEND, TO REWARD YOU FOR WORKING SO HARD!
SHWEEN
ANY NORMAL PERSON WOULD BE THINKING ALL KINDS OF THINGS WHILE GOING THROUGH THOSE GAMES OF THEIRS.
GLUK GLUK
THINGS LIKE, "WHY I AM DOING THIS?" OR, MORE TO THE POINT, "WHY ARE THEY MAKING ME DO THIS?"
GLUK GLUK

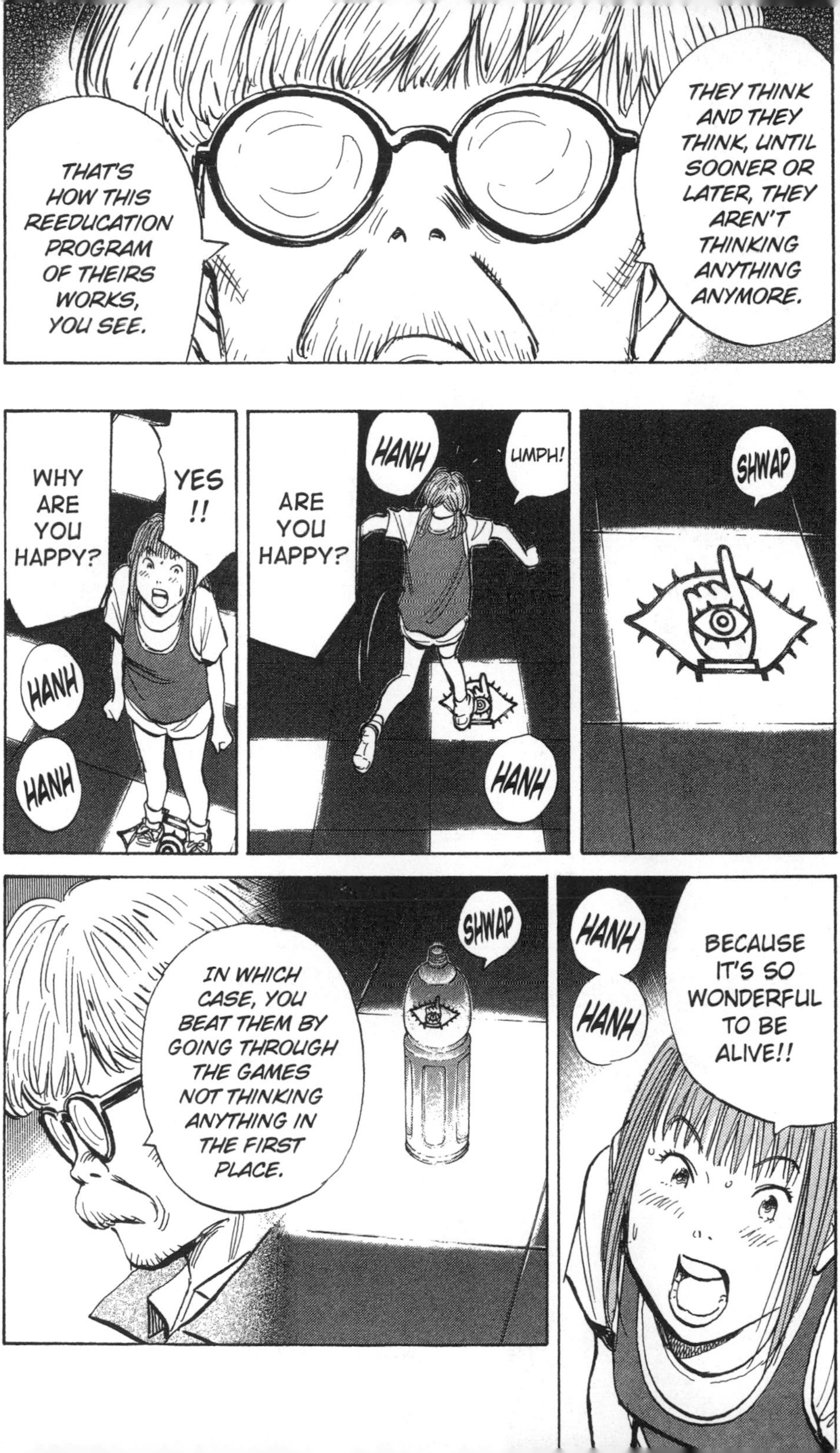
THEY THINK AND THEY THINK, UNTIL SOONER OR LATER, THEY AREN'T THINKING ANYTHING ANYMORE.
THAT'S HOW THIS REEDUCATION PROGRAM OF THEIRS WORKS, YOU SEE.
SHWAP
UMPH!
HANH
ARE YOU HAPPY?
HANH
YES!!
WHY ARE YOU HAPPY?
HANH
HANH
BECAUSE IT'S SO WONDERFUL TO BE ALIVE!!
HANH
HANH
SHWAP
IN WHICH CASE, YOU BEAT THEM BY GOING THROUGH THE GAMES NOT THINKING ANYTHING IN THE FIRST PLACE.

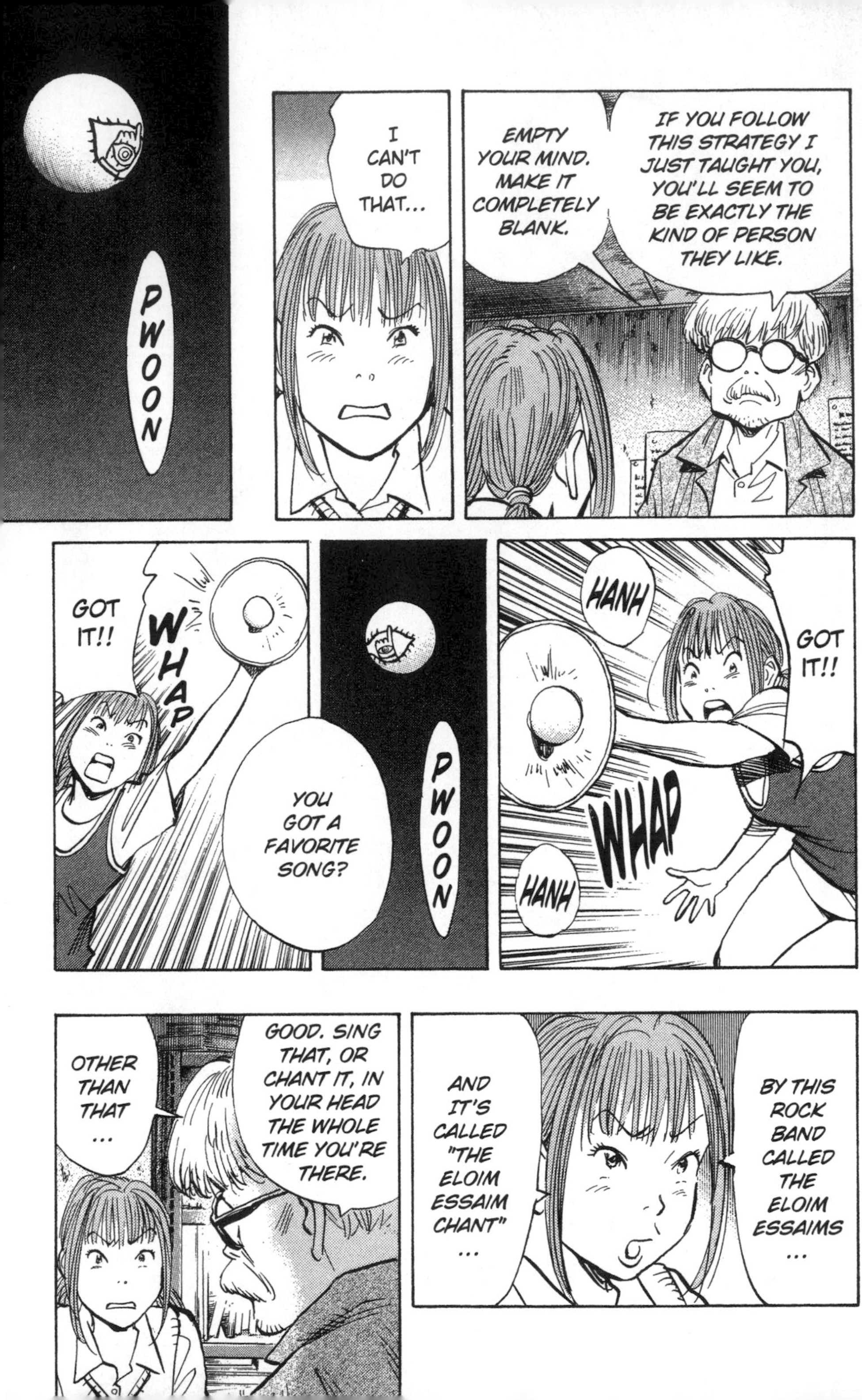
IF YOU FOLLOW THIS STRATEGY I JUST TAUGHT YOU, YOU'LL SEEM TO BE EXACTLY THE KIND OF PERSON THEY LIKE.
EMPTY YOUR MIND. MAKE IT COMPLETELY BLANK.
I CAN'T DO THAT…
PWOON
HANH
GOT IT!!
WHAP
HANH
PWOON
YOU GOT A FAVORITE SONG?
GOT IT!!
WHAP
BY THIS ROCK BAND CALLED THE ELOIM ESSAIMS …
AND IT'S CALLED "THE ELOIM ESSAIM CHANT" …
GOOD. SING THAT, OR CHANT IT, IN YOUR HEAD THE WHOLE TIME YOU'RE THERE.
OTHER THAN THAT …

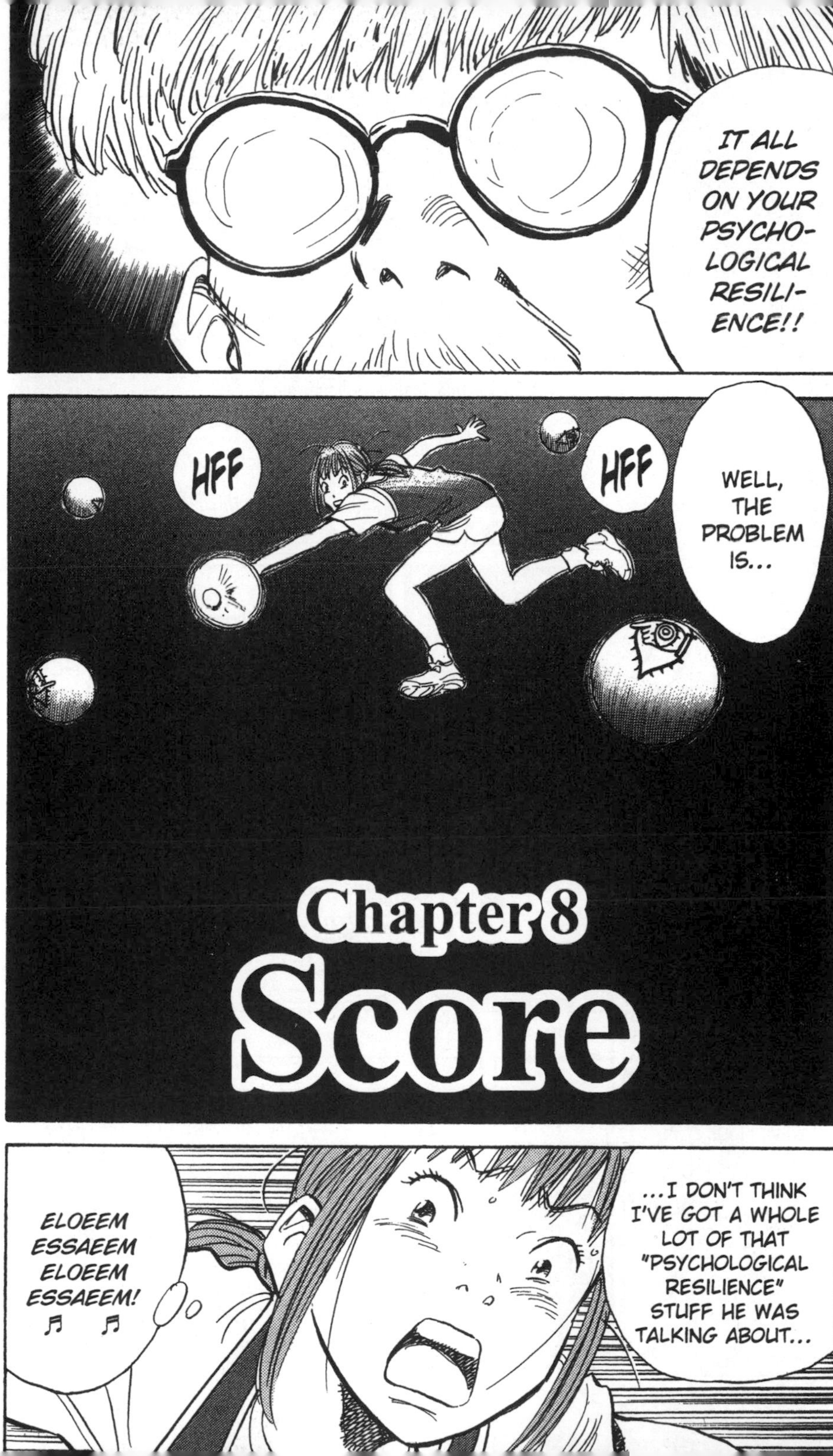
IT ALL DEPENDS ON YOUR PSYCHO-LOGICAL RESILI-ENCE!!
WELL, THE PROBLEM IS...
HFF
HFF
Chapter 8
Score
...I DON'T THINK I'VE GOT A WHOLE LOT OF THAT "PSYCHOLOGICAL RESILIENCE" STUFF HE WAS TALKING ABOUT...
ELOEEM ESSAEEM ELOEEM ESSAEEM! ♬ ♬

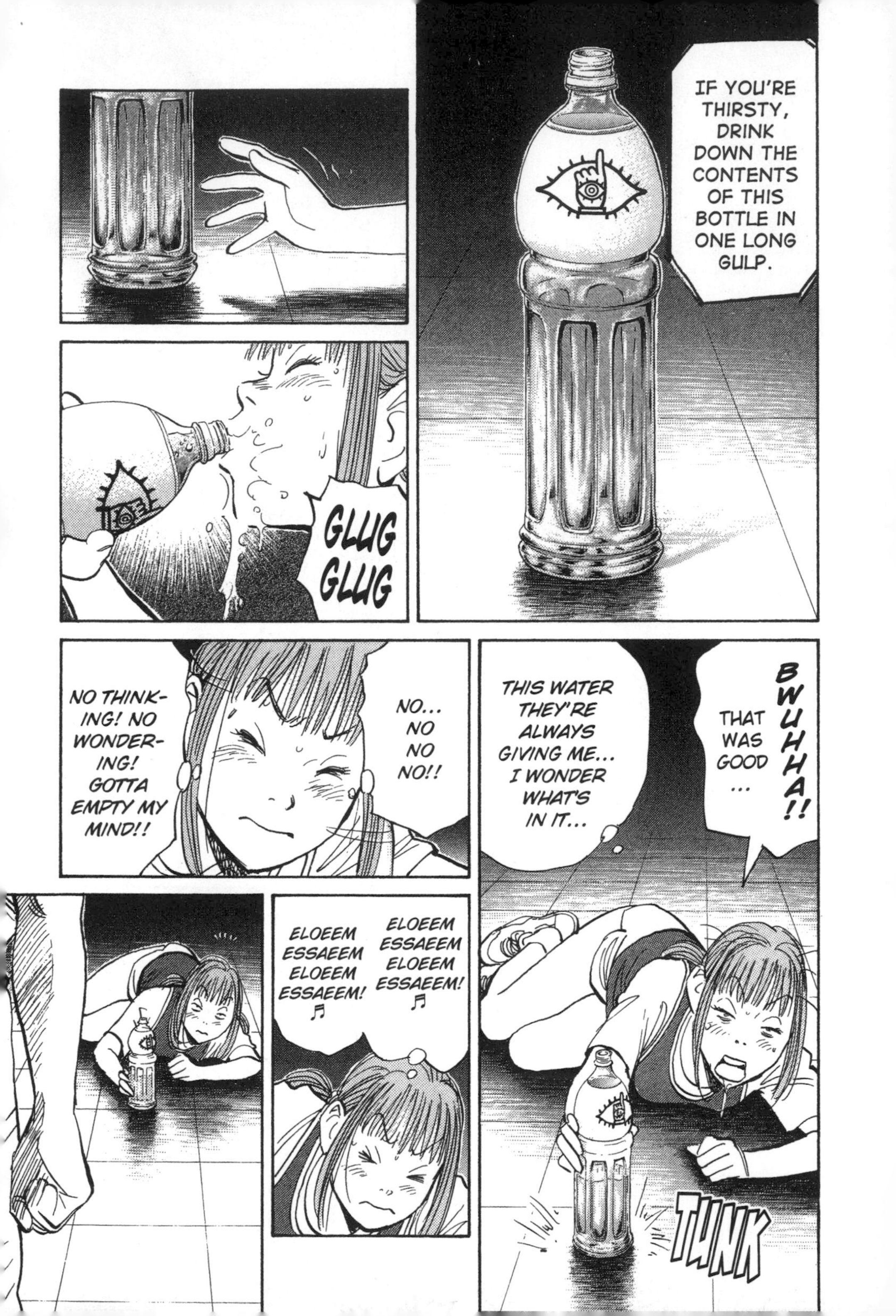
IF YOU'RE THIRSTY, DRINK DOWN THE CONTENTS OF THIS BOTTLE IN ONE LONG GULP.
GLUG GLUG
BWUHHA!!
THAT WAS GOOD ...
THIS WATER THEY'RE ALWAYS GIVING ME... I WONDER WHAT'S IN IT...
TUNK
NO... NO NO NO!!
NO THINKING! NO WONDERING! GOTTA EMPTY MY MIND!!
ELOEEM ESSAEEM ELOEEM ESSAEEM! ♬
ELOEEM ESSAEEM ELOEEM ESSAEEM! ♬

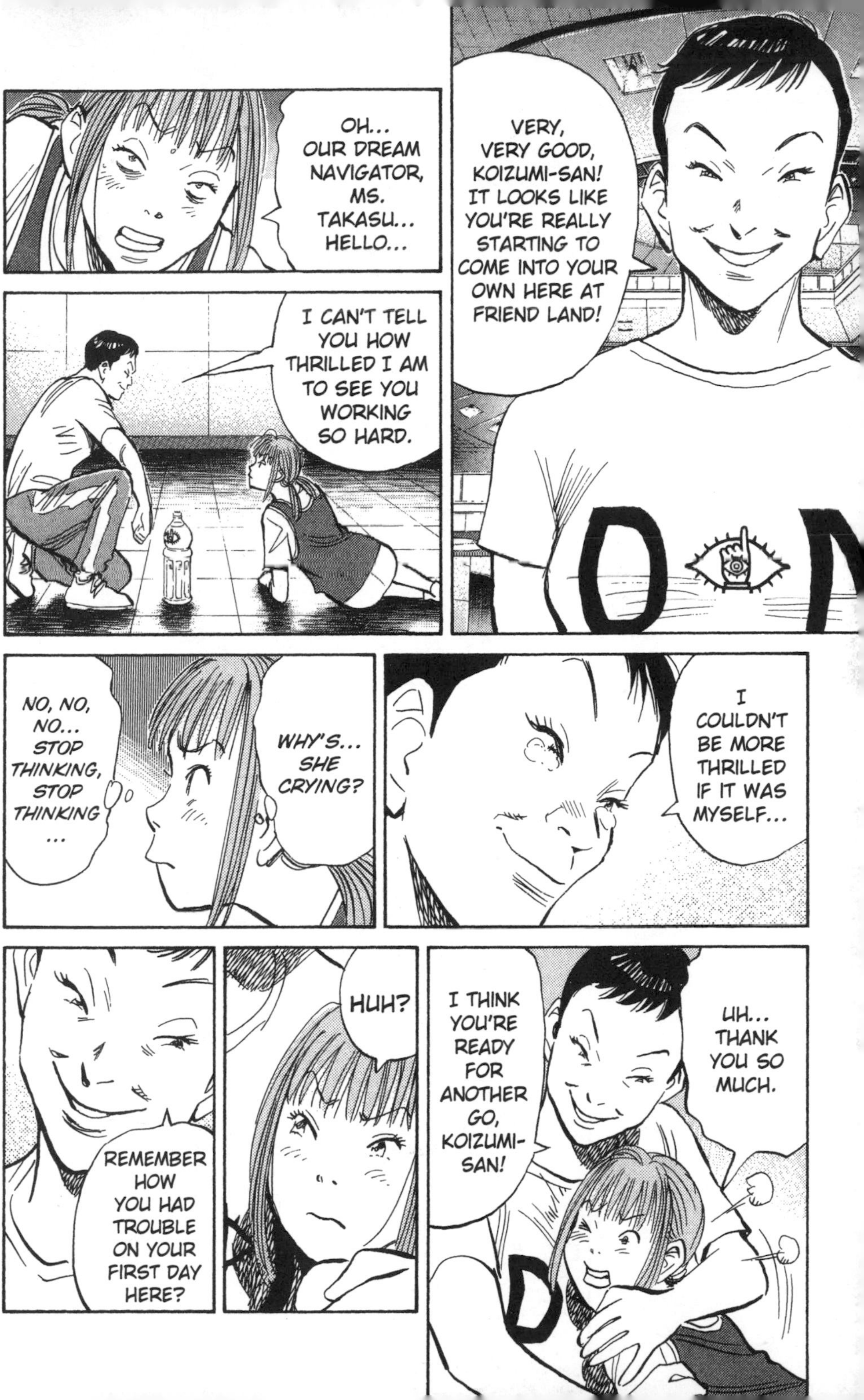
VERY, VERY GOOD, KOIZUMI-SAN! IT LOOKS LIKE YOU'RE REALLY STARTING TO COME INTO YOUR OWN HERE AT FRIEND LAND!
OH... OUR DREAM NAVIGATOR, MS. TAKASU... HELLO...
I CAN'T TELL YOU HOW THRILLED I AM TO SEE YOU WORKING SO HARD.
I COULDN'T BE MORE THRILLED IF IT WAS MYSELF...
WHY'S... SHE CRYING?
NO, NO, NO... STOP THINKING, STOP THINKING...
I THINK YOU'RE READY FOR ANOTHER GO, KOIZUMI-SAN!
UH... THANK YOU SO MUCH.
HUH?
REMEMBER HOW YOU HAD TROUBLE ON YOUR FIRST DAY HERE?

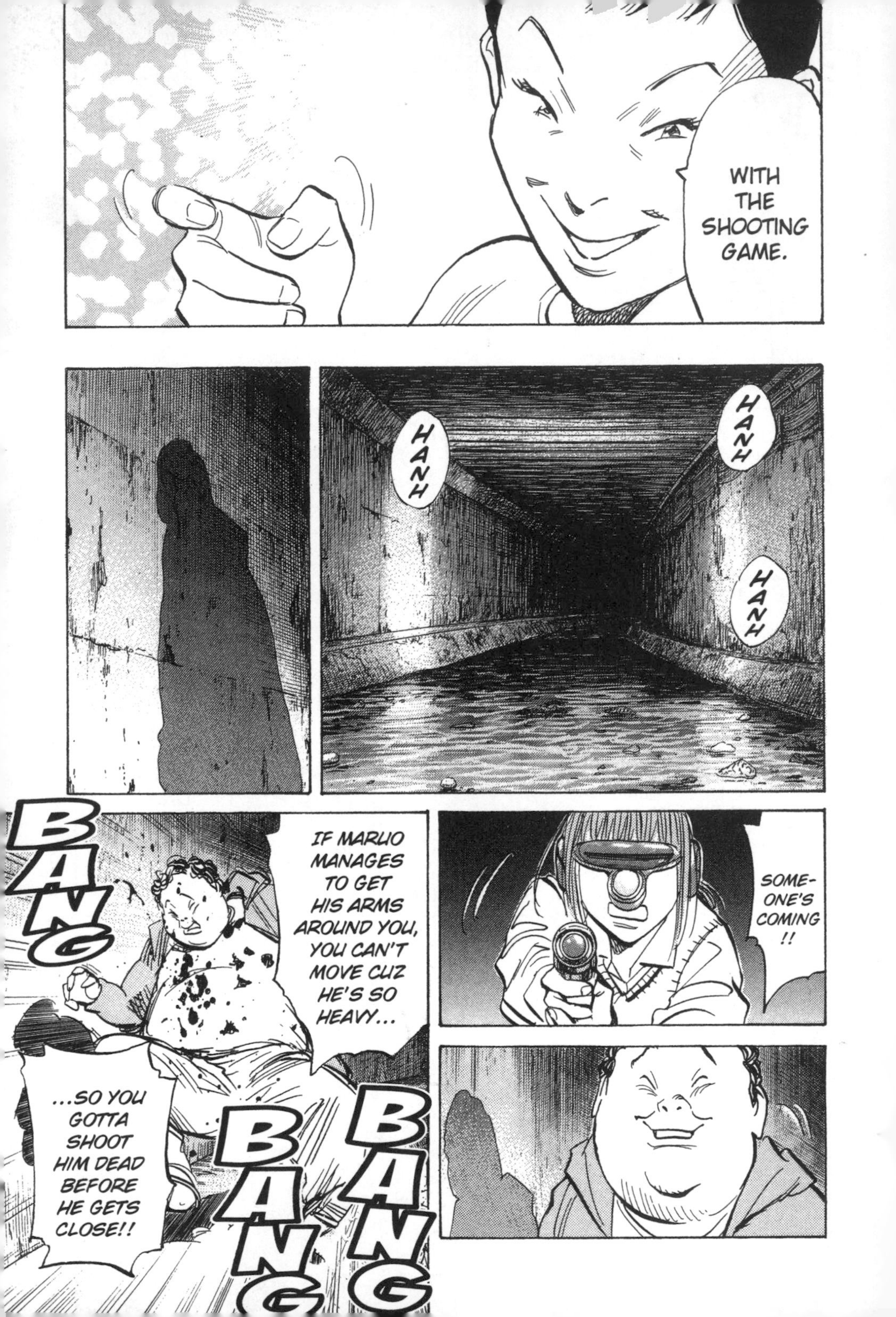

WITH THE SHOOTING GAME.
HANH
HANH
HANH
SOME-ONE'S COMING!!
IF MARUO MANAGES TO GET HIS ARMS AROUND YOU, YOU CAN'T MOVE CUZ HE'S SO HEAVY...
BANG
...SO YOU GOTTA SHOOT HIM DEAD BEFORE HE GETS CLOSE!!
BANG
BANG

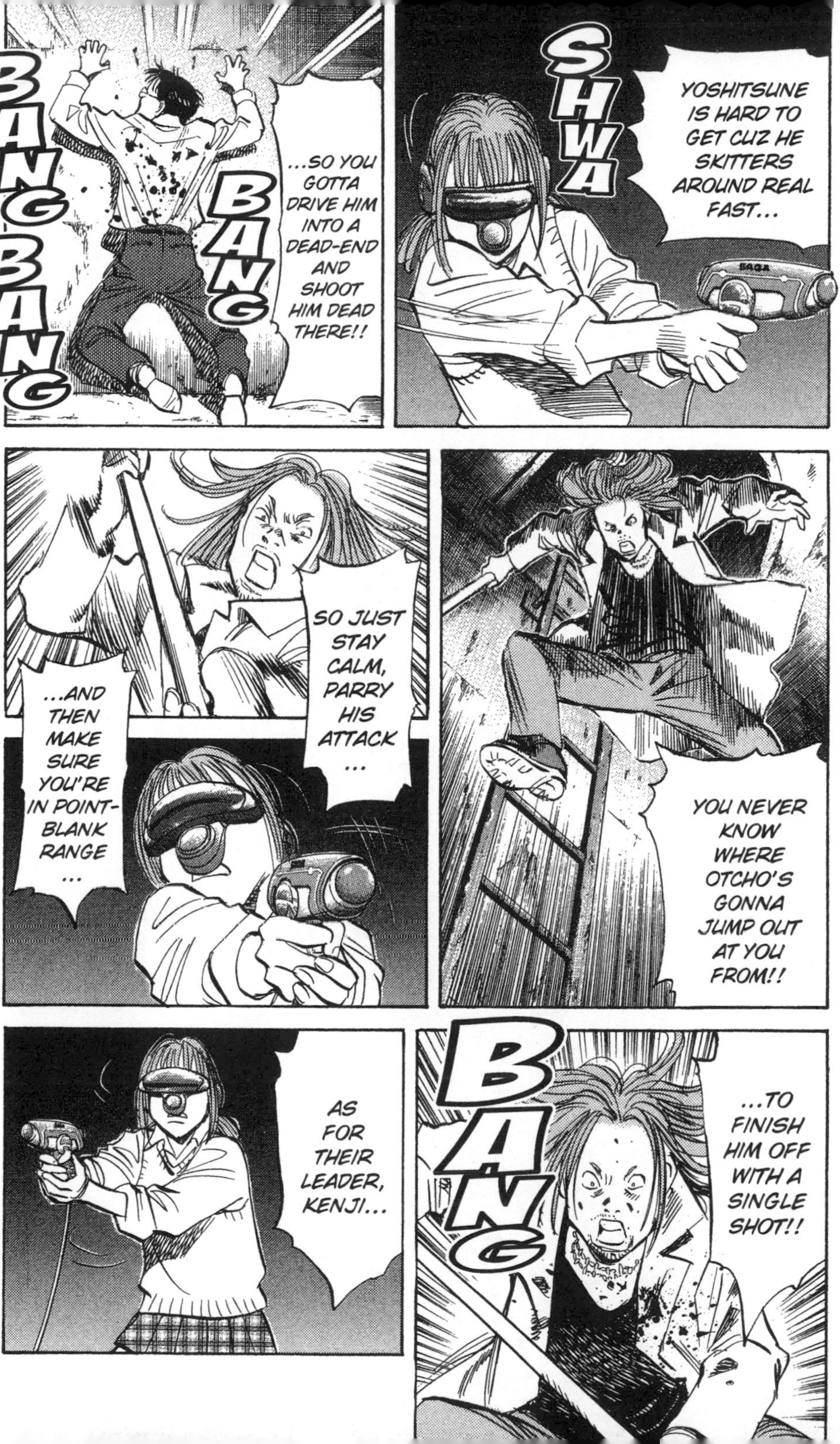
SHWA
YOSHITSUNE IS HARD TO GET CUZ HE SKITTERS AROUND REAL FAST...
BANG BANG
BANG BANG
...SO YOU GOTTA DRIVE HIM INTO A DEAD-END AND SHOOT HIM DEAD THERE!!
YOU NEVER KNOW WHERE OTCHO'S GONNA JUMP OUT AT YOU FROM!!
SO JUST STAY CALM, PARRY HIS ATTACK...
...AND THEN MAKE SURE YOU'RE IN POINT-BLANK RANGE...
BANG
...TO FINISH HIM OFF WITH A SINGLE SHOT!!
AS FOR THEIR LEADER, KENJI...

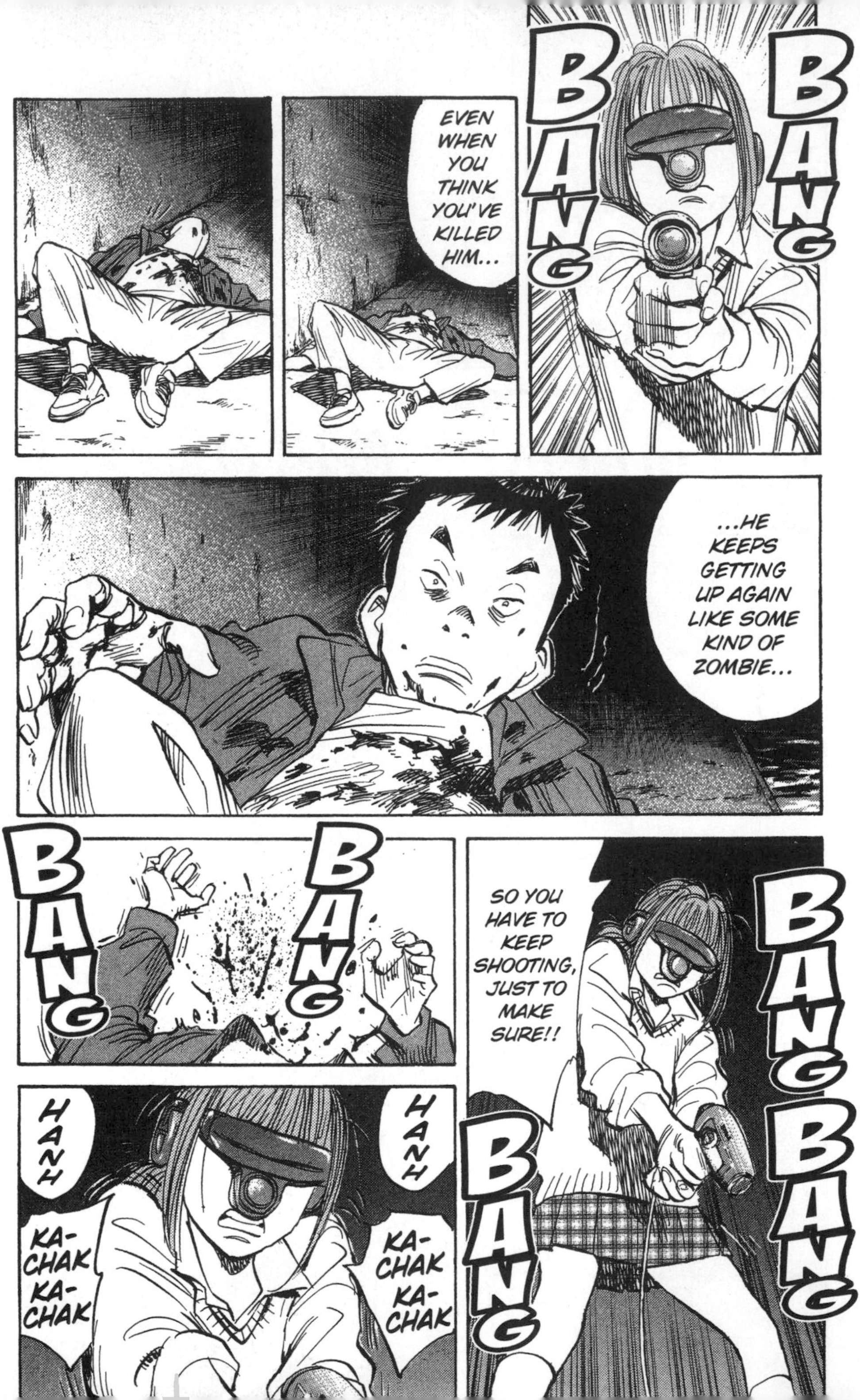
BANG
BANG
EVEN WHEN YOU THINK YOU'VE KILLED HIM...
...HE KEEPS GETTING UP AGAIN LIKE SOME KIND OF ZOMBIE...
SO YOU HAVE TO KEEP SHOOTING, JUST TO MAKE SURE!!
BANG
BANG
BANG
BANG
BANG
BANG
HANH
HANH
KA-CHAK KA-CHAK
KA-CHAK KA-CHAK

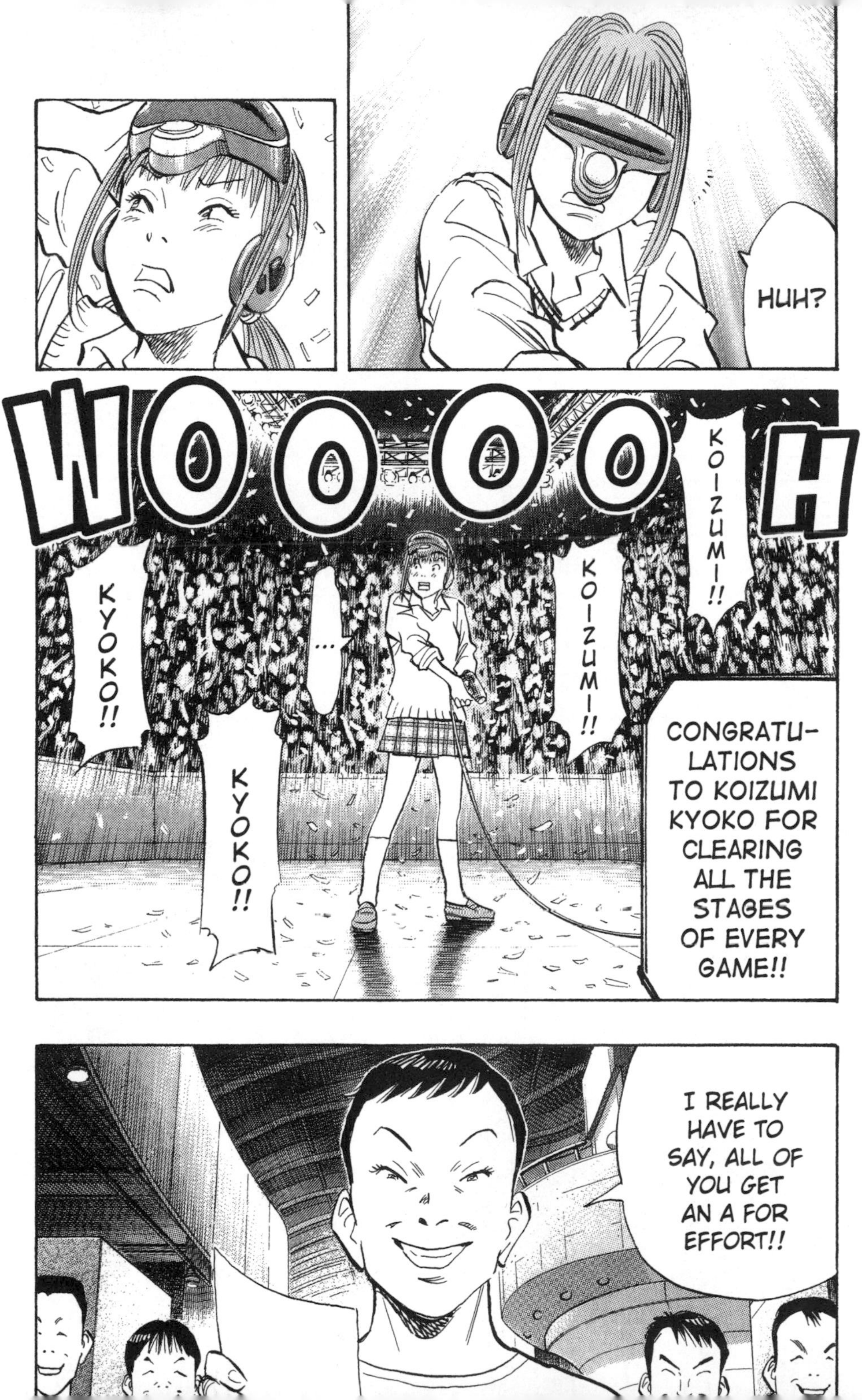
HUH?
WOOOOH
KOIZUMI!!
KOIZUMI!!
CONGRATULATIONS TO KOIZUMI KYOKO FOR CLEARING ALL THE STAGES OF EVERY GAME!!
...
KYOKO!!
KYOKO!!
I REALLY HAVE TO SAY, ALL OF YOU GET AN A FOR EFFORT!!

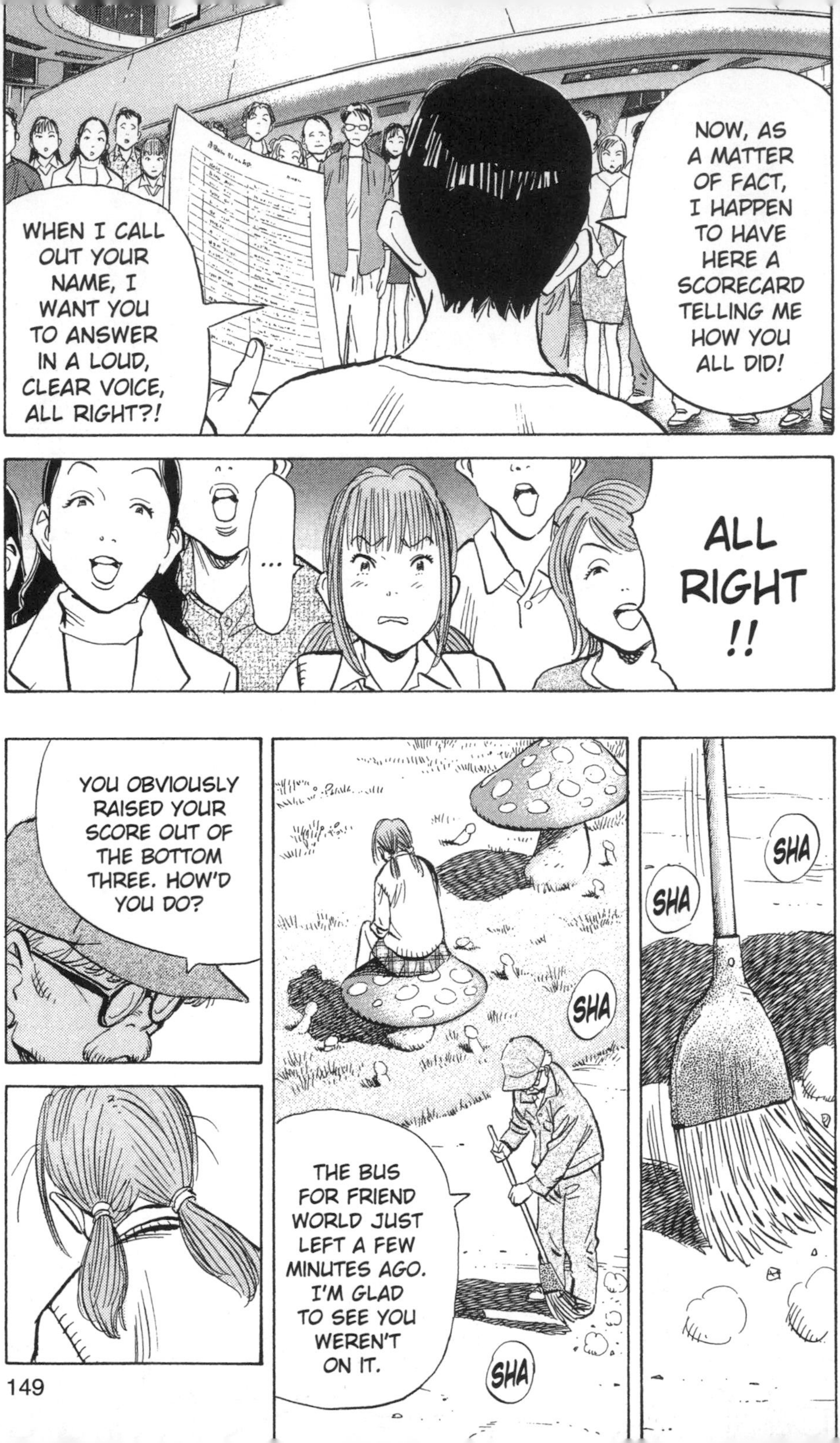
NOW, AS A MATTER OF FACT, I HAPPEN TO HAVE HERE A SCORECARD TELLING ME HOW YOU ALL DID!
WHEN I CALL OUT YOUR NAME, I WANT YOU TO ANSWER IN A LOUD, CLEAR VOICE, ALL RIGHT?!
ALL RIGHT !!
...
SHA
SHA
SHA
THE BUS FOR FRIEND WORLD JUST LEFT A FEW MINUTES AGO. I'M GLAD TO SEE YOU WEREN'T ON IT.
SHA
YOU OBVIOUSLY RAISED YOUR SCORE OUT OF THE BOTTOM THREE. HOW'D YOU DO?

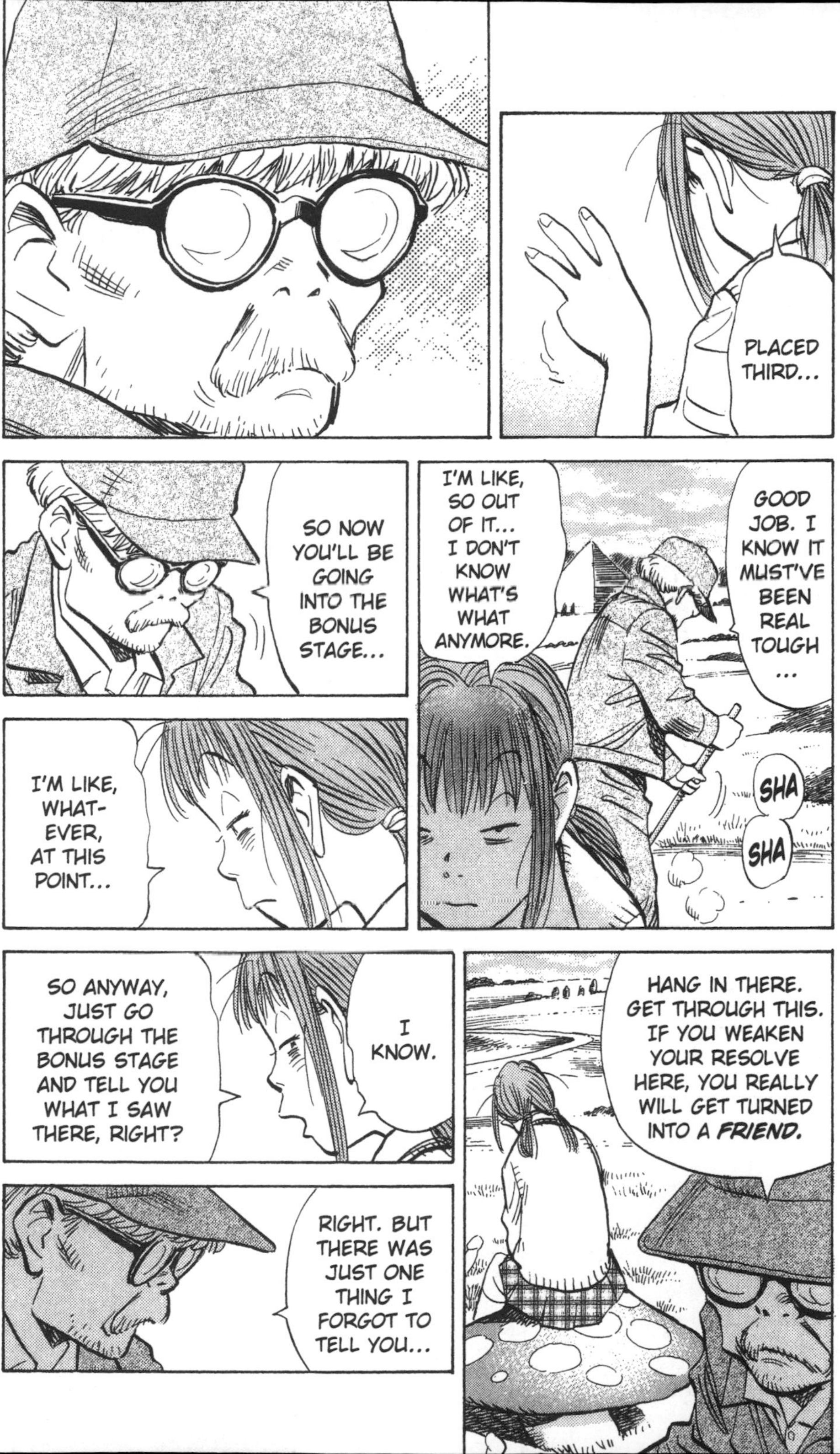
PLACED THIRD...
GOOD JOB. I KNOW IT MUST'VE BEEN REAL TOUGH...
I'M LIKE, SO OUT OF IT... I DON'T KNOW WHAT'S WHAT ANYMORE.
SHA
SHA
SO NOW YOU'LL BE GOING INTO THE BONUS STAGE...
I'M LIKE, WHATEVER, AT THIS POINT...
HANG IN THERE. GET THROUGH THIS. IF YOU WEAKEN YOUR RESOLVE HERE, YOU REALLY WILL GET TURNED INTO A FRIEND.
I KNOW.
SO ANYWAY, JUST GO THROUGH THE BONUS STAGE AND TELL YOU WHAT I SAW THERE, RIGHT?
RIGHT. BUT THERE WAS JUST ONE THING I FORGOT TO TELL YOU...

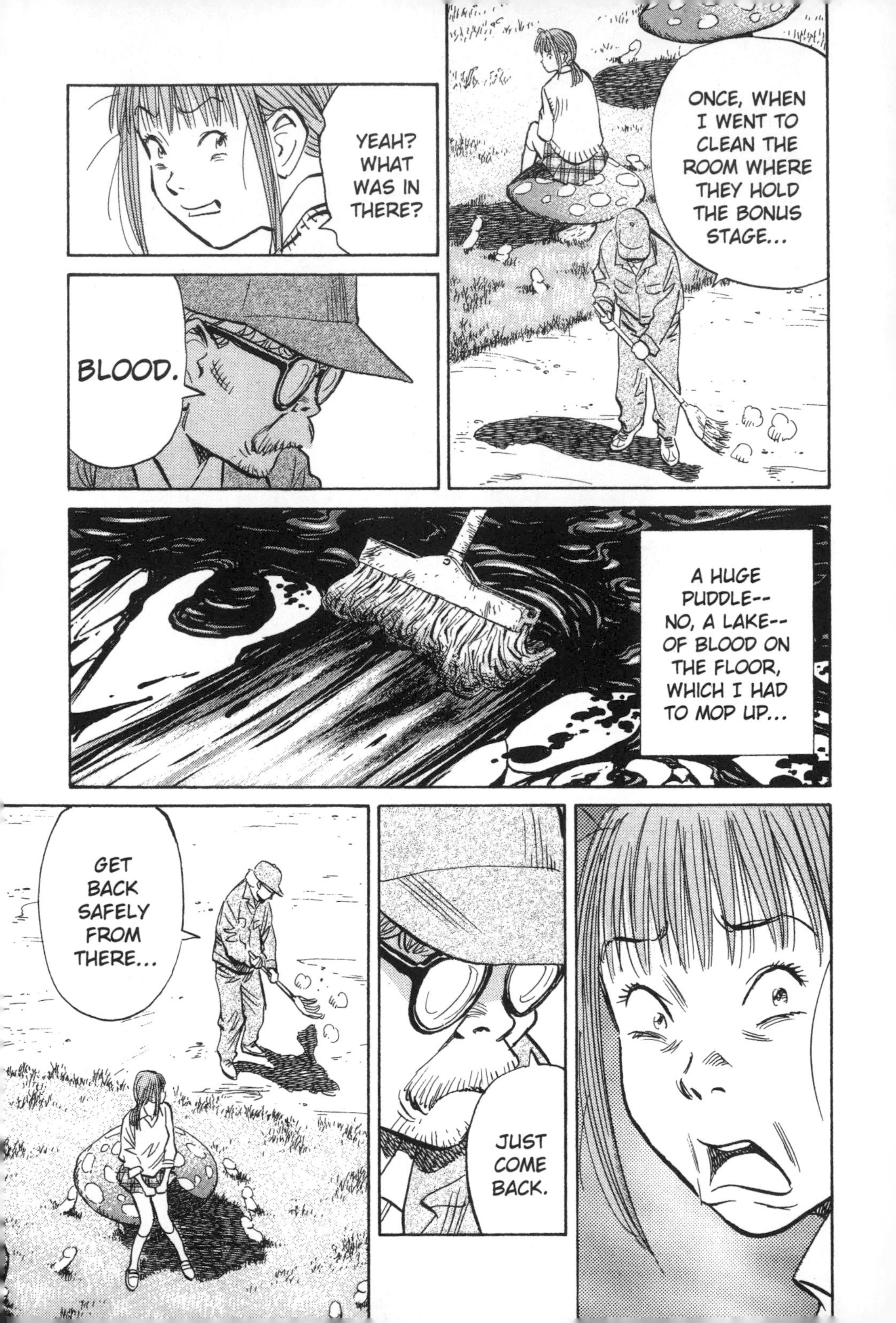
ONCE, WHEN I WENT TO CLEAN THE ROOM WHERE THEY HOLD THE BONUS STAGE...
YEAH? WHAT WAS IN THERE?
BLOOD.
A HUGE PUDDLE-- NO, A LAKE-- OF BLOOD ON THE FLOOR, WHICH I HAD TO MOP UP...
JUST COME BACK.
GET BACK SAFELY FROM THERE...

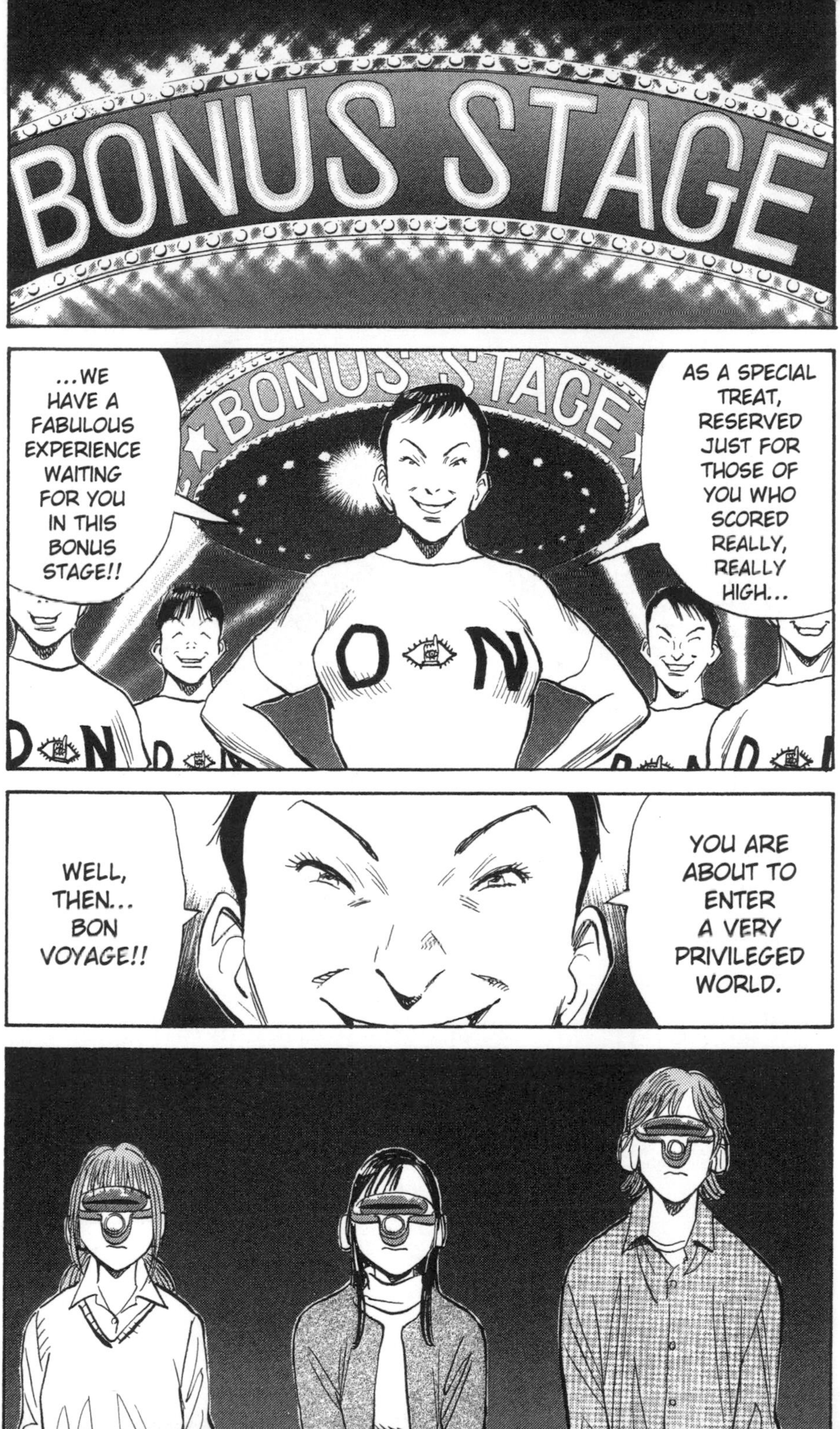
BONUS STAGE
BONUS STAGE
AS A SPECIAL TREAT, RESERVED JUST FOR THOSE OF YOU WHO SCORED REALLY, REALLY HIGH...
...WE HAVE A FABULOUS EXPERIENCE WAITING FOR YOU IN THIS BONUS STAGE!!
YOU ARE ABOUT TO ENTER A VERY PRIVILEGED WORLD.
WELL, THEN... BON VOYAGE!!

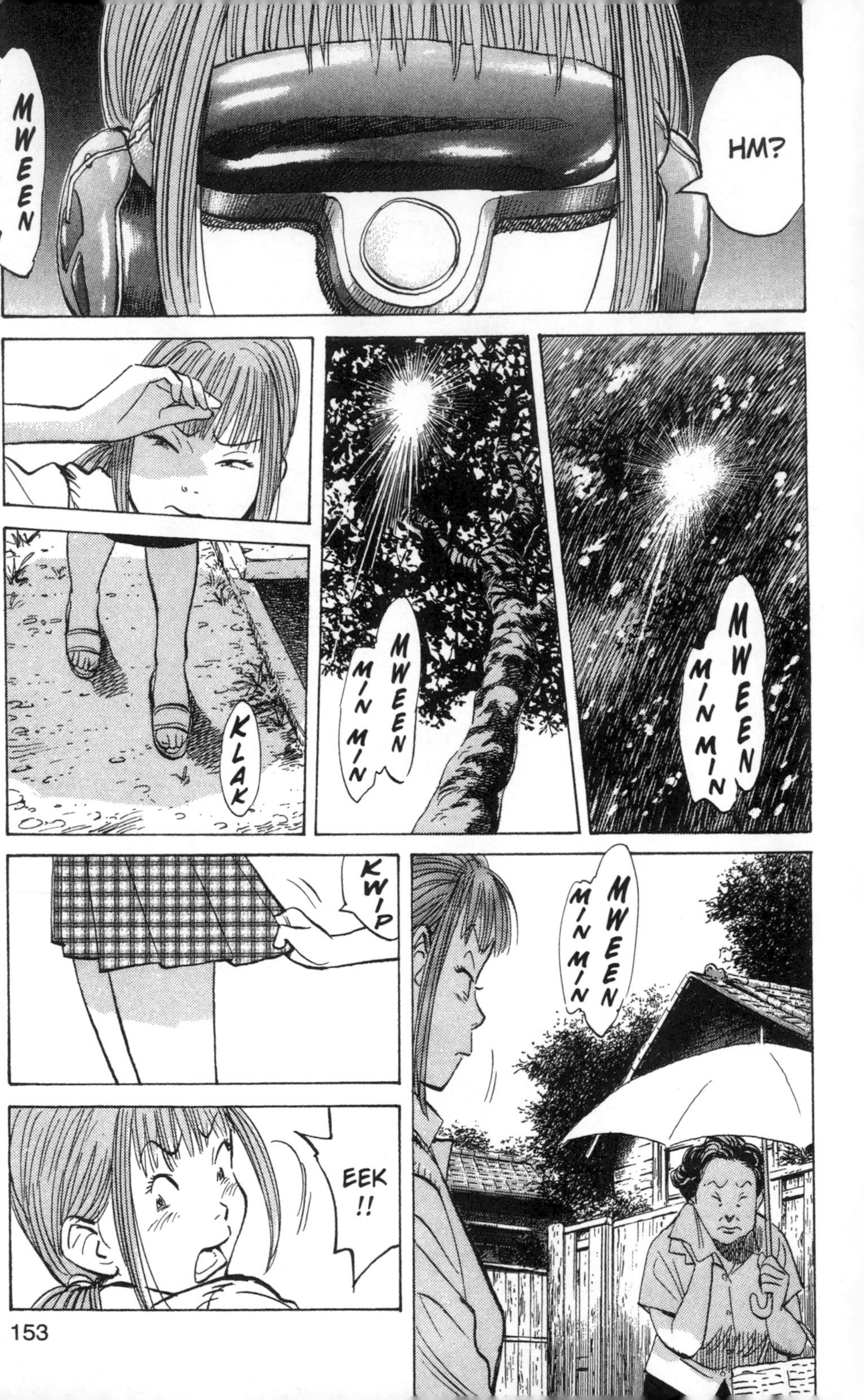
HM?
MWEEN MIN MIN
MWEEN MIN MIN
MWEEN MIN MIN
KLAK
MWEEN MIN MIN
KWIP
EEK !!

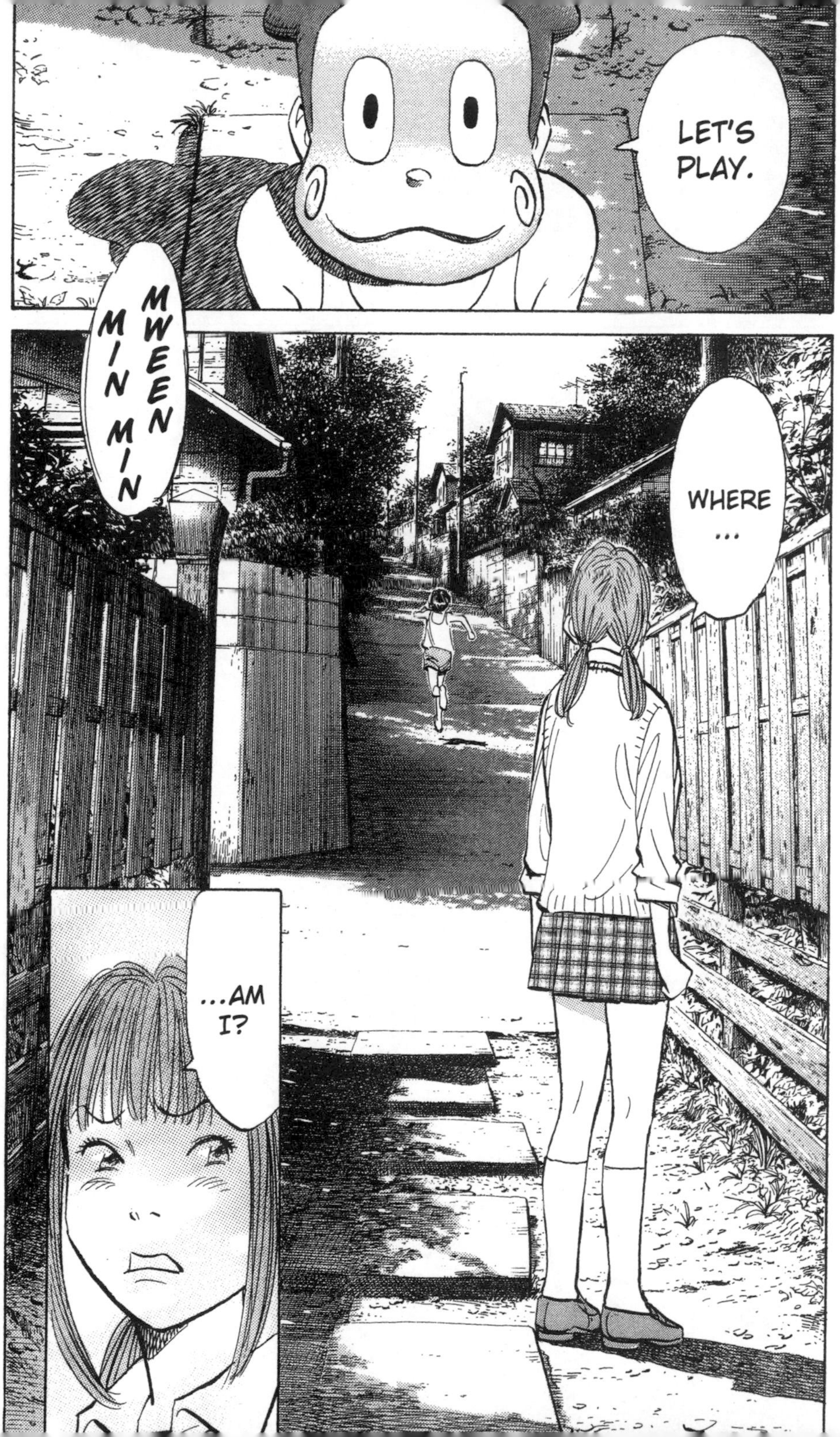
LET'S PLAY.
MWEEN MIN MIN
WHERE ...
...AM I?

Chapter 9 Plan

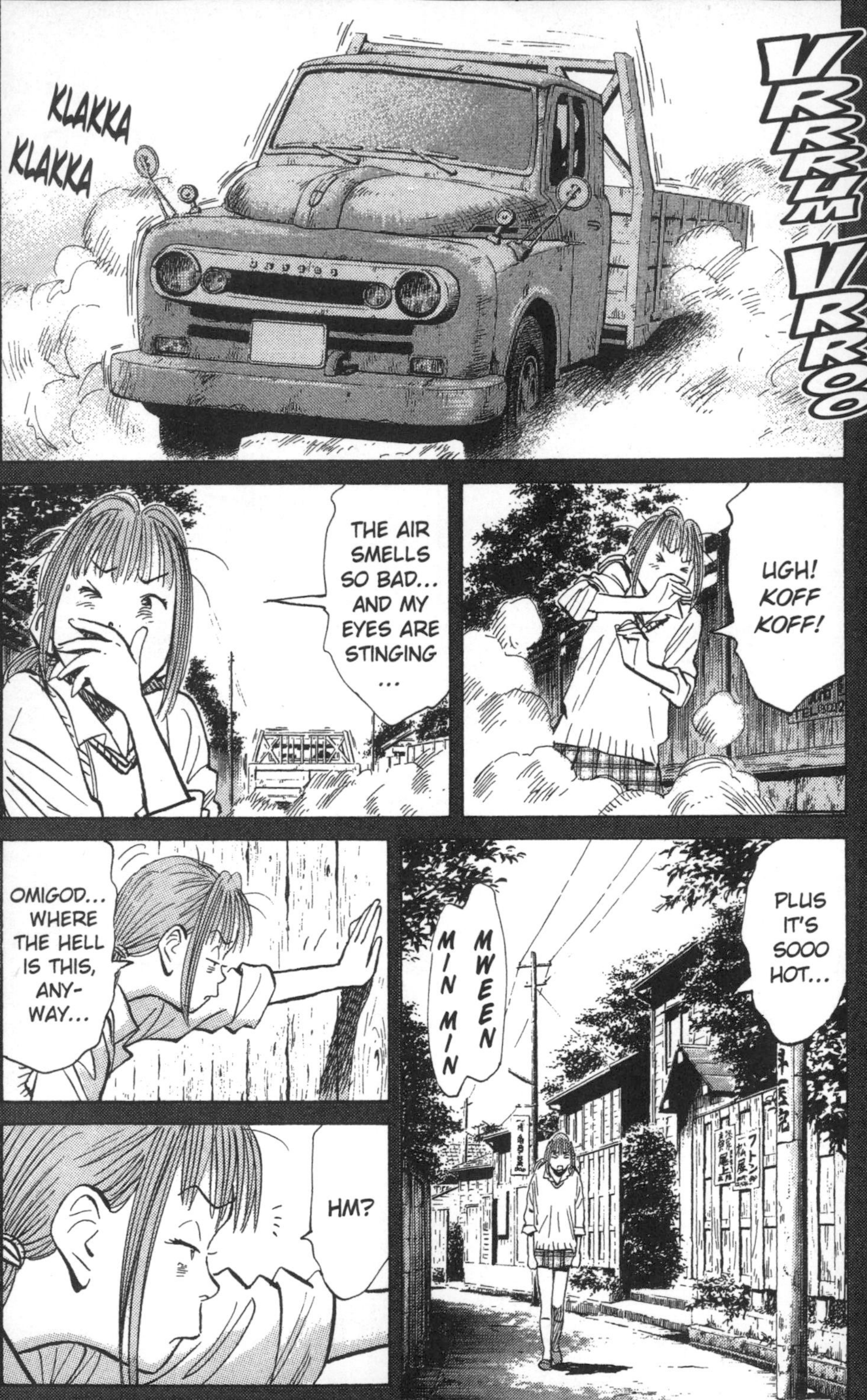
VRRRM VRROO
KLAKKA KLAKKA
UGH! KOFF KOFF!
THE AIR SMELLS SO BAD... AND MY EYES ARE STINGING ...
PLUS IT'S SOOO HOT...
MWEEN MIN MIN
OMIGOD... WHERE THE HELL IS THIS, ANY-WAY...
HM?

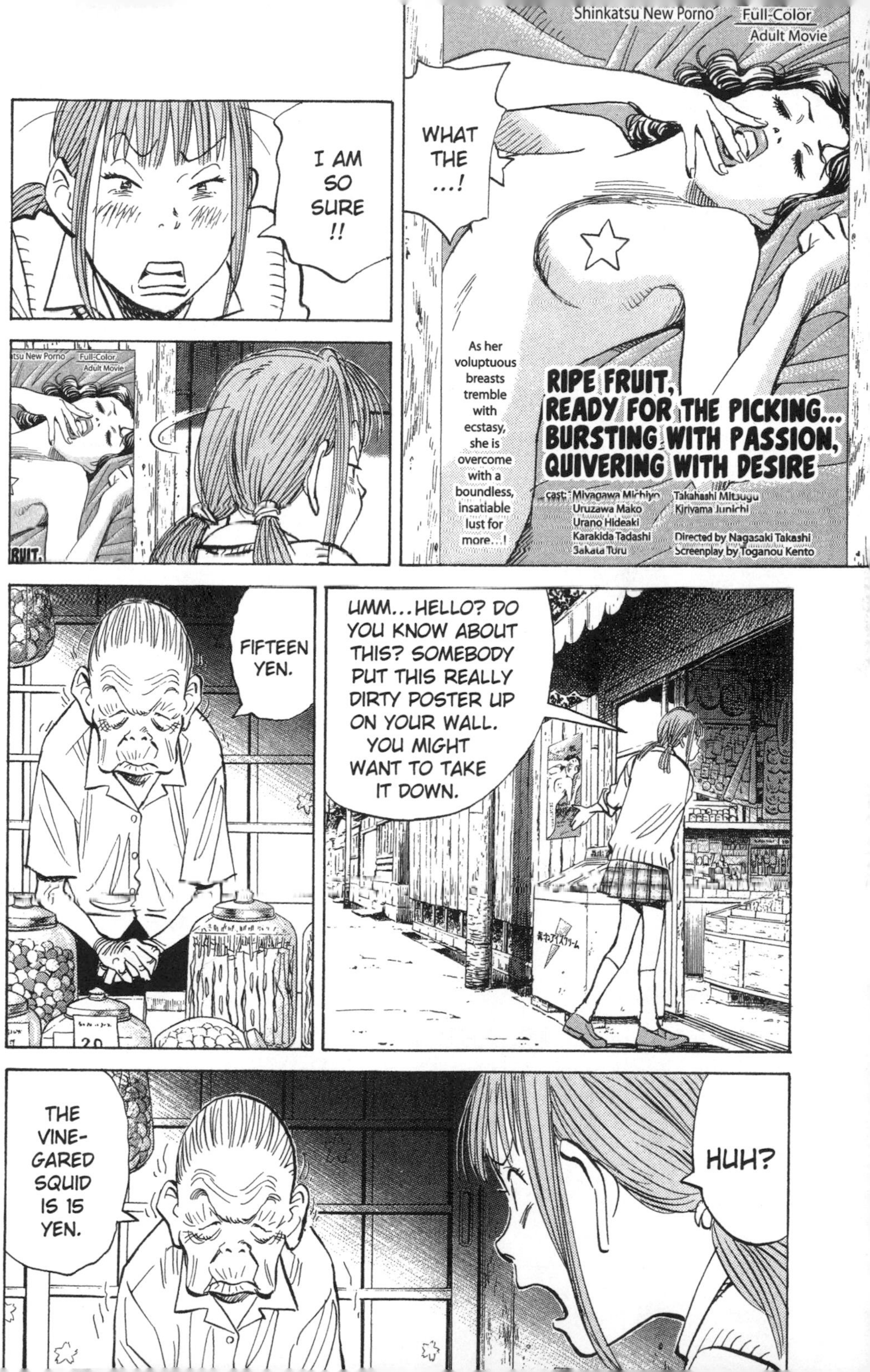
Shinkatsu New Porno
Full-Color Adult Movie
WHAT THE ...!
As her voluptuous breasts tremble with ecstasy, she is overcome with a boundless, insatiable lust for more...!
RIPE FRUIT, READY FOR THE PICKING... BURSTING WITH PASSION, QUIVERING WITH DESIRE
cast: Miyagawa Michiyo Uruzawa Mako Urano Hideaki Karakida Tadashi Sakata Toru
Takahashi Mitsugu Kiriyama Junichi
Directed by Nagasaki Takashi
Screenplay by Toganou Kento
I AM SO SURE !!
UMM...HELLO? DO YOU KNOW ABOUT THIS? SOMEBODY PUT THIS REALLY DIRTY POSTER UP ON YOUR WALL. YOU MIGHT WANT TO TAKE IT DOWN.
FIFTEEN YEN.
HUH?
THE VINE-GARED SQUID IS 15 YEN.

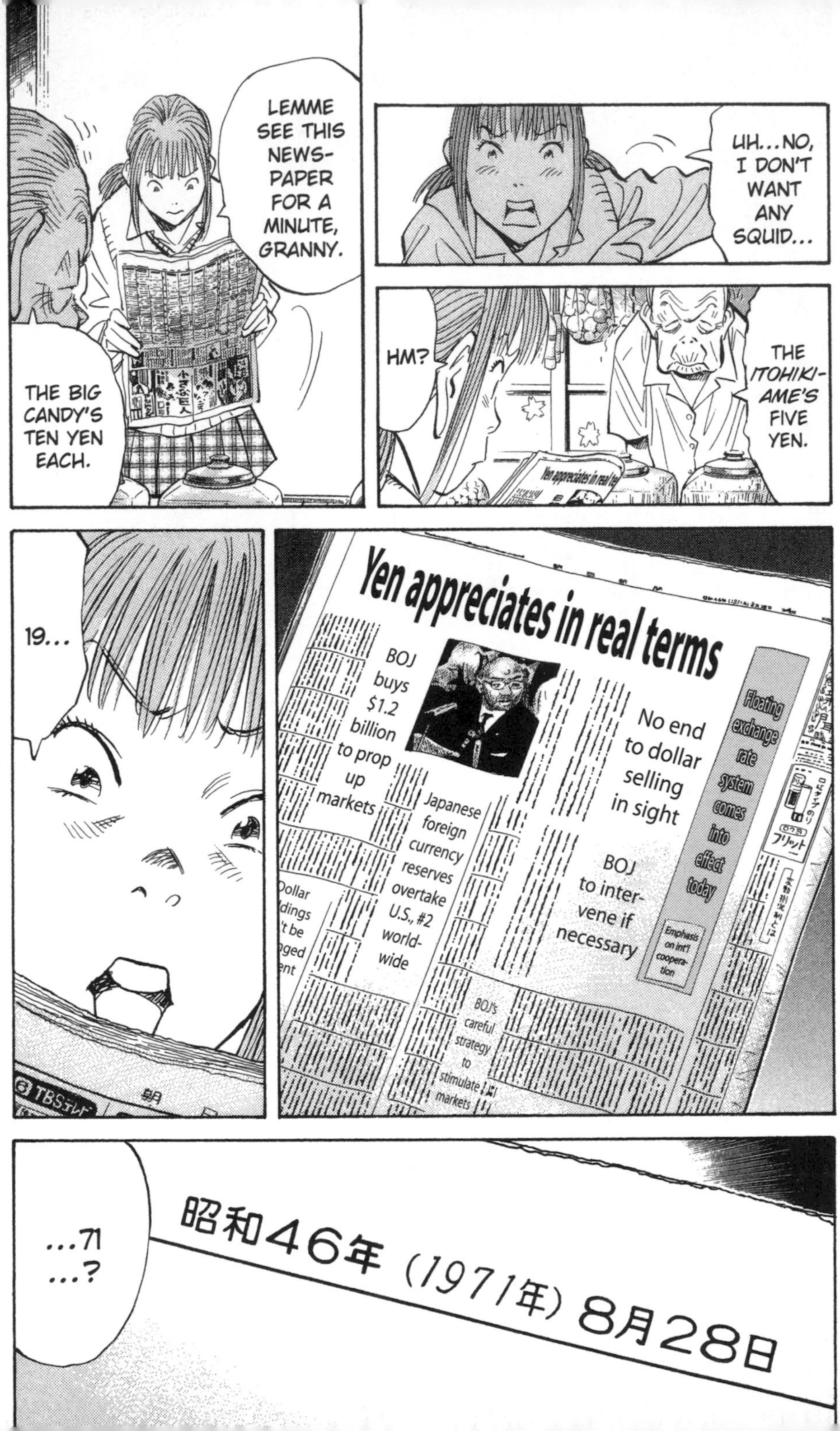

UH...NO, I DON'T WANT ANY SQUID...
THE ITOHIKI-AME'S FIVE YEN.
HM?
LEMME SEE THIS NEWSPAPER FOR A MINUTE, GRANNY.
THE BIG CANDY'S TEN YEN EACH.
Yen appreciates in real terms
Floating exchange rate system comes into effect today
Emphasis on int'l cooperation
No end to dollar selling in sight
BOJ to intervene if necessary
BOJ buys $1.2 billion to prop up markets
Japanese foreign currency reserves overtake U.S., #2 worldwide
BOJ's careful strategy to stimulate markets
19...
昭和46年（1971年）8月28日
...71 ...?

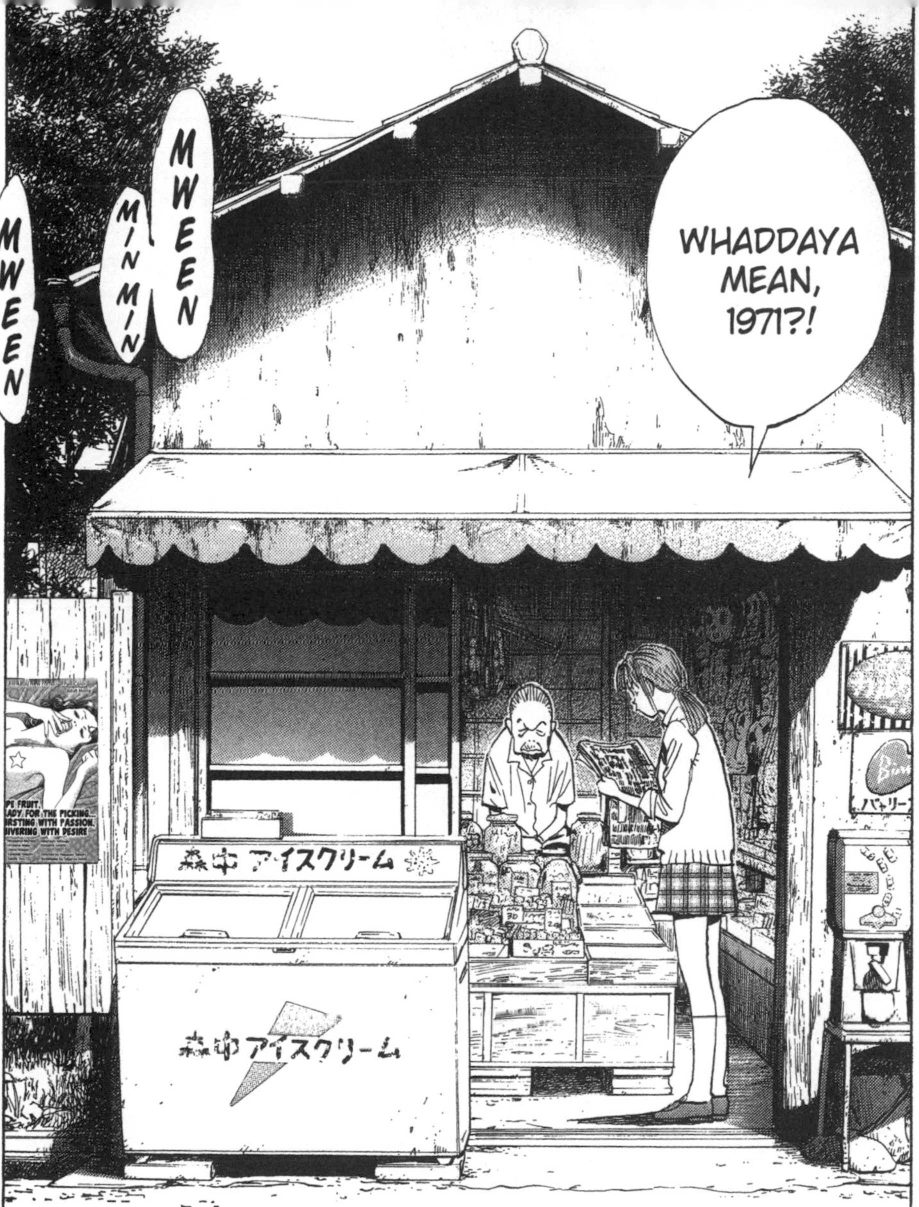
WHADDAYA MEAN, 1971?!
MWEEN
MINMIN
MWEEN
森中アイスクリーム
森中アイスクリーム

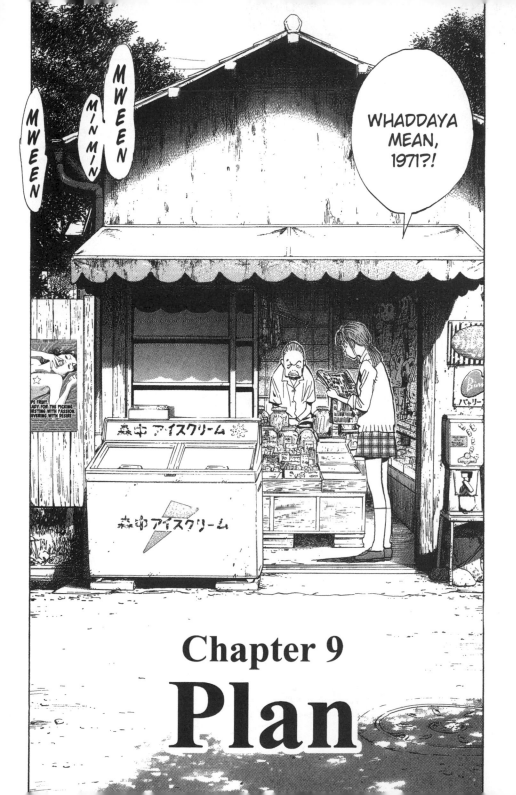

Chapter 9
Plan

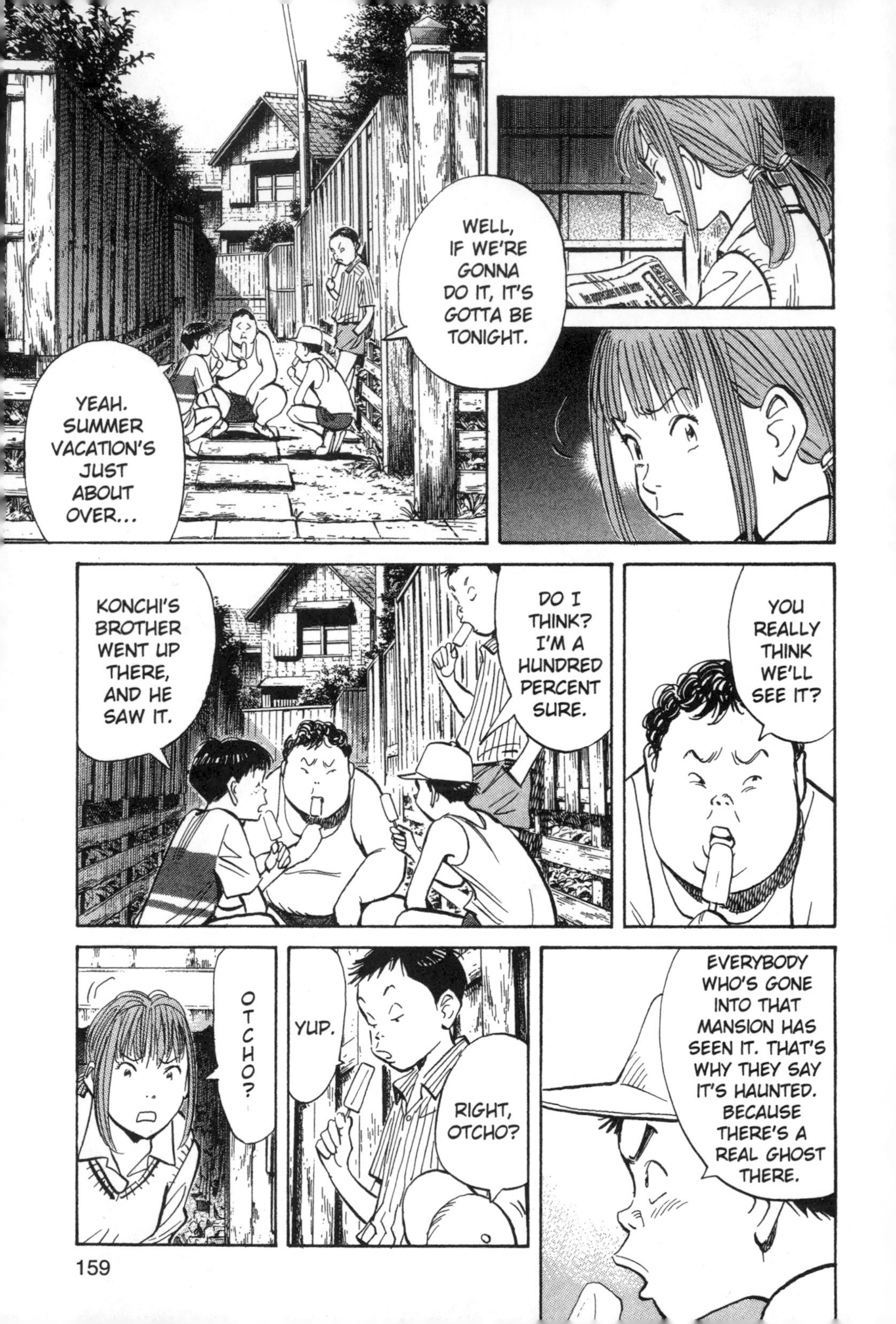
WELL, IF WE'RE GONNA DO IT, IT'S GOTTA BE TONIGHT.
YEAH. SUMMER VACATION'S JUST ABOUT OVER...
YOU REALLY THINK WE'LL SEE IT?
DO I THINK? I'M A HUNDRED PERCENT SURE.
KONCHI'S BROTHER WENT UP THERE, AND HE SAW IT.
EVERYBODY WHO'S GONE INTO THAT MANSION HAS SEEN IT. THAT'S WHY THEY SAY IT'S HAUNTED. BECAUSE THERE'S A REAL GHOST THERE.
RIGHT, OTCHO?
YUP.
OTCHO?

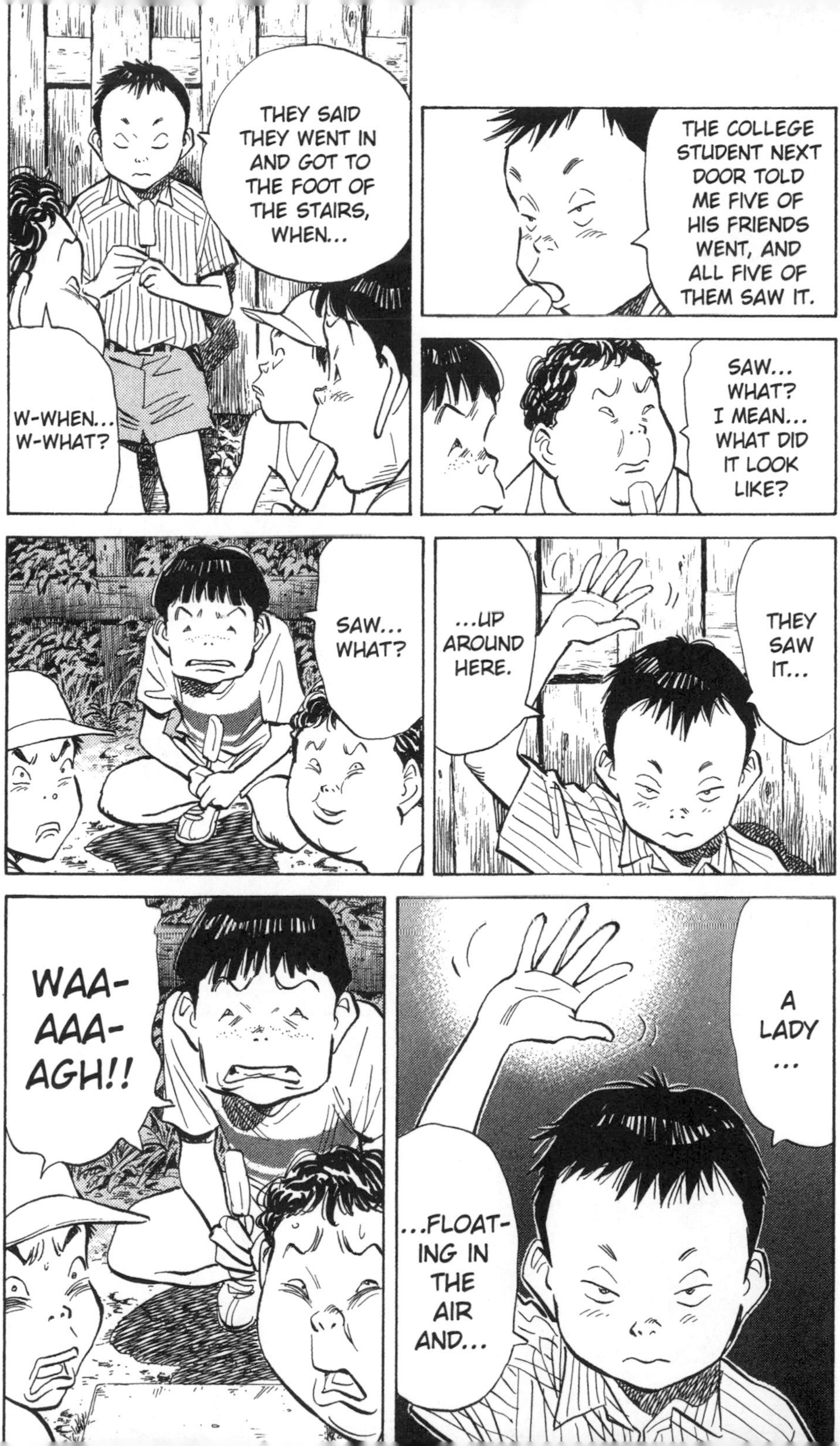
THE COLLEGE STUDENT NEXT DOOR TOLD ME FIVE OF HIS FRIENDS WENT, AND ALL FIVE OF THEM SAW IT.
SAW... WHAT? I MEAN... WHAT DID IT LOOK LIKE?
THEY SAID THEY WENT IN AND GOT TO THE FOOT OF THE STAIRS, WHEN...
W-WHEN... W-WHAT?
THEY SAW IT...
...UP AROUND HERE.
SAW... WHAT?
A LADY ...
...FLOAT-ING IN THE AIR AND...
WAA-AAA-AGH!!

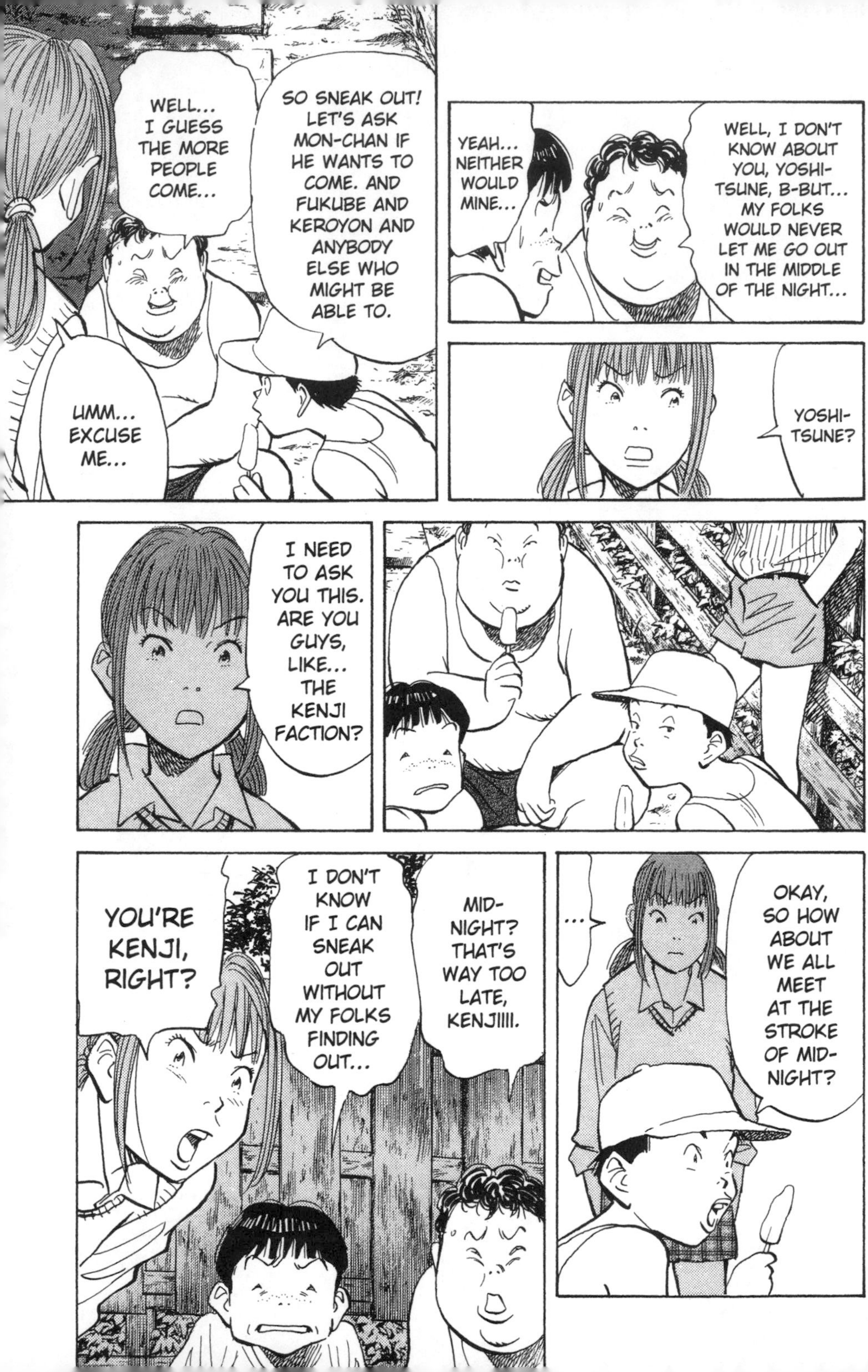

WELL, I DON'T KNOW ABOUT YOU, YOSHI-TSUNE, B-BUT... MY FOLKS WOULD NEVER LET ME GO OUT IN THE MIDDLE OF THE NIGHT...
YEAH... NEITHER WOULD MINE...
YOSHI-TSUNE?
SO SNEAK OUT! LET'S ASK MON-CHAN IF HE WANTS TO COME. AND FUKUBE AND KEROYON AND ANYBODY ELSE WHO MIGHT BE ABLE TO.
WELL... I GUESS THE MORE PEOPLE COME...
UMM... EXCUSE ME...
I NEED TO ASK YOU THIS. ARE YOU GUYS, LIKE... THE KENJI FACTION?
OKAY, SO HOW ABOUT WE ALL MEET AT THE STROKE OF MID-NIGHT?
...
MID-NIGHT? THAT'S WAY TOO LATE, KENJIIII.
I DON'T KNOW IF I CAN SNEAK OUT WITHOUT MY FOLKS FINDING OUT...
YOU'RE KENJI, RIGHT?

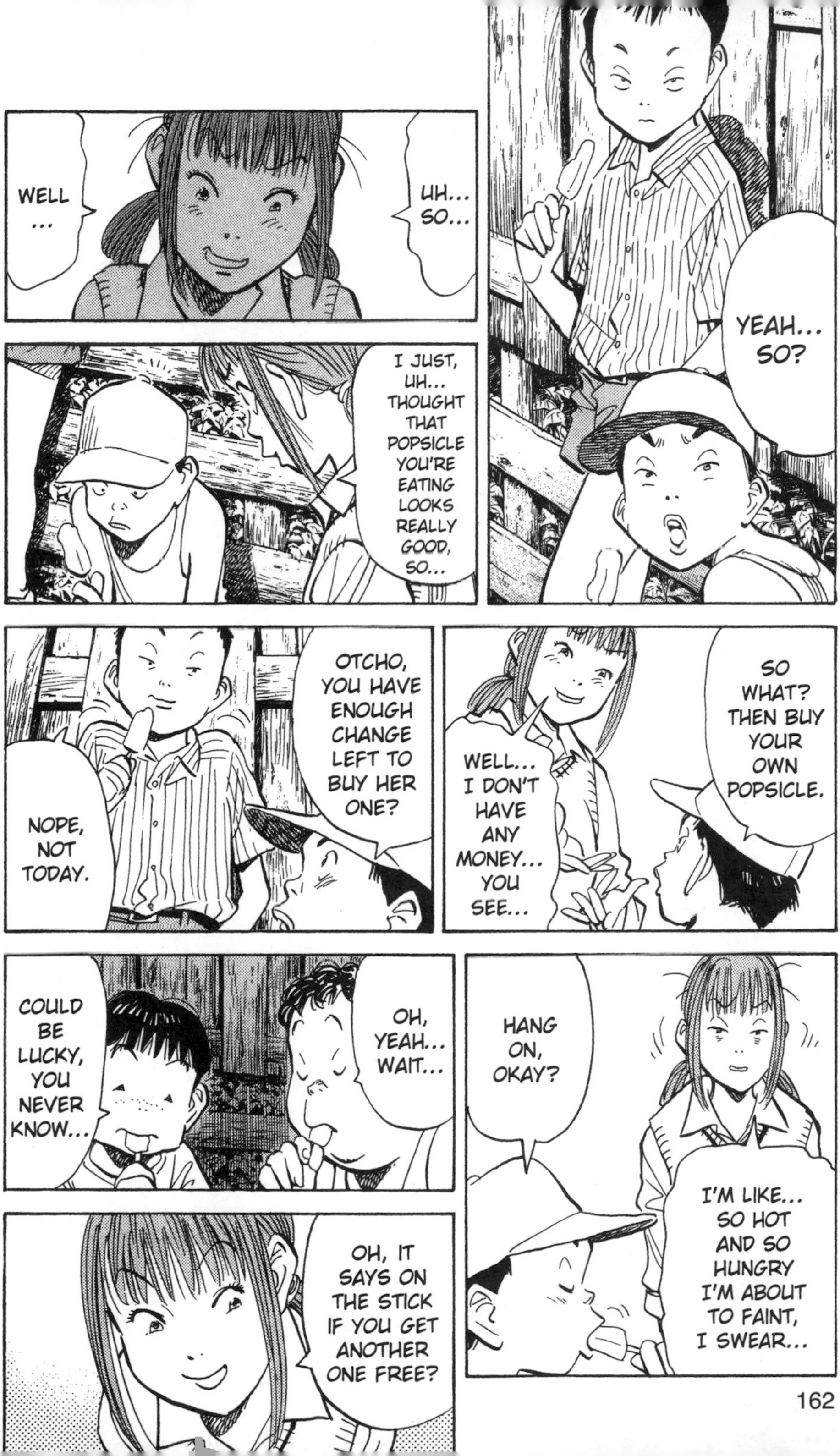
YEAH... SO?
UH... SO...
WELL ...
I JUST, UH... THOUGHT THAT POPSICLE YOU'RE EATING LOOKS REALLY GOOD, SO...
SO WHAT? THEN BUY YOUR OWN POPSICLE.
WELL... I DON'T HAVE ANY MONEY... YOU SEE...
OTCHO, YOU HAVE ENOUGH CHANGE LEFT TO BUY HER ONE?
NOPE, NOT TODAY.
HANG ON, OKAY?
I'M LIKE... SO HOT AND SO HUNGRY I'M ABOUT TO FAINT, I SWEAR...
OH, YEAH... WAIT...
COULD BE LUCKY, YOU NEVER KNOW...
OH, IT SAYS ON THE STICK IF YOU GET ANOTHER ONE FREE?

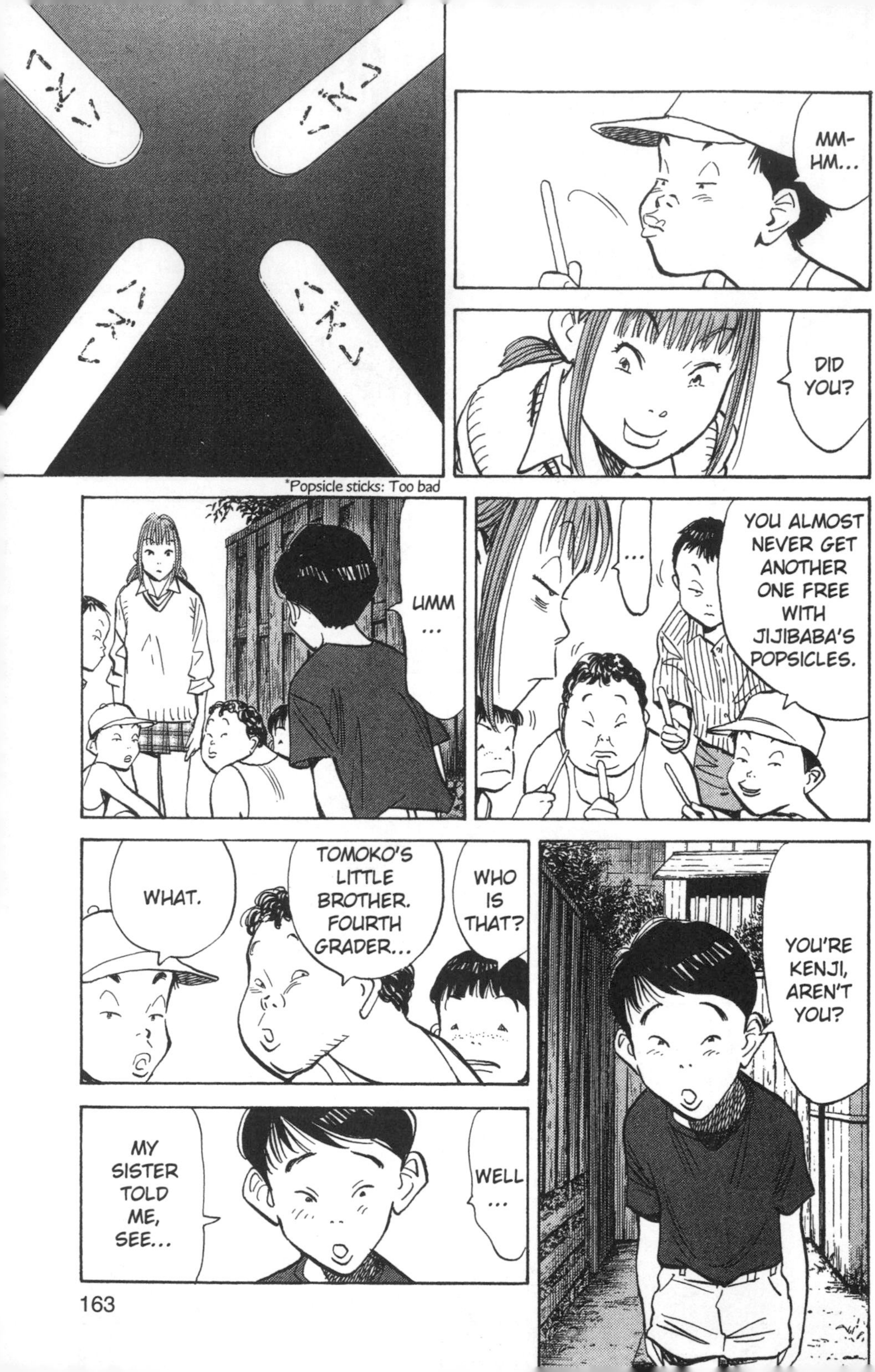
MM-HM...
DID YOU?
ハズレ
ハズレ
ハズレ
ハズレ
*Popsicle sticks: Too bad
...
YOU ALMOST NEVER GET ANOTHER ONE FREE WITH JIJIBABA'S POPSICLES.
UMM ...
YOU'RE KENJI, AREN'T YOU?
WHO IS THAT?
TOMOKO'S LITTLE BROTHER. FOURTH GRADER...
WHAT.
WELL ...
MY SISTER TOLD ME, SEE...

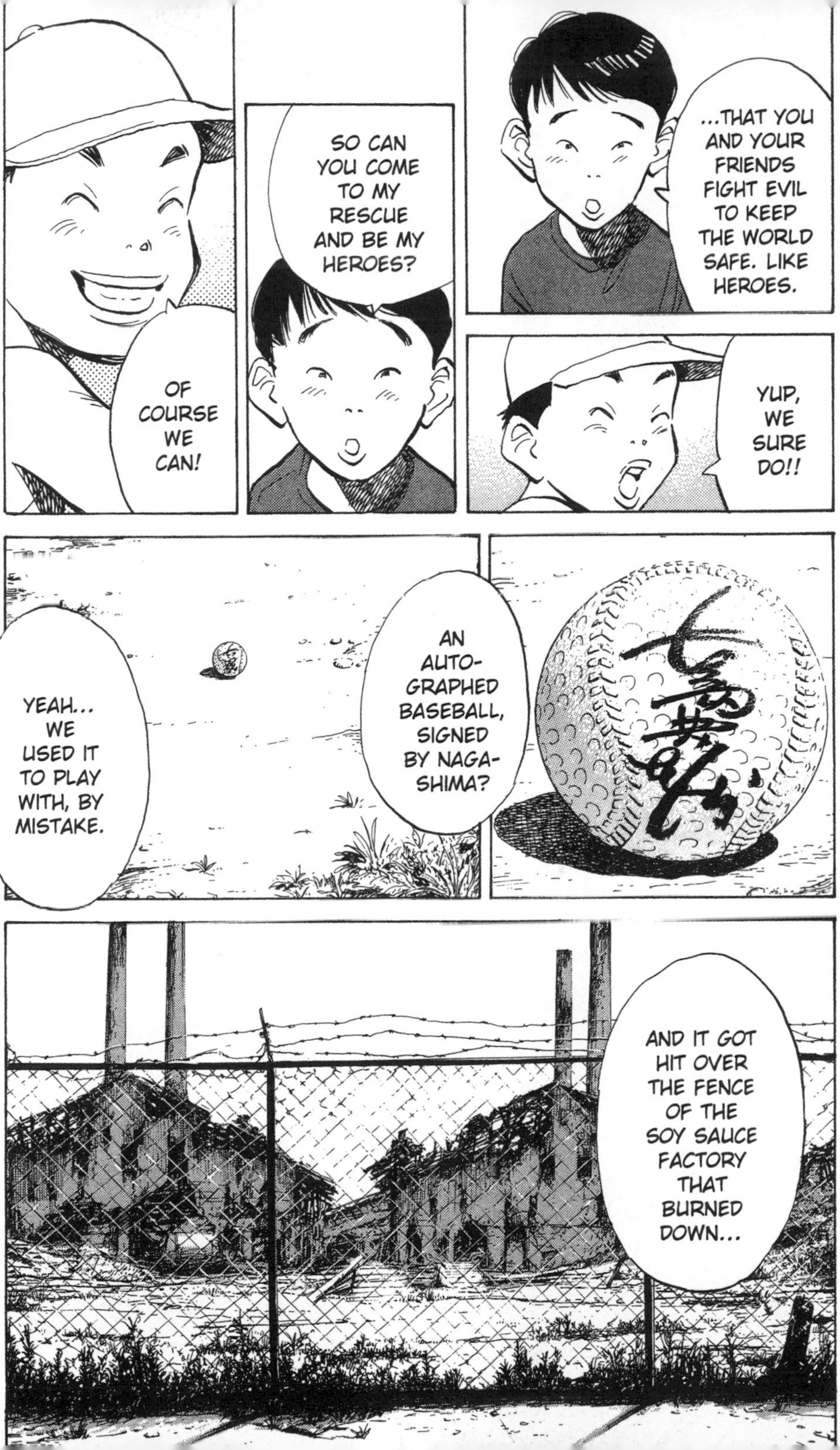
...THAT YOU AND YOUR FRIENDS FIGHT EVIL TO KEEP THE WORLD SAFE. LIKE HEROES.
YUP, WE SURE DO!!
SO CAN YOU COME TO MY RESCUE AND BE MY HEROES?
OF COURSE WE CAN!
AN AUTO-GRAPHED BASEBALL, SIGNED BY NAGA-SHIMA?
YEAH... WE USED IT TO PLAY WITH, BY MISTAKE.
AND IT GOT HIT OVER THE FENCE OF THE SOY SAUCE FACTORY THAT BURNED DOWN...

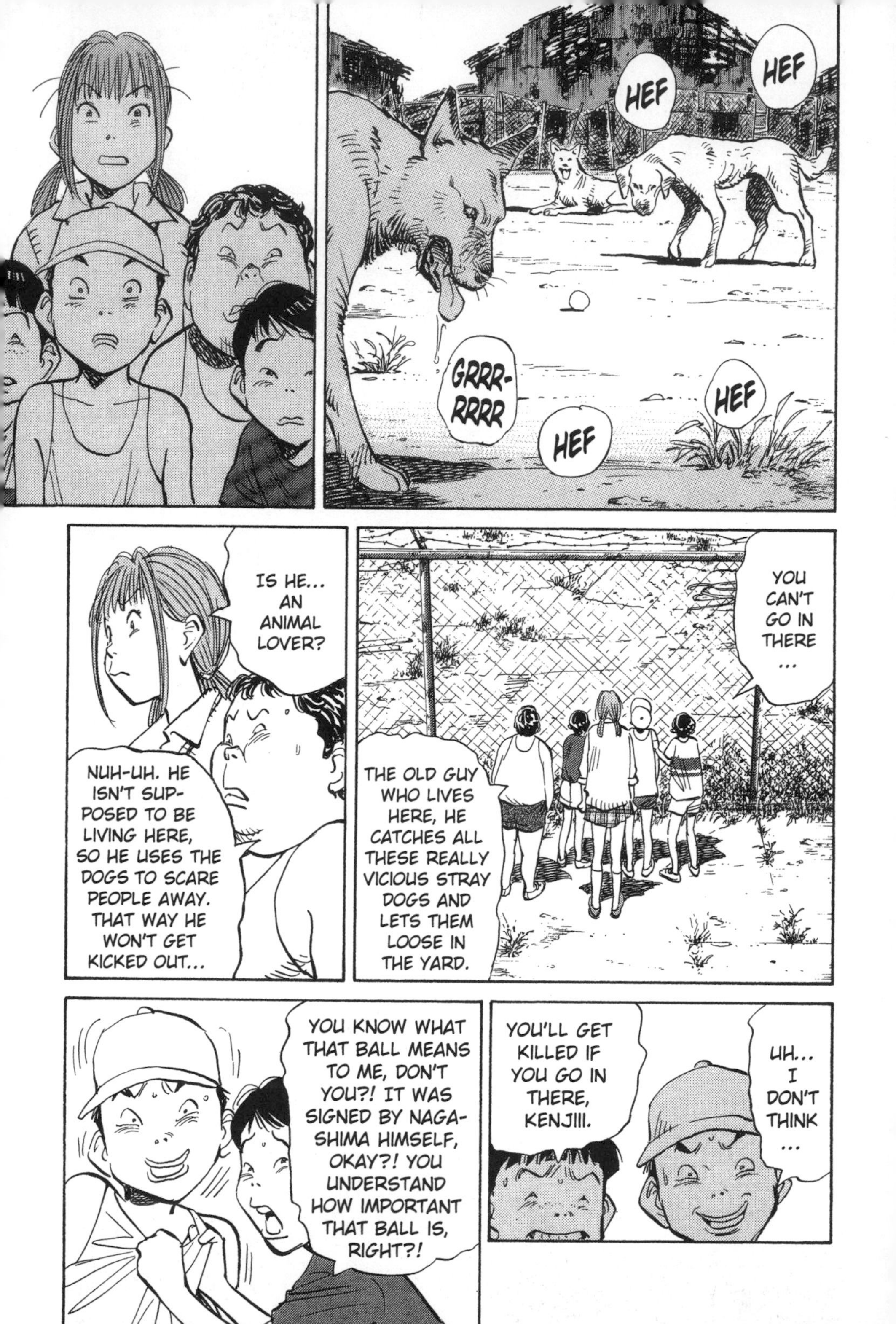
HEF
HEF
HEF
HEF
GRRR-RRRR
YOU CAN'T GO IN THERE...
THE OLD GUY WHO LIVES HERE, HE CATCHES ALL THESE REALLY VICIOUS STRAY DOGS AND LETS THEM LOOSE IN THE YARD.
IS HE... AN ANIMAL LOVER?
NUH-UH. HE ISN'T SUP-POSED TO BE LIVING HERE, SO HE USES THE DOGS TO SCARE PEOPLE AWAY. THAT WAY HE WON'T GET KICKED OUT...
UH... I DON'T THINK...
YOU'LL GET KILLED IF YOU GO IN THERE, KENJIII.
YOU KNOW WHAT THAT BALL MEANS TO ME, DON'T YOU?! IT WAS SIGNED BY NAGA-SHIMA HIMSELF, OKAY?! YOU UNDERSTAND HOW IMPORTANT THAT BALL IS, RIGHT?!

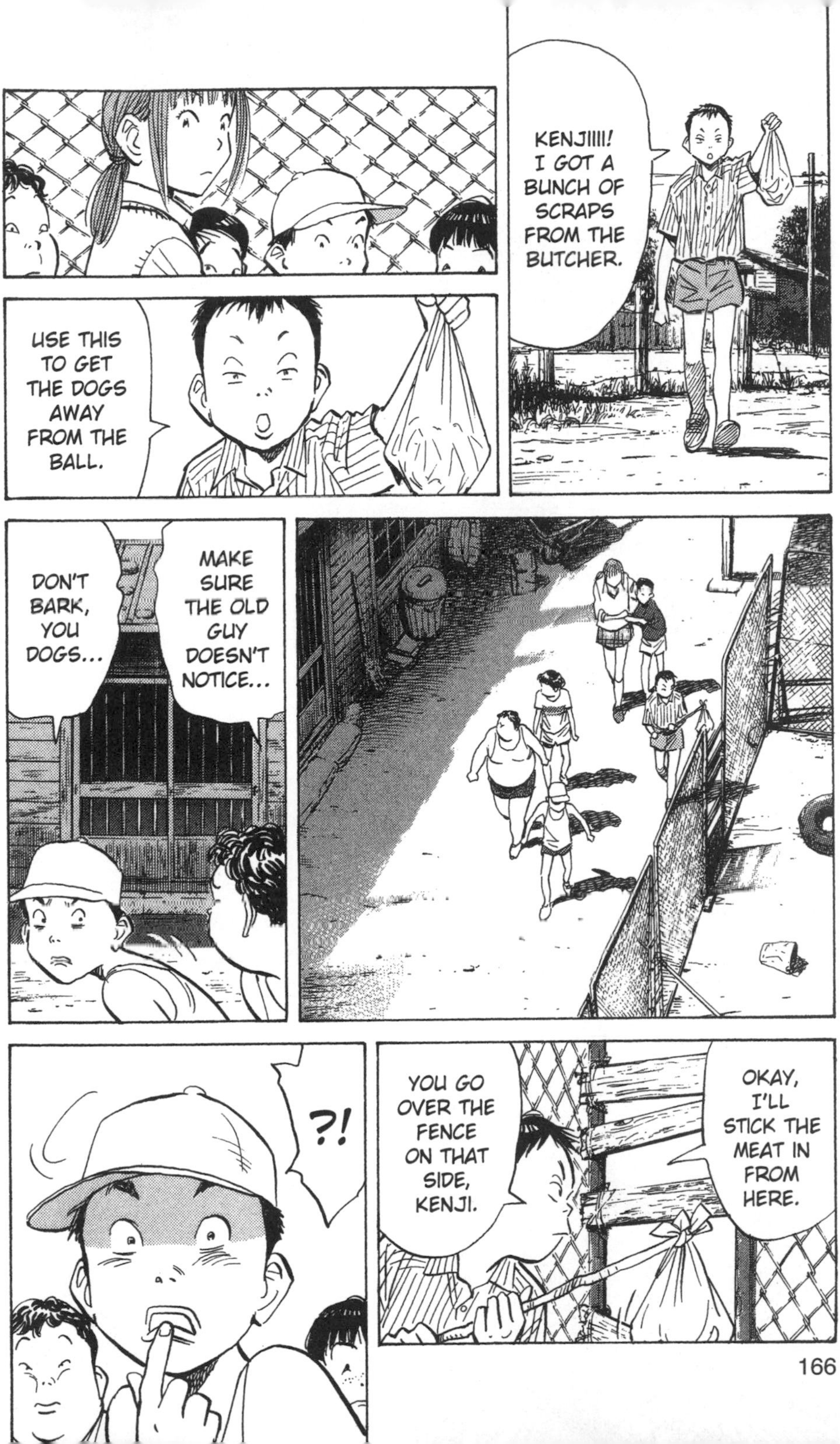
KENJIIII! I GOT A BUNCH OF SCRAPS FROM THE BUTCHER.
USE THIS TO GET THE DOGS AWAY FROM THE BALL.
MAKE SURE THE OLD GUY DOESN'T NOTICE...
DON'T BARK, YOU DOGS...
OKAY, I'LL STICK THE MEAT IN FROM HERE.
YOU GO OVER THE FENCE ON THAT SIDE, KENJI.
?!

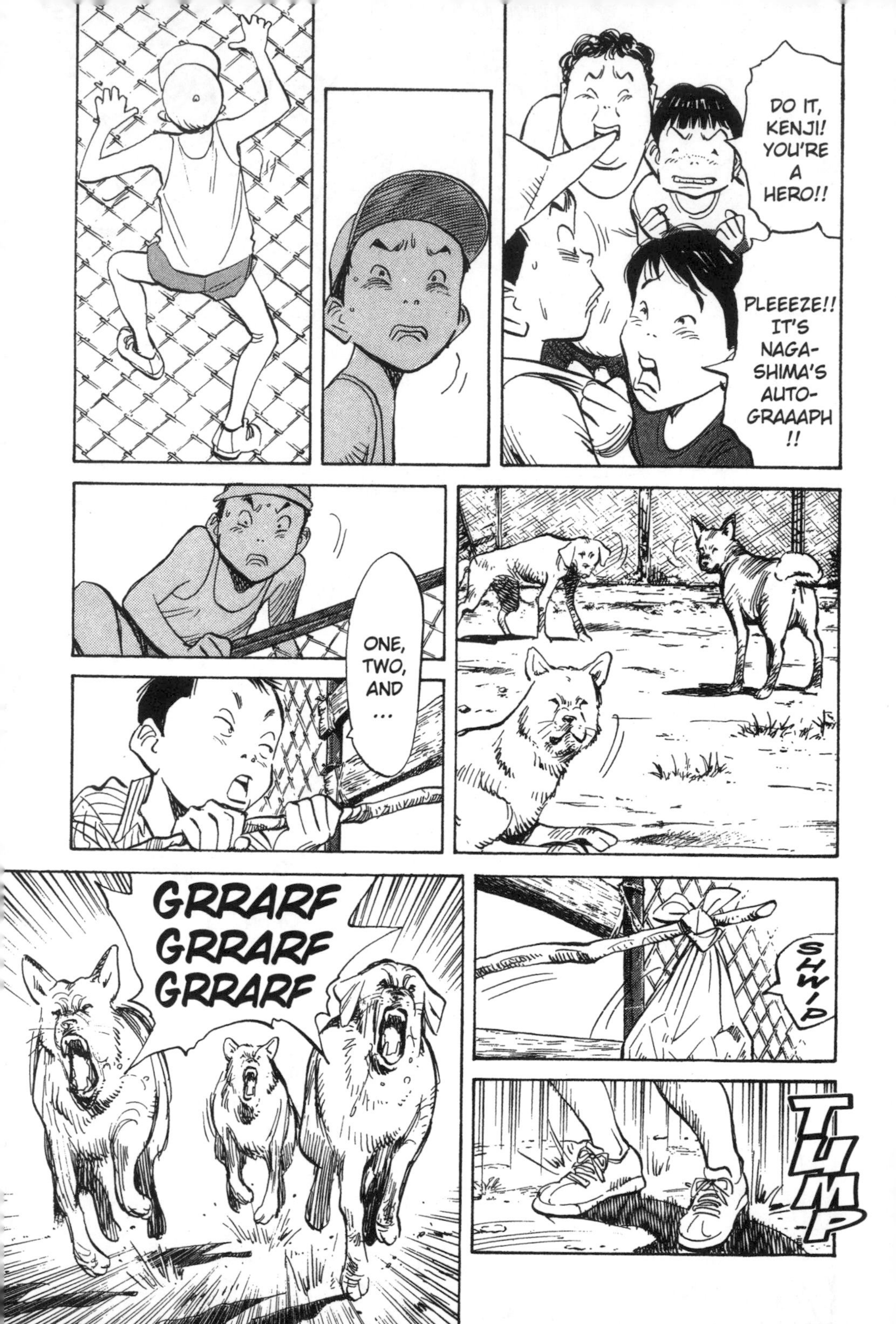
DO IT, KENJI! YOU'RE A HERO!!
PLEEEZE!! IT'S NAGA-SHIMA'S AUTO-GRAAAPH !!
ONE, TWO, AND ...
SHWIP
TUMP
GRRARF GRRARF GRRARF

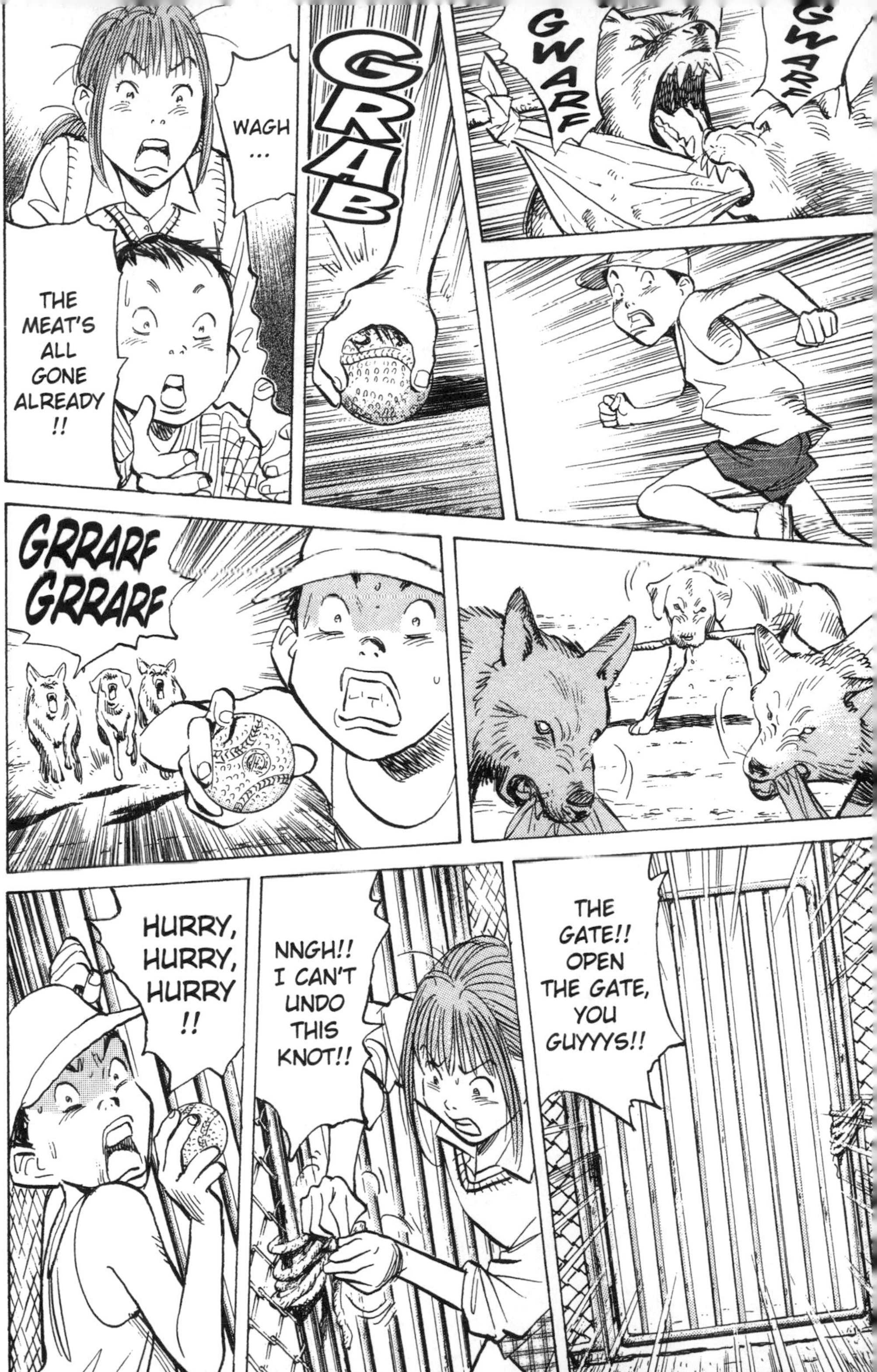
GWARF
GWARF
GRAB
WAGH ...
THE MEAT'S ALL GONE ALREADY !!
GRRARF GRRARF
THE GATE!! OPEN THE GATE, YOU GUYYYS!!
NNGH!! I CAN'T UNDO THIS KNOT!!
HURRY, HURRY, HURRY !!

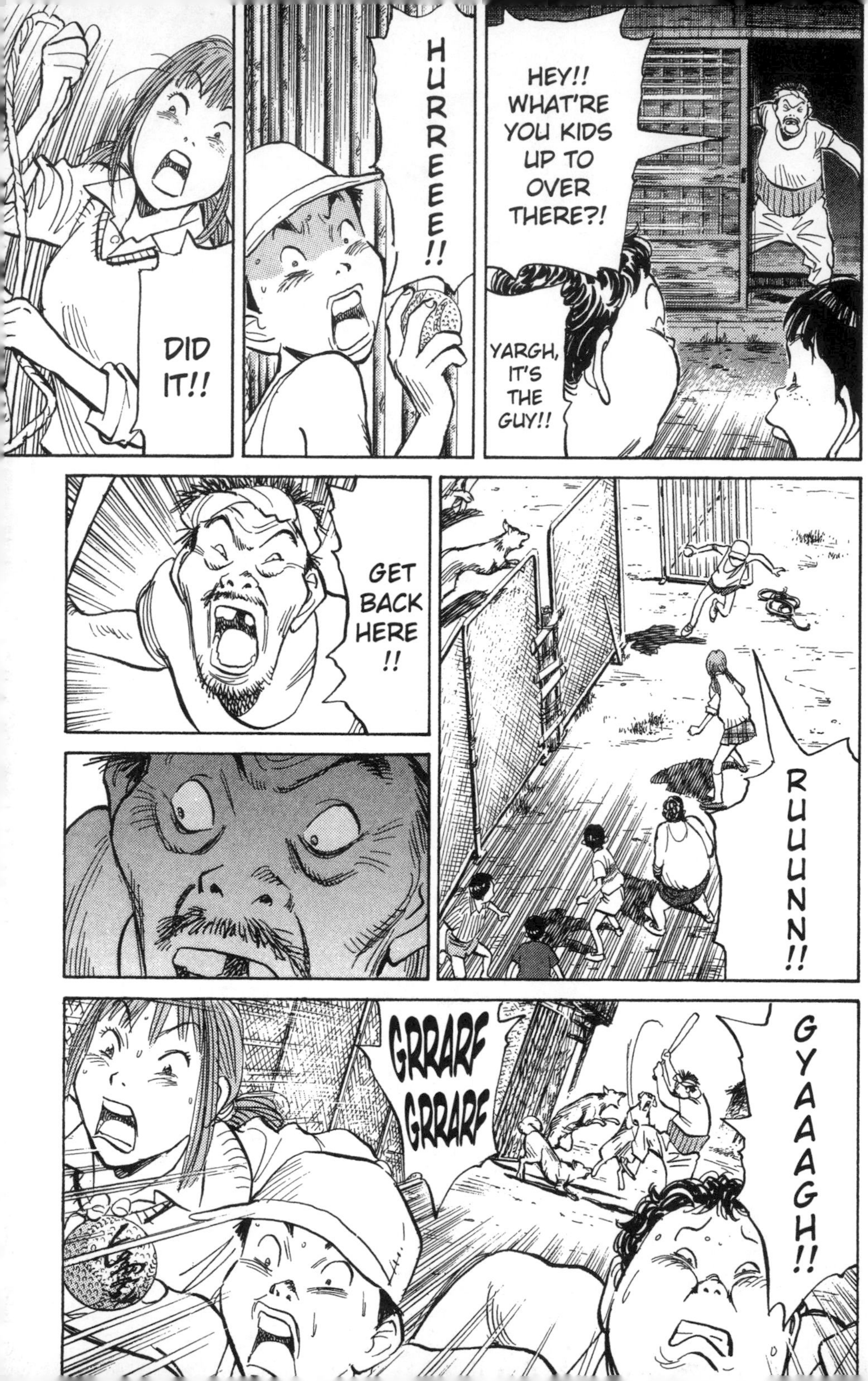
HEY!! WHAT'RE YOU KIDS UP TO OVER THERE?!
YARGH, IT'S THE GUY!!
HURREEEE!!
DID IT!!
RUUUNNN!!
GET BACK HERE!!
GYAAAAGH!!
GRRARF GRRARF

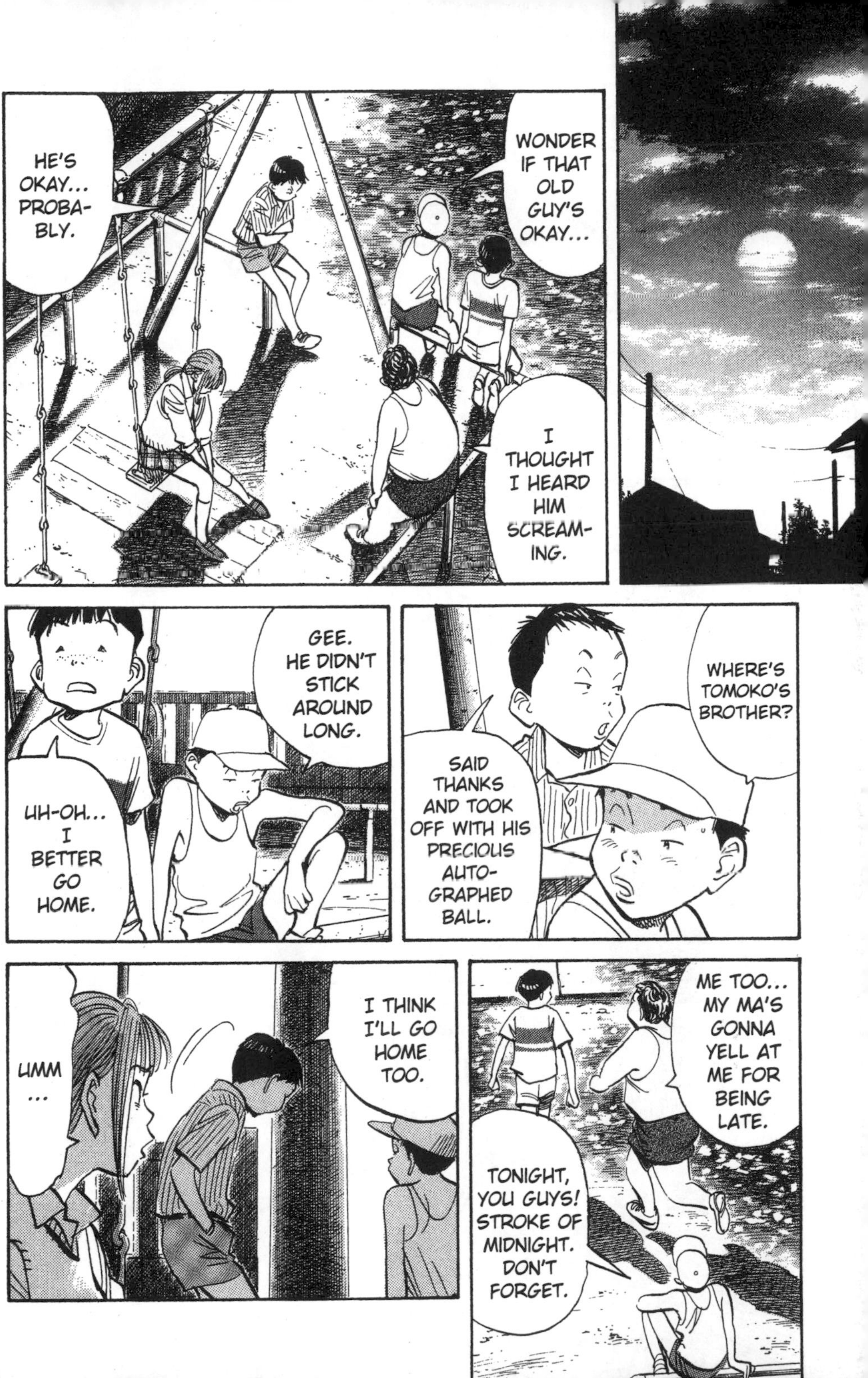
WONDER IF THAT OLD GUY'S OKAY...
I THOUGHT I HEARD HIM SCREAMING.
HE'S OKAY... PROBABLY.
WHERE'S TOMOKO'S BROTHER?
SAID THANKS AND TOOK OFF WITH HIS PRECIOUS AUTOGRAPHED BALL.
GEE. HE DIDN'T STICK AROUND LONG.
UH-OH... I BETTER GO HOME.
ME TOO... MY MA'S GONNA YELL AT ME FOR BEING LATE.
TONIGHT, YOU GUYS! STROKE OF MIDNIGHT. DON'T FORGET.
I THINK I'LL GO HOME TOO.
UMM...

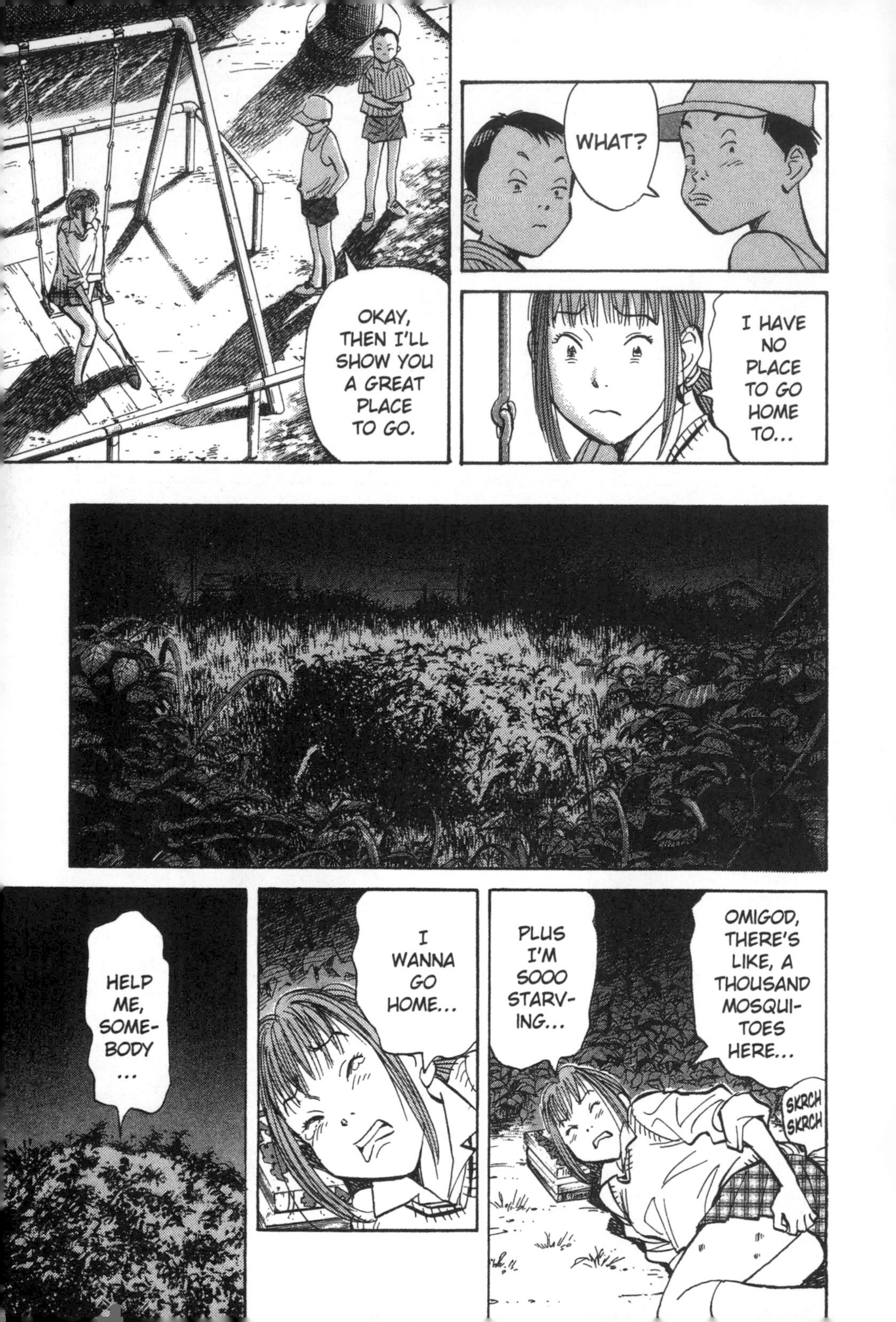
WHAT?
I HAVE NO PLACE TO GO HOME TO...
OKAY, THEN I'LL SHOW YOU A GREAT PLACE TO GO.
OMIGOD, THERE'S LIKE, A THOUSAND MOSQUI-TOES HERE...
PLUS I'M SOOO STARV-ING...
SKRCH SKRCH
I WANNA GO HOME...
HELP ME, SOME-BODY ...

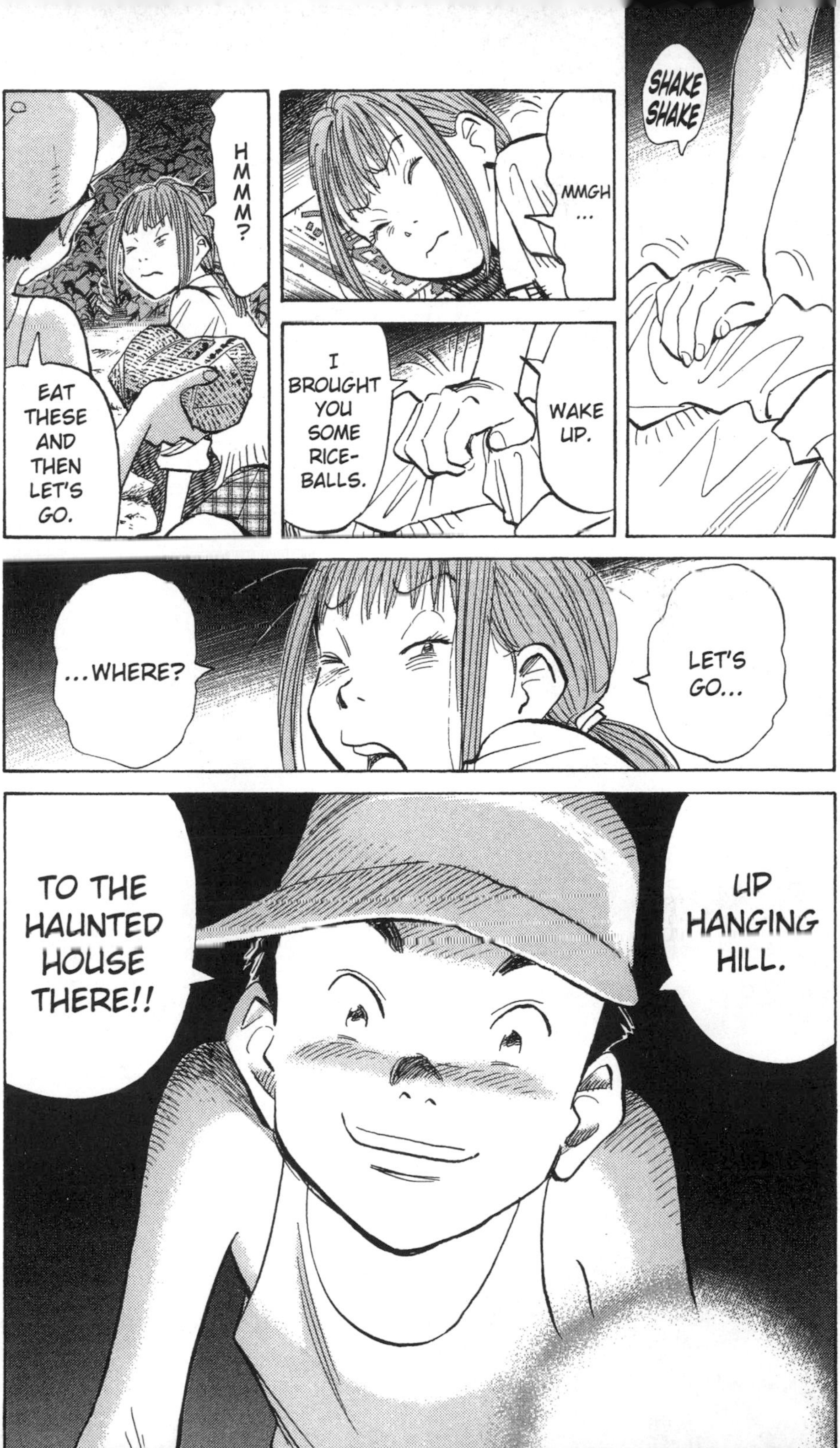
SHAKE SHAKE
MMGH ...
WAKE UP.
I BROUGHT YOU SOME RICE-BALLS.
HMMMM?
EAT THESE AND THEN LET'S GO.
LET'S GO...
...WHERE?
UP HANGING HILL.
TO THE HAUNTED HOUSE THERE!!

Chapter 10 Hanging Hill

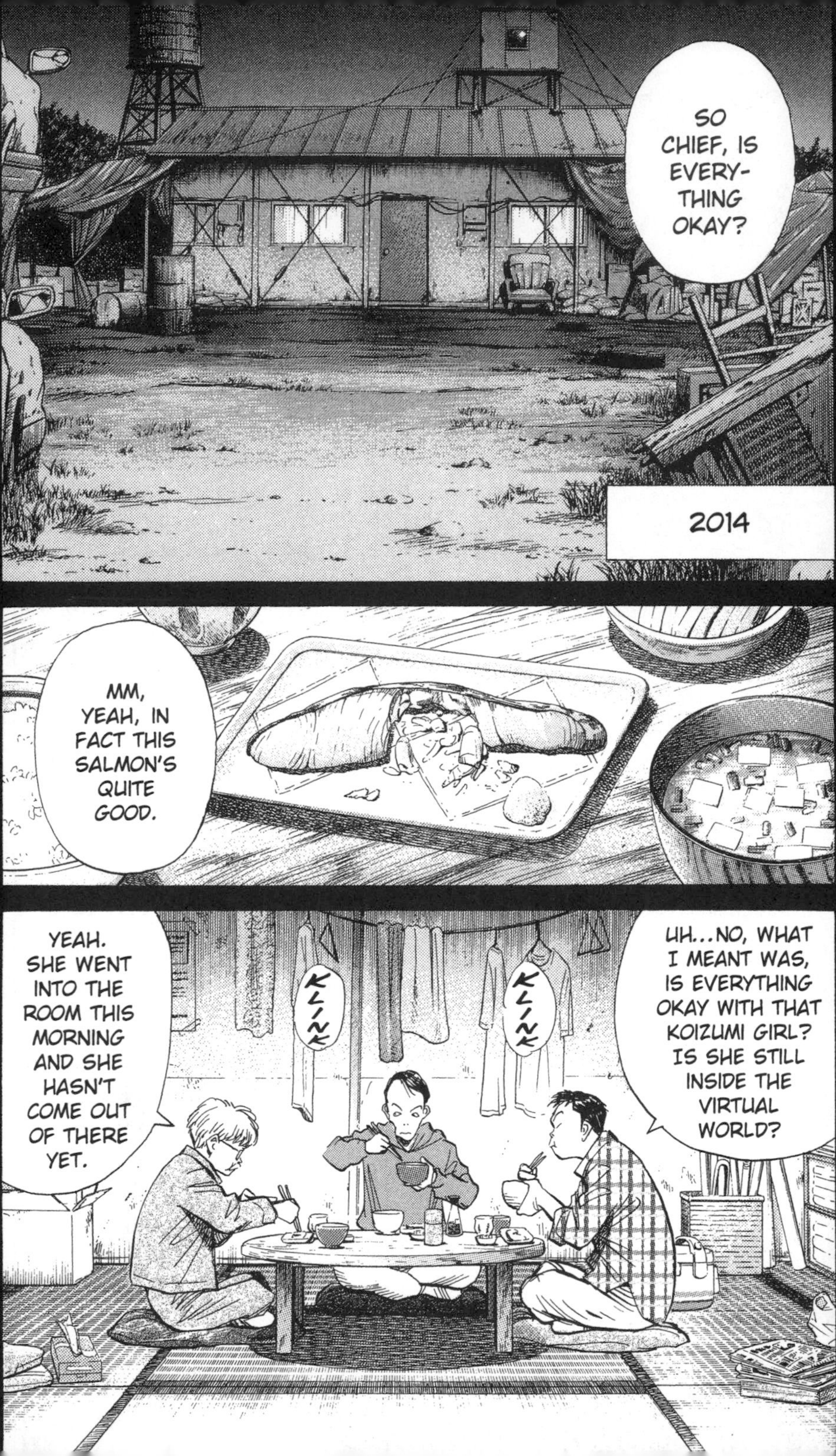
SO CHIEF, IS EVERY-THING OKAY?
2014
MM, YEAH, IN FACT THIS SALMON'S QUITE GOOD.
UH...NO, WHAT I MEANT WAS, IS EVERYTHING OKAY WITH THAT KOIZUMI GIRL? IS SHE STILL INSIDE THE VIRTUAL WORLD?
KLINK
KLINK
YEAH. SHE WENT INTO THE ROOM THIS MORNING AND SHE HASN'T COME OUT OF THERE YET.

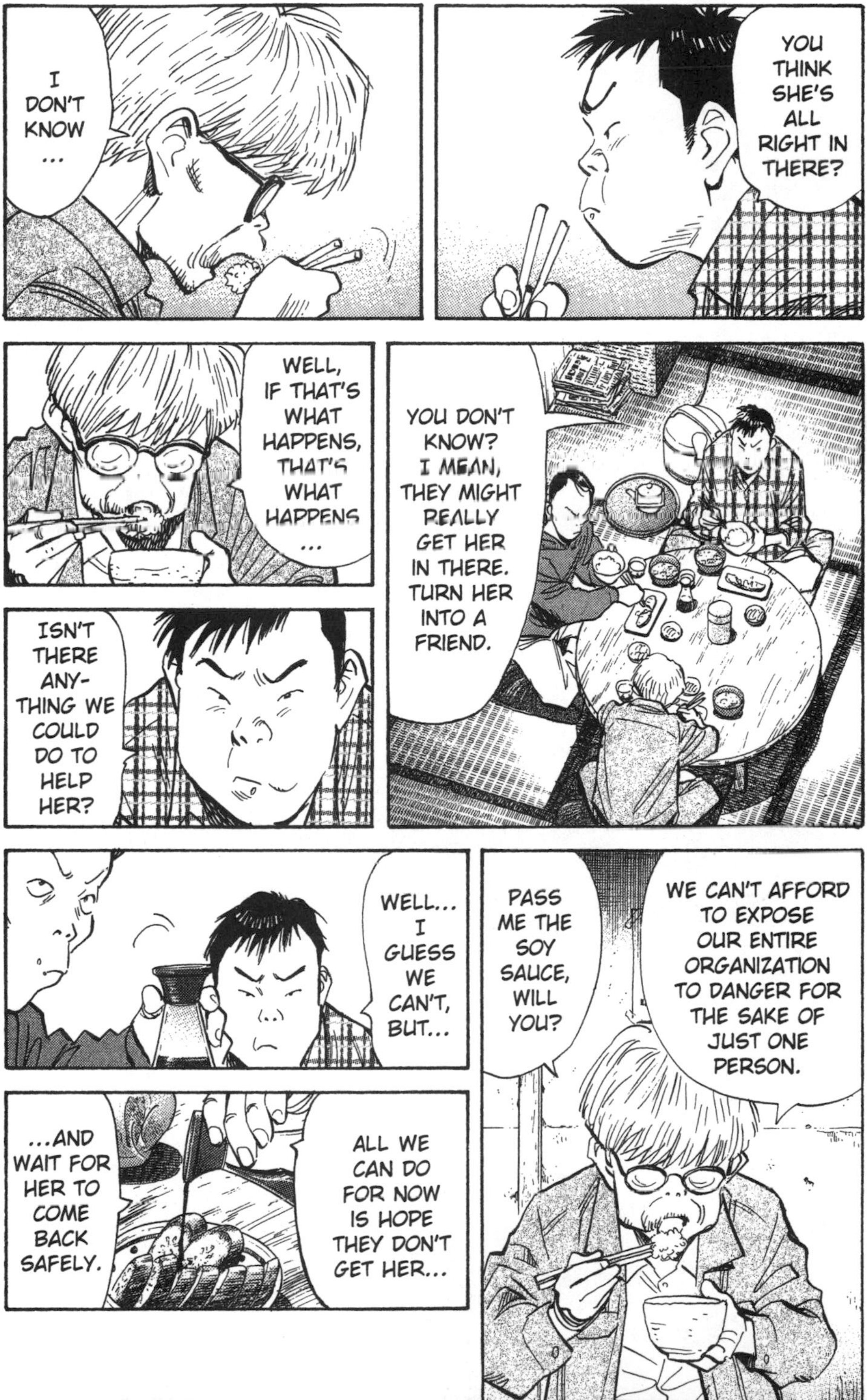
YOU THINK SHE'S ALL RIGHT IN THERE?
I DON'T KNOW ...
YOU DON'T KNOW? I MEAN, THEY MIGHT REALLY GET HER IN THERE. TURN HER INTO A FRIEND.
WELL, IF THAT'S WHAT HAPPENS, THAT'S WHAT HAPPENS ...
ISN'T THERE ANY-THING WE COULD DO TO HELP HER?
WE CAN'T AFFORD TO EXPOSE OUR ENTIRE ORGANIZATION TO DANGER FOR THE SAKE OF JUST ONE PERSON.
PASS ME THE SOY SAUCE, WILL YOU?
WELL... I GUESS WE CAN'T, BUT...
ALL WE CAN DO FOR NOW IS HOPE THEY DON'T GET HER...
...AND WAIT FOR HER TO COME BACK SAFELY.

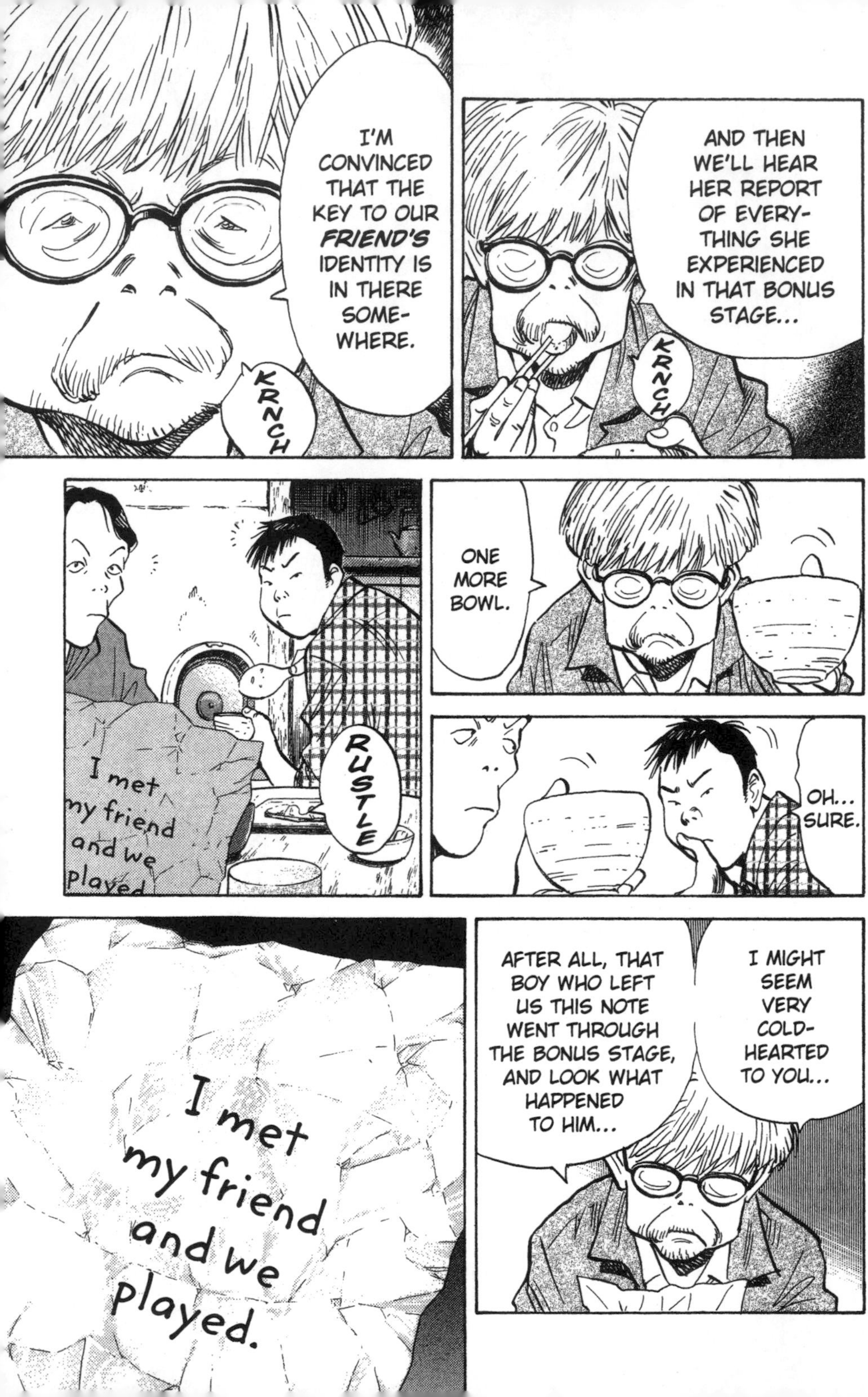
AND THEN WE'LL HEAR HER REPORT OF EVERY-THING SHE EXPERIENCED IN THAT BONUS STAGE...
KRNCH
I'M CONVINCED THAT THE KEY TO OUR ***FRIEND'S*** IDENTITY IS IN THERE SOME-WHERE.
KRNCH
ONE MORE BOWL.
OH... SURE.
RUSTLE
I met my friend and we played
I MIGHT SEEM VERY COLD-HEARTED TO YOU...
AFTER ALL, THAT BOY WHO LEFT US THIS NOTE WENT THROUGH THE BONUS STAGE, AND LOOK WHAT HAPPENED TO HIM...
I met my friend and we played.

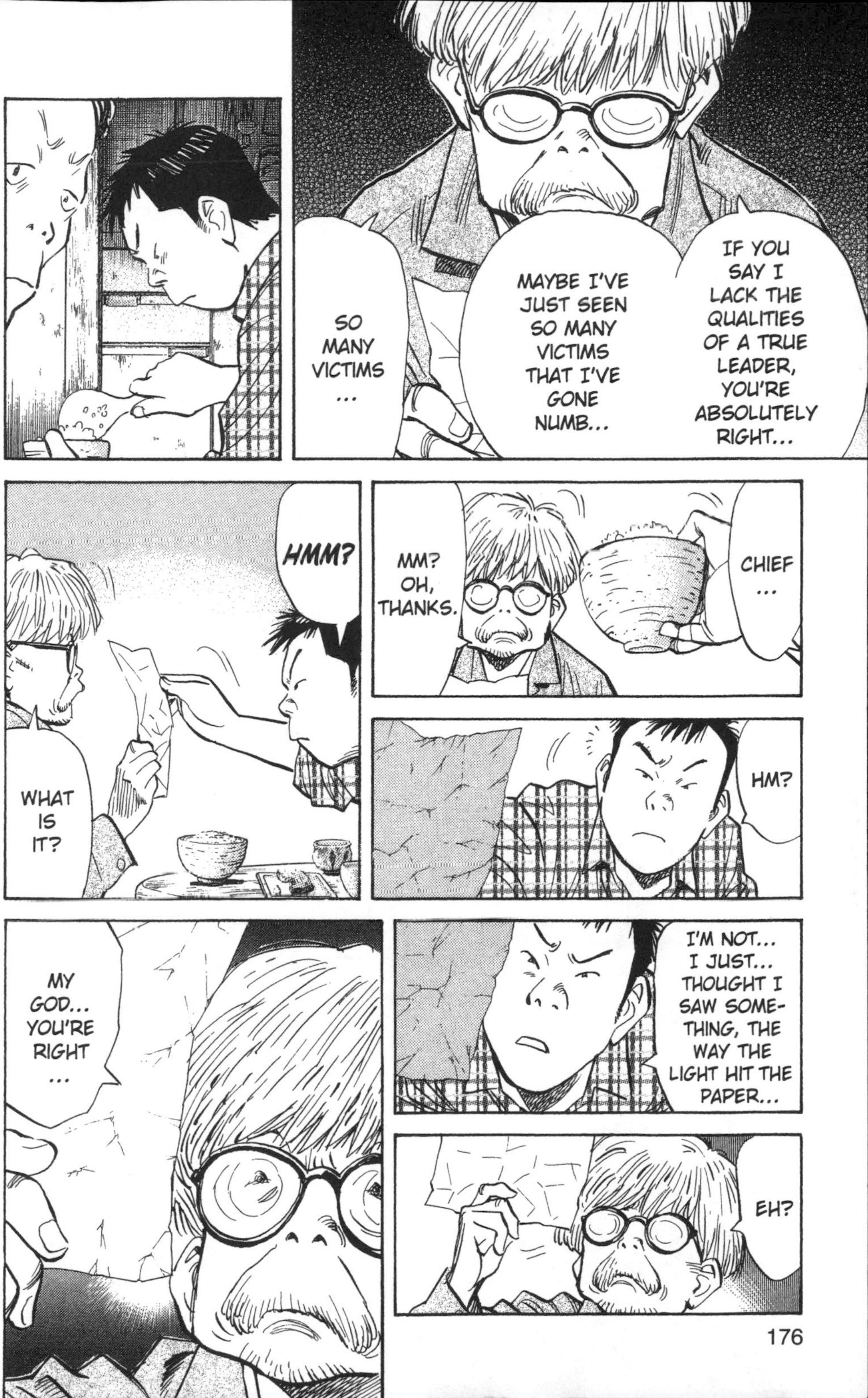
IF YOU SAY I LACK THE QUALITIES OF A TRUE LEADER, YOU'RE ABSOLUTELY RIGHT...
MAYBE I'VE JUST SEEN SO MANY VICTIMS THAT I'VE GONE NUMB...
SO MANY VICTIMS ...
CHIEF ...
MM? OH, THANKS.
HM?
HMM?
WHAT IS IT?
I'M NOT... I JUST... THOUGHT I SAW SOME-THING, THE WAY THE LIGHT HIT THE PAPER...
EH?
MY GOD... YOU'RE RIGHT ...

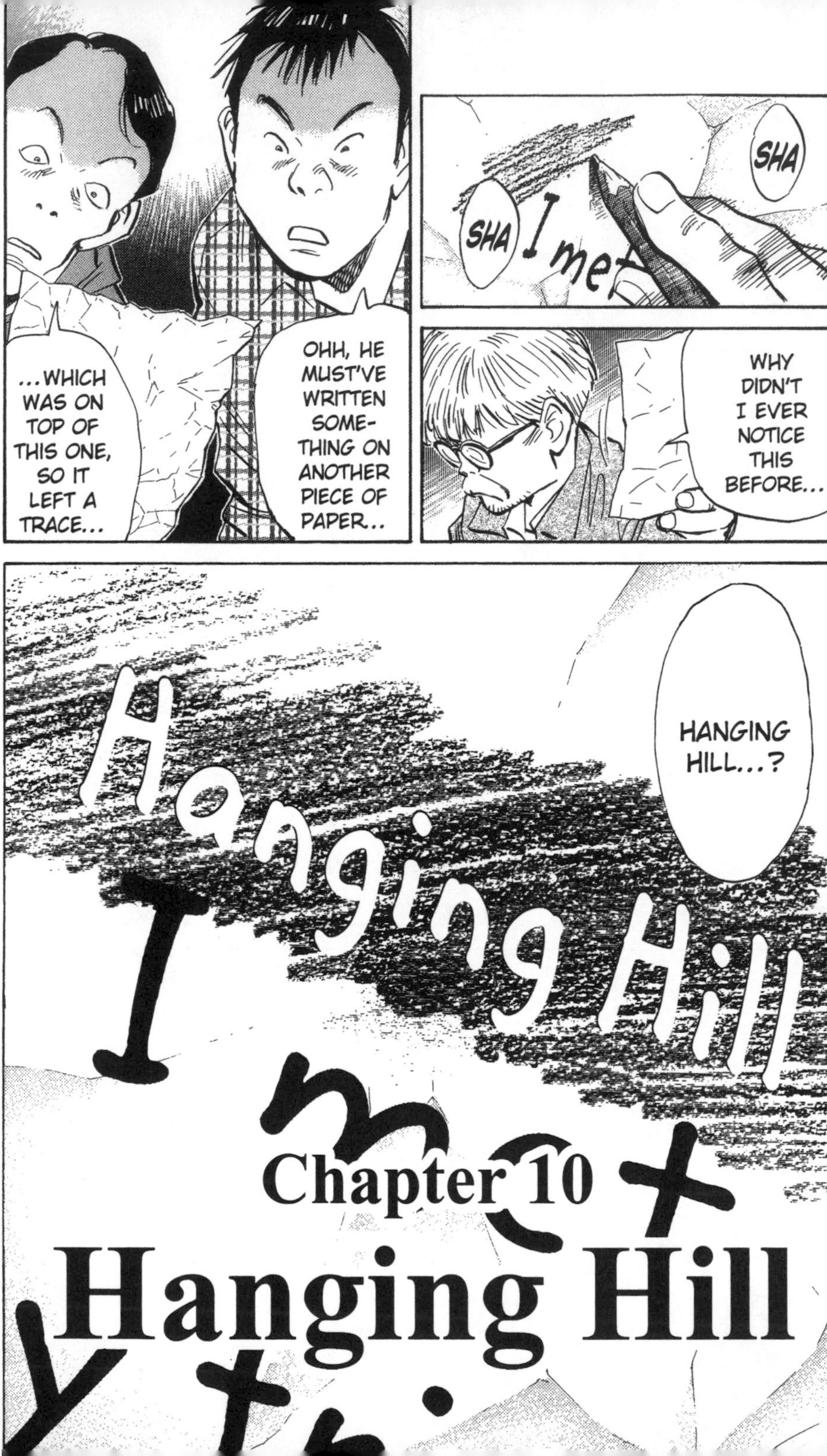
SHA
SHA
I met
WHY DIDN'T I EVER NOTICE THIS BEFORE...
OHH, HE MUST'VE WRITTEN SOME-THING ON ANOTHER PIECE OF PAPER...
...WHICH WAS ON TOP OF THIS ONE, SO IT LEFT A TRACE...
HANGING HILL...?
Hanging Hill
Chapter 10
Hanging Hill

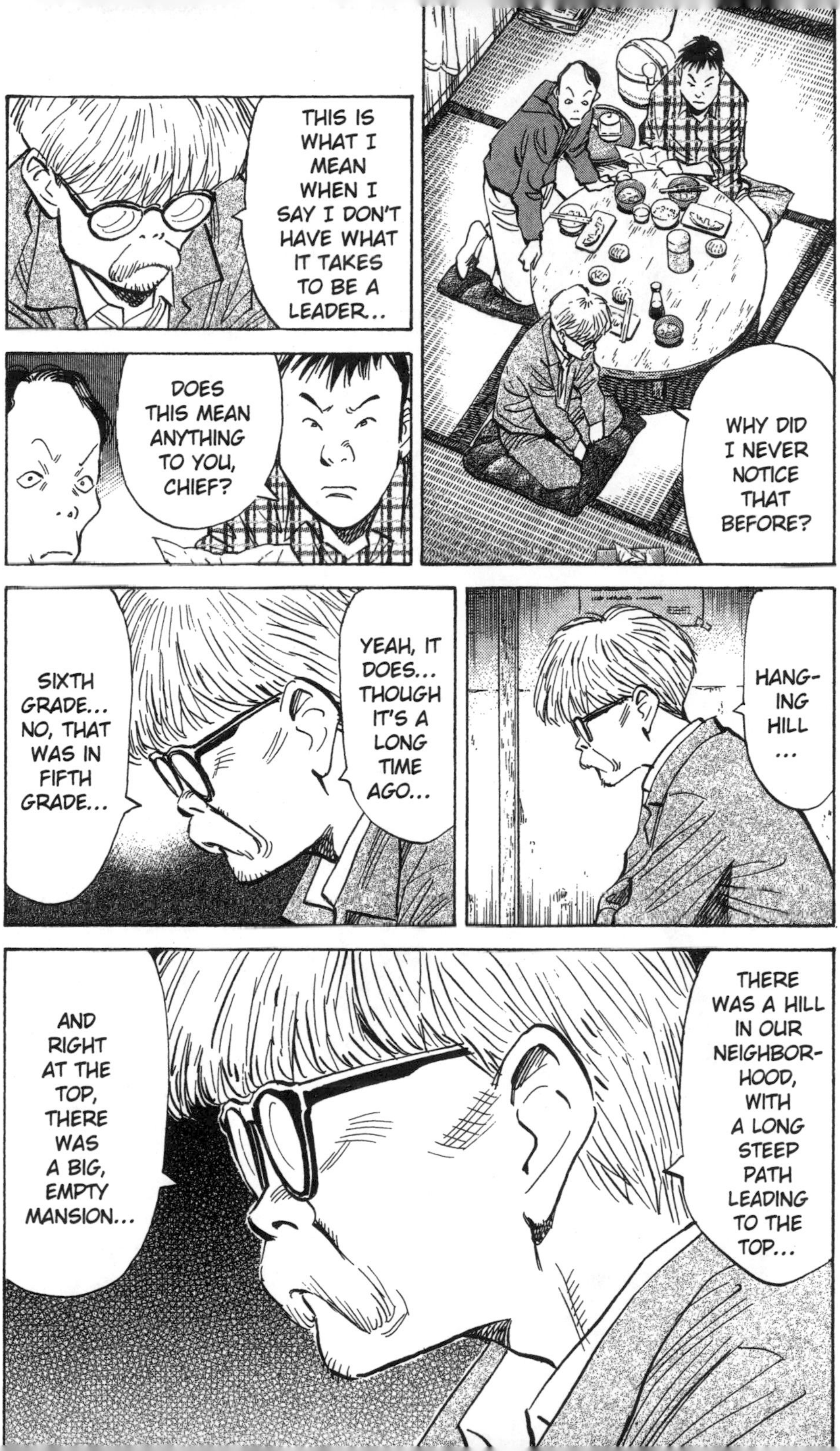
WHY DID I NEVER NOTICE THAT BEFORE?
THIS IS WHAT I MEAN WHEN I SAY I DON'T HAVE WHAT IT TAKES TO BE A LEADER...
DOES THIS MEAN ANYTHING TO YOU, CHIEF?
HANG-ING HILL ...
YEAH, IT DOES... THOUGH IT'S A LONG TIME AGO...
SIXTH GRADE... NO, THAT WAS IN FIFTH GRADE...
THERE WAS A HILL IN OUR NEIGHBOR-HOOD, WITH A LONG STEEP PATH LEADING TO THE TOP...
AND RIGHT AT THE TOP, THERE WAS A BIG, EMPTY MANSION...

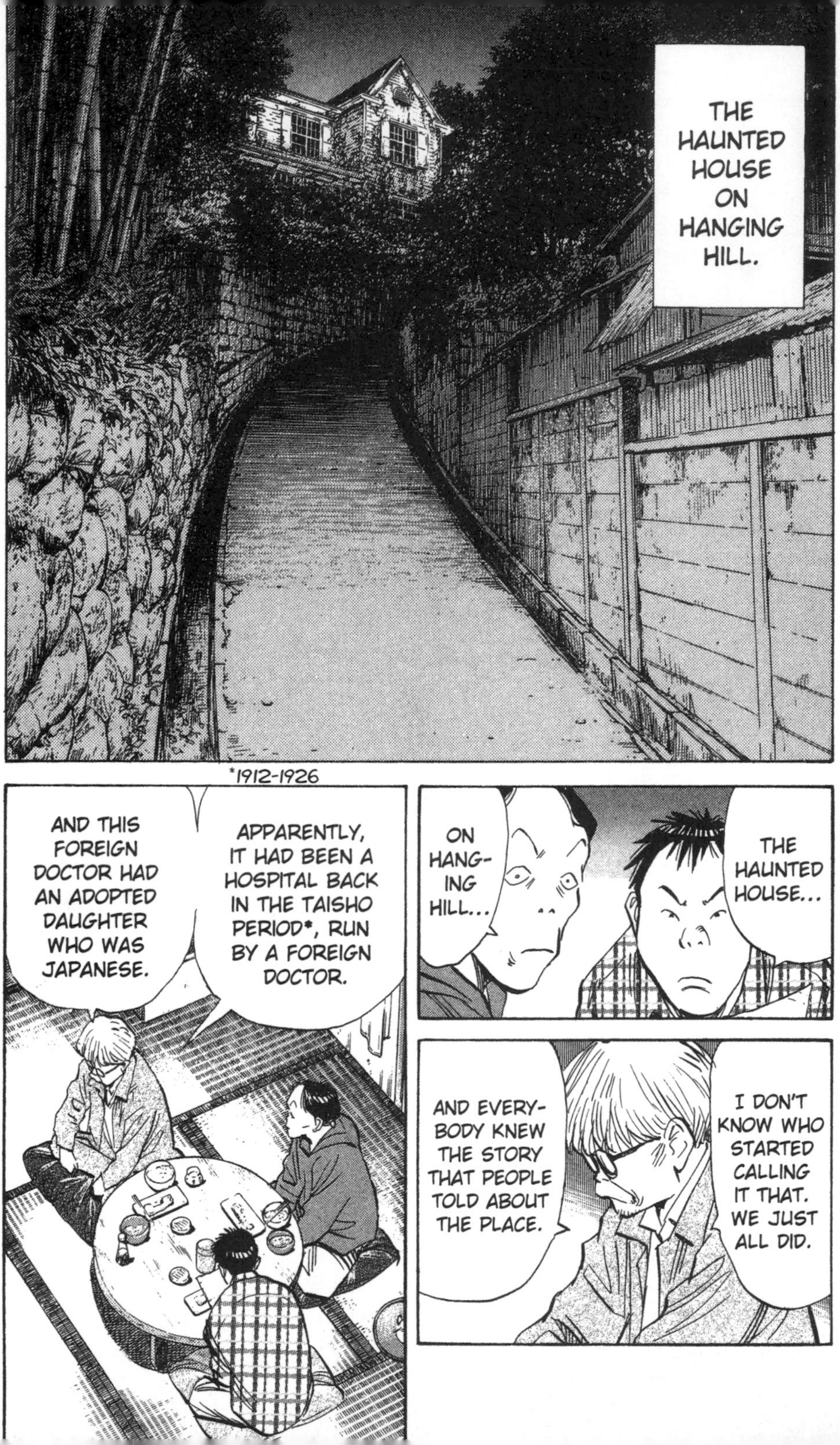
THE HAUNTED HOUSE ON HANGING HILL.
THE HAUNTED HOUSE...
ON HANG-ING HILL...
I DON'T KNOW WHO STARTED CALLING IT THAT. WE JUST ALL DID.
AND EVERY-BODY KNEW THE STORY THAT PEOPLE TOLD ABOUT THE PLACE.
APPARENTLY, IT HAD BEEN A HOSPITAL BACK IN THE TAISHO PERIOD*, RUN BY A FOREIGN DOCTOR.
AND THIS FOREIGN DOCTOR HAD AN ADOPTED DAUGHTER WHO WAS JAPANESE.

*1912-1926

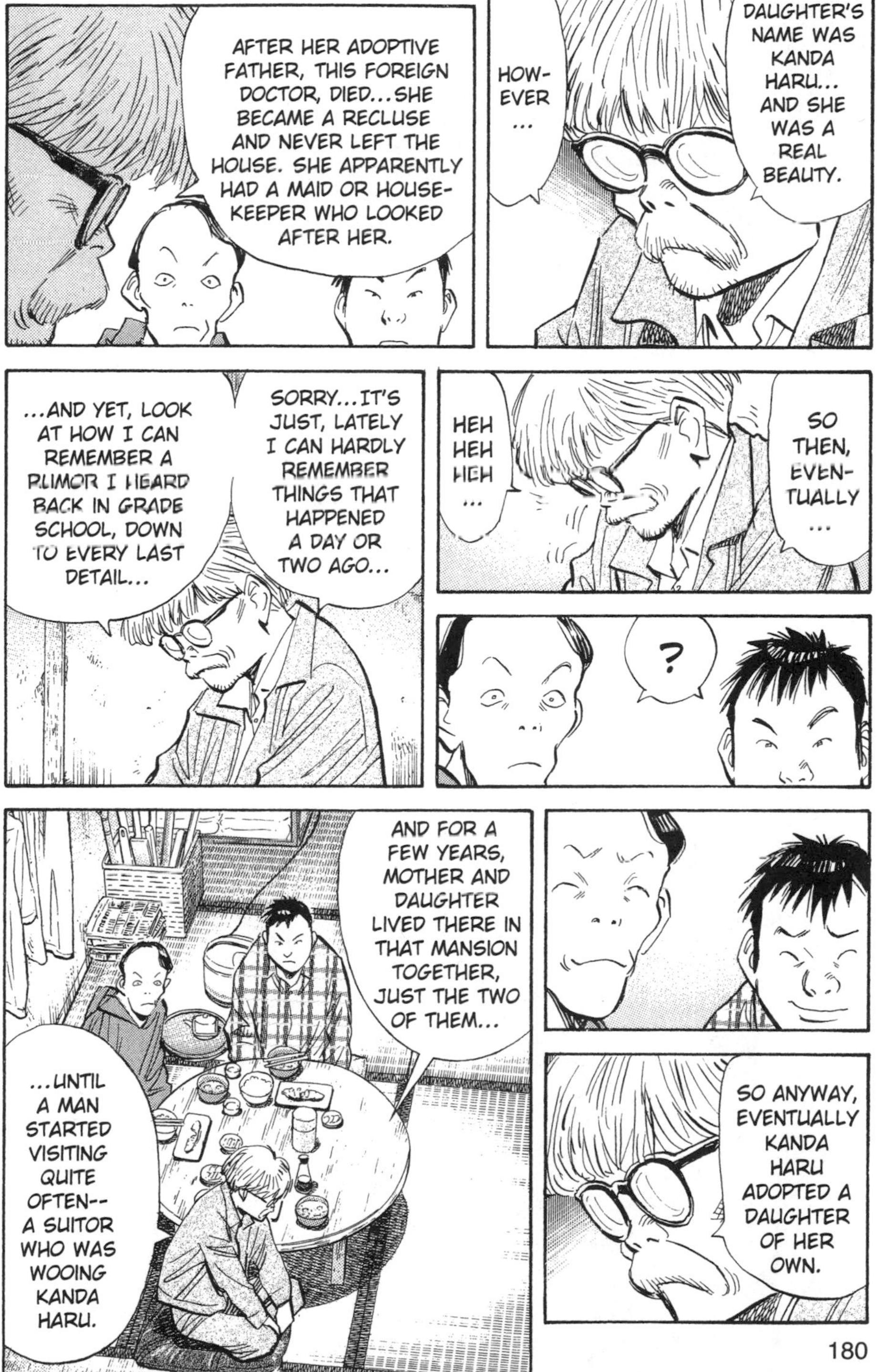
THIS DAUGHTER'S NAME WAS KANDA HARU... AND SHE WAS A REAL BEAUTY.
HOW-EVER ...
AFTER HER ADOPTIVE FATHER, THIS FOREIGN DOCTOR, DIED...SHE BECAME A RECLUSE AND NEVER LEFT THE HOUSE. SHE APPARENTLY HAD A MAID OR HOUSE-KEEPER WHO LOOKED AFTER HER.
SO THEN, EVEN-TUALLY ...
HEH HEH HEH ...
?
SORRY...IT'S JUST, LATELY I CAN HARDLY REMEMBER THINGS THAT HAPPENED A DAY OR TWO AGO...
...AND YET, LOOK AT HOW I CAN REMEMBER A RUMOR I HEARD BACK IN GRADE SCHOOL, DOWN TO EVERY LAST DETAIL...
SO ANYWAY, EVENTUALLY KANDA HARU ADOPTED A DAUGHTER OF HER OWN.
AND FOR A FEW YEARS, MOTHER AND DAUGHTER LIVED THERE IN THAT MANSION TOGETHER, JUST THE TWO OF THEM...
...UNTIL A MAN STARTED VISITING QUITE OFTEN-- A SUITOR WHO WAS WOOING KANDA HARU.

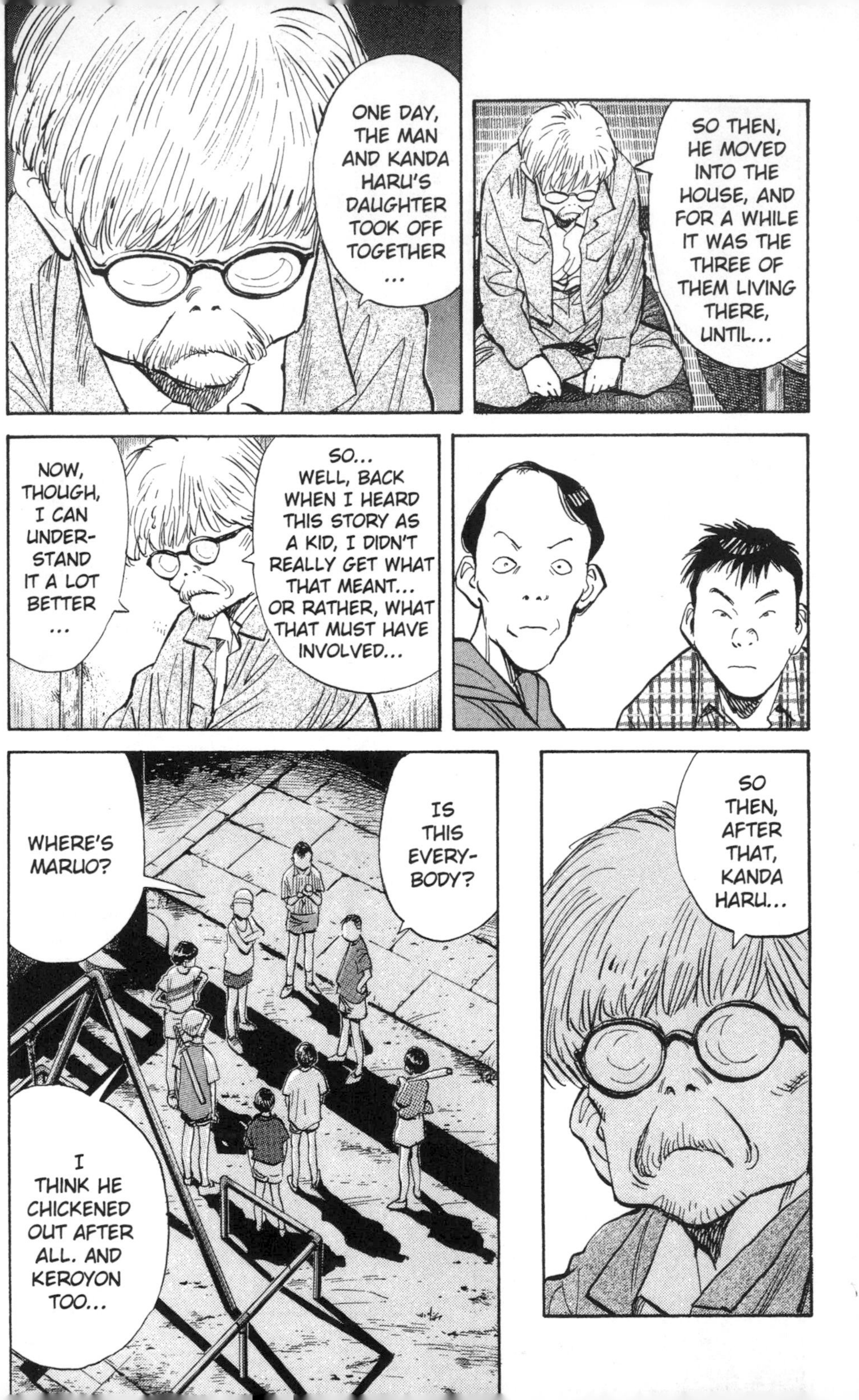
SO THEN, HE MOVED INTO THE HOUSE, AND FOR A WHILE IT WAS THE THREE OF THEM LIVING THERE, UNTIL...
ONE DAY, THE MAN AND KANDA HARU'S DAUGHTER TOOK OFF TOGETHER ...
SO... WELL, BACK WHEN I HEARD THIS STORY AS A KID, I DIDN'T REALLY GET WHAT THAT MEANT... OR RATHER, WHAT THAT MUST HAVE INVOLVED...
NOW, THOUGH, I CAN UNDER-STAND IT A LOT BETTER ...
SO THEN, AFTER THAT, KANDA HARU...
IS THIS EVERY-BODY?
WHERE'S MARUO?
I THINK HE CHICKENED OUT AFTER ALL. AND KEROYON TOO...

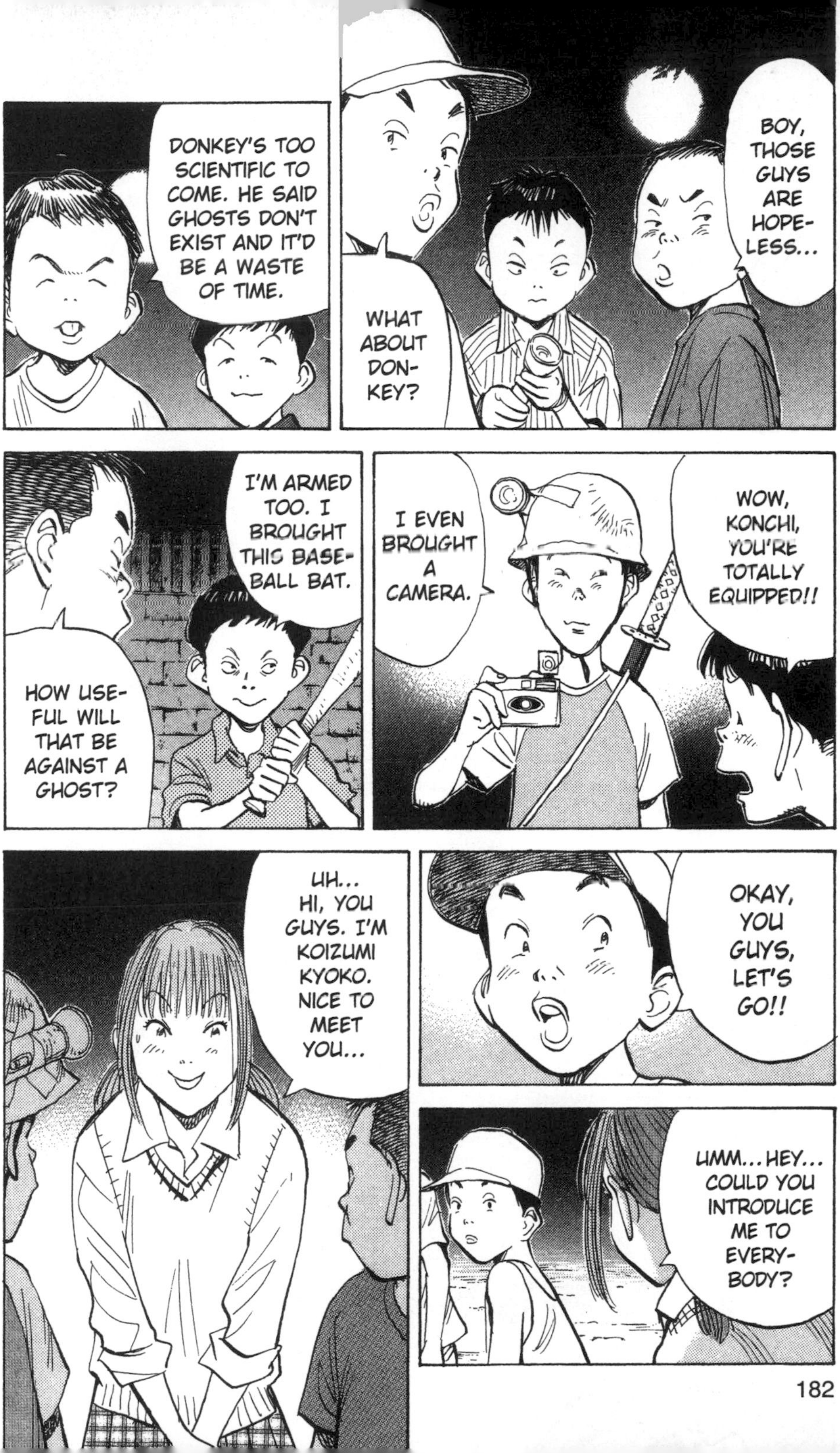
BOY, THOSE GUYS ARE HOPE-LESS...
WHAT ABOUT DON-KEY?
DONKEY'S TOO SCIENTIFIC TO COME. HE SAID GHOSTS DON'T EXIST AND IT'D BE A WASTE OF TIME.
WOW, KONCHI, YOU'RE TOTALLY EQUIPPED!!
I EVEN BROUGHT A CAMERA.
I'M ARMED TOO. I BROUGHT THIS BASE-BALL BAT.
HOW USE-FUL WILL THAT BE AGAINST A GHOST?
OKAY, YOU GUYS, LET'S GO!!
UMM...HEY... COULD YOU INTRODUCE ME TO EVERY-BODY?
UH... HI, YOU GUYS. I'M KOIZUMI KYOKO. NICE TO MEET YOU...

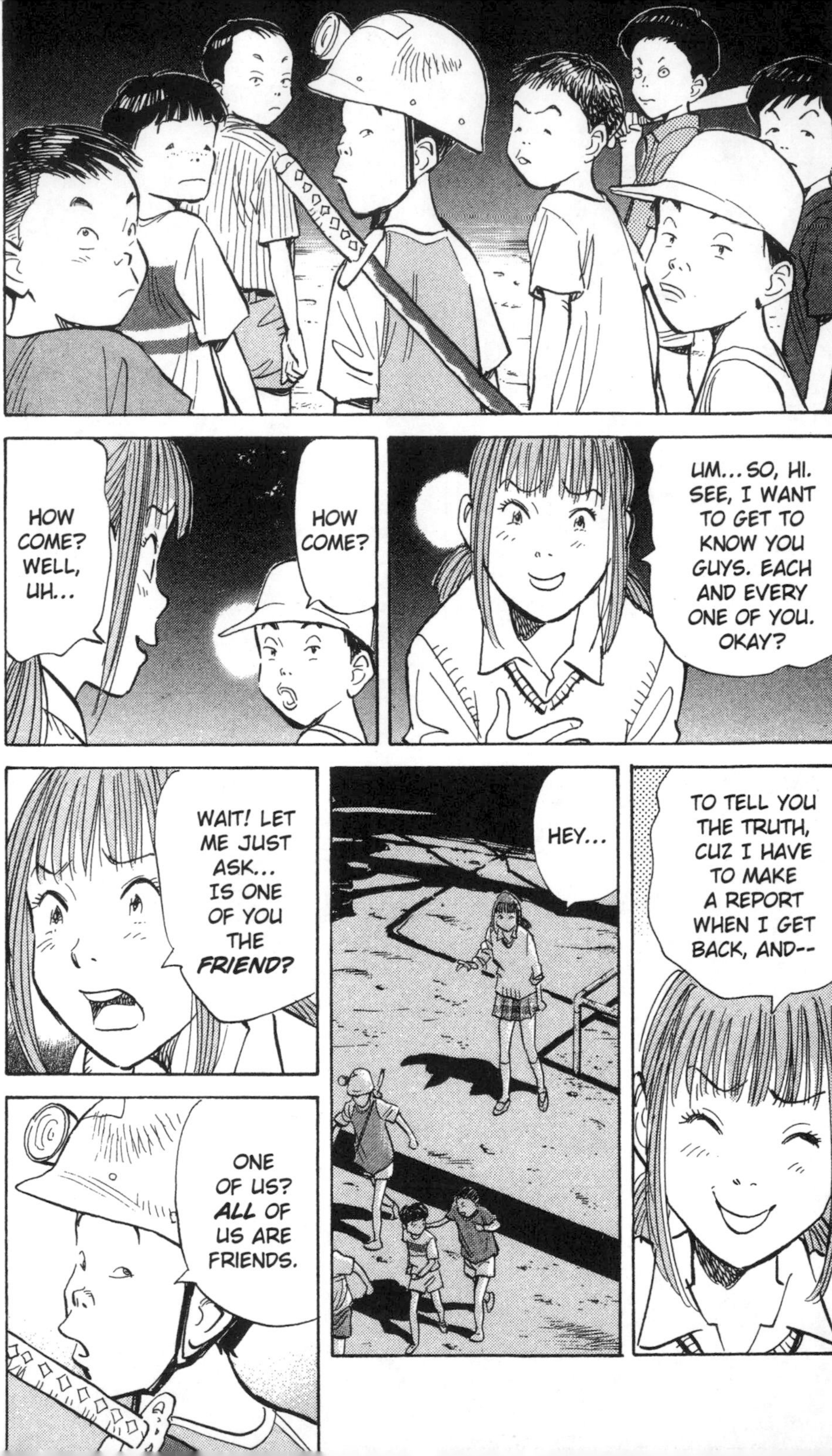
UM... SO, HI. SEE, I WANT TO GET TO KNOW YOU GUYS. EACH AND EVERY ONE OF YOU. OKAY?
HOW COME?
HOW COME? WELL, UH...
TO TELL YOU THE TRUTH, CUZ I HAVE TO MAKE A REPORT WHEN I GET BACK, AND--
HEY...
WAIT! LET ME JUST ASK... IS ONE OF YOU THE FRIEND?
ONE OF US? ALL OF US ARE FRIENDS.

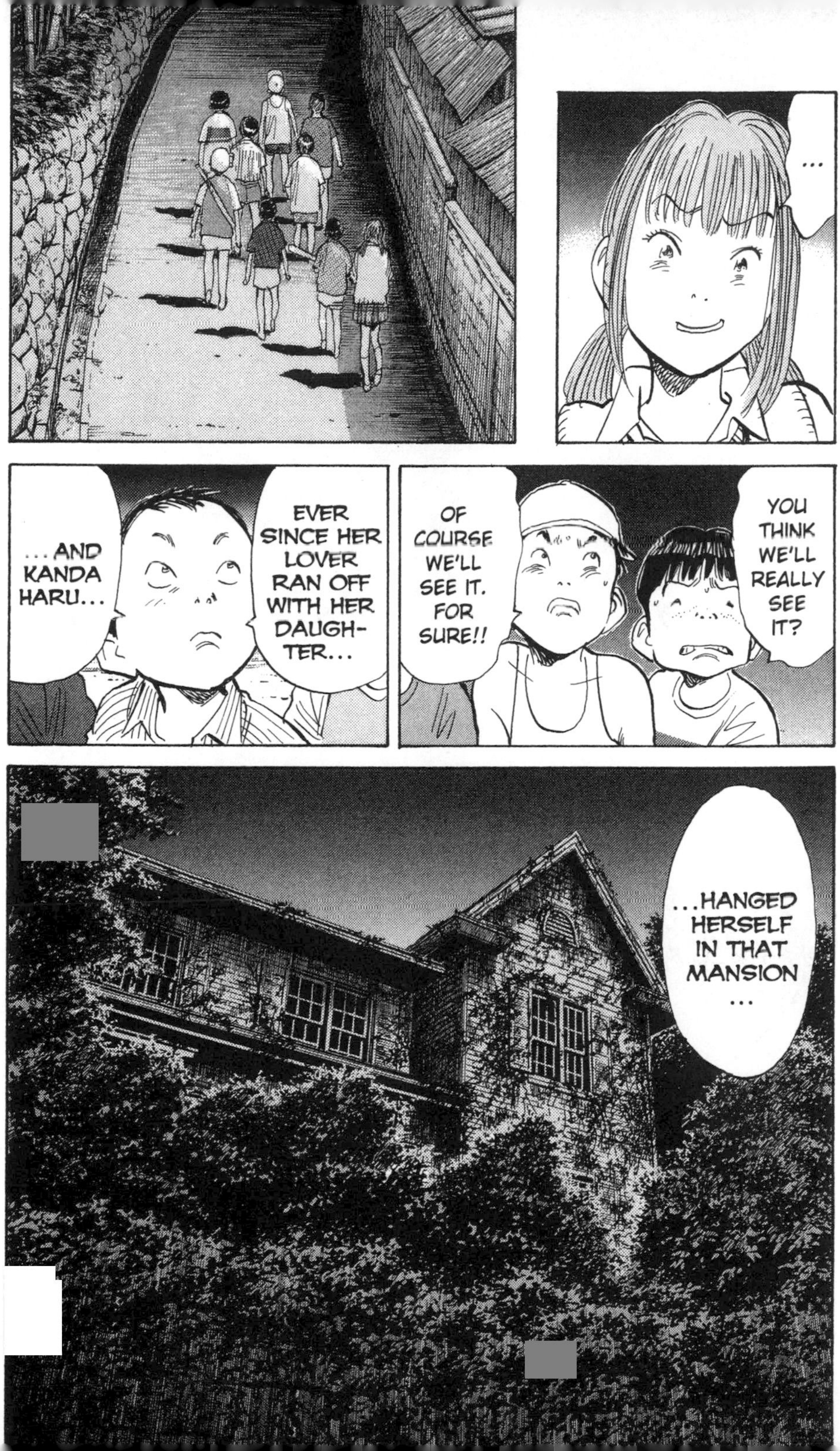
...
YOU THINK WE'LL REALLY SEE IT?
OF COURSE WE'LL SEE IT. FOR SURE!!
EVER SINCE HER LOVER RAN OFF WITH HER DAUGHTER...
...AND KANDA HARU...
...HANGED HERSELF IN THAT MANSION...

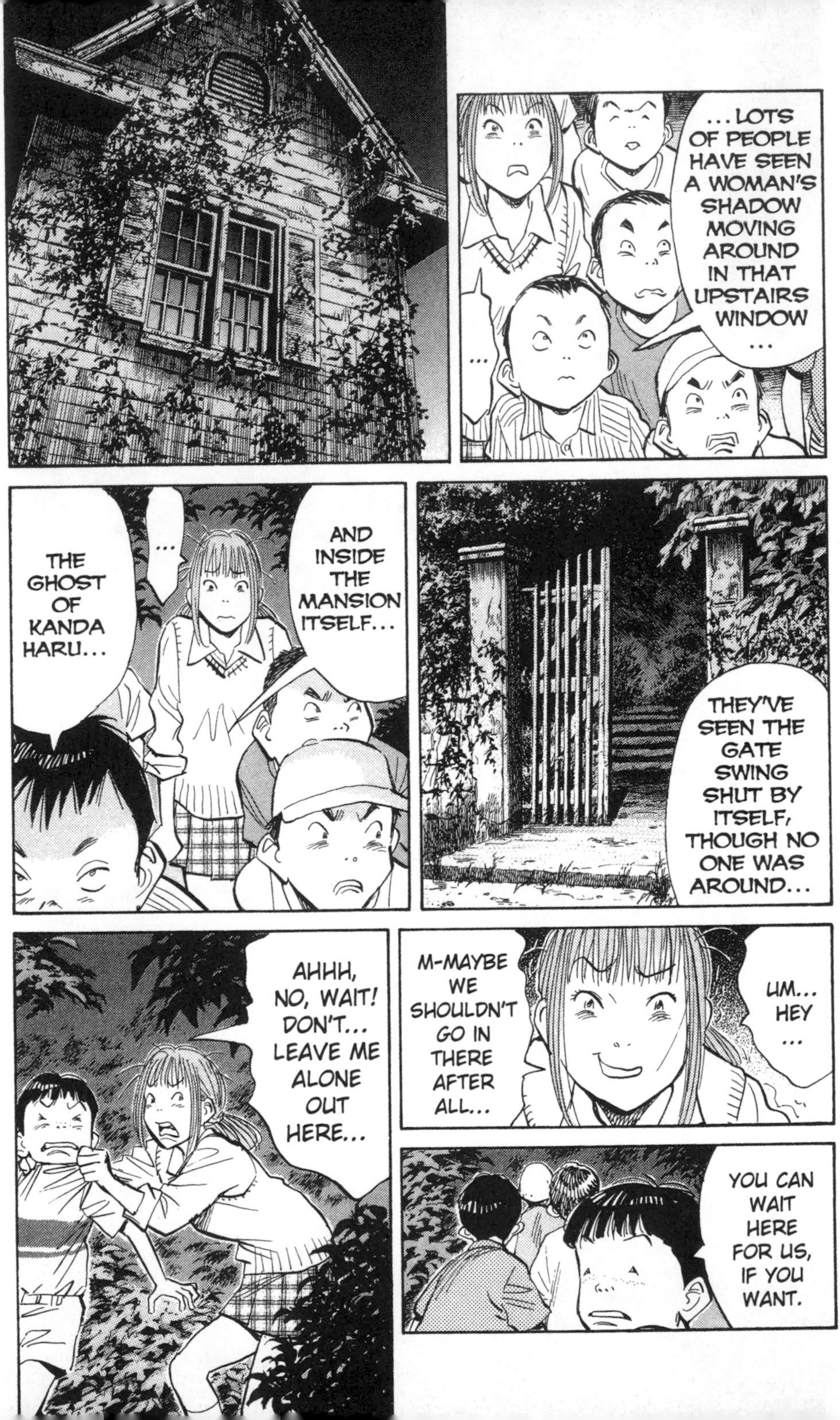
...LOTS OF PEOPLE HAVE SEEN A WOMAN'S SHADOW MOVING AROUND IN THAT UPSTAIRS WINDOW ...
...
THEY'VE SEEN THE GATE SWING SHUT BY ITSELF, THOUGH NO ONE WAS AROUND...
AND INSIDE THE MANSION ITSELF...
...
THE GHOST OF KANDA HARU...
UM... HEY ...
M-MAYBE WE SHOULDN'T GO IN THERE AFTER ALL...
YOU CAN WAIT HERE FOR US, IF YOU WANT.
AHHH, NO, WAIT! DON'T... LEAVE ME ALONE OUT HERE...

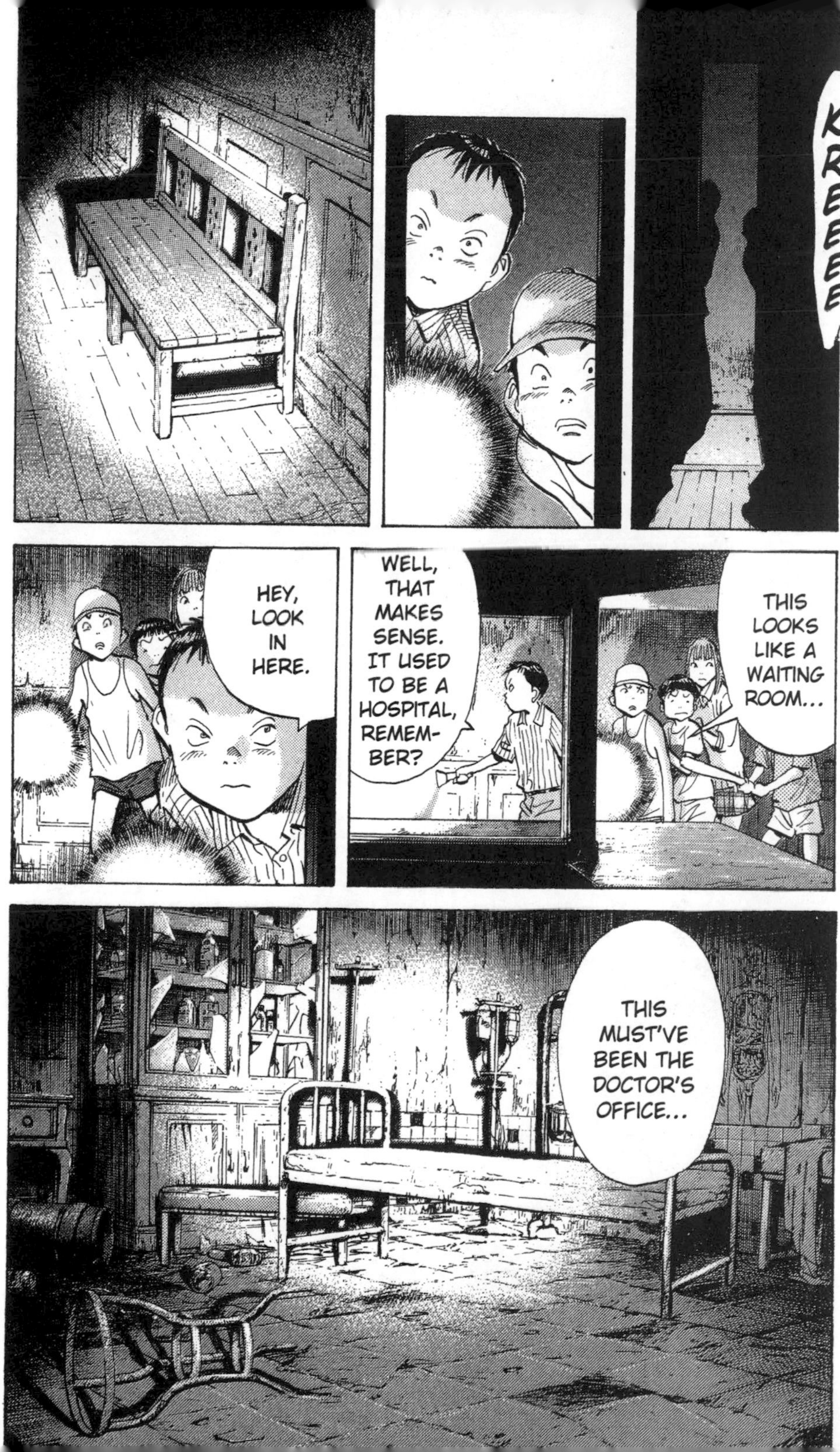
KREEEE
THIS LOOKS LIKE A WAITING ROOM...
WELL, THAT MAKES SENSE. IT USED TO BE A HOSPITAL, REMEMBER?
HEY, LOOK IN HERE.
THIS MUST'VE BEEN THE DOCTOR'S OFFICE...

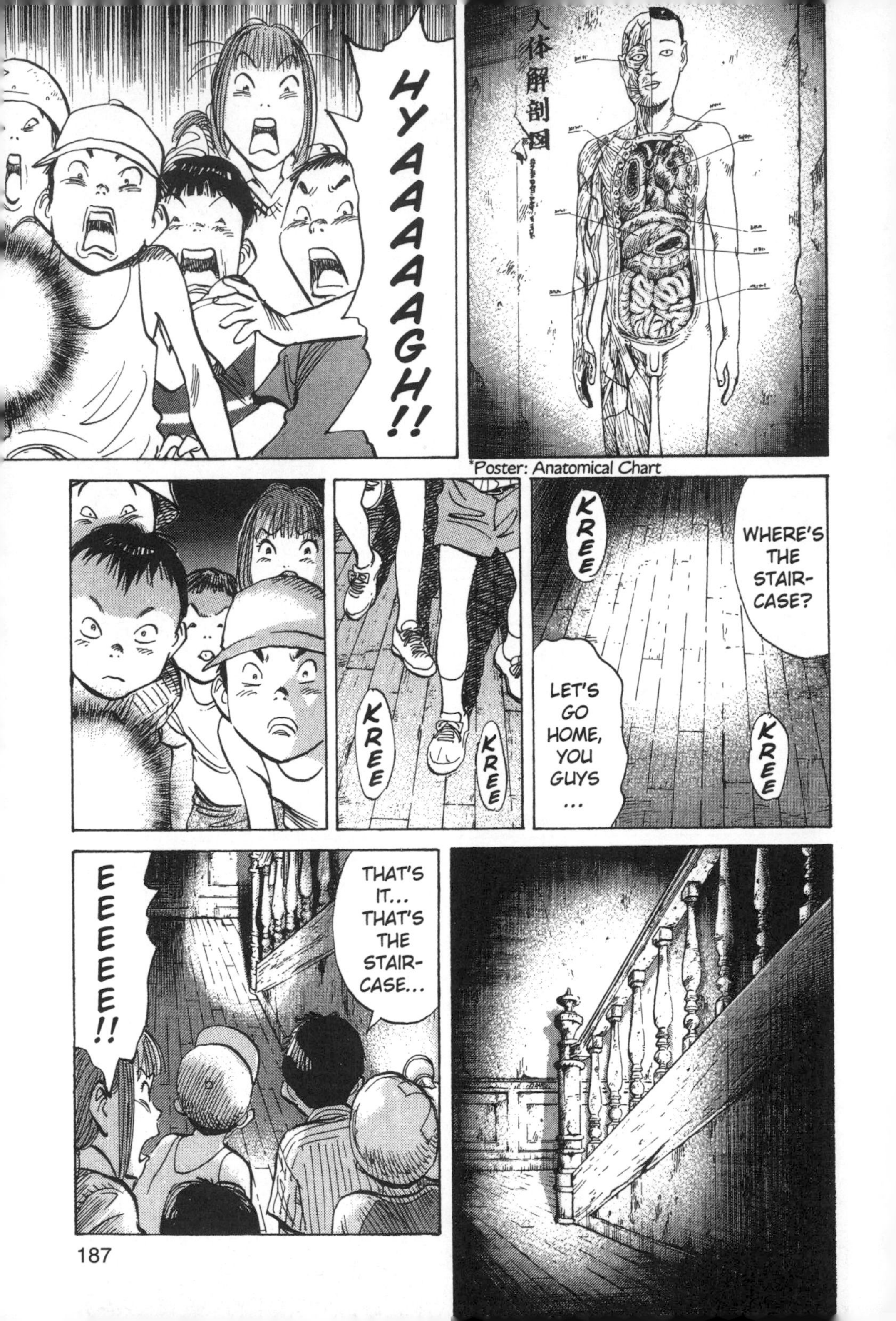
人体解剖図
*Poster: Anatomical Chart
HYAAAAAAGH!!
KREE
WHERE'S THE STAIR-CASE?
LET'S GO HOME, YOU GUYS ...
KREE
KREE
KREE
THAT'S IT... THAT'S THE STAIR-CASE...
EEEEEE!!

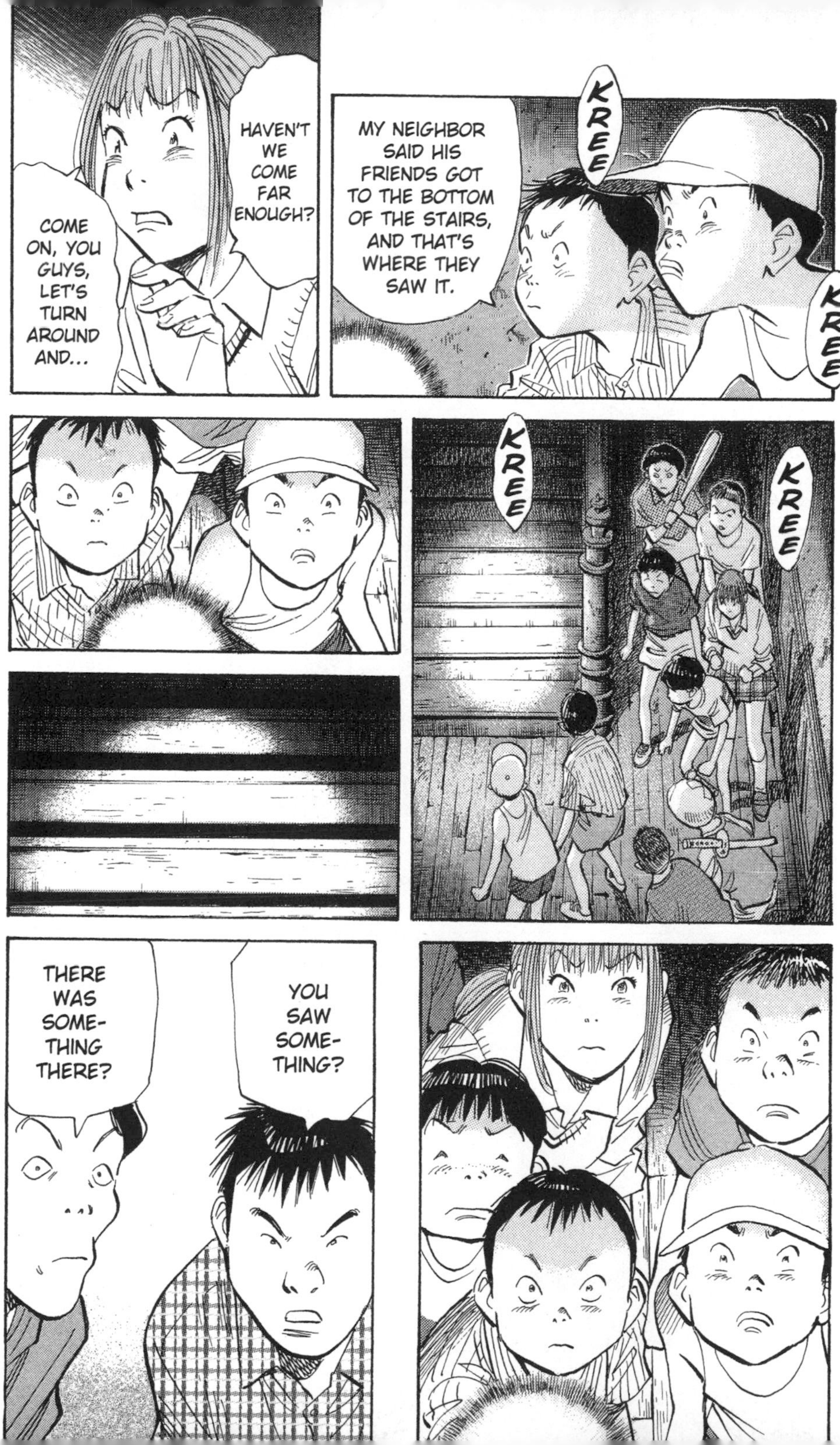
KREE
MY NEIGHBOR SAID HIS FRIENDS GOT TO THE BOTTOM OF THE STAIRS, AND THAT'S WHERE THEY SAW IT.
KREE
HAVEN'T WE COME FAR ENOUGH?
COME ON, YOU GUYS, LET'S TURN AROUND AND...
KREE
KREE
YOU SAW SOME-THING?
THERE WAS SOME-THING THERE?

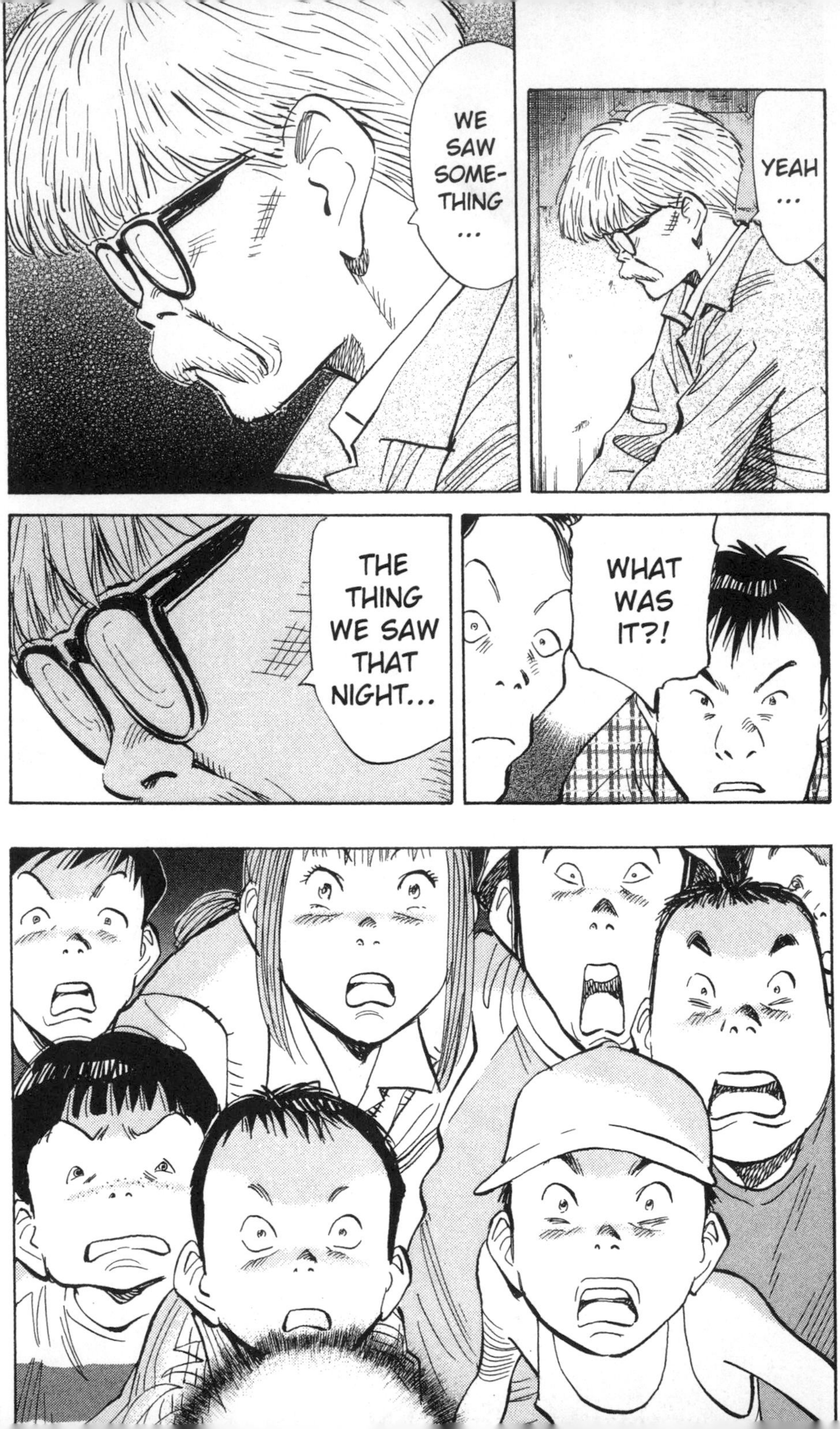
YEAH ...
WE SAW SOMETHING ...
WHAT WAS IT?!
THE THING WE SAW THAT NIGHT...

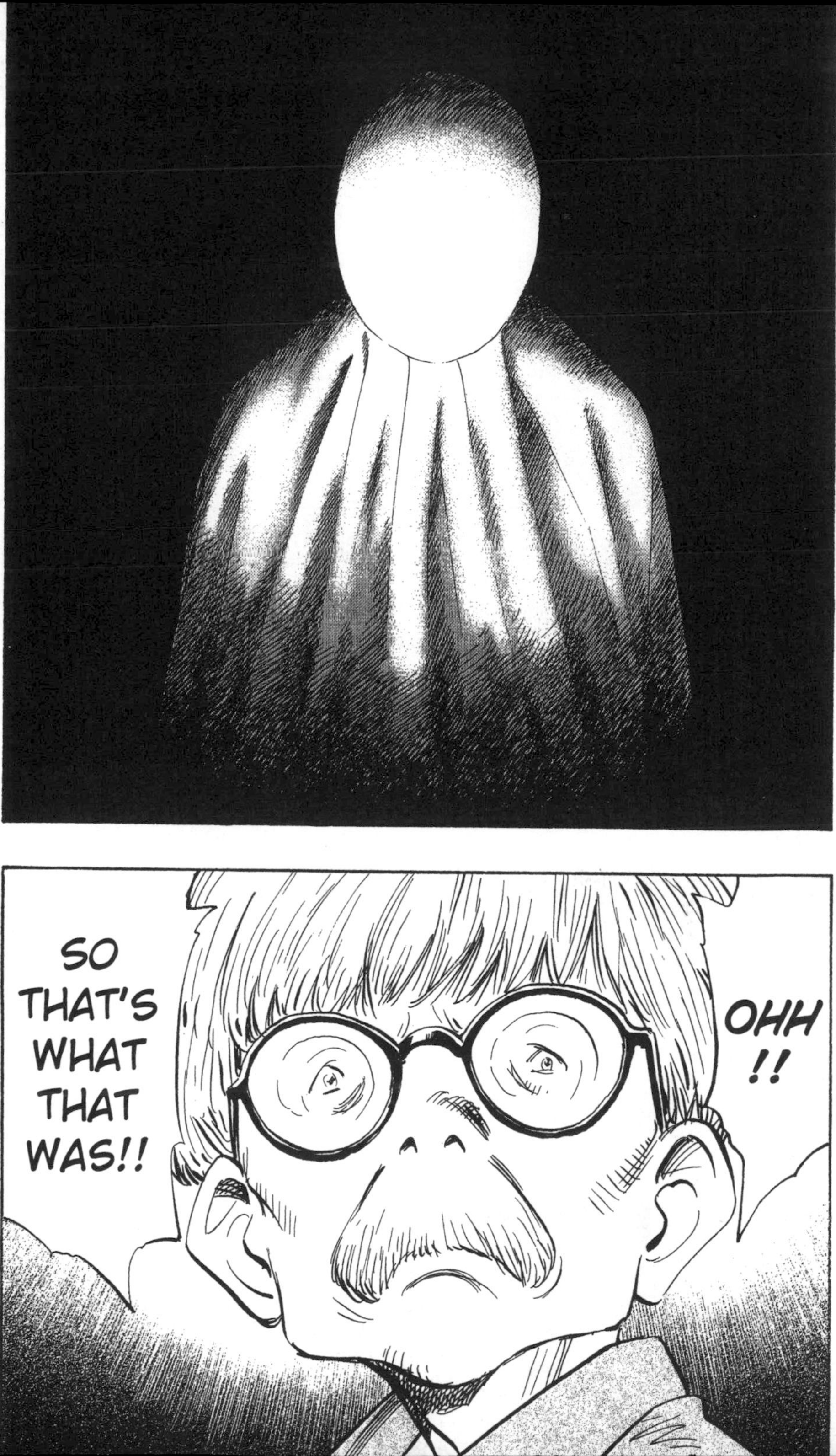
OHH !!
SO THAT'S WHAT THAT WAS!!

Chapter 11 Voices

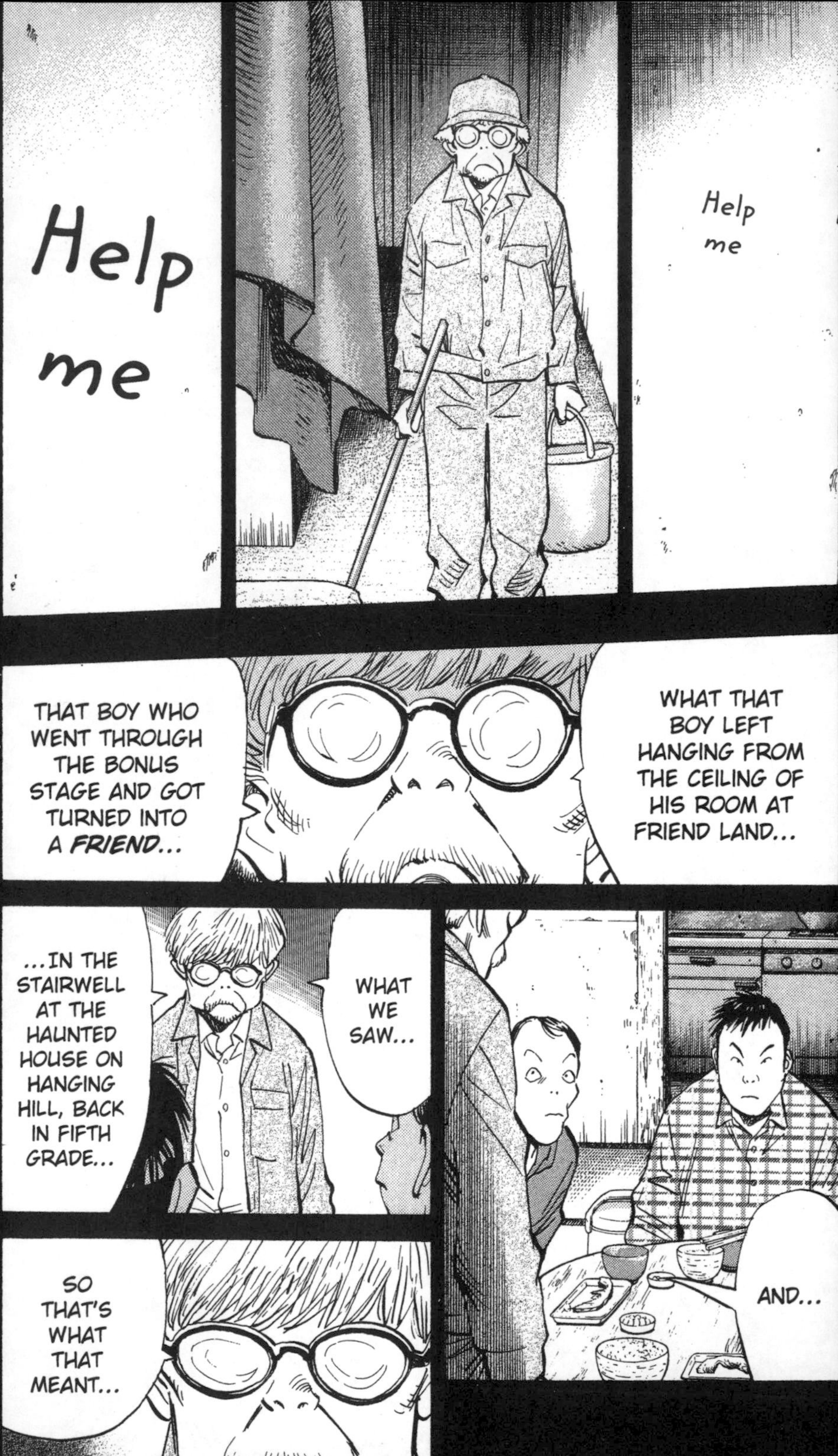

Help me
Help me
WHAT THAT BOY LEFT HANGING FROM THE CEILING OF HIS ROOM AT FRIEND LAND...
THAT BOY WHO WENT THROUGH THE BONUS STAGE AND GOT TURNED INTO A *FRIEND*...
AND...
WHAT WE SAW...
...IN THE STAIRWELL AT THE HAUNTED HOUSE ON HANGING HILL, BACK IN FIFTH GRADE...
SO THAT'S WHAT THAT MEANT...

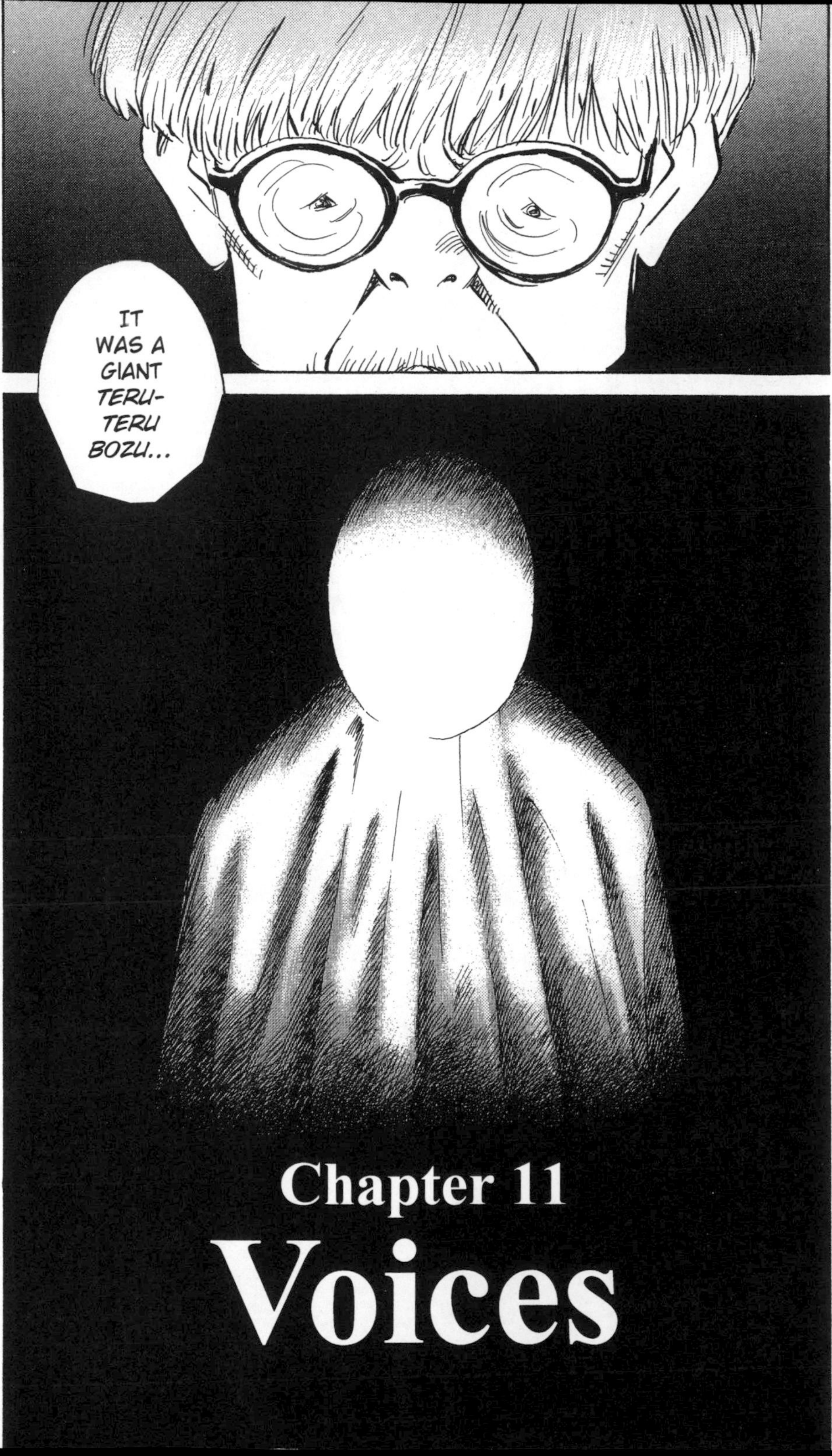
IT WAS A GIANT TERU-TERU BOZU...

Chapter 11

Voices

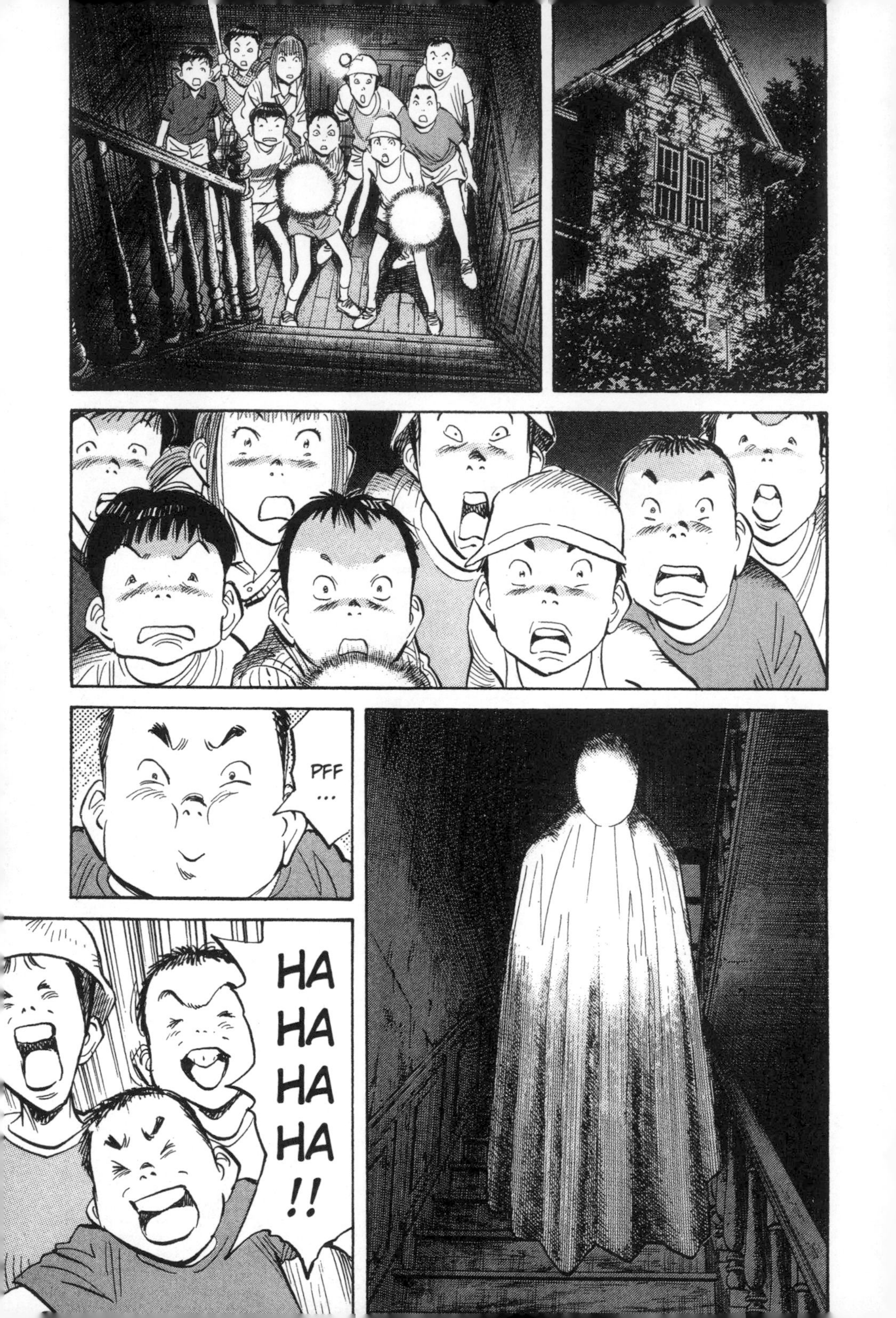
PFF ...
HA HA HA HA!!

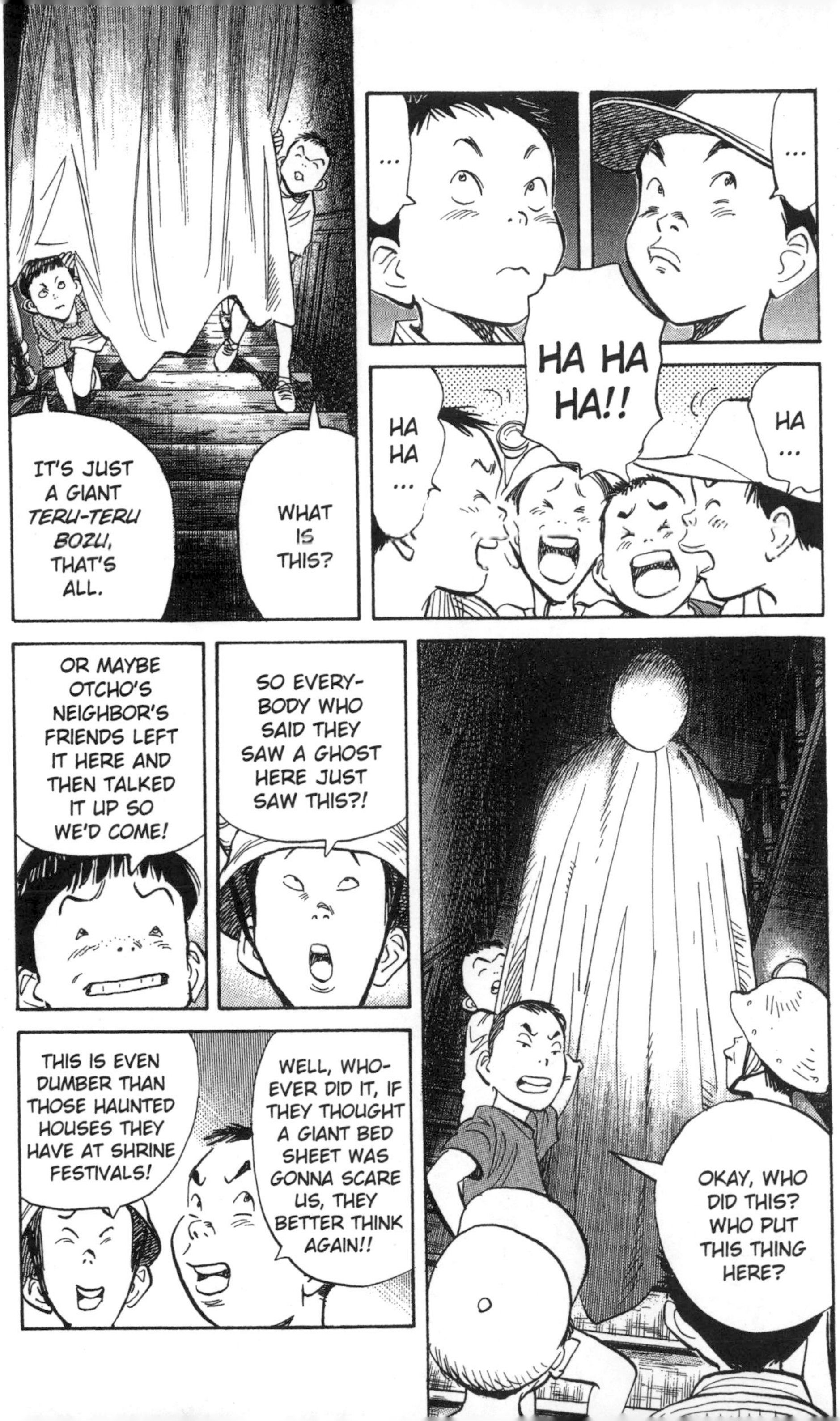
...
...
HA ...
HA HA HA!!
HA HA ...
WHAT IS THIS?
IT'S JUST A GIANT *TERU-TERU BOZU*, THAT'S ALL.
OKAY, WHO DID THIS? WHO PUT THIS THING HERE?
SO EVERY-BODY WHO SAID THEY SAW A GHOST HERE JUST SAW THIS?!
OR MAYBE OTCHO'S NEIGHBOR'S FRIENDS LEFT IT HERE AND THEN TALKED IT UP SO WE'D COME!
WELL, WHO-EVER DID IT, IF THEY THOUGHT A GIANT BED SHEET WAS GONNA SCARE US, THEY BETTER THINK AGAIN!!
THIS IS EVEN DUMBER THAN THOSE HAUNTED HOUSES THEY HAVE AT SHRINE FESTIVALS!

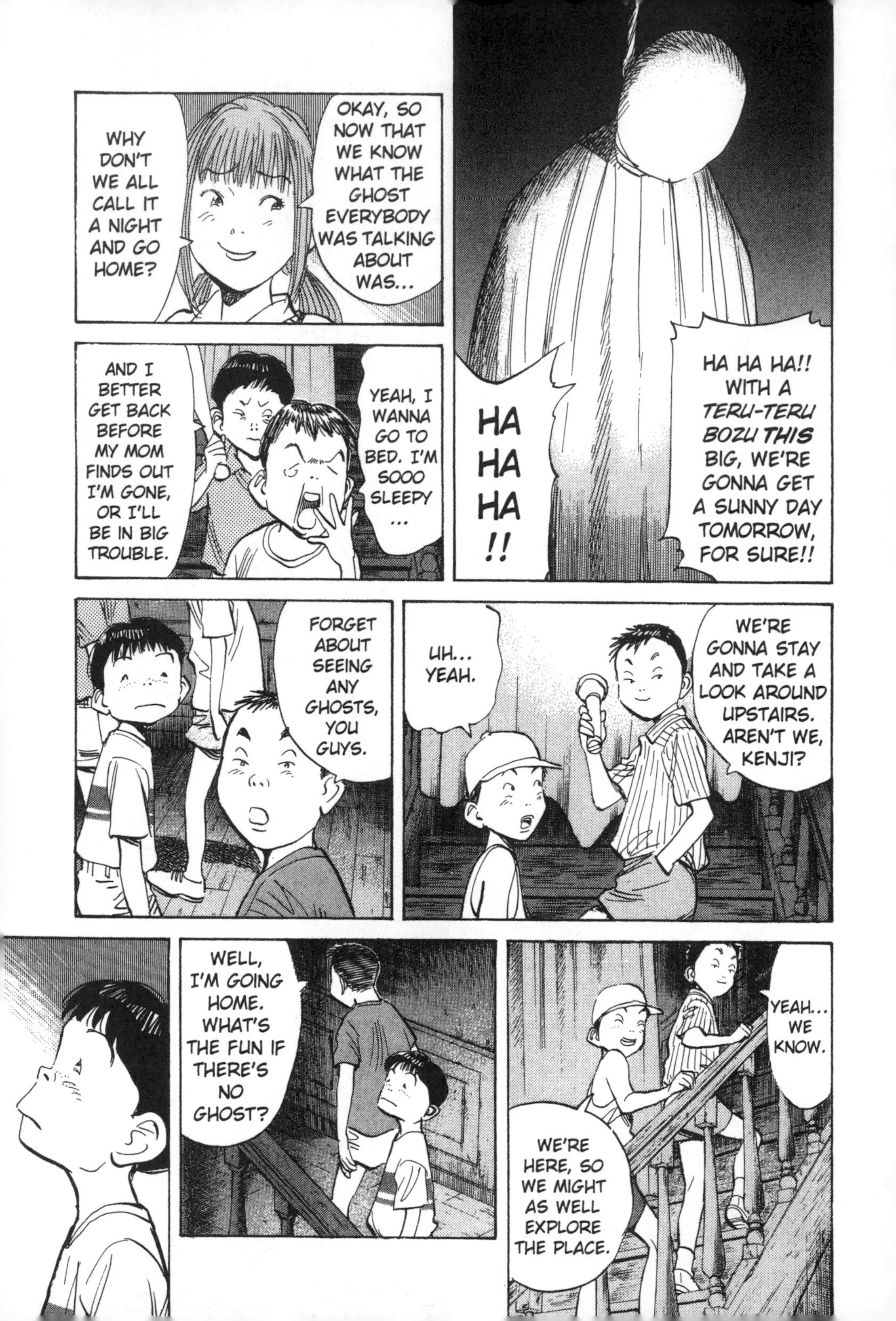
HA HA HA!! WITH A *TERU-TERU BOZU* **THIS** BIG, WE'RE GONNA GET A SUNNY DAY TOMORROW, FOR SURE!!
HA HA HA !!
OKAY, SO NOW THAT WE KNOW WHAT THE GHOST EVERYBODY WAS TALKING ABOUT WAS...
WHY DON'T WE ALL CALL IT A NIGHT AND GO HOME?
YEAH, I WANNA GO TO BED. I'M SOOO SLEEPY ...
AND I BETTER GET BACK BEFORE MY MOM FINDS OUT I'M GONE, OR I'LL BE IN BIG TROUBLE.
WE'RE GONNA STAY AND TAKE A LOOK AROUND UPSTAIRS. AREN'T WE, KENJI?
UH... YEAH.
FORGET ABOUT SEEING ANY GHOSTS, YOU GUYS.
YEAH... WE KNOW.
WE'RE HERE, SO WE MIGHT AS WELL EXPLORE THE PLACE.
WELL, I'M GOING HOME. WHAT'S THE FUN IF THERE'S NO GHOST?

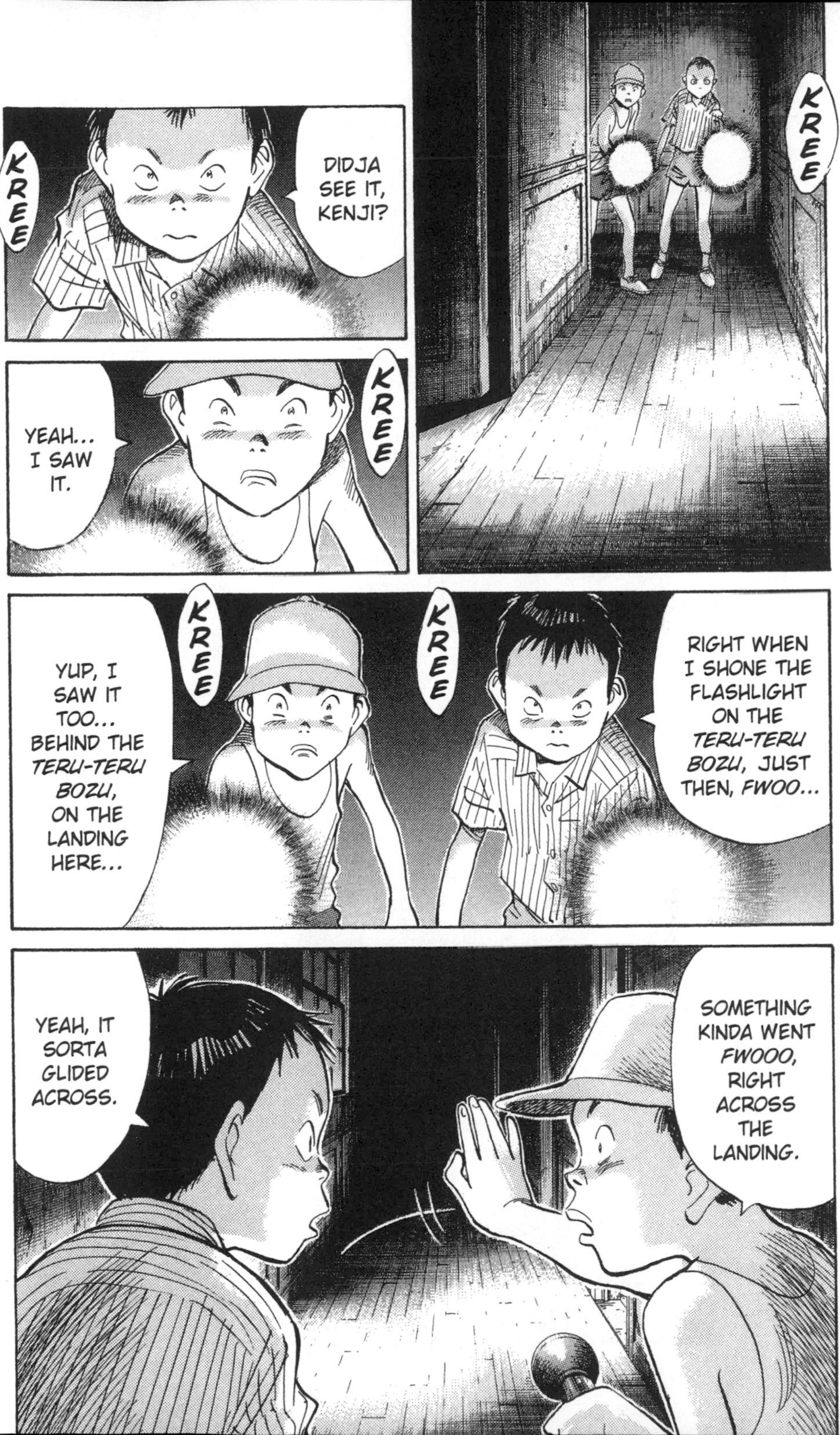
KREE
DIDJA SEE IT, KENJI?
KREE
KREE
YEAH... I SAW IT.
RIGHT WHEN I SHONE THE FLASHLIGHT ON THE *TERU-TERU BOZU*, JUST THEN, *FWOO*...
KREE
KREE
YUP, I SAW IT TOO... BEHIND THE *TERU-TERU BOZU*, ON THE LANDING HERE...
SOMETHING KINDA WENT *FWOOO*, RIGHT ACROSS THE LANDING.
YEAH, IT SORTA GLIDED ACROSS.

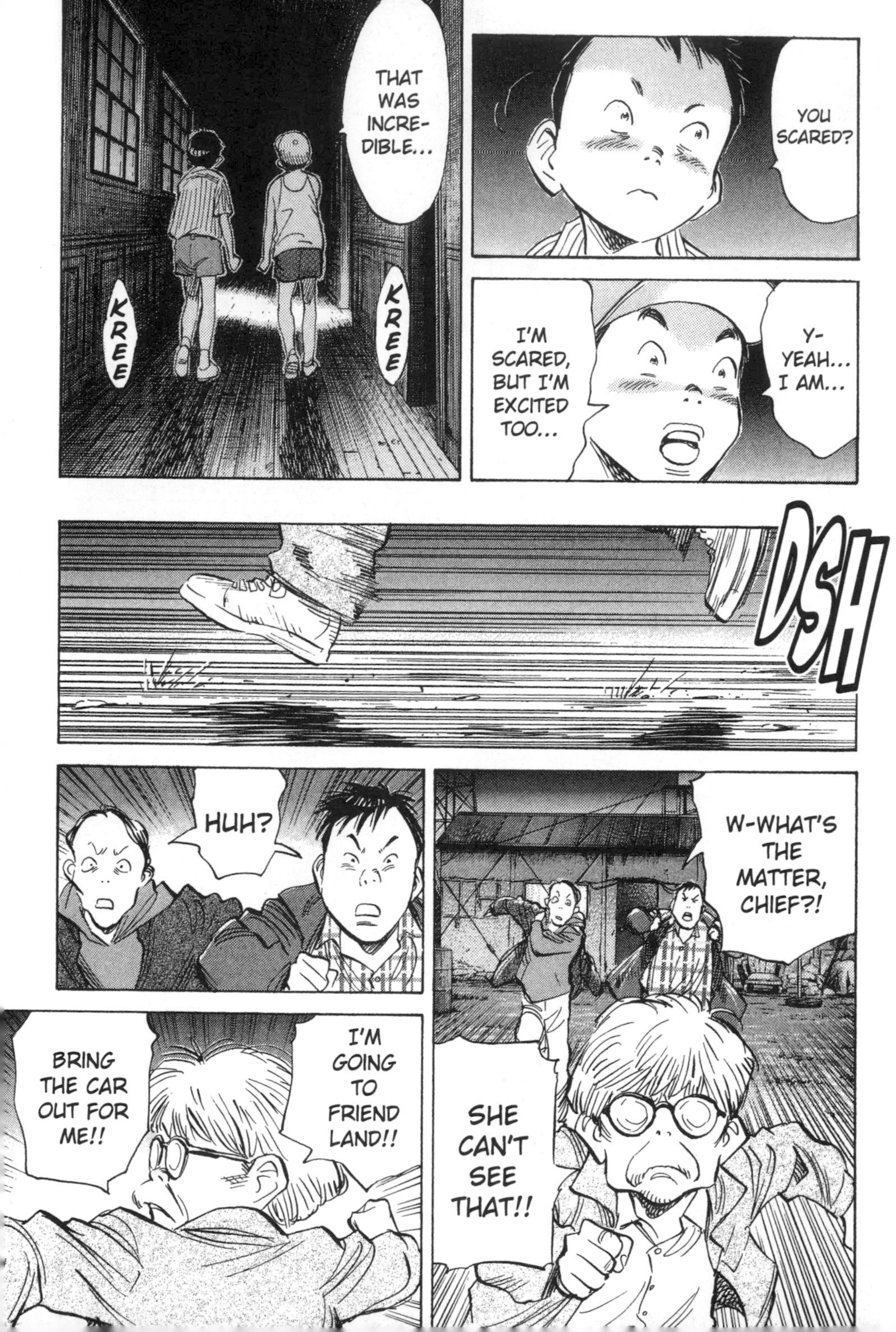
YOU SCARED?
Y-YEAH... I AM...
I'M SCARED, BUT I'M EXCITED TOO...
THAT WAS INCREDIBLE...
KREE
KREE
DSH
W-WHAT'S THE MATTER, CHIEF?!
SHE CAN'T SEE THAT!!
HUH?
I'M GOING TO FRIEND LAND!!
BRING THE CAR OUT FOR ME!!

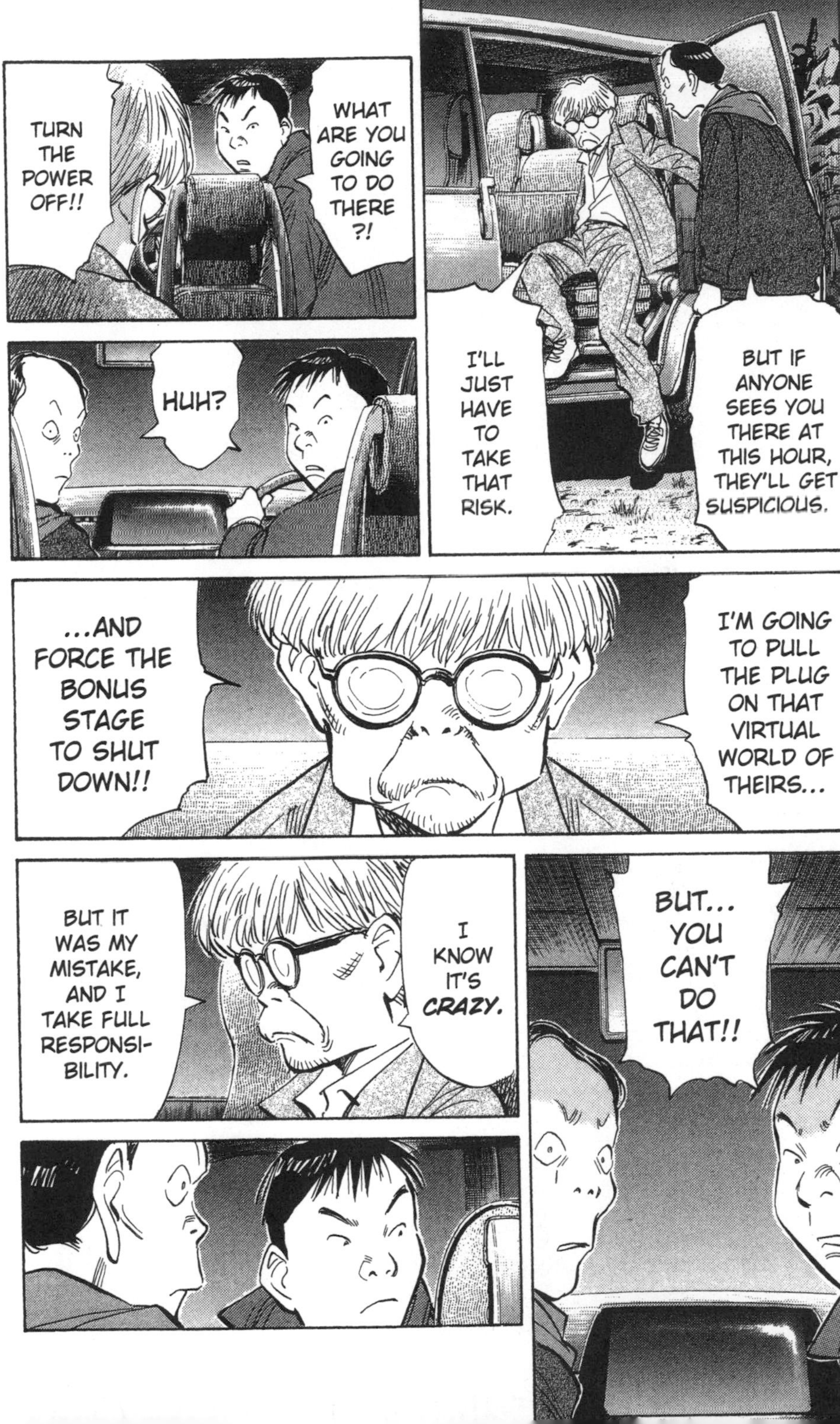
BUT IF ANYONE SEES YOU THERE AT THIS HOUR, THEY'LL GET SUSPICIOUS.
I'LL JUST HAVE TO TAKE THAT RISK.
WHAT ARE YOU GOING TO DO THERE?!
TURN THE POWER OFF!!
HUH?
I'M GOING TO PULL THE PLUG ON THAT VIRTUAL WORLD OF THEIRS...
...AND FORCE THE BONUS STAGE TO SHUT DOWN!!
BUT... YOU CAN'T DO THAT!!
I KNOW IT'S *CRAZY*.
BUT IT WAS MY MISTAKE, AND I TAKE FULL RESPONSI-BILITY.

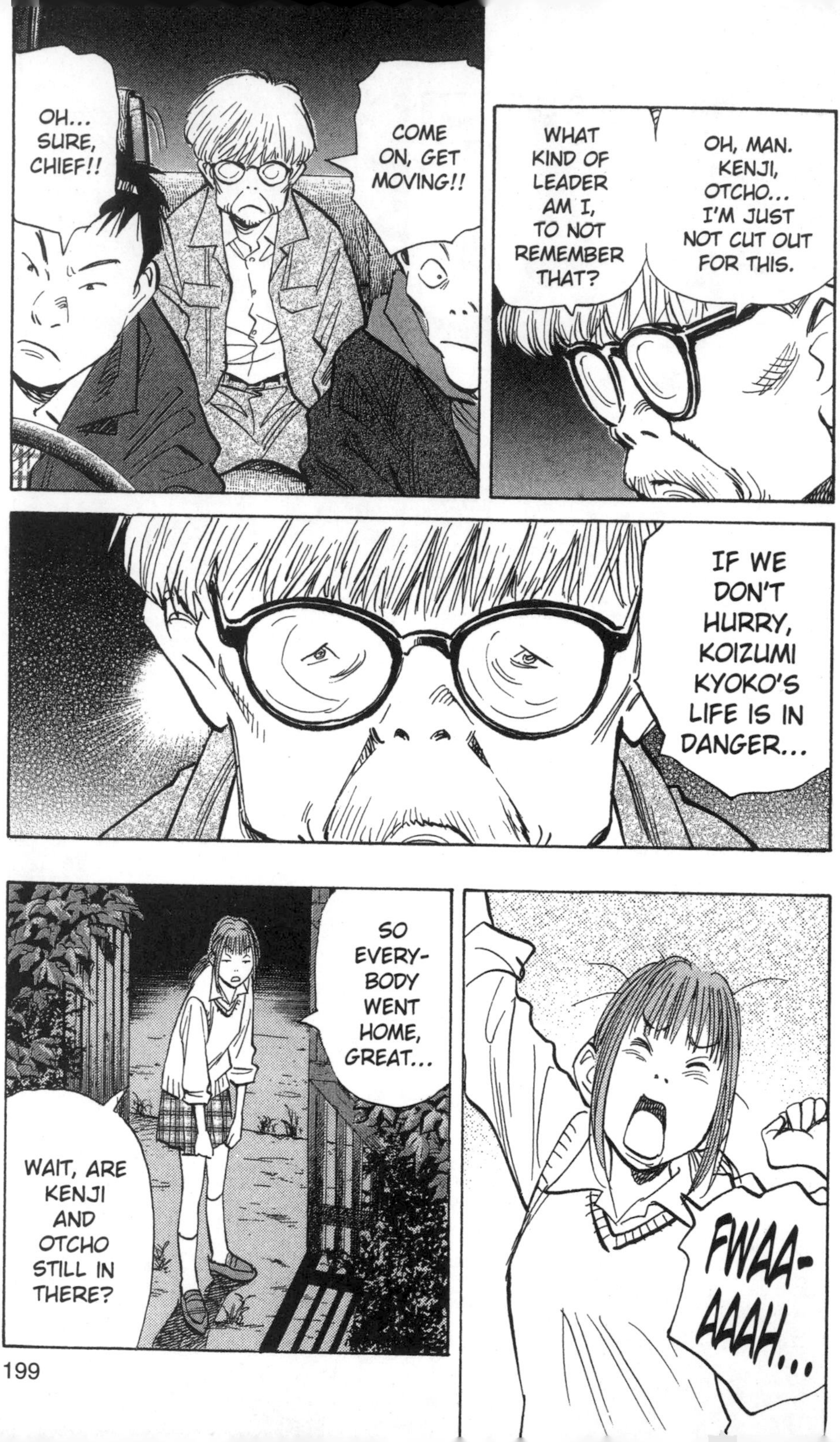
OH, MAN. KENJI, OTCHO... I'M JUST NOT CUT OUT FOR THIS.
WHAT KIND OF LEADER AM I, TO NOT REMEMBER THAT?
COME ON, GET MOVING!!
OH... SURE, CHIEF!!
IF WE DON'T HURRY, KOIZUMI KYOKO'S LIFE IS IN DANGER...
FWAA-AAAH...
SO EVERY-BODY WENT HOME, GREAT...
WAIT, ARE KENJI AND OTCHO STILL IN THERE?

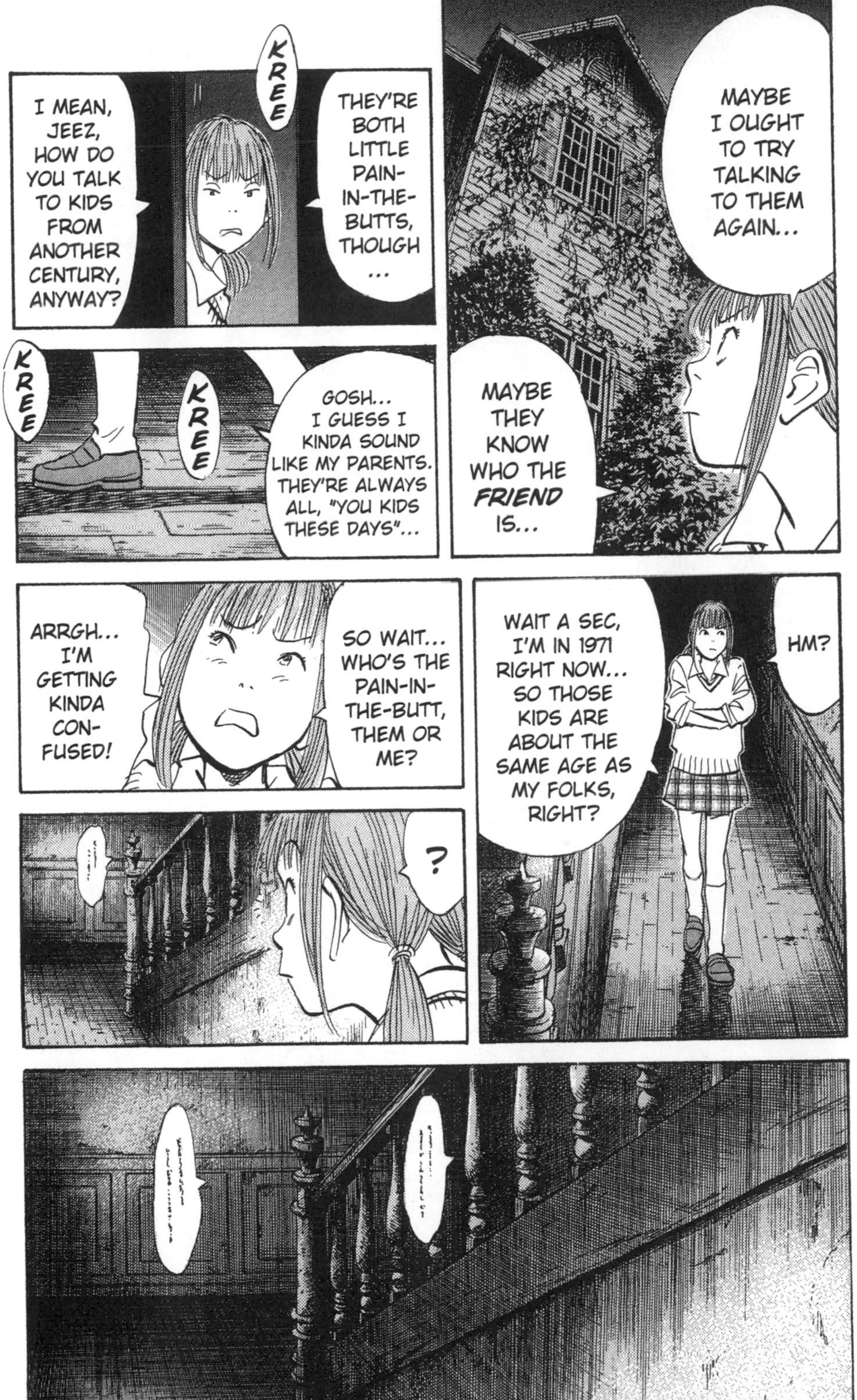
MAYBE I OUGHT TO TRY TALKING TO THEM AGAIN...
MAYBE THEY KNOW WHO THE ***FRIEND*** IS...
KREE
THEY'RE BOTH LITTLE PAIN-IN-THE-BUTTS, THOUGH ...
I MEAN, JEEZ, HOW DO YOU TALK TO KIDS FROM ANOTHER CENTURY, ANYWAY?
GOSH... I GUESS I KINDA SOUND LIKE MY PARENTS. THEY'RE ALWAYS ALL, "YOU KIDS THESE DAYS"...
KREE
KREE
HM?
WAIT A SEC, I'M IN 1971 RIGHT NOW... SO THOSE KIDS ARE ABOUT THE SAME AGE AS MY FOLKS, RIGHT?
SO WAIT... WHO'S THE PAIN-IN-THE-BUTT, THEM OR ME?
ARRGH... I'M GETTING KINDA CON-FUSED!
?

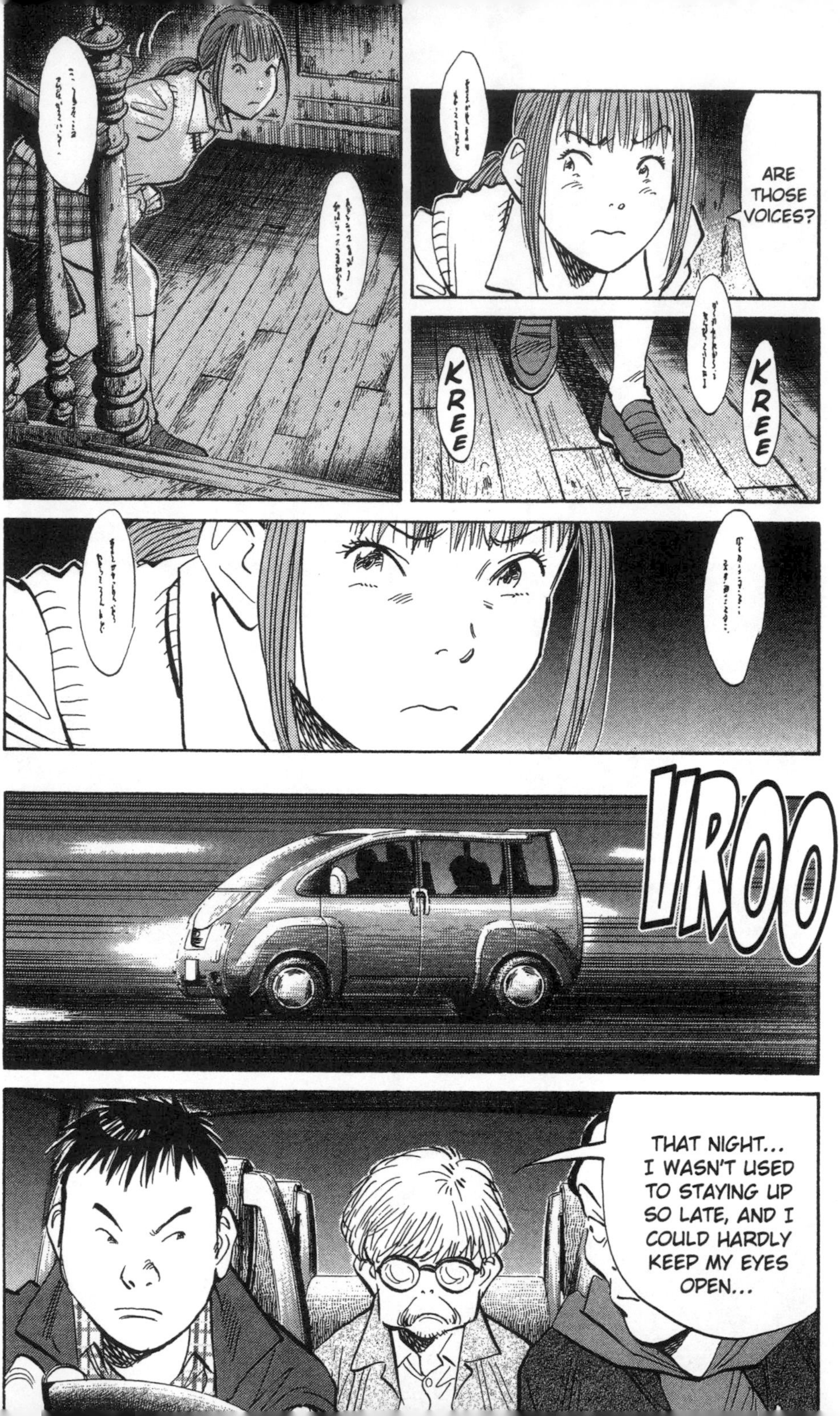
ARE THOSE VOICES?
KREE
KREE
VROO
THAT NIGHT... I WASN'T USED TO STAYING UP SO LATE, AND I COULD HARDLY KEEP MY EYES OPEN...

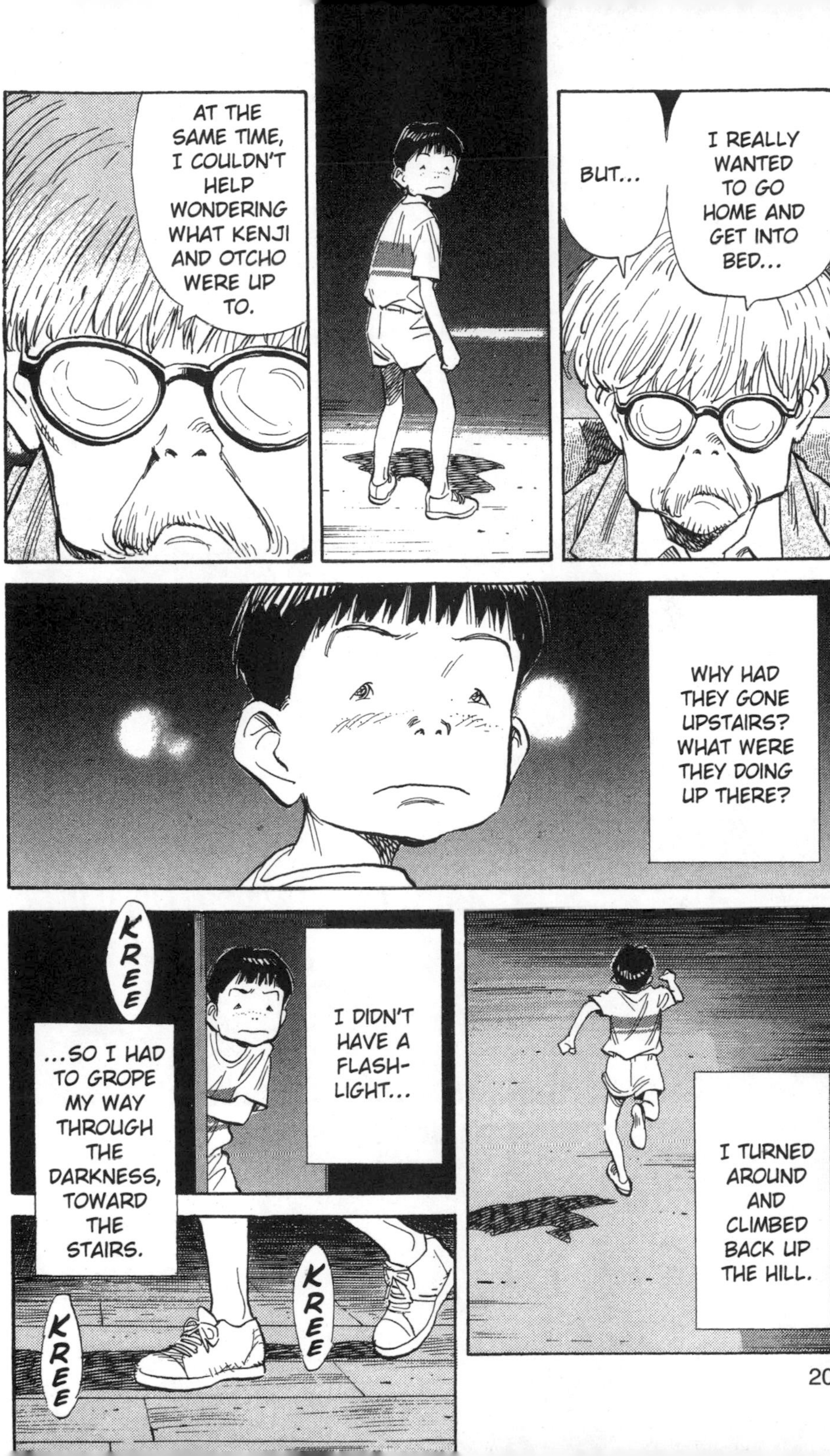
I REALLY WANTED TO GO HOME AND GET INTO BED...
BUT...
AT THE SAME TIME, I COULDN'T HELP WONDERING WHAT KENJI AND OTCHO WERE UP TO.
WHY HAD THEY GONE UPSTAIRS? WHAT WERE THEY DOING UP THERE?
I TURNED AROUND AND CLIMBED BACK UP THE HILL.
I DIDN'T HAVE A FLASH-LIGHT...
KREE
...SO I HAD TO GROPE MY WAY THROUGH THE DARKNESS, TOWARD THE STAIRS.
KREE
KREE

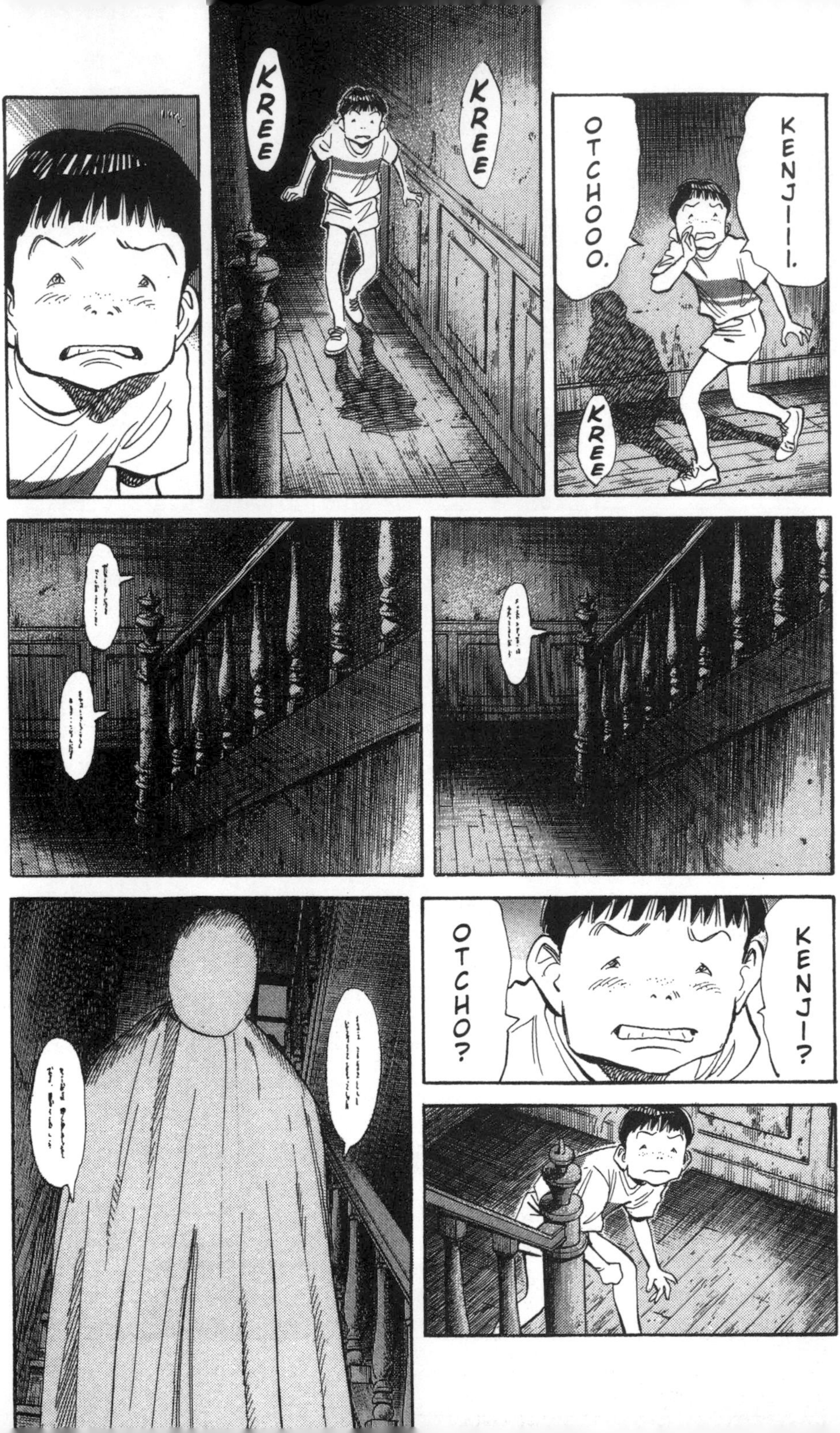
KENJIII.
OTCHOOO.
KREE
KREE
KREE
KENJI?
OTCHO?

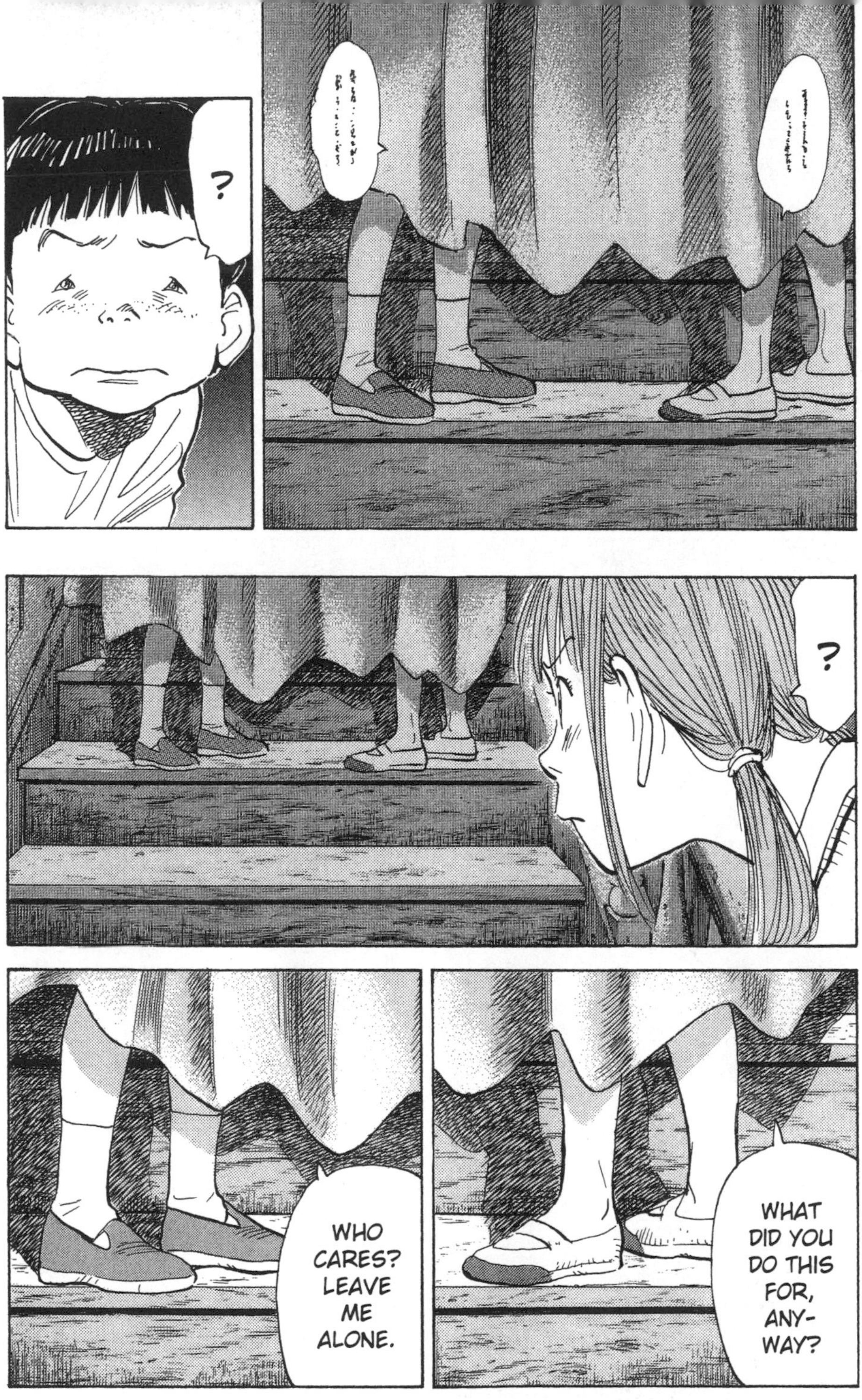
?
?
WHAT DID YOU DO THIS FOR, ANY-WAY?
WHO CARES? LEAVE ME ALONE.

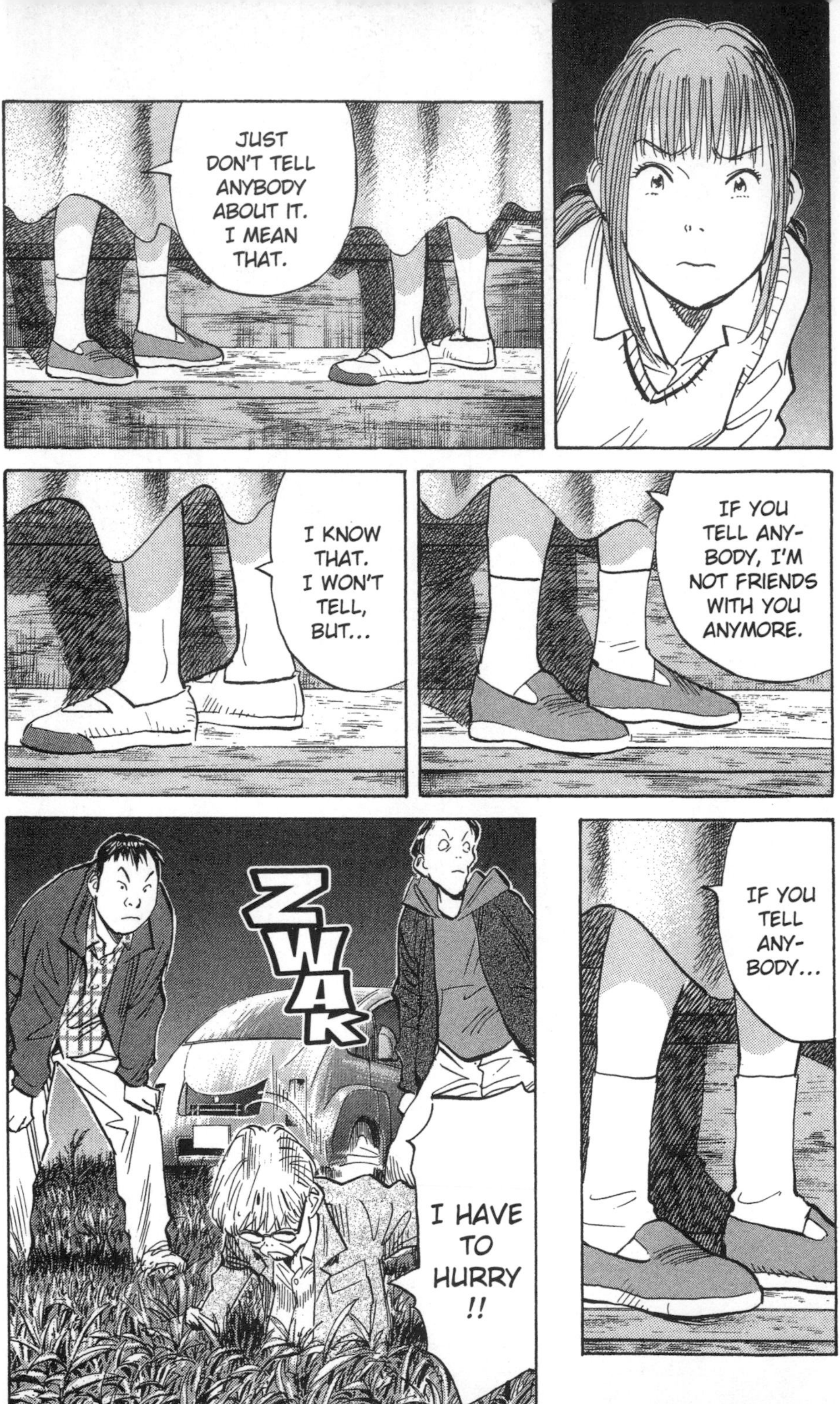
JUST DON'T TELL ANYBODY ABOUT IT. I MEAN THAT.
IF YOU TELL ANY-BODY, I'M NOT FRIENDS WITH YOU ANYMORE.
I KNOW THAT. I WON'T TELL, BUT...
IF YOU TELL ANY-BODY...
ZWAK
I HAVE TO HURRY !!

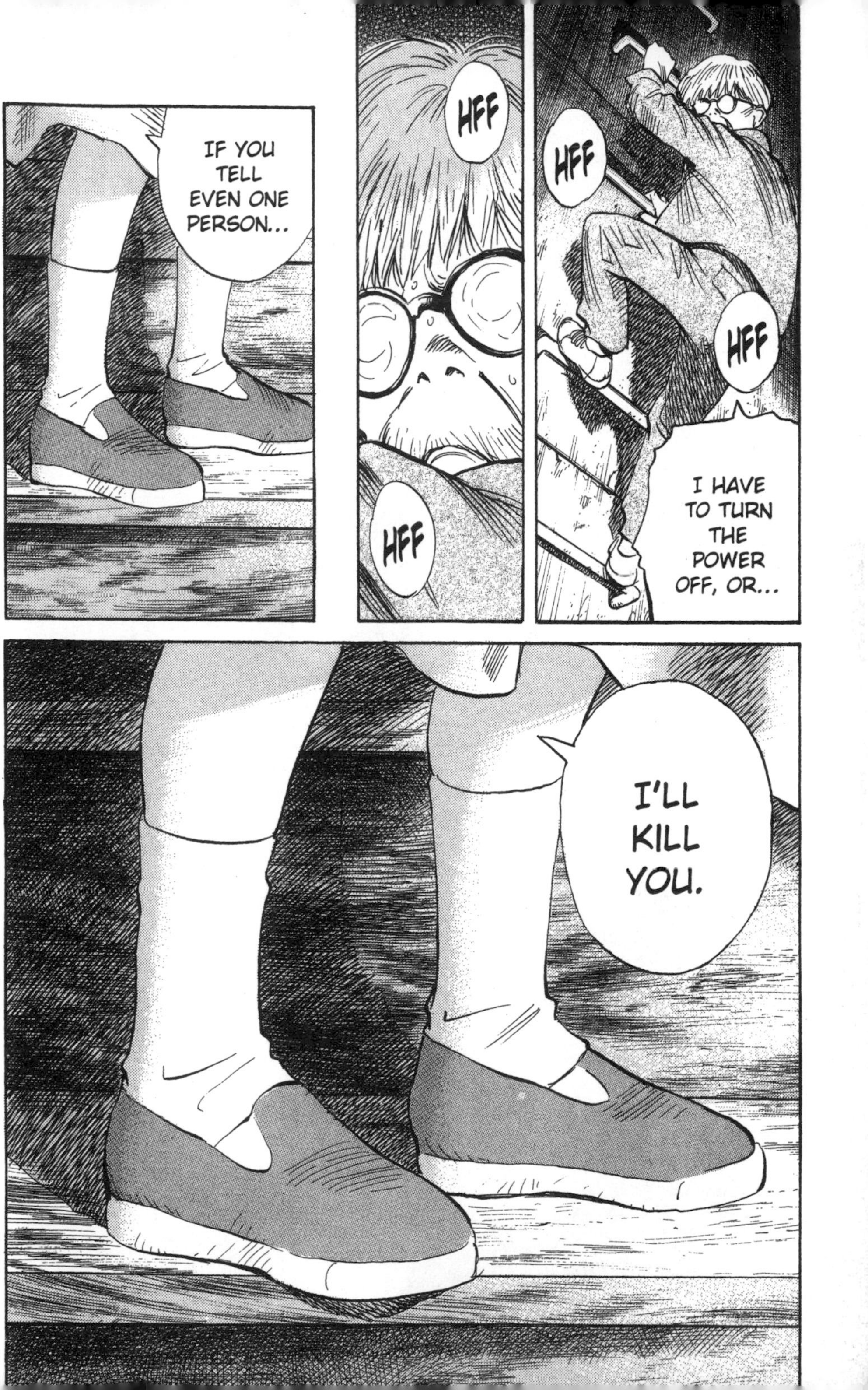
HFF
HFF
I HAVE TO TURN THE POWER OFF, OR...
HFF
HFF
IF YOU TELL EVEN ONE PERSON...
I'LL KILL YOU.

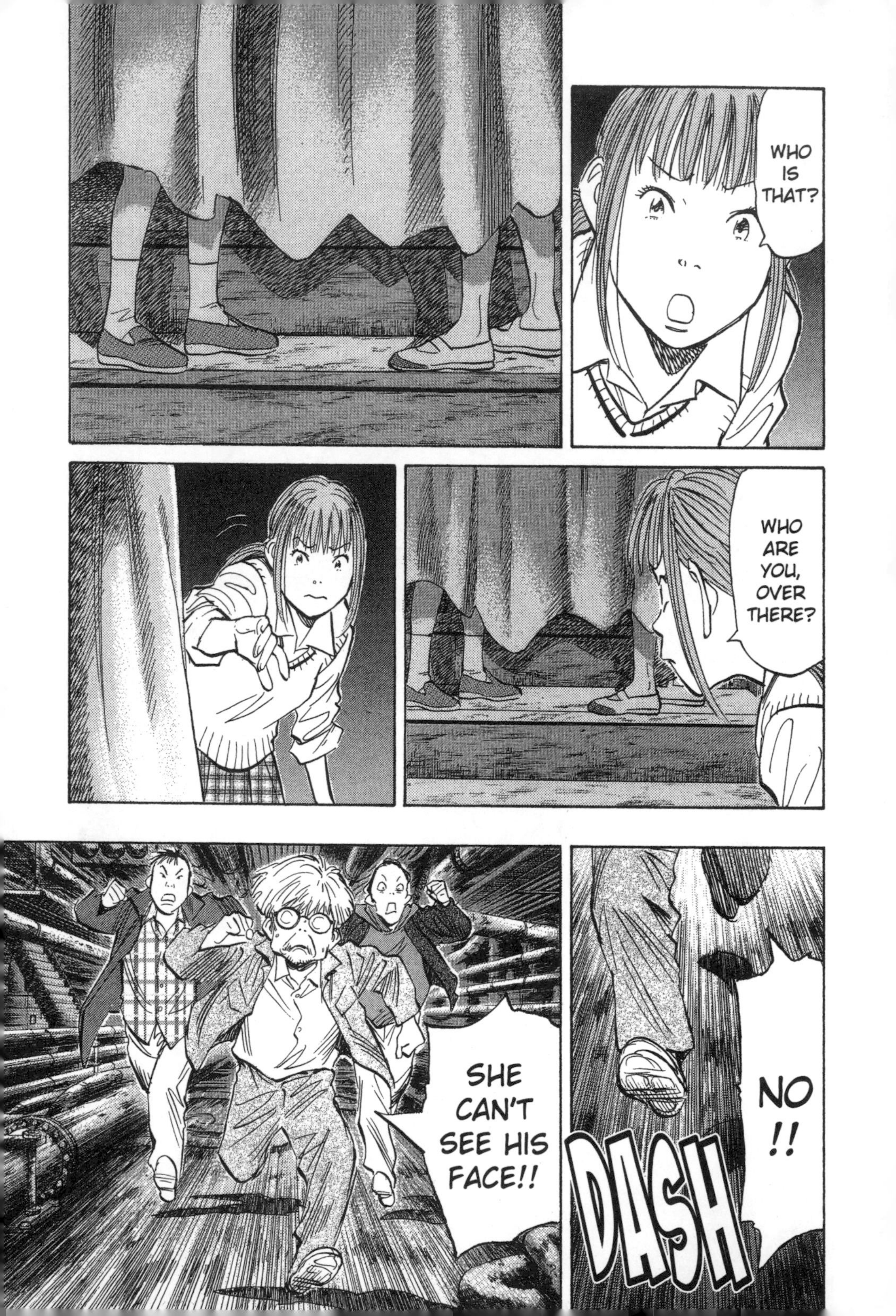
WHO IS THAT?
WHO ARE YOU, OVER THERE?
NO!!
DASH
SHE CAN'T SEE HIS FACE!!

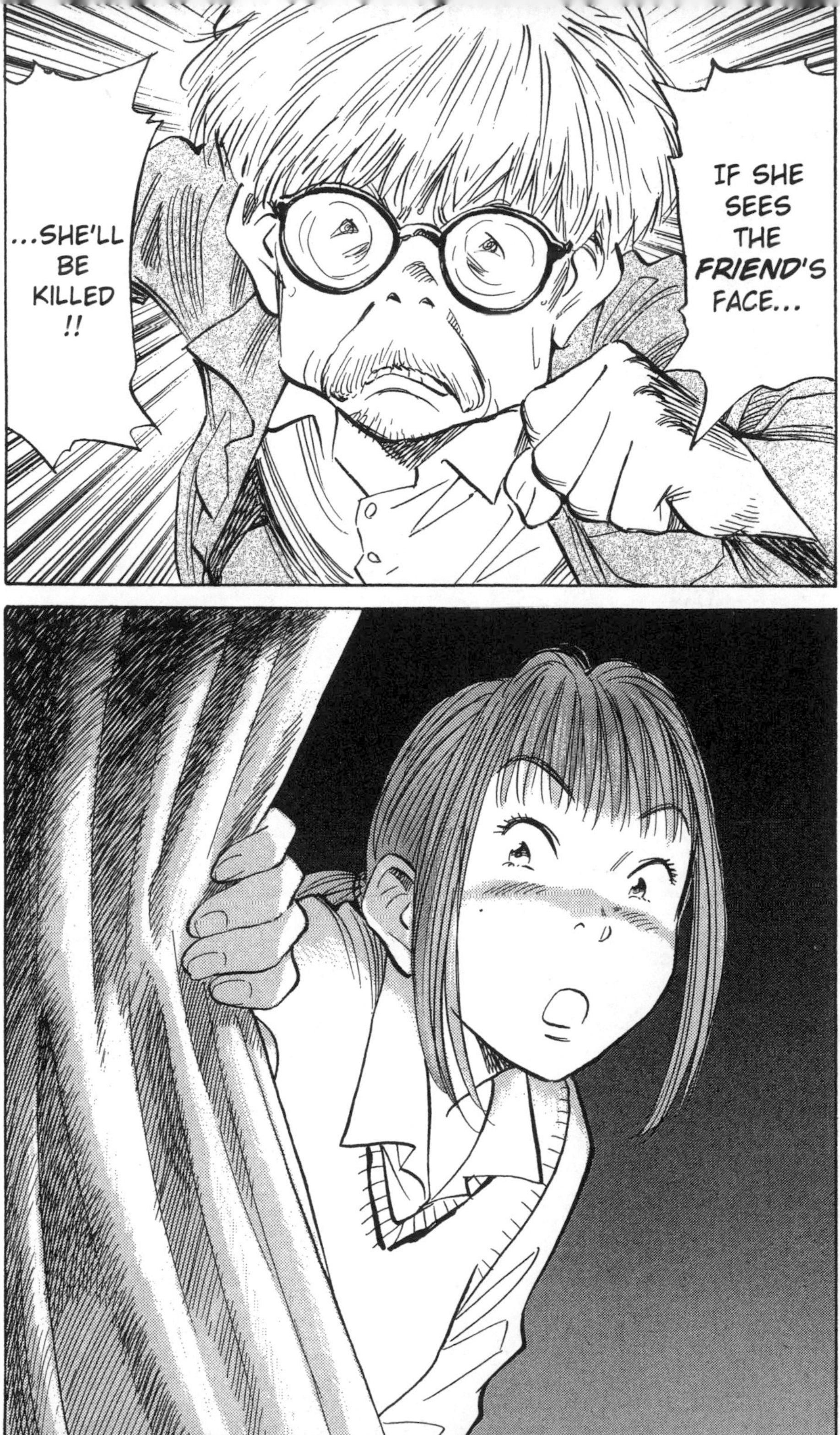
IF SHE SEES THE *FRIEND*'S FACE...
...SHE'LL BE KILLED!!

TO BE CONTINUED

NOTES FROM THE TRANSLATOR

This series follows the Japanese naming convention, with a character's family name followed by their given name. Honorifics such as -san and -kun are also preserved.

Page 25: Kenji is singing the theme song from the *Tetsuwan Atomu* anime. In the U.S., the series is more commonly known as *Astro Boy*, and was created by Tezuka Osamu.

Page 26: Created by manga legend Yokoyama Mitsuteru, both *Giant Robo* and *Tetsujin 28-go* (known as *Gigantor* in the U.S.) were precursors of the "giant robot" genre of manga and have both been turned into anime series.

Page 28: The *Seaview* is the name of the submarine in *Voyage to the Bottom of the Sea*.

Page 76: Oshio Heihachiro was a Confucian scholar and philosopher who led a popular uprising during the Tokugawa era in 1837 in response to those who were suffering during a widespread famine.

Page 112: This is what the "Re-re-re no Ojisan" in Akatsuka Fujio's *Tensai Bakabon* series often says while he is sweeping.

Page 135: A *teru-teru bozu*, or "sunshine doll," is usually made of tissue paper and hung by the window, or the eaves, the night before you need good weather.

Page 157: *Itohiki-ame*, or "thread-pull candy," is a lottery-type candy found at most *dagashiya* (candy stores).

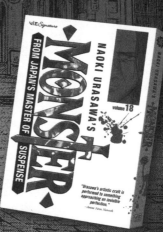

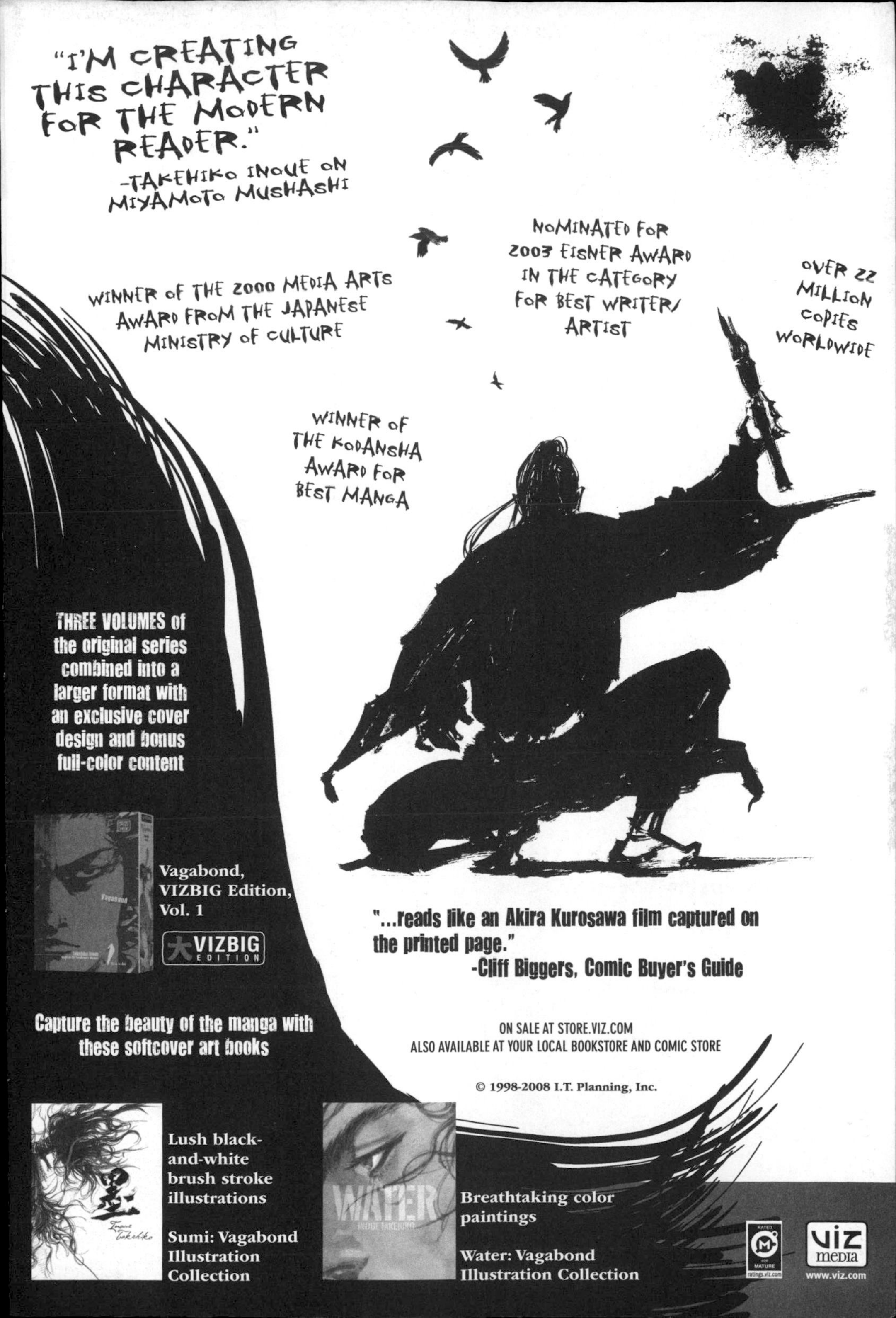
"I'M CREATING THIS CHARACTER FOR THE MODERN READER."
-TAKEHIKO INOUE ON MIYAMOTO MUSHASHI
WINNER OF THE 2000 MEDIA ARTS AWARD FROM THE JAPANESE MINISTRY OF CULTURE
NOMINATED FOR 2003 EISNER AWARD IN THE CATEGORY FOR BEST WRITER/ARTIST
OVER 22 MILLION COPIES WORLDWIDE
WINNER OF THE KODANSHA AWARD FOR BEST MANGA
THREE VOLUMES of the original series combined into a larger format with an exclusive cover design and bonus full-color content
Vagabond, VIZBIG Edition, Vol. 1
大 VIZBIG EDITION
"...reads like an Akira Kurosawa film captured on the printed page."
-Cliff Biggers, Comic Buyer's Guide
ON SALE AT STORE.VIZ.COM
ALSO AVAILABLE AT YOUR LOCAL BOOKSTORE AND COMIC STORE
© 1998-2008 I.T. Planning, Inc.
Capture the beauty of the manga with these softcover art books
Lush black-and-white brush stroke illustrations
Sumi: Vagabond Illustration Collection
Breathtaking color paintings
Water: Vagabond Illustration Collection
viz media
www.viz.com

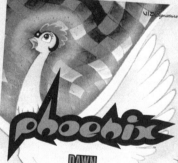
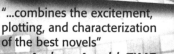

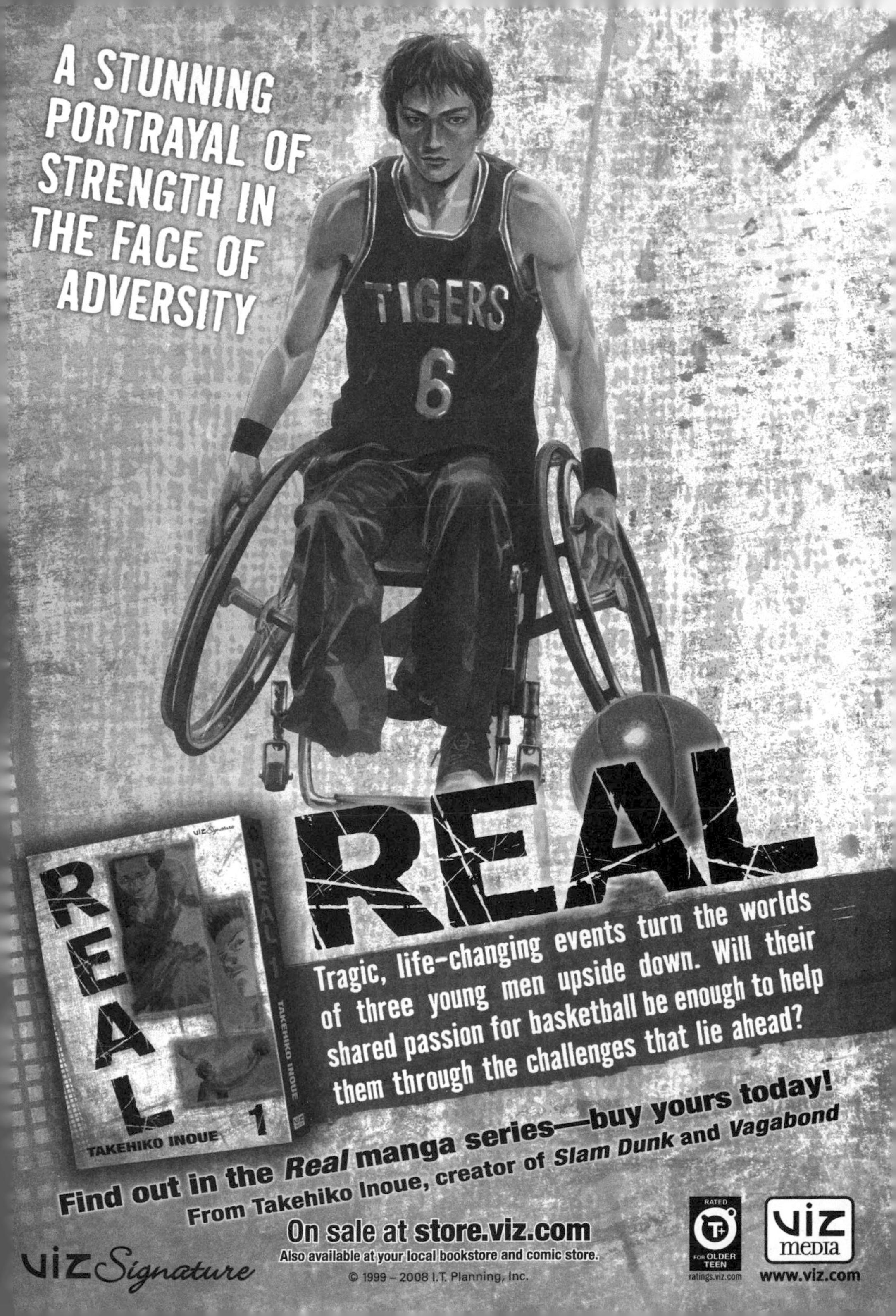
A STUNNING PORTRAYAL OF STRENGTH IN THE FACE OF ADVERSITY
TIGERS
6
REAL
VIZ Signature
REAL 1
TAKEHIKO INOUE
Tragic, life-changing events turn the worlds of three young men upside down. Will their shared passion for basketball be enough to help them through the challenges that lie ahead?
Find out in the Real manga series—buy yours today!
From Takehiko Inoue, creator of Slam Dunk and Vagabond
On sale at store.viz.com
Also available at your local bookstore and comic store.
VIZ Signature
© 1999 – 2008 I.T. Planning, Inc.
RATED T+ FOR OLDER TEEN
ratings.viz.com
VIZ media
www.viz.com

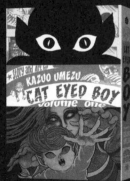
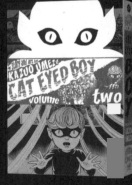
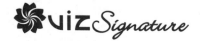

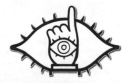